RELIGIOUS REALISM

THE MACMILLAN COMPANY
NEW YORK · BOSTON · CHICAGO · DALLAS
ATLANTA · SAN FRANCISCO

MACMILLAN & CO., LIMITED
LONDON · BOMBAY · CALCUTTA
MELBOURNE

THE MACMILLAN COMPANY
OF CANADA, LIMITED
TORONTO

RELIGIOUS REALISM

By

A. K. ROGERS, J. B. PRATT, J. S. BIXLER, A. G. WIDGERY,
H. HARTSHORNE, H. N. WIEMAN, G. A. COE, R. L.
CALHOUN, E. W. LYMAN, W. M. HORTON,
D. C. MACINTOSH, H. R. NIEBUHR,
W. K. WRIGHT, J. E. BOODIN,
W. P. MONTAGUE

Edited by

D. C. MACINTOSH

NEW YORK
THE MACMILLAN COMPANY
1931

SET UP BY BROWN BROTHERS LINOTYPERS
PRINTED IN THE UNITED STATES OF AMERICA
BY THE FERRIS PRINTING COMPANY

PREFACE

RELIGIOUS Realism, as the term is used in this volume, means centrally the view that a religious Object, such as may appropriately be called God, exists independently of our consciousness thereof, and is yet related to us in such a way that through reflection on experience in general and religious experience in particular, and without any dependence upon the familiar arguments of epistemological idealism, it is possible for us to gain either (as some would maintain) adequately verified knowledge or (as others would be content to affirm) a practically valuable and theoretically permissible faith not only that that religious Object exists but also, within whatever limits, as to what its nature is.

In the essays here presented—brought together and edited in consultation from time to time with Professors Lyman, Wright and Calhoun—the critical reader will discover under the common label of Religious Realism a considerable variety of philosophical and religious beliefs. Thus he may feel that the first two essays incline, in their theory of religious knowledge, toward the dualistic Left, whereas the third and especially the fourth develop some of the possibilities of the extreme monistic Right in a way that is distinctly reminiscent of the English school of "new realists." Most of the remaining papers fall into two groups, particularly when considered from an ontological or theological point of view. The first two and perhaps three of the eleven will no doubt be set down as showing, especially in relation to theism, more or less of a tendency toward the Left, whereas the others will be regarded as distributed variously along the way toward the theological Right.   15066

It is to be hoped, however, that readers will find the variety which undeniably exists in point of view and conclusion stimulating rather than confusing. Each contributor has worked in unhampered freedom, investigating individually the results of applying realistic principles and methods to problems of religious thought; and while to some extent the differences arrived at may represent different positions logically tenable within a common religious realism, it may well be that there are conclusions indicated which must eventually be modified or given up. In any case, criticism is needed and desired. At the same time it is strongly felt that our common presuppositions and procedure are likely to find increasing recognition among religious thinkers, and that some of the significant agreements independently arrived at will be found to have enduring value.

In timely support of the opinion just expressed, and since it was written down, there has come to hand, in a volume entitled *The Growth of the Idea of God,* evidence that Dean Shailer Mathews of the University of Chicago is also fairly to be numbered among the exponents of Religious Realism in the sense in which we have employed the term in this volume. Insisting that the starting point for religion must be "a relationship with the universe described by the scientist" and that religion is itself essentially a directed, "help-gaining adjustment" to "those cosmic activities which the word God represents," Dr. Mathews defends a "conceptual theism" in which a metaphysically exact definition of God is regarded as "less basic" than "personal relations with personality-creating, personally responsive, personally conceived activities of the cosmos."

D. C. Macintosh.

New Haven,
July 1, 1931.

CONTENTS

PAGE

PREFACE v

I. IS RELIGION IMPORTANT? 3
By ARTHUR KENYON ROGERS, formerly of Yale University

II. THE IMPLICATIONS OF HUMAN CONSCIOUSNESS . . 35
By JAMES BISSETT PRATT, of Williams College

III. A PHENOMENOLOGICAL APPROACH TO RELIGIOUS
REALISM 57
By JULIUS SEELYE BIXLER, of Smith College

IV. RELIGIOUS REALISM AND THE EMPIRICAL FACTS OF
RELIGION 101
By ALBAN G. WIDGERY, of Duke University

V. AN EMPIRICAL APPROACH TO A THEORY OF CHAR-
ACTER 133
By HUGH HARTSHORNE, of Yale University

VI. GOD AND VALUE 155
By HENRY NELSON WIEMAN, of the University of Chicago

VII. A REALISTIC VIEW OF DEATH 179
By GEORGE ALBERT COE, formerly of Teachers College,
Columbia University

VIII. PLATO AS RELIGIOUS REALIST 195
By ROBERT LOWRY CALHOUN, of Yale University

IX. CAN RELIGIOUS INTUITION GIVE KNOWLEDGE OF
REALITY? 255
By EUGENE WILLIAM LYMAN, of Union Theological
Seminary

X. AUTHORITY WITHOUT INFALLIBILITY 277
By WALTER MARSHALL HORTON, of the Oberlin Graduate
School of Theology

CONTENTS

PAGE

XI. EXPERIMENTAL REALISM IN RELIGION 307
By DOUGLAS CLYDE MACINTOSH, of Yale University

XII. RELIGIOUS REALISM IN THE TWENTIETH CENTURY . 413
By HELMUT RICHARD NIEBUHR, of Yale University

XIII. GOD AND EMERGENT EVOLUTION 431
By WILLIAM KELLEY WRIGHT, of Dartmouth College

XIV. GOD AND THE COSMOS 479
By JOHN ELOF BOODIN, of the University of California at Los Angeles

XV. THE TRINITY: A SPECULATION 495
By WM. PEPPERELL MONTAGUE, of Barnard College, Columbia University

I

IS RELIGION IMPORTANT?

By
ARTHUR KENYON ROGERS

Formerly Professor of Philosophy
Yale University

IS RELIGION IMPORTANT?

ANY defense of religion is in these days met by an initial obstacle which is peculiarly baffling to the earnest controversialist. In the past it has happened not infrequently that religious convictions have seemed on the point of being for the cultivated mind engulfed in a wave of unbelief, usually under the influence of one of two main motives; but neither of these historic motives is of the sort to cause the enlightened apologist nowadays very grave concern. Prior to the middle of the last century skepticism found its chief occasion in the identification of religion with the creed and ecclesiastical polity of a dominant church, and the reaction against it was in large measure a reaction against obscurantism, intolerance and the other vices which a religious establishment harbors. As such it had its own degree of moral and even of religious zeal—a zeal still in evidence among the remnant of sectarian atheists at the present time. But militant atheism outside the communistic movement exerts a small and vanishing influence as an intellectual force, and even in its palmier days the religious advocate always was able to blunt its weapons simply by dissociating his cause from that of current theology and ecclesiasticism. That religion is a more inclusive term than Catholicism, or Calvinism, or Christianity even, is plain to all except the excited partisan; in point of fact the older type of skeptic was very apt himself to emerge with a residual creed of deism. In the present-day philosophy of communism hostility to religion is, it is true, more thoroughgoing, because of the conviction that any faith whatever in a divine economy is calculated to act as a narcotic and make men disinclined to sympathize with radical departures from the established economic order.

3

But this is a *non sequitur* and easily might disappear once the hold of vested religious interests was broken.

The case for the apologist changed appreciably with the advent of modern science more particularly in the form of evolution. Here also at the outset it was an intrenched theology rather than religion in its more universal aspects that aroused the fighting spirit of the scientist, who for the most part would have been content to let religion go its way if it had not presumed to set preconceived limits to the methods and results of scientific inquiry. Nevertheless it soon grew evident that the new science was demanding even of the most liberal conceptions of religion a more thorough overhauling than its earlier defenders had felt the need of undertaking; not secondary doctrines only but the whole notion of meaning in the universe, of divine purpose and direction, and even of any settled validity attaching to human ideals and moral preferences, seemed to be undermined by some of the assumptions on which science was proceeding when these were pushed to their logical conclusion.

I shall make no effort here to adjudicate the speculative quarrel thus arising; it is enough to call attention to one new character which the controversy now assumed. The earlier skeptics had mainly been concerned with the tactics of offense against plainly vulnerable aspects of the current creeds, and while this left their polemics ineffective against opponents who might elect not to identify religion with theology, it also relieved them from the need of going to much trouble to defend a positive doctrine of their own. This immunity the newer opponents of religion could no longer claim. In so far as they were not content with sticking to the proper work of science in detail but undertook to add to this a philosophy purporting to set forth the final nature of the universe— and only by so doing were they in a position to confound rival philosophies of a religious or idealistic cast—they ceased to enjoy the undisputed prestige of science and scientific method. In adopting this more ambitious aim

they put themselves on even terms with their opponents
and were forced to defend their views in the same speculative fashion. And whatever one personally may think
about the outcome, at least it very soon became apparent
that they had nothing like the same advantage here that
science in the proper sense could claim over current theological opinions. On the whole most critics probably
would agree that idealism has had rather the better of a
scientific materialism or naturalism; at any rate it has
had more numerous and equally capable defenders.

Meanwhile it is the less necessary to decide the issue
since for the moment the opposition to religion has taken
still another turn which, in intention if not in practice
always, has abandoned the metaphysical pretensions of
the earlier naturalists. The distinctive presumption that
modernism brings to the religious problem is, in other
words, that the whole point of the controversy now has
lapsed; religion has lost its intellectual hold on cultivated
minds and has dropped in consequence out of the region
of profitable debate. This it is obvious leaves the would-
be disputant rather at a disadvantage. Former opponents
did at least take the matter seriously. They were very
much in earnest about certain positive convictions of their
own, rational or ethical, to which religion stood in what
was at any rate an important negative relation; and so
long as a man is prepared to enter into argument there
is always a chance he may be brought to see reason on
the other side. But once he genuinely has lost interest in
a subject of debate there is nothing much left to do
about it.

Now this as I say has come to be the fashion in influential circles at the present moment. In a way it is defensible enough. There is no law human or divine to force a
man to waste his time on matters about which he feels no
real concern; and since the human capacity for interest
is limited at best it perhaps is just as well that he should
keep to the things to which his special bent inclines him.
If music does not stir me there is no good reason why I
should be asked to listen to operas or symphonies, any

more than I am called on to insist that the artist concern himself with trade or politics if he is not so disposed. However there is a common infirmity of mind which does not stop with this. My natural disposition is to say not merely that so and so is lacking in sufficient interest for me, but that it has legitimately no interest for anyone and ought therefore to be ruled out from the list of human values altogether. This last attitude is not so easy to defend; and it is this that characteristically the modernist adopts in his dealing with religion. His measure of value purports to be definitive, not personal; religion is relegated outright to an earlier and less sophisticated age, and of those still disposed to take its claims in earnest it is enough to say that they are outmoded and have lost touch with modern ways of thinking.

In what I am going on to say I shall not be attempting more than very incidentally a defense of religion against this judgment of insignificance and obsolescence; I am too well aware that you cannot hope to make anyone accept an ultimate premise of debate unless he is ready of his own accord to grant it. Primarily I shall be engaged with a less controversial task. This is the task of determining what more precisely the considerations are that lead the modernist to take the stand he does. On two questions in particular one is justified in asking for more light than usually is volunteered. Exactly where in the first place is the value in dispute supposed to lie? This is an indispensable preliminary, since religion has meant many things to many men and in the mouth of present-day liberalism certainly has lost much of its historic connotation. And what are the reasons in detail that lead the modernist to discredit its importance? Such a problem as I say is one for critical analysis rather than polemics; and if the history of human thought has any lesson it is that opinions which dispense with such exact analysis have a precarious standing. A good deal of current skepticism lies on this account outside the field of edifying disputation; so far as it is easy to discover its only basis is the rather naïve faith that the last word of reason has been spoken by a handful of contemporary thinkers, and such a faith has been too often disappointed in the past to meet the needs of a critical standard. Occasionally however the modernist has paid religion the compliment of a more respectful treatment; and it is one of the more recent of these treatises—that of Mr. Walter Lippmann [1]—that I propose using as a text.

Before however taking up the grounds for Mr. Lippmann's rejection of religion it will be useful first to call attention to certain general aspects of the situation in the light of what he himself conceives to be the essential thing that religion tries to do. With this conception I have personally no quarrel. Briefly it amounts to saying that for the religionist the world in which he lives is thought of as at bottom a friendly sort of world that offers some insurance against loss to the interests he has most at heart. By holding fast to this simplified issue we shall automatically rule out a number of considerations which in the past have tended to complicate and confuse discussion. The superstitions of religion, its absurd and stupid dogmas, the humanity and bigotry of sects and hierarchies, the self-centered pettiness of much religious piety, are largely if not entirely irrelevant, and their intrusion marks either a failure in intellectual precision or a desire to make capital by arousing an initial prejudice.

Such a judgment of exclusion is perhaps not wholly warranted however unless we first draw one distinction— a distinction of enough importance for my thesis to make desirable some emphasis on it at the start. It is not hard to draw up historically an indictment of religion on the score of what is supposed to be the trivial nature of its service to private and subjective ends. No one is likely to deny that men very often have conceived of God as a mere instrument for furthering their desires whatever these may chance to be. Not only has "salvation" been on the whole the commonest religious motive, but for this present life as well the believer has demanded that

[1] *A Preface to Morals.*

the universe should guarantee his right to happiness; and it has been more or less his habit to interpret happiness in terms that hardly merit much intellectual respect. It has been assumed that if a man is "good," if he performs with reasonable regularity accepted moral and religious duties, God is put under some obligation to see to it that his business thrives and that he escapes at least the major ills of life; while conspicuous prosperity for men or nations has been taken as a sign that God is pleased.

I am not prepared to go along with those who would regard this underlying demand as in every respect objectionable. It is I think quite impossible to assign to the word "value" any concrete meaning which dissociates it from happiness, and happiness is always in the end a personal affair; so that if the world does really have a concern for anything that men call good it cannot be blind to the concrete forms of human satisfaction. Still it is undeniable that in the way this has often been construed it justifies those who would object to it as repugnant alike to cosmic and to human dignity. There must be something better for cosmic energies to do than to nurse human ailments or assist man in his quest for small pleasures and successes, to say nothing of the lack of evidence that the world does actually much concern itself with such affairs directly. The problem of evil with which the human intellect has wrestled so long and unsuccessfully would hardly have been started were it not that man gets rather forcibly the impression of a large indifference on the part of nature to his personal wishes; and on the whole, to a rationally disinterested mind, this very well may seem a more complimentary view than that which makes out of the illimitable universe a foster mother to a race of beings for whose importance to anyone except themselves it is not always easy to find convincing reasons.

However it is possible to put the matter in a way to lessen somewhat the force of this contention, in so far as it rests at any rate not on the evidence of facts but on an intellectual distaste for allowing the "subjective" to interfere with a realistic understanding. When we speak of values we are likely to think first of the satisfaction of desire, and desires are to be sure subjective and, it may be, in detail more or less irrelevant to rational interpretation. But in strictness desire is not equivalent to a value judgment; at best it is only the object of this judgment. And the judgment itself, whether successfully or unsuccessfully, professes to make a straightforward statement about the constitution of reality; when we go on to say not that desires are desired but that desires as such are good, we no longer are feeling a desire simply but are making an objective affirmation which may be as free from personal bias and as coolly and disinterestedly intellectual as the contrary judgment that desires have no such universal bearing.

And once this objective reference is recognized we can go on to a distinction which as I say takes something from the force of the conventional disparagement of human ends. If a value is not primarily a personal claim to happiness but a relatively disinterested form of intellectual approval, a considered opinion that some things are more genuinely worth while than others irrespective of what this or that man may be disposed to aim at for his momentary pleasure, it is not so self-evidently bound to be deserving of our disesteem. Men can scarcely avoid passing some judgments of relative significance which naturally impress them as having a more solid ground than mere private feeling; indeed the critic himself commonly is doing this when he censures religion as detracting from the proper respect and honor due the cosmic scheme. Whether value judgments in this interpretation can in the end be justified is a question I am not for the moment raising. I am only trying to say that when a man asserts that justice in some objective sense is better than injustice or decency better than indecency his judgment is not obviously absurd and inconsequential, as if it carried an implication of discourtesy toward scientific reason or the universe which reason aims to understand.

As a matter of historical fact our human judgments of unworthiness or pettiness do not in the first instance spring from a comparison of mankind with an impersonal nature. They arise from comparing the *merely* personal with a more general human good; and it is just to these shared forms of a common good that disinterested judgments of approval are most solidly attached.

As a point of departure then what I am contending is that one ought not in fairness to rely upon an indiscriminate appeal to the futilities of human life for rendering plausible his assumption that there is something intrinsically ridiculous and unworthy of belief in a faith that what man approves has some relevance also to the universal nature. By picking one's facts it is not hard to make out a case that emotionally may seem persuasive. But if its plausibility depends on this selectiveness it is hardly in a position to constrain our rational assent. And it seems to me fairly evident that if we substitute for the confused and inconsequential aims of individuals those larger and more substantial values that enter into a general human good we are in sight of something that does not carry to the natural mind any necessary sense of triviality to which the universe has a right to condescend; on the contrary the world would be a more imposing spectacle for man could it find a place for these qualities which he values most. At any rate I am going to assume that this is so, and that if we are to set the religious hypothesis aside it will need to be for more specific reasons still to be disclosed.

It will help clear the ground if I start with one reason which I freely grant is unanswerable once its premises are admitted. If one honestly thinks that there is nothing in human life worth the effort of attaining and that all values so called are mere illusions he is logically invulnerable; he has found the infallible way of emptying religion of significance or interest because the thing religion is supposed to guarantee does not for him exist. One may to be sure suspect that a substantial strain of self-deception enters into the current vogue of disillusionment; life has not lost all its savor so long as one continues to get a thrill out of talking and writing fluently about its general worthlessness. But to the extent that disillusionment is real the argument for religion naturally will fail. In fact it is not necessary to go so far as this; a consistent Cyrenaicism will be equally effective in dispelling interest. If one identifies the good solely with the emotions and pleasures of the passing moment there is again no reason to concern himself with the grounds for a permanence and stability that by definition is not to be desired; it is enough to take pleasure as it comes and decline to look beyond its empirical presence.

I have no intention of trying to argue with the hedonist, nor is this because of any presumption that his philosophy is logically absurd or morally indefensible. It is sufficient for my purpose to point out that if it cuts the ground from under an effective presentation of religious claims it leaves in so far the skeptic in precisely the same argumentative dilemma. The issue is reduced simply to a clash of temperaments: one man tells us, I am indifferent toward a possible cosmic backing for what men call values because these seem to me unimportant; another says, Since to me they do appear important the question is still to my mind of consequence. What alone would give to the first alternative something like a rationally objective backing would be the sharing of this indifference by so preponderant a part of humankind as to make plausible the inference that the judgment of history has been pronounced. But this outcome is not here as yet, and until the time arrives the Cyrenaic or the nihilist has nothing on which to base a rational generalization except his own feeling of significance or the lack of it.

Meanwhile a denial that human ends have any value is not the only or on the whole the most important source of modern skepticism. Religion has critics of a more serious turn of mind, critics who are themselves committed to positive value preferences but who in spite of this, sometimes because of it, think they see reasons why the traditional quest for a cosmic guarantee ought now to be abandoned. I shall as I have already said be concerned more with identifying these reasons than with refuting them; at most my polemics will be limited to suggesting grounds for the suspicion that the argument commonly involves a complication of motives not very carefully discriminated, and that when these are disentangled and examined separately their cogency will be found to suffer. But it is possible at least to feel that here we are dealing with a state of mind that does not render discussion and mutual understanding hopeless. And I am ready now to turn to Mr. Lippmann more directly.

Briefly summarized, Mr. Lippmann's argument starts from the assumption that the demand for a religious guarantee arises out of emotional requirements natural to the human mind perhaps but not supported by our modern scientific insight. A true perspective calls not for a universe subservient to man's wishes; it directs us to mold our wishes to reality as this reveals itself through the disinterested eyes of science. And if this seems to dash the hopes that have solaced man for the many ills and disappointments that attend his earthly life and to leave him a bit of flotsam borne by chance currents to an unknown goal, he must turn instead to the inner resources which after all are what lend to him his proper human dignity and excellence—courage, and self-reliance, and the intellectual satisfactions that derive from seeing things as they truly are and accepting their duress.

This is a human attitude for which unquestionably a good deal can be said. But before accepting it as final one needs to ask again what in particular the reasons are that have led the modernist to take it as the one sole alternative open to a discriminating mind. Why in other words, allowing that a sober acquiescence in reality is man's only safety, is it to be assumed that one of the things to which reality constrains him is the adoption of a particular philosophical opinion that denies any place to value in the cosmic scheme? Such a question is not one that calls for a wholesale and impressionistic judgment but for analysis in detail.

I start with the point that seems most distinctive of Mr. Lippmann's own explicit treatment and most central to his argument as a whole. Briefly it amounts to saying that religion stands in need of certainty, complete assurance; and since this is something which science and philosophy have pretty thoroughly discredited by now we are compelled, whether reluctantly or not, to turn elsewhere than to religion for a practicable method of salvation. Without complete certainty religion does not offer genuine consolation, Mr. Lippmann writes; without certainty there can be no profound sense that a man's own purpose has become part of the purpose of the whole creation. On this thesis the force of his reasoning as a connected whole depends.

To estimate the force of such an argument it is necessary first to note that it rests on two things—a fact and an assumption. At least for my own part I am ready to take it as a fact that the reign in religion of authority and dogma is definitely over; and for purposes of argument at any rate I shall agree that the hope for any logically water-tight defense of a religious philosophy which claims to exercise a comparable authority in the courts of reason is equally delusive. But Mr. Lippmann's second step does not appear to me so unequivocal. If one defines religion as of necessity involving certitude, then with the loss of certainty religion goes; but is such a definition compulsory?

I think Mr. Lippmann is not guiltless here of the logical fault I have just deprecated—the lumping uncritically of reasons for a conclusion one wants to draw without estimating carefully enough their individual force. What in the first instance he seems to have in mind is the fact that popular religion historically has got much of its driving force from the craving of the average man for an authoritative guide to supplement his own perplexed and groping reason; for the mass of men who are not naturally suited to the religion of the spirit, so he tells us, an external machinery is indispensable, and the essence of such an organization is the title to say with apostolic certainty that the message is true. But such a contention runs the risk of getting away from the real point at issue. At any rate if it only represents, as at times it seems to do, a sociological judgment about the historic function of the church as a practical device for securing social order we hardly need to reckon with it; this doubtless contains a large element of truth, but it is irrelevant to what Mr. Lippmann calls the religion of the spirit. What we are concerned with is not the function of an institution but the psychological state of mind of the religious believer toward the content of his belief.

But here again there is a possibility of confusion unless we discriminate. With his beliefs robbed of their certainty, Mr. Lippmann says, each man is thrown back on his own resources; he is denied the support which all popular religion offers him, the conviction that outside himself there is a power on which he can and must lean for guidance. The mass of men cannot have a faith of which the only foundation is their need and desire to believe; something is left out—the conviction that the religion comes from God. Ethical codes cannot lay claim to unhesitating obedience when they are based on the opinion of a majority or on notions of wise men or on an estimate of what is socially useful or on an appeal to patriotism. A human morality has no such sanction as a divine, and the sanction of a divine morality is the certainty of the believer that it originated with God. If he once had come to think that the rule of conduct has a purely human, local and temporal origin its sanction is gone.

But here I think that an alternative exists of which Mr. Lippmann does not take account. It is true that however religions may have come about they do and must claim to have a divine rather than a merely human reference. But there is a middle ground between a conviction based on certainty and one whose only foundation is the desire to believe. One may conceivably have concrete reasons for believing which fall short of the complete assurance he might wish but which still lead him to acquiesce in the belief as on the whole reasonable and sane; indeed it would be hard to point out any human conviction of real importance of which this is not true. The objectivity of the belief, in other words, is something we can distinguish from its certainty; if religion is only a reasonable faith this does not in the least prevent me from identifying the object of such a faith with a divine reality rather than with human utility or subjective wants. It may be that such an attitude of mind is one in which the mass of men can find no satisfaction; I do not know and I suspect that Mr. Lippmann has no decisive means of knowing whether this is true or not. But while if it is true it may have some bearing on the sociological aspects of religion it still leaves the issue as it affects the modern individual undetermined; and it is in this latter form that we need to put the problem with which Mr. Lippmann supposedly is dealing. What we want to know has to do with the right of intelligent people at the present day to entertain certain beliefs, or hopes, and not with the causes that have led mankind to acquiesce in historic creeds. To be in a position to meet such an issue we shall need to call in a different sort of motive.

To be logically compelling, this motive will have to be looked for not in the demand of the undisciplined mind for an impressive external authority, but in something intrinsic to the nature of reason itself which justifies the insistence on certitude as a prerequisite before a belief can be rationally entertained. In other words we are pointed to that peculiar philosophic temper which goes by the name of absolutism. This disposition to refuse to call anything valid knowledge unless it can be shown to be undeniable has had in the past an enormous philosophic vogue; and I do not find it easy to account for Mr. Lippmann's confidence in his own reasoning unless we suppose a lurking sympathy with such a prepossession. He declines indeed to follow the absolutist

in supposing that the quest for philosophic certainty can
be successful; but none the less he appears to feel that
in default of this outcome we are left without anything
acceptable to reason. As a matter of fact it would not
I think be difficult to find a strong rationalistic bias such
as this presupposes elsewhere in Mr. Lippmann's writings; despite his pretensions to empiricism and realism
his social and political conclusions not infrequently reveal a tendency to start from some abstract premise and
follow a restricted line of logic which does less than
justice to the concrete facts.

Meanwhile if my suspicion here is justified it will have
a bearing on the cogency of Mr. Lippmann's argument
about religion. For it leaves this resting on an individual preference; and however convincing therefore it may
be to those who feel the same way about the requirements
of reason at least it leads into a blind alley and renders
discussion useless. One might raise the query also
whether it does not fall into the same error that Mr.
Lippmann himself is so anxious to avoid; to insist that
the universe cannot be of a certain kind because only
reality of a different kind will meet the requirements we
set up as the price of an intellectual complacency looks a
little like trying to force reality to acquiesce in our
demands instead of adjusting these demands to conditions as we find them. However all I am much concerned
in pointing out is the temperamental prepossession which
limits the power of Mr. Lippmann's argument to carry
conviction to those whom he might be supposed to be
trying to persuade. Religion does not need to take the
form either of traditionalism or of a philosophic absolutism; it is quite possible to reject alike current theologies and the pretension to philosophic certainty and still
find oneself able to retain, for specific reasons that appear plausible to him, a belief or at least a not entirely
unfounded hope that the nature of things is of a sort
that does not exclude some deep-seated relationship to
what he conceives to be his worthiest conceptions of the
good. I do not say that he would not be glad to see his

way to proof that goes beyond such a tentative assurance. But he has learned, as Mr. Lippmann recommends, to take what he can get without growing petulant because the world does not offer more; and he refuses in consequence to root out an interest and hope that means something to him simply because other men with other minds choose to identify the acceptable with the incontrovertible. So long as people exist who feel this way—and I suspect they exist in very considerable numbers—the sort of argument I have so far been considering will of course leave them cold. If they are to be approached by reason it must be through other channels; and it is to the further possibilities here that I have next to turn.

The main brunt of such a possible argument rests on one particular kind of consideration at the present day— the claims, supposed or actual, of science. It is to the authority of science that the modernist almost invariably betakes himself when he wishes to give intellectual prestige to a personal decision to turn religion out of doors. And here I might of course extend my remarks, indefinitely; all I really wish to say however can be brought within a fairly narrow compass. I propose once more merely to distinguish several forms that the argument might take and to indicate why none of them seem to me entirely adequate to the task in hand; though when, as is usually the case, they are drawn on without any nice discrimination to back a presumption already emotionally congenial they undeniably can be made to seem impressive.

The availability of science as a weapon for invalidating religion lies in the merited prestige which it enjoys in the modern world. Science has revolutionized all our ways of thought and practice, has substituted an ideal of experimental caution and a respect for unadulterated fact in place of vague and haphazard thinking, has opened up the possibility for the first time of something like order and intelligent progress in social life, and— what specially recommends it to the general temper of the age—has added vastly to the material comfort and security of man. All this is undeniable, and because it is undeniable it has tended to promote a new human interest which is proving a formidable rival to all the older interests—not religion simply, but culture and nationalistic fervor and traditional moralities as well.

About this the first and most obvious thing to say is that the vogue of science on its more invulnerable side by no means of necessity sets it up as a claimant for exclusive honors. Because science cultivates an interest of its own which is distinct from that of religion or of art it is natural that in the degree of its impressiveness it should tend to absorb attention to the exclusion of competing claims; human versatility is limited, and for the time being any new enthusiasm is likely to drive out the old. But unless there is some fatal incompatibility the balance sooner or later is bound to get readjusted, as has happened many times before in human history. Few instructed minds will be apt to think that culture is never again to have its innings because temporarily it has been eclipsed; and conceivably this may be the case too with religion. For it seems evident that in the form which gives it its most indisputable authority science does not really trespass on the peculiar province of religion. The working scientist to whom all the credit for its high prestige is due does not when he knows his business assume to pass metaphysical judgments about the ultimate meaning of reality or its lack of meaning; such a pretentious enterprise he leaves to other men and confines himself to his proper task of formulating in detail the way things actually work—what he calls the laws of nature. No interpretation by philosophy or religion is a substitute for such factual laws; on any showing definite sequences of events must still occur which can only be discovered by the methods of experiment and verification to which science is committed. But because the tasks are different ones they ought not to be confounded; and before one is in a position therefore to confute religion by an appeal to science he is bound to produce further and more explicit arguments.

It is worth noting to begin with that the popular claim that science has displaced religion as a serious contender for belief runs some risk itself of violating scientific canons. There is no such thing as science in the large except as a metaphysical abstraction. When one declares that science rejects religion he either means that scientists generally—for it is only through its endorsement by flesh and blood scientists that a scientific doctrine gets its standing—are in actual agreement here, or else he means that there exists at any rate a settled body of conclusions from which the agreement ought to follow as a necessary inference whether it does so in point of fact or not.

If the first alternative were really true it would of course still not settle things conclusively; it has happened more than once that experts have passed verdicts that later have had to be recanted. Nevertheless anything like a consensus among scientists undoubtedly would prove a strong handicap to overcome and would justify a certain arrogance in the skeptic. In point of fact however no consensus here exists. I am not inclined myself to take too seriously the pronouncements in favor of religion that constantly are issuing from scientists more or less eminent in their special fields; on the whole they seldom seem to me entirely well advised. But the existence of a strong faction of religious sympathizers does at least debar the modernist from this particular sort of claim. All he can do at best is to assure us that dissenters from his own preferred opinion are to be disqualified for incompetence; and whatever the truth of this it does not represent the judgment of science but a layman's judgment about the relative capabilities of scientists.

For the second alternative more is to be said. I have already had occasion to remark that the typical skeptic of the last century was apt to look for the overthrow of religion to a positive metaphysics of his own. It was supposed that through the aid of science a rival theory had been solidly established which left no place in the world for meaning or ideals; and this is of course a thesis that can be more or less plausibly defended. It may even for the sake of argument be granted that it is the most plausible contender in the field; for my present purpose it will be enough to enter two provisos.

One is that for the position to be tenable a man should be open about it and consistent. It is legitimate to reject one theory of reality because it seems to contradict another and better theory. But in case one elects to shelve metaphysics and avail himself of the immunity that comes from having no positive dogmas of his own to bolster up it is not legitimate then to shift his ground and fall back on a presumption that he has positive knowledge on his side. The individual soul, writes Mr. Bertrand Russell in a passage which Mr. Lippmann quotes approvingly, must struggle alone with what of courage it can command against the whole weight of a universe that cares nothing for its hopes and fears. As a personal attitude on the part of one who finds for himself no sufficient reason for believing that the universe is concerned with his desires this is unobjectionable. But it is more than a personal attitude for Mr. Russell; he has positive information as to what the universe is like, and he knows as a fact that it is careless of human aims. As a convinced philosopher he may in his own case have the right to this assurance. But the everyday modernist at least, who assumes no responsibility for a system, has no such right thus tacitly when he finds it a convenience to take for granted that the dogma of the world's indifference is for purposes of argument a settled truth. A truth perhaps it may be, but not at any rate a truth of science. If it can be justified at all it is not by scientific methods but through an interpretation of scientific findings by philosophy or metaphysics. And whatever may be true of science proper no philosophy as yet has reached a stage where its validity can be taken as a postulate. Mr. Russell with his air of serene and somewhat intolerant finality might be impressive as a spokesman of science if that were what he really had a claim to be; he is much less impressive as spokesman of a particular and subtle brand of metaphysics which has entered very recently the field of historic systems and which quite conceivably may in a few years be found to have suffered the fate of its numerous predecessors. The distinction is at any rate one that no appeal to science can afford to overlook. Superadded dogmas may as I say be true; but they offer a subject for debate rather than an authoritative premise. That the laws of science have as such no reference to human meanings is of course indisputable; but at least it still remains to show that the human mind is bound to stop with purely scientific formulations.

I have been giving reasons for supposing that the enlistment of science against religion has as yet no sufficient warrant either from the unanimity of scientists or from a body of assured scientific laws which in their own right rather than through the assistance of dubious metaphysical deductions drive the scientific mind to skepticism. There is a third way however of interpreting the appeal to science distinguishable from the other two though commonly mixed up with them, and to this I am willing to assign considerably more weight. Regardless of whether or not the feeling can be backed by compelling arguments, there can be little doubt I think that the picture which modern science offers us does exercise an emotional constraint not altogether favorable to an assured conviction of man's importance in the world. It is in vain that the mind endeavors to take in the unimaginable vastness of nature's processes going their way eons before man comes upon the scene and destined to continue after the same forces that brought him into being have swept away the fragments of the tiny planet which offers him a temporary foothold. We follow man himself in his ephemeral existence, undistinguishable at the start from the brutes that prey upon him, waging an internecine strife where ferocity and guile seem to have all the best of it, winning his way gradually indeed and almost in his own despite to a relative security in something which he calls civilization, but to a security which almost at any moment runs the risk of crumbling through his stupidity and his unruly passions, and which harbors so much misery and disillusionment and such heartless exploitation of the many by the few that his mind keeps turning to the past with all its manifold shortcomings as a refuge from his dissatisfaction with his own achievements. To gaze steadily on such a picture with no abatement in the exuberance of one's faith argues I should say some imaginative lack; and it is not without a large degree of fellow feeling with those who find themselves forced to abandon any confidence in human destinies that I go on to inquire whether or to what extent this really is a necessary outcome.

It is important as a background to keep in mind what has just been said about the limitations of this new motive to negation. If to immediate impressions one could add grounds for some logical assurance that the world is of a nature actively to rule out human values there would not be a great deal left to say; but it is on our right to rely very much on this assistance that my previous remarks have been intended to cast doubt. The motive we are now considering is imaginative and impressionistic, not rational in the stricter sense; that it starts from scientific or semi-scientific data does not change the fact that its logic is emotional or æsthetic rather than of the sort that gives prestige to scientific method. I am perfectly prepared to grant the difficulties that any competing view will have to face; there is no short and easy way to reconcile the universe of science with the claims of human good, or to see just *how* values are to be conceived as entering into combination with its impersonal laws and forces. But so long as science does not set itself up as a metaphysics which on the authority of the human mind denies the significance of all things human, we cannot shut out the possibility at least that there may be some reconciliation; the more indeed we dwell on the wonder and mystery of existence and the insignificance of man the less right we have to dogmatize about what sort of thing reality can *not* do or be. It is on probability then that the issue turns. And the case no doubt may be so stated as to make the probability appear remote. But first impressions are not always final; at any rate it is on his ability to modify such a first impression that the claim of the apologist to attention will depend.

It is not hard to see where in general he will need to look. The world of physical nature can hardly constitute his initial problem; everyone alike must accept this from the hands of science as a datum, and while in the end philosophy may undertake to reconstrue it, no belief that rests on some special type of metaphysics is likely to satisfy normal human needs. The point to be settled first is not how we conceivably may view the world so as to bring it into line with human aspirations, but whether we can vindicate man's rational right to retain at least his historic interest in such a task without having to feel from the start that he can have no expectation of success; and for this we shall need to turn from nature to the human scene.

It will hardly I imagine be disputed that the picture of man and his history to which I have just adverted briefly is far less unequivocal and scientifically compelling than the picture of his entourage. It unfortunately has large elements of truth—so large as to excuse if not to justify a readiness to adopt it as the final truth. But unquestionably too there is another side; the picture leaves out things that equally are real and that we have no right to treat with disrespect without at least going to the trouble first of a critical interrogation. The cynic and nihilist, that is, no less than the optimist and sentimentalist, is as such not a scientist but an impressionistic artist selecting his facts to suit his humor; and until the missing data are restored there is no safe basis for a judgment.

The new consideration is the sporadic appearance in human life of qualities that defy the mood of cynical disfavor or indifference. I want to avoid making claims that go beyond the evidence. Whether history in the large shows any real improvement in the human stock, whether man in these latter days is better or happier than his progenitors, I should not care to say with any great assurance; I hope the case is so, but too many things can be offered in rebuttal for one to be very positive about it. This much however is beyond a reasonable doubt, that the human race has sometimes flowered into products that kindle our unforced admiration and respect. In the mass of human folly and credulity there are gleams of a sober and impartial wisdom, self-love and self-indulgence are leavened by generosity and friendliness and true affection, the love of beauty fights successfully at times against the ugliness and vulgarities of the common life, and out of the brutal or sordid rivalry for wealth and power there emerges here and there a passion for justice and a universal good that has small connection with the hope of personal reward. That the possessors of these qualities are seldom supermen or saints and that they have their share of human frailties is true enough and worth remembering. But one does not need to go to the undiscriminating lengths of the hero worshipper to feel assured that there are some human traits that really merit his sincere appreciation, and that the cynic who tries to explain them all away in terms of hidden selfishness, hypocrisy or self-deception is only revealing his own lack of a sensitive understanding.

Granting the facts then—and I am not greatly interested in arguing with those who would refuse to call them facts—what are the inferences which one is safe in drawing? These will depend a good deal on the method of approach. As social historians or observers to begin with—if it were possible for anyone to be a *mere* historian or scientist—it may be doubtful whether sufficient grounds exist for a decisive judgment. One might argue that the presence of such emergent traits is a signpost to indicate the direction in which reality is traveling and ought therefore to be given weight in any essay at determining what reality is like; on the other hand it is just as easy to view them as casual products of the

amazing fertility of nature, as fitful and insignificant as
the spume of the windswept ocean. If it were not for
one further point it might well seem the part of wisdom
to drop the matter altogether as beyond our competence
to settle.

The new consideration is the fact that normally we
approach the problem not as unattached critics and observers but with a personal stake in its solution. These
qualities which we pick out as lending a touch of dignity
to the futilities and stodginess of human life are qualities
with which we are ourselves identified through a sympathetic fellow feeling; apart from thus representing values
that enlist our own approval there is little to make them
stand out from the undistinguished mass so as to constitute a problem. I am not trying just now to argue that
our acceptance of such special qualities is in itself a proof
of anything whatever. But it is a motive, a source of
curiosity and interest, a claim to intellectual as well as to
emotional importance; and as such it carries with it a
certain natural presumption. For it is the essence of anything we look upon as valuable that we should want to
attach it firmly to reality, to give it rational substance
and stability, to be able to believe that from the universal
source it derives some chance of guiding human destinies.
That social justice for example in the long run may be
expected to prevail because reality is on its side may or
may not be so; but at least for any mind oppressed by the
weight of man's inhumanity to man it is absurd to say
that the question holds no interest or appeal. The burden
of proof is on the other side.

Assuming then that we have already for our purpose
gained the right to dismiss the thoroughgoing type of
skepticism that denies all reality to values, as well as the
dogmatic claim to a positive knowledge that the world is
a sort of world from which the values one does approve
are definitely excluded, it remains to ask what motives
still may be left to justify the current indifference to religious hopes. And there are two final considerations which
seem to me chiefly to account for this, both of them im-

plicit for the most part rather than plainly stated, and both once again a matter more of temperament than of reason.

The one that lends itself most readily to exposition is primarily an æsthetic motive. I quite understand, as I have said, that there may be a strong appeal to the imagination in the spectacle that is offered by the valiant soul which sets itself to defeat a hostile or apathetic universe by the sheer force of a disinterested intellect that abandons fanciful hopes and accepts facts as it finds them; and while for myself I see no reason why as matters go a courageous realism does not find in practice quite enough room for exercise without the need to dogmatize over ultimates, undoubtedly its æsthetic force is heightened in the degree in which one plays up the world's indifference to man. It is plainly his attachment to such a particular ideal of human character and dignity that constitutes one powerful motive in determining the point at which Mr. Lippmann chooses to set the bounds of a legitimate human curiosity and faith. A rational ethics he identifies with "maturity," and maturity is the recognition of the vast indifference of the world and a revision of natural desires in the light of this truer understanding of reality. One develops to a human stature by growing out of the childish belief that each of us is the center of an adoring and solicitous universe. The mature man can no longer count on possessing whatever he may happen to want and therefore he must learn to want what he can possess. He can no longer hold forever the things at which he grasps, for they change and slip away; and therefore he must learn to hold on to things not by grasping them but by understanding them and by remembering them. Then he is wholly an adult. For he has ceased to expect anything of the world which it cannot give, and he has learned to love it under the only aspect in which it is eternal. To attain such a mind harmonious with itself and with reality, to attain detachment, understanding and disinterestedness in the presence of reality itself, is man's only rational ideal.

For my purpose it is enough to say one thing about this outcome. Such a particular ideal of what constitutes the highest good is of course a valid human end in so far as for anyone it really works. But I fail to see why we should try to force it on another man if he objects; to offer it as a universal formula and identify it with *the* human good is simply to follow the path that has strewn man's history with so many absolute values more or less mutually irreconcilable. Certainly the empiricist has no right to this procedure. What he does have a perfect right to do is to decide that here lies for him the best method of salvation in a world which he cannot persuade himself has any relevance to human values; and he may recommend the same faith to those like-minded with himself. But to imply that one who looks elsewhere for his good is stultified thereby and must needs be out of step with the march of true intelligence is quite another matter; it either means a tacit shift once more from a modest agnosticism to a claim to know categorically the nature of man's destiny, or else it means giving arbitrarily a preeminence to one empirical form of good that appeals to a special and sophisticated human type.

There is one other side to the æsthetic motive which also is worth noticing; it issues in an aristocratic rather than a democratic ethics. No one I think is likely to suppose that Spinozism as an ethical ideal will ever be adopted very widely; indeed the fact that the common run of men are unsuited to the rarefied atmosphere of a disinterested intellectual contemplation is plainly one source of its attraction. I am not putting this forward as a criticism; it may be that the good *is* for the exceptional man alone. The reason I am noting this aristocratic quality is that I may call attention to a certain logical advantage which the æsthetic motive possesses over the one I am going on next to mention. One may object as I have done to generalizing the ideal of the self-sufficient intellect, for the reason that it is just one particular ideal which is powerful in so far, and only in so far, as it carries to this or that man an emotional appeal; however

once accepted it does provide a working motive that can
get along without the assistance of religion. The exceptional man, through his exceptional gifts, may actually
find his satisfaction in the way proposed; this is because its source lies wholly in himself and is independent of what happens in the world of nature. To
win it he may stand alone; he is not at the mercy
of unmanageable forces such as are at work in society
about him.

But along with the Spinozistic motive goes another
which is even more characteristic of the modern temper—
the "social" interest namely. The two not infrequently
are held together, as they happen to be in Mr. Lippmann's
case. But trouble is always apt to come from mixing
things; and in combining the intellectualism of the seeker
for salvation with the intellectualism of the social reformer I think Mr. Lippmann has not escaped some measure of confusion.

The point I wish to make I have just anticipated in the
preceding paragraph. In so far as salvation depends on
one's inner resources it is possible to urge that the interest in a cosmic background has been undermined; the case
is not so clear when it is a social good we are aiming to
secure. Social justice is not an individual achievement;
it depends on forces which in the end are natural forces
and which implicate the structure of the natural world.
Now it of course is so that no belief on my part in the
existence of such forces sympathetic to the cause of
human good is going to make out of this a fact provided
the fact is otherwise. But granting that any direct knowledge to the contrary is beyond our limited capacities, the
ability to retain a working faith in a friendly world may
in terms of its psychological effects be distinctly pertinent to an effective social program. Naturally it will have
no such effect if it induces men to lie back at their ease
in the expectation that nature is going to take care of
everything. But this last consequence is by no means so
inevitable as conventional criticisms of religion make it
out to be; the faith equally might serve as a spur to men's

flagging energies and so further the chances that the ends which they approve will get accomplished.

That this possibility is so often left unnoticed by the reformer at the present day and that the vogue of a pragmatic and secularistic intelligence as the solution of our social problems is so apt to be accompanied by an active repugnance toward the intrusion of religious hopes I can only account for by two considerations. One is the surreptitious influence of the various secondary motives I have been trying to sift out; the other is the peculiar limitations of the practical or pragmatic mind.

The fact is of course that a type of mind exists which prefers not to range beyond the field in which empirically verifiable consequences may be looked for; it resents or at least it declines to interest itself in the less tangible sentiments that enlist feeling and emotion. Such an attitude has been enormously reinforced by the career of modern science; under its influence many have been led to feel that the application of scientific intelligence to the field of human life offers all the intellectual opportunity they need without encroaching on the more dubious premises of sentiment and faith. And it is very likely true that this has advantages in practice—the advantages which a specialized interest can almost always show; one hardly can refuse to grant indeed that to the utilitarian with his scientific leaning the growth of a social philosophy of progress in the last century has been very largely due. But one or two additional remarks are needed to qualify such a judgment.

First and most generally, I want to reiterate that the absence in one man of some special interest is not an adequate excuse for a general denial of the legitimacy of this interest in case other people feel it. Such a denial is the product not of reason but of a certain hardheadedness and lack of imaginative sympathy, and is only one more instance of man's inveterate disposition to standardize the human race after a pattern determined by his own emotional range.

But also a positive reason in the present case exists for

questioning such an attitude. There is one respect in
which a "science of society" needs to be distinguished
sharply from the sciences that deal with physical nature.
In the latter case the investigator has no reason whatever
to desire one result rather than another; he only wants
to know the facts. But the social scientist is not in the
same degree unbiased. Provided he expects his investigations to bear fruit he is bound to be committed to a
preference for one sort of future outcome over others;
and this brings in considerations that affect his purely
scientific status. His special task as a pragmatist is to
supply a technique for social progress. But effective
social reform needs something besides technique. It needs
motivation also; and this is a need which the pragmatist
is less successful in supplying. Secure in his own possession of a coolly intellectual interest in his scientific
problem plus a not very highly emotionalized sense of
abstract justice, he is apt to forget that these are motives
little likely to be widely shared; and democracy has gone
far enough by now to make it highly improbable that
without incentives that make a general appeal the grave
difficulties in the way of progress can successfully be
overcome. I am not of course intending to suggest that
these hindrances to a decent human society can be exor-
cised by religion. The road to such a goal is on any showing long and arduous, and no faith in an eventual destiny
does anything to point the actual way to its attainment.
The only conclusion I am drawing is that the goal is
visionary unless we can enlist the active coöperation of
the ordinary man; and it is scarcely conceivable, man
being what he is, that he will do his part if he is not
upheld by a conviction that the things which meet the
approval of his deepest instincts are in fact somehow the
law of universal nature, so that he has not to think of himself as pulling against the stream of human destiny.

And to some extent at least such a conclusion will have
a rational bearing on the reformer's own state of mind.
If the momentum of his interest is not eventually to fail
he cannot afford not to pay some attention to the obvious

chance that his task may be hopeless from the start; and
for this such a seeming requirement of human nature
introduces a disturbing complication. That men generally
ever can be expected to work for a large and generous
aim in the spirit solely of an intellectual self-reliance and
without the support of more ultimate convictions calls for
a faith almost equally robust with that which he rejects;
if on the other hand he concedes the imbecility of the
average man and still hopes to meet the handicap by
enlisting the superior wisdom of the few, among other
things he runs the risk I fear of damaging the prestige
of science. He is pointed to the conception of a society in
which an impassable gulf exists, and where the masses
are directed for their own good by an intellectual aris-
tocracy that does not share their opinions and their common sentiments though it is bound in some degree to
cater to these in order to get its way; and it is impossible
without loss to its own integrity that the scientific mind
should build thus upon indirection, shams and mental
reservations.

As a matter of fact however most of the protagonists
of a scientific secularism are by no means so lacking as
their principles might suggest in an assurance that goes
beyond the scientific facts. They have their own brand
of faith—a faith in the potential rationality of humankind. Apart from some presumption that men generally
may learn to see straight, and act accordingly, on the
basis of an enlightened selfishness sufficient to overcome
the disrupting influence of greed and personal ambition,
the new science of society though it might set up an agreeable ideal would have very little application to the actual
world. But such a conviction obviously does not spring
directly from the empirical data; the scientist would, it
is likely, be himself be the first to grant that facts on
the surface do not seem to bear it out. His own task is set
for him by the conspicuous lack of reason which man's
past reveals, and which on first view may very well seem
to justify the cynic rather than the optimist. I do not
say that the cynical inference is really justified; but it is

one for which very impressive arguments can be adduced. Meanwhile it is enough for me that in so far as the factual evidence goes the issue lies in the balance; if one subscribes to the more pleasing view it will not be because history and human experience prove his case but for some reason more personal and implicit.

And I see nowhere to look for such a reason save in man's proneness to believe that somehow, though it may be he is quite unable to say how, natural forces are on the side of reason and the sentiments which social reason presupposes, so that the reformer can be allowed to entertain some reasonable assurance that his work will not go for nothing. But this is religion as I have been defining it—in an attenuated form perhaps but still religion. I am not insisting that the conclusion is inevitable; if one can combine a belief in the insignificance of all things human with a continued faith in the destined triumph of a human reason which even as such has been so little in evidence up to date, I have no wish to unsettle his conviction. But I do question his right to make for himself the claim that he alone is being rational. And at the very least I do not admit that he has any call to use the presumption that a faith in ultimate values retains no assignable meaning or interest for the modern man as a ground for feeling superior to those who still ask the privilege of holding to such a faith.

II

THE IMPLICATIONS OF HUMAN CONSCIOUSNESS

By
JAMES BISSETT PRATT

Professor of Philosophy
Williams College

THE IMPLICATIONS OF HUMAN CONSCIOUSNESS [1]

It has been a favorite suggestion, a beloved belief, of many philosophers throughout the history of European, or at least of Christian thought, that man is a "microcosm," and that from a study of this small and easily handled specimen of the universe one can come to a knowledge of the universe in the large. That such a belief involves an immense and undemonstrable assumption is obvious, and a philosophy which starts by taking for granted that cosmic nature and human nature run closely parallel is, with all its fascination, far too daring—at any rate for me. Yet there was an element of true insight in the suggestion which even the most cautious of us can hardly deny. Man and the universe may be exceedingly unlike; yet, after all, man is a product of the universe, and, so far as we know, the latest and most consummate product, and his nature must therefore be taken into serious consideration by anyone who would seek to determine the nature of the world. Long ago Aristotle taught us that a thing is what it does; and doubtless we are all pragmatists enough to agree that an individual's character or a thing's nature is best indicated by the results that flow from it. From this point of view it may well be that we shall find few methods of attacking the mystery of the cosmos so promising as a study of human nature, or an attempt to answer the question put so long ago by the Psalmist: "What is man?"

To this question there are two obvious answers. "A little lower than the angels," says the Psalmist, "crowned with glory and honor, with all things under his feet." "A little higher than the brutes," replies Natural

[1] Reprinted, in large part, from the *Harvard Theological Review*, Vol. XVI, No. 4, by permission.

Science, "sprung from them not long ago and inheriting still most of their nature." Far apart as these answers seem, they may both be true. They are not really inconsistent; for the being that evolved but yesterday from the brutes and who is as yet in many ways very like them, may be already well upon the upward path and at least in promise and potency only a little lower than the angels. This would be a mediating view and also in a sense a dualistic view, for it would find in man two natures, which the biblical nomenclature of our predecessors would have called the earthly and the heavenly. For though it is conceivable that the two may somehow ultimately be taken up into a supreme unity, short of that ultimate cosmic unity the brute's nature and the angel's, the earthly and the heavenly, are certainly two; and not merely are they two—they are in some ways antithetical and often found in deadly conflict.

Those to whom all dualism is anathema will, therefore, have nothing to do with this mediating position, but will insist either that man is all from heaven or all from earth, with no mingling of different principles in his nature. So far as I know, the former of these extreme monistic views has never been held; no one has regarded man as already full-formed angel with no smirch of the earth upon him. The Psalmist himself puts man at least a *little* lower than the angels. And Genesis tells us that in the beginning he was made from clay. But the other extreme view has often been taken—is, in fact, the increasingly popular belief of our day, at least in circles that call themselves scientific. It is the view of Naturalism. For it is the aim of Naturalism to reduce all beings and all activities to one type of being and one type of change; and the type of being and of change which it takes as fundamental and to which it would reduce all others is that made familiar to us in natural science. It is no idle impulse that has led to the construction of this ideal. The great practical aim of science—in pursuit of which man has conquered the earth and subdued the elements—has been to enable us to know what to expect from nature. Science has worked

out a system of physical concepts and laws by the application of which we are able to foresee the course of physical changes and the consequences of physical conditions.
That all changes and the consequences of all conditions
should be subject to the same laws, that all reality should
be capable of being written down and described under
one set of formulæ is, indeed, not an hypothesis of science; but that many a courageous scientific mind should
make this postulate was almost inevitable. The postulate
is a bold one, and the desire to test it thoroughly and if
possible to prove it is a worthy ambition. And no one can
deny that Naturalism has gone much farther in verifying
its hypothesis than most of our ancestors would have supposed possible. Material nature has been unified under
the naturalistic formula; and man has been shown to be
in large measure a product and a part of nature.

But the question is still to be settled: Is man *wholly* a
part and product of nature? Much of him doubtless is.
All of him, of course, is, if we take nature in the widest
sense as including all reality, as in Shakespeare's lines:

> Nature is made better by no means
> But nature made those means.

This, however, is not the meaning of the word nature
which Naturalism attributes to it; for Naturalism means
to be more than mere tautology. If Naturalism is right,
man and all there is to him is ultimately to be explained,
and completely explained, in terms of the physical and
the mechanical. The question, therefore, still remains
open: Is such an explanation really adequate? Is man
wholly a product and a part of physical nature, or is there
in him an additional element which cannot be described
in naturalistic terms nor evolved out of Naturalism's
monistic formula? Here is the real issue.

Plainly the issue centers about consciousness and personality. Can consciousness, in its lower and its higher
forms, be included within the formulæ of Naturalism?
Can personality be so analyzed as to be statable in terms
of chemistry, physics, and mechanics? As all must see,

these questions with their necessary correlates stretch out almost endlessly into the world of thought, and involve two-thirds of contemporary philosophical discussion. To be more specific, they involve the three great problems of the nature of consciousness and its relation to its object, the relation of consciousness to the body, especially to the brain, and the nature of the self. To discuss three such complex problems with any detail in one paper is, of course, out of the question. I do, however, hope to show in a general way the sort of position which monistic Naturalism takes and must take on these three problems, together with the consequences which must necessarily follow from the acceptance and from the denial of these naturalistic views.

If consciousness be something different in kind from the physical, it is plainly going to be difficult to make man —and for that matter even the animals—fit into a formula which avoids all dualism by basing itself ultimately upon the physical alone. All the greater will be this difficulty if knowledge be considered in the traditional fashion as involving a subjective and an objective factor, a relation, let us say, between a mind and its object, a relation of such a sort that in knowing the mind transcends its own immediate psychic states, *means* more than it experiences, refers to more than it directly senses, and grasps in intention the distant in space and the absent in time. One would search in vain through the files of Naturalism for a formula that could include such a power; and if the mind really possesses it—is able really to have knowledge in this sense—it is going to be extraordinarily difficult to derive the mind of man from physical nature without the addition of any new element. Hence we find the two great schools of epistemology which are most sympathetic with Naturalism attempting to build up an entirely new view of knowledge and even denying the existence of consciousness in the ordinary sense altogether; attempting, in short, to do away with the subjective aspect of experience and to substitute for the older philosophical view a kind of pan-objectivism.

This attempt to do away with the unique nature of knowledge and with the subjective in general sometimes takes the form of interpreting consciousness as a unique kind of control over behavior—a control exerted by the environment. This control is brought about by a peculiar kind of stimulus, namely, one that has a peculiar kind of incompleteness or reference to the future. Thus a sound wave, in addition to its physical characteristics, has the additional quality of causing the hearer to cock the ear and turn the eyes and set on foot activities which are directed toward getting a better stimulus. This quality, we are told, *is* consciousness. Consciousness, therefore, is not something different from the physical, something inner and subjective. It is the peculiar quality of a stimulus by virtue of which the environment is enabled to control behavior by reference to the future. There is nothing, therefore, in man's consciousness or his knowledge to prevent him from being described wholly in naturalistic terms—a conclusion surely beyond cavil, once we accept the definition of consciousness suggested.

But to found a philosophical view upon the invention of a new definition for an old word is to build a house upon the sand. One may, of course, define one's words as one likes, and if one wishes to define consciousness as a peculiar quality of a peculiar stimulus one may do so, though it will be admitted, I think, that the definition is a bit peculiar. But after one has disposed of "consciousness" in this neat and simple way, the really important question is still to be answered as to how we shall deal with those indubitable experiences which are not qualities of physical stimuli—pains, pleasures, memories, intentions, images, meanings, processes of will and of attention. It is these that press for interpretation, and it is equally idle to assert that they are qualities of physical stimuli, or to evade them by a new and arbitrary definition of the word "consciousness."

The other method by which it is sought to make consciousness and knowledge consistent with naturalistic monism is much more ingenious and persuasive. It consists, namely, in analyzing consciousness and its processes into content, and identifying this content either with bodily processes or (in the case of perception and knowledge) with the objects to which consciousness is commonly said to refer. Psychic states thus turn out to be identical with physical objects and physical objects are identical with psychic states, except for their order of arrangement or mode of collection. In fact, taken in themselves objects are neither psychical nor physical, they are neutral; and we call a given object psychical or physical purely because of the collection with which it is related in reference to our judgment. My watch is in itself, like all things else, neutral; but as a part of that collection of things to which my nervous system responds it is called psychical; as one of the things in my room it is physical. Thus both matter in the old sense and mind in the old sense are banished. Reality is a collection of neutral entities and there is nothing in it that is really subjective. Ideas and mental processes in the old sense are done away with, and thus the world is one in substance and one in the laws of its workings.

We must look a little further to get the full meaning of this doctrine. It means, for one thing, that all mental processes and attitudes—such as those we experience in an effort of will or of attention or in the attitude of belief —consist in sensations and images or are to be identified with physiological processes. Such an experience, for example, as believing or meaning or intending is to be construed not as the *feeling* of a bodily process, but as identically the bodily process itself; or else it is to be interpreted as a succession of sensuous images—images which even the chief exponent of this doctrine, Mr. Bertrand Russell, admits that neither he nor anyone else has ever been able to find by analysis, but which for entirely nonempirical reasons somehow *must* constitute all mental processes.

The theory of knowledge and of consciousness we are considering takes, moreover, a rather interesting position on the question of the process found in perception.

Physiological psychologists assure us that your percept of my watch is brought about by the reflection of ether waves from its surface to your retina and by processes which are thereupon set up in your optic nerve and eventually in your brain. Either immediately after this brain event or concomitantly with it, a sensation is born which we call a sensation of the watch. Now the doctrine we are examining, which would abolish the subjective by identifying psychic content with its object, is bound to hold that the sensation and the watch are one and the same, in spite of the fact that the watch started the whole process which ended with the sensation, and in spite of the fact that between the two are intercalated the entire physical and physiological series of the events of the perceptive process.

Not only shall we get into trouble with psysiological psychology if we accept this doctrine, but we shall also be forced to do astonishing things with the spatial and temporal characters of all things and all events. For if my visual image of the watch which I hold in my hand be identical with the watch, and your visual image of the watch be also the watch, then it would seem that your image and mine are identical with each other, in spite of the fact that my image is several times as large as yours, much more vivid, and of an entirely different shape. The only way we could get out of this manifest contradiction would be by asserting that the watch is not anywhere in particular but that it is actually everywhere. In other words, every object would have to be identified with all its actual and all its possible appearances at any and every angle, and any and every distance, each object being thus exploded to the extreme bounds of space, and interpenetrating with every other object in the universe. In similar fashion every *event* would have to be exploded to the extremes of time—both future and past. For the perception of an event—for example our perception of the reflection of light from a star—plainly occurs at a time subsequent to the event perceived, since the physical and physiological processes involved take time.

Even more obviously is it true that memory, anticipation, and the conceptual references we make to the past and the future occur at points in the time-series very different from the events which we remember, anticipate, and refer to, as when, for example, we think of the battle of Marathon. There is nothing particularly difficult about this if we recognize subjective conscious states in the old and usual way, as different from their objects, and if we admit that in knowing or meaning its objects the mind transcends in intention its immediate content. But such admissions are of course just the things which the pan-objective view that we are considering is most bound to refuse. Hence it finds great difficulty in the temporal facts I have just cited, namely, that perception, memory, and conceptual reference occur at different times from the events to which they refer. How, for example, can my present thought of the death of Socrates or of the end of the world be identical with its objects—separated as it is from those objects by thousands of years? The only way this can be done is by asserting that no event ever happens at any one particular time, but that every briefest event is an eternal process, identifiable with all actual and possible thoughts of it, past and future. In other words, every event must be exploded to the extremes of time, backward and forward, just as every object had to be exploded to the extremes of space.

Furthermore, the pan-objective view under consideration is forced to deny the privacy and separateness of individual minds, and is faced with a particularly awkward situation in dealing with such psychical entities as emotions, impulses, values, qualities like clearness, and ideas of admittedly nonexistent objects. For in these cases there is no object with which to identify the mental content. The denial of its peculiarly mental nature, therefore, seems doubly difficult. And much the same difficulty reappears when one comes to deal with error, illusion, and hallucination. In spite of many labored attempts to explain away this very patent obstacle, most students of the subject, I think, still fail to see how illusion and error are going to be at all possible if every idea or thought *is* its object.

In this examination of the methods by which contemporary naturalistic epistemology seeks to avoid the necessity of admitting consciousness as something different in kind from physical or purely logical entities, I have not sought to give an actual refutation of the doctrines involved. My aim has been rather to point out the extremes to which the upholders of these views are necessarily driven. If one denies the reality of the subjective and denies that in knowledge the mind transcends its immediate content, one must maintain all the strange positions of pan-objectivism which I have been outlining, or others like them.

Why, then, are these paradoxical positions maintained? Why do many of the keenest thinkers of our day insist upon denying the subjective in spite of the difficulties involved in such denial? In answer they will tell us that they have taken this position because of the difficulties they find in the doctrines of those schools which, like Idealism, Critical Realism, and much of the British New Realism, admit the existence of the subjective in some form or other. I do not for a moment doubt the sincerity of this statement. But at the same time I cannot help feeling that the strongest motive at work in the denial of consciousness in the old sense has largely escaped the notice of many of those who make the denial. This motive, I believe, has very little to do with epistemological considerations. It is, in my opinion, the fear that an epistemology which recognizes consciousness as different in kind from matter and not to be identified with its objects, conscious processes as different in kind from physical processes, and knowledge as the activity of a mind which is able to transcend its content—that an epistemology, I say, which takes these or any of these positions, is pretty sure to lead in the end to a metaphysics which will prove fatal to the claims of monistic Naturalism.

That naturalistic epistemology is justified in cherishing this fear and right in maintaining this opinion is my own conviction. If the images and processes and mental states by which the mind thinks its objects are not to be identified with those objects but are instead actual entities, actual though not discoverable in all the world of physical space nor parts of the executive order of the physical world, if the activity of knowing is something very different from the "flat piece of substantive experience" to which William James sought to reduce it, if in thinking of the distant in space and the remote in time the mind really transcends its immediate content and becomes, in Plato's phrase, at least potentially, "a beholder of all time and all existence," then it is plain that the mind is something that can hardly be explained by any of the laws of physical nature, and to which even the most refined formulæ of evolutionary Naturalism are fundamentally inadequate.

If, then, consciousness or mind, in something like its traditional sense, cannot successfully be explained away by the new epistemology, we must resolutely face the metaphysical question of the relation of the mind to the physical world in which it has its setting. The central and crucial part of this question is, of course, to be found in the mind-body problem. Obviously we cannot here deal with this great question. I wish merely to point out the general nature of the situation. If we refuse to accept the pan-objective epistemology already considered which would do away with consciousness in the subjective and traditional sense, we must recognize that the relation of the mind to the body forms a real and unescapable problem, and unless we are weakly to evade it by an ostrich-like refusal to look it in the face, the alternatives open to us are reduced to two: the acceptance of the doctrine of interaction, on the one hand, or the adoption of one of the naturalistic positions on the other. That interaction has its difficulties it would be impossible to forget, so often have they been pointed out and so emphatically have they been stressed by the advocates of the naturalistic school these many centuries. The classical diffi-

culties most commonly emphasized are two. The first is
usually expressed in the oft-heard question: How can
two things so different from each other as mind and body
interact? To which, it seems to me, the sufficient answer
is to be found in the rather obvious query, Why may they
not? Are we so sure that unlike things cannot influence
each other? The only way really to decide this question
is to go to experience and see. And when we do this, we
certainly seem very plainly to find in sensation body
acting upon mind, and in volition mind acting upon body.
The obvious testimony of our everyday normal experience seems to be corroborated by various pathological
conditions and by various curative methods. I need
hardly mention such things as the age-long use of drugs
as stimulants and sedatives, nor the equally ancient and
efficacious mental treatment of physical disorders,
psycho-analysis and Christian Science; the much talked
of influence of the ductless glands upon personality; and,
on the other hand, the unquestionable power of Coué's
methods and of auto-suggestion in general upon very real
physiological derangements. Surely he who would roundly
deny all influence of body and mind upon each other
has a heavy burden of proof resting upon his shoulders.
And, in fact, the only kind of proof he has to offer for his
astounding position is an appeal not *to* experience but
away from experience; an appeal, namely, to what he
regards as the antecedent improbability of any such
mutual influence. This so-called antecedent improbability
is, in fact, the second of the two difficulties of interaction
to which I referred. More specifically it consists in the
impossibility of reconciling interaction with the universality of mechanical law. But of course the question
whether mechanical law *is* universal is just the question
at issue; and it can hardly be called logic to use this
affirmed universality both as major premise and as conclusion.

But we can better estimate the importance or negligi-
bility of the difficulties of interaction if we go on to consider the consequences of denying it; or, in other words,

the necessary implications of the naturalistic theories of mind and body. Very briefly, then—for we have no time for a detailed consideration of the matter—each of these theories is faced with the dilemma of either denying the efficiency of consciousness or identifying consciousness with matter, motion, or physical energy. One may take one's choice, but choose one must. And the seriousness of either choice must not be overlooked. If we deny all efficiency to consciousness, maintaining that the laws of physical nature determine all the actions of human bodies, we make the evolutionary development of consciousness a hopeless mystery, and we shall be forced to maintain the astounding position that the strategy of Napoleon, the plays of Shakespeare, and the acts of love of all the lovers and all the mothers of the world have in no wise been influenced by thought or feeling. There is no getting around this. It is an identical equation, a tautologous assertion. If the laws of physical nature completely determine all actions and all events, then all actions and all events are determined completely by the laws of physical nature; and though emotions, desires, ideas, plans, purposes, voluntary acts may be admitted to exist, they must be denied the least particle of influence upon any of our deeds. No event in the whole history of the race, on this conception, is different from what it would have been had all human beings from *pithecanthropus erectus* to the latest naturalistic philosopher been mere unconscious automata. Even his own writings, such an up-to-date philosopher must assert, are in no wise the product of thought or memory or conscious experience. They were composed, not by his mind, but by his cortex and his typewriter. The naturalistic thinker does not like to dwell upon this aspect of his own theory, but it is an inevitable consequence of his fundamental position, inevitable, at least, unless he is prepared to choose instead the other horn of the naturalistic dilemma and affirm that consciousness is to be identified with the physical. If he chooses this course, he may indeed escape the unwelcome necessity of denying efficiency to consciousness; but he does so only at the cost of basing his whole position upon an assertion that is in the last analysis essentially meaningless. I do not say that his assertion is undemonstrable; I do not say that it is improbable. I say that it has no meaning. The sentence, *Consciousness is physical energy,* is grammatically a perfectly good sentence. It has a subject and a predicate. You can parse it. You can parse it and you can repeat it; but you cannot think it. It is exactly on a par with such a sentence as, *A logarithm is green cheese.* The tongue runs glibly along each of these sentences, but the thought, starting out bravely enough, simply stops, or turns into the sort of thing our behaviorist friends describe their own thought as being, namely, just the unconscious activity of the language mechanism. We know what we mean by conscious ideas, emotions, intentions, and the rest; and we know what we mean by the physiological processes that go on in the brain; and to assert the absolute identity of the two is to put words together out of which all meaning has evaporated. If such an assertion be not nonsense, there is no such thing as nonsense.

I am making no elaborate attempt to refute the naturalistic position on the mind-body problem. My purpose is simply to draw attention to the quite unescapable implications of that position. If one wishes to accept the naturalistic view, of course one may; but one should realize fully all that must be accepted with it. One cannot take it and refuse the implications of which I have been speaking. They go inevitably together. Doubtless interaction has its difficulties, the two most important of which we have considered. As we have seen, these difficulties have little or nothing that is empirical about them. They rest, instead, upon what is called the antecedent improbability of interaction. But, as I have already indicated, and as I think I could clearly show did time permit, this asserted improbability is itself based simply upon an ideal of scientific explanation which we ourselves have constructed and have more or less dogmatically set up. And for the rest, weight the improbability of interaction as greatly as you like, you will have to rouse your emotions of naturalistic enthusiasm to an extraordinary pitch before you can make it compare with the astounding assertion that consciousness never has any influence upon conduct, or with the meaningless assertion that consciousness *is* brain activity.

At an early point in this paper I spoke of three problems relating to man upon which Naturalism, if it is to be thorough and consistent, must take extreme views. Two of these we have now briefly considered, namely, the relation of the mind to its objects and its relation to the body. The third question had to do with the nature of the self. If we accept the pan-objective epistemology discussed in the early part of this paper, the self of course either vanishes together with consciousness into the various objects to which the organism responds, or else has to be identified with the physical organism itself. If we accept that form of naturalism which identifies consciousness with the physiological processes of the brain, the self hardens, so to speak, together with its psychic states, into gray and white matter. If, for reasons such as those I have suggested, we find ourselves unable to accept either this view of the mind-body problem or the pan-objective epistemology, but still wish to hold to a naturalistic position, we must, I suppose, identify the self with the ineffectual mental states which, for some unaccountable reason, accompany brain-states—the stream of inactive epiphenomena. The self will thus become, in Hume's phrase, "a bundle of sensations and ideas." The untenability of such a position was brought to light long ago by William James. Doubtless there is diversity in the stream of consciousness, but there is unity as well, and the major portion of this unity is the unity of the judging thought, the unity of the active mind. James, to be sure, refused to refer this unity of judgment and action to a self; it belonged rather, he said, to what he called the present judging thought. This present thought was not mere passive content; it was active, and it actively claimed and owned all the memories, all the past states of the conscious stream, as its own. It not only claimed them; it inherited them from its predecessor and passed them on to its successor. It was, in a word, a real, though momentary self. It had unity, activity, in short all the essential characteristics that are usually attributed to the self, except continuity. Instead of the one continuous self of Personal Realism, James gives us a cinematographic succession of momentary selves, flashing into existence and out of it, each cut off from its predecessor and from its successor by the sharp lines of birth and death.

Now there are two obvious comments to be made upon this view. In the first place, introspection shows no such sharp division between successive judging thoughts, no such jumping, jumping of the moving pictures of our inner life, as James implies. Instead there is continuous progress with no lines of cleavage between successive selves. And the second comment is this: if we recognize this steady continuity of our inner lives, as I think we must, and therefore give up James's notion of a succession of momentary and disparate selves, we have left on our hands, as a result of careful introspection, a modification of James's doctrine which turns out to be in no important respect distinguishable from the view taken by Personal Realism. The doctrine of the reality of the self does not necessarily maintain the existence of an unknowable something outside of experience and transcending time. It means rather the active unity of experience itself as it goes forward in time, cleaving time as a spear head steadily cleaves the air, and identical with its own past in much the same way that anything is identical with its own past. Taken in this sense, the self is both active, unitary, continuous, and real; and it is to this real and discoverable kind of self that, as it seems to me, James's conception is ultimately reducible.

There is only one way, so far as I can see, in which this conclusion can be avoided—at least by those who admit consciousness in the subjective sense at all; and that is by denying the trustworthiness of introspection and chal-

lenging James's fundamental assertion that the essence
of feeling is to be felt, and that as a psychic existent feels
so it must be. This course is therefore adopted by the
bolder and more clear-sighted upholders of Naturalism.
All real activity is thus denied to the mind; processes
such as those of attention, meaning, volition, are analyzed
into passing and passive sensations and images; and then
all these different sorts of passive content are asserted
to be composed ultimately of a single homogeneous element. Inasmuch as introspection has been declared fallacious, and the feeling of a feeling has been ruled out
of court as giving no evidence concerning the feeling's
real nature, almost anything may be true, and the requirements of Naturalism are allowed to dictate the conclusion. Thus by a reduction of the multiplicity which introspection discovers to a stark homogeneity we are enabled
to reduce quality to quantity. Having done this successfully, we are encouraged to go on and identify this one
homogeneous psychical element with some sort of physical element, or the physical with the psychical, it matters
little which. In the words of the chief supporter of this
view, we must interpret matter in motion as feeling, ''but
not feeling just as it is introspectively given; feeling,
rather, having more spatial divisions and less continuity, and more change of place among the divisions,
than we are aware of introspectively; in a word, something truly of the nature of feeling, but in arrangement
more like matter in motion.''

The conception of a self or personality—a center of
emotion and reason and conscious volition—doubtless has
its difficulties, difficulties due chiefly to the fact that if
there be a self at all, in any meaningful sense, it must be
sui generis and not susceptible of description in the categories of natural science. But I submit that, paradox for
paradox, the inherent improbability of personality as we
seem to find it in ourselves is surely not greater than the
improbability of a position which abolishes both personality and conscious activity, gives the lie to introspection,
reduces the diversity which we actually find to a blank

homogeneity, and ends by asserting that feeling is not what we feel but, "is in arrangement more like matter in motion."

The extreme positions which Naturalism is forced to defend, once its logical implications are understood, are such as to make one wonder how they could ever be accepted. But it is not for nothing that Naturalism pays the price of these tremendous paradoxes. The naturalistic philosopher realizes that unless he has the courage to accept all these extremes, he must recognize in the world a dualism of process which will make the universal sway of purely naturalistic laws forever impossible. In the recognition of this fact he is unquestionably right. If consciousness be irreducible to the physical, if the laws of mechanism do not fully determine human conduct, if there be such a thing as conscious personality—a real center of spontaneous activity—then there is a realm of spirit which has its own laws and whose activities are not to be forecast by the laws of physical science, since they are not determined by those laws. If, now, we define nature as that realm to which natural science applies, we may properly recognize the realm of the spirit as supernatural in a very real and significant sense. And to the acknowledgement of this realm we are driven if we refuse to accept the extreme and seemingly preposterous views of naturalistic monism. Some more or less vague sense of the necessity of choosing between these rival alternatives there has always been; but it is only in our own day that the fact has been brought home to us in sharp, clear outline. No one is more keenly aware of it than the leaders of naturalistic thought. Passage after passage from their writings could be quoted in which they defend their seeming paradoxes explicitly upon the ground that if they be not accepted there is no alternative but what they—quite properly—call supernaturalism. The word supernaturalism is of course sometimes used as synonymous with superstition, but it is not in this sense that either the naturalists or we are using it. What both of us mean by the word is a dualistic view of reality, a view which finds in the world two kinds of power and of process, a spiritual as well as a physical, a realm of free and conscious activity as well as a realm of passive scientific and unconscious regularity.

Which of these views, the dualistic or the monistic, is the true one? Upon the answer to this question depends the answer to the further question, Is religion merely a case of the will to believe, a collection of comforting illusions and deceptive hopes, or is its view of the nature of reality essentially true?

I have tried to point out in this paper that if we look at the matter in empirical fashion we can hardly deny that the facts of experience and the testimony of consciousness seem plainly to point toward the dualistic view. The argument against this position is based not upon any solid fact but on what is called the inherent and antecedent improbability of dualism. Now when we analyze this improbability, we find that it comes down ultimately to the *improbability of there being in the world any such creature as man.* That is exactly the situation. Let me repeat it. Such a creature as man—a being with a mind that is not a brain, a thought that is not identifiable with its distant object, a will that is capable of affecting the actions of the body, a personality that is not reducible to a succession of sensations—such a creature cannot be made to fit into the naturalistic scheme, and it is for this reason that the naturalistic philosophers deny his existence.

Here let me turn aside for a moment from the direct course of our thought to point out the interesting bearing of the conclusions to which we have been forced upon what is known as religious Humanism. The attentive reader has probably long since noted what I have here in mind. The advocates of the "New Religion" advertise to the world in no uncertain tones that Humanism is based upon and grows out of the naturalistic point of view. It turns away from God and the Supernatural and centers its attention upon man. One of its leading spokesmen defines Humanism as "faith in the supreme value and self-perfectibility of human personality," and defines human personality as "that unity of qualities and powers making up the self-recognizing, self-directing, self-giving individual." Now if this be Humanism (and the definition is not a bad one) it would seem to me pretty plain that instead of being based upon Naturalism, Humanism is essentially incompatible with it. Instead of being forced by Naturalism into Humanism, one must choose between the two. For the naturalistic philosopher the existence of a "self-recognizing, self-directing, self-giving individual" is hardly conceivable. In short, on naturalistic doctrines it is most unlikely that there ever could be such a universe—such a queer universe—as the one which the Humanists and the rest of us find ourselves living in.

But after all, we cannot dictate to reality. We cannot reframe its nature to suit our *a priori* notions of probability. With Margaret Fuller we had best accept the universe. The world we live in is the kind of universe we find it to be—a world that is full of a number of things, and, most surprising of all, a world that has a place in it for that most unlikely of beings, *man*. Man with his spiritual nature is a fact, the fundamental and central fact from which our whole interpretation of the universe may well start. And if we start with man as he is, we shall be led to recognize that Reality stretches out beyond the realm of the merely natural, that it contains a sphere which may well be called the Realm of the Spirit.

This is the conception which religion has always stood for. With unwavering faith it has persistently maintained that the world of matter and force, of mechanical laws and physical evolution is not the whole. Doubtless we belong in part—in large part—to the natural world. We grow out of the soil, perhaps, but we are not wholly of the soil. Our bodies were made of clay; but before we could be fully men, God breathed into us the breath of life.

It is, then, to the reality of a supernatural realm, a realm of the spirit, that all the religions have in some sense consistently and persistently testified. There are many roads that lead to the conviction that this testimony is true. Only one of them have we had time to follow in this paper. But I am convinced that this road, though leading through lowly regions and over no great heights of speculation or inspiration, may safely be trusted to lead us at last to our goal. We know that there is a spiritual realm, because we find that man cannot be adequately understood or described without recognizing the independent reality of the spirit. We know that there is a supernatural realm because we find that we ourselves are in part members of it. We are able to answer religion's question as to reality in the large, because we have seen that man is not merely one of the higher brutes, not merely an outgrowth of the earth, but also a little lower than the angels.

III

A PHENOMENOLOGICAL APPROACH TO RELIGIOUS REALISM

By
JULIUS SEELYE BIXLER

Professor of Religion and Biblical Literature
Smith College

III

A PHENOMENOLOGICAL APPROACH TO RELIGIOUS REALISM

THE phenomenological movement in modern Germany, in so far as it has busied itself with problems of religion, has supplemented in a striking way the movement toward religious realism in this country. With American religious realism it has made the analysis of religious experience its chief concern. Using the autonomy of the religious consciousness both as a point of departure and as a hypothesis to be constantly verified it has done much to deliver the philosophy of religion out of the hands of that "psychologizing" tendency which looks for the final interpretation and evaluation of all experience in the psychological statement of the processes involved. In its analysis of the religious consciousness it has combined a rigorous logical method with a remarkable degree of sensitiveness to that which is of value in the historical religious tradition. The result has been a high degree of precision without emptiness, and a wealth of content which has not been sacrificed to purely formal considerations.

The name which, in this connection, stands out most significantly in the phenomenological movement is that of Max Scheler, the most prolific writer among recent German philosophers, who died in 1928 at the age of fifty-five, a few days after entering upon his duties as professor of philosophy at Frankfurt. Although he wrote much, Scheler has left only sketchy outlines of his thought behind him. Like other gifted minds whose main interest was religion—one thinks of Pascal, Schleiermacher, Renan, William James—his work is notable for the penetrating quality of its insights rather than for its completeness as a system. Scheler's career was a tempestuous one, marked by a restless urge for new ideas and new experiences, and his philosophy in many ways reflects its unsettled quality. In his youth a Protestant, the son of a Jewish mother, by nature, as his friends have said, a pagan, he became a leader in the Roman Catholic youth movement and an exponent of Augustinianism in Catholic circles. Later he left the Church, and before his death he opposed it vigorously for its interference with scientific inquiry. The teachers who had the most influence on his thought were Rudolf Eucken and Edmund Husserl. Although he differs from Husserl on important points he is regularly identified in Germany with the phenomenological group of which Husserl has for some years been the leader. Scheler brought to philosophy not only the eagerness of the restless seeker for new truth, but the sensitiveness of an artist and a capacity for scientific research which won him recognition in the field of psychology. The range of his interests and flexibility of his intellectual temper make his work especially significant for the study of religious realism.

For a running start toward an understanding of Scheler's phenomenology it is necessary to pay some attention to a few of its forerunners. From the outset we must be prepared to use conceptions which imply somewhat unfamiliar attitudes toward philosophical problems. We must face first of all the fact that phenomenology is concerned with such things as essences, with "pure consciousness," with what is called the "intentional" nature of thought, and with possibilities that belong to the world of immanent inspection rather than that of objective scientific verifiability. For the time being we must free ourselves from any hope of linking the subject matter of phenomenology with the data of science or the interests of everyday life. Phenomenology asks questions about consciousness, but it means "pure consciousness," not the ordinary thinking and feeling processes of our usual life. Its interest is not in a psychological, but in a logical consciousness, one whose contents must be of a certain sort because no other logical possibilities exist, and in the kind of objects which such a pure or refined or abstracted consciousness can have. Since these objects are really all thinkable or experienceable objects the inquiry becomes, looked at from one angle, an inquiry into what is thinkable or experienceable, and into the conditions which govern the rightful objects of our thought and experience. The name "phenomenology" (*Phänomenologie*) comes from the fact that the objects of its study are phenomena, not in the traditional sense of appearances as contrasted with reality, but as data present to consciousness, phenomena in the Aristotelian rather than the Kantian sense. In studying these phenomena it makes much of the fact that all consciousness is correlative. That is, all consciousness is consciousness-of-something; all consciousness has objects as truly as it has a subject. The objects are to be found by a kind of immanent inspection, for it is as resident in consciousness that they are known. The question of their external reality, their existence in and for themselves, is thus left at one side by phenomenology as excluded from its special field of inquiry. What these objects are, not that they are, is its concern. Questions such as existence, position in space and time, relation to sense experience, important as they may be for the man in the street, are for phenomenology irrelevant. It is this unusual circumscription of its field which gives phenomenology its originality and also threatens as its greatest danger.

Phenomenology has drawn much from Franz Brentano (1838-1917) who formulated what has been called the "acts" psychology. Husserl was for a time a pupil of Brentano, and his *Logische Untersuchungen* studies the logical aspect of processes in which Brentano was interested psychologically. According to the "acts" psychology all mental life is activity. Experience is a way of acting rather than a body of content. Psychology is the study of acts, or psychical functions; it is the science of experiences or acts which are psychical and which "intend" or are directed toward material or physical objects. A psychical act is not complete or self-contained,

but has within itself its "intentional" object, the object
toward which it points. The view of mind as "intentional," a view which has resemblances to scholastic conceptions, Brentano developed as a natural part of the
"acts" psychology. To say that consciousness is functional means that it is "intentional" in the sense that
it is always pointing to objects. To love is to love an
object, to judge is to judge concerning an object, and to
imagine is to imagine an object as well. The act of consciousness is separable both from reflection upon the act
and from all judgments as to truth or falsity, reality or
unreality of that which is contained in the act. The different classes of consciousness such as judgment, feeling,
will, are to be distinguished by their intentional direction, that is, by the way in which something becomes an
object for them.

To explain what this view means the expression, "I
present something to myself in consciousness" as contrasted with the mere "there is something," has been
used. It may be illuminating to notice that a somewhat
similar conception is used to-day by *Gestalt* psychology
as a means of opposing the current behaviorism. The
relation studied by psychology, according to this claim, is
not that of stimulus provoking response, but a more conative relation in which the subject has more than a passive
part. The love of child for parent, for example, is not
determined by the fact that the child is fed by the parent.
There is rather from the beginning an emotional attitude
on the child's part which makes it possible for the stimulus to exert its own influence. Or an illustration from
a book called *Absolute Stellungnahmen* [1] by Kurt Stavenhagen may help to make the point clear. This author
claims that an analysis of an experience, say that involved in religion, must be made from the subjective as
well as the objective side. We must know what the ego
itself contributes, what its "intention" is. Feeling, doctrine, and rite involve different "intentions" on the part
of the subject, different directions which his conscious-

[1] Erlangen, 1925.

ness takes. It is possible to think of æsthetic enjoyment as directed toward an object which is not æsthetic and as in itself predicating something about that object. If I love, this fact alone tells something about the object loved. It is the intentional direction of consciousness which here counts.

After Brentano, Alexius Meinong (1853-1920) in his analysis of objects betook himself so far from the world of real things as to assert that objects can be referred to which so far from existing, do not even "subsist," as numbers or universal truths are supposed by some philosophers to do, but which can be pointed to, impossible though it be, as in the case of a "round square," to describe them or to imagine their existence. Meinong is a forerunner of phenomenology in the ease with which he abstracts objects from considerations of existence and also in his view that the task of philosophy is that of taking objects as presented in consciousness. Wilhelm Dilthey (1833-1912) also helped to prepare the ground in his plea, as against Ebbinghaus, for the method of understanding as against explaining. In true understanding, with sympathetic insight, we see life as it is, in its wholeness and not broken up into atoms, in its connections and relationships. An inseparable connection which we should try to understand rather than explain, as we might explain a process in nature, is that between consciousness and its world, between subject and object. We perceive an object in its relationships to us, including those of use and familiarity as well as sense content. The philosopher should not lose his sense of the complex character of the connections which the subject-object relation brings.

Edmund Husserl, who in 1929 celebrated his seventieth birthday in Freiburg, is the man who brought phenomenology to Scheler's attention. In dealing with Husserl's view of consciousness let us keep in mind that we are talking not of any empirical consciousness but of consciousness as such, the kind of consciousness which would hold good for angels or centaurs as much as for human

beings. The objects which we meet here are objects of
consciousness as such and our inquiry is as to what
objects are possible for consciousness of this pure and
refined sort. Husserl wishes to formulate a philosophy
which shall deal with absolutely fundamental and basic
data, which shall treat them with exactness as complete
as that of mathematics itself, and which shall thereby
become with right the first philosophy, a basis for all
other philosophy and no less for science. The method
best fitted to accomplish this is, he believes, Descartes'
method of rigorous doubt carried further than Descartes
was himself able to carry it. Descartes did not doubt himself. Husserl doubts everything but a stream of experience. Instead of a *cogito* he will allow only a succession
of *cogitata* or *cogitationes* as he sometimes calls them.
These *cogitationes* have a subjective aspect and an objective aspect. If we study the objective side we cannot get
beyond the realm of that which is absolutely given, for
there they are, presented in experience and waiting only
for our analysis. This saves us also from the difficulty
into which Descartes plunged himself and all subsequent
philosophy by his distinction between *res cogitans* on the
one hand and *res extensa* on the other. We no longer
have to ask how the knower can get out of himself and
into the known because the two are simply complementary parts of one experience. With Dilthey, Husserl
reaches out beyond the current idealistic-realistic dualism to a realm which lies beyond either. He attains it
with the aid of Brentano's notion of the "intentional"
character of consciousness, where thought is regarded as
necessarily *of* something beside itself.

But even more important than the elimination of Descartes' dualism which this view gives us is its clue to a
more complete assurance than he was able to attain. We
want to doubt all that can be doubted. Very well, then,
let us strike out or cancel everything contingent, everything except the essence of the subject matter in hand.
All questions of relation to sense experience or to the
world of space and time, all factual considerations or

questions of "existence" must be "bracketed." It is not
that we deny them for other purposes, but simply that
we refuse to admit their relevance to the present inquiry.
The electric current which animates them is for the moment turned off. When we have done this and have given
our attention to the thing itself we are able to see what it
is by nature, what it *must be* and cannot help being, what
it is not in existence but as essence. This process Husserl
calls the "phenomenological reduction" and he makes it
preliminary to all philosophical investigation. This is the
positive side of the method of systematic doubt. When all
that can be cancelled has been crossed off that which is
truly possible remains. It is the business of phenomenology to take account of these possibilities and to record
them as they present themselves. Philosophy as phenomenology thus becomes a process not of deducing that
which is logical but of describing that which is conceivable. The possibilities which are seen and described are,
it should be said, not possibilities in the sense that they
may be realized and may not. They are *essential* possibilities, necessities in that they are part of the nature of
the subject in hand and cannot be neglected or doubted.
They are seen in a form of intuition which Husserl calls
Wesenerschauung, or intuition of essences. And there
can be no question about them for the one who has faithfully bracketed all extraneous considerations.

A trivial illustration may help to make the point clear.
If I hear a tone I can take the tone that I hear and by
putting it through this phenomenological reduction can
testify certainly as to what is true not only of the tone
itself as an individual thing but what the essence of tone
must be as distinct from color. The illustration seems
obvious, but in its very obviousness lies the point. Whatever phenomenology reveals will seem obvious because
it clearly cannot be otherwise. The great aim is clearness. We want to see what is undeniably true of essences
whether individual things corresponding to them exist or
not, what is true of the universal proposition $A = A$
which endures throughout all changes among empirical

instances and indeed whether or not empirical instances are given at all. This is what Husserl means when he says that the scientific and philosophical world needs to have the phenomenological method applied to its conceptions before further progress can be made.

The similarity between these essences and Platonic universals is undeniable, although Husserl will not admit their identity. The kind of existence which his essences have is different from that of the Platonic forms, and the *eidos* is only one of many kinds of essences. But he admits his dependence on Plato and says it was Lotze who first made him aware of the phenomenological implications in the Platonic dialogues. Students of Husserl see to-day, however, a tendency away from the realism of Plato toward the idealism of Descartes. It is true that his bracketing of considerations of existence and his attack on psychologism make his "transcendental idealism" in a way something which borders on the logical realism of the new realists. When he talks of the object as different from the act and as transcending the act he shows affiliations with realism. But those who have followed his development see to-day a shifting of interest on Husserl's part from the Platonic *eidos* to the Cartesian *cogito,* from the *Wesen* or essence to the *Wesensschau* or act of intuiting the essence, from the *noëma* or objective aspect of the datum of experience to the *noësis* or subjective aspect. Husserl speaks of his own attitude as idealistic, and of the realm which he explores as that of "pure" or "transcendental" consciousness. He is concerned with the object, yet the object must itself be presented to consciousness.

What Husserl gives us, then, is an *a priori* science of pure experience. It is *a priori* not in the sense that it follows rules laid down by a unified mind, but in the sense that it admits only what is necessary—necessary, that is, from the point of view of logic, not from that of the world of space and time. It is also in the largest sense empirical, since it relies upon intuitions, though these are of course not related to sense experience. It assumes

nothing, but merely describes what it sees. What it sees
is, however, absolutely sure. The object is accepted for
just what it is. The phenomenological intuition touches
no unknown world but examines merely what is necessarily immanent in consciousness.

It is interesting to notice that Husserl came to philosophy from mathematics and with the conviction that the
clue to mathematical as well as to logical truth was to be
found in psychology. In a book on arithmetic published
in 1891 he accepted the idea that it is psychology on which
logic is based. But this view, called *"Psychologismus"*
in Germany to-day, now finds in Husserl one of its most
powerful antagonists. Husserl says himself that it was
partly his reading of Dilthey, known in Germany as one
of the ablest defenders of *Geisteswissenschaften,* or sciences of the spirit as contrasted with natural science,
which convinced him of the need for different methods
in science and philosophy respectively. In a famous article published in the magazine *Logos* in 1910 Husserl
claimed that the procedures of natural science were not
suitable even for all psychological investigation. It is
interesting to know that the line of argument pursued by
both Dilthey and Husserl played a part in the founding
of the new *Gestalt* movement in psychology. The leaders
of this movement took over the phenomenological method
to the extent of claiming that mental processes should be
judged by what they themselves had to offer, for the
meanings resident in them as presented to experience,
and not exclusively in relation to the physiological processes which accompany them. *Gestalt* psychology allows
experiences to speak for themselves and so finds qualitative distinctions among them which are not otherwise
apparent. It has thus purified its basic conceptions just
as phenomenology asserts all sciences must do.

Whether or not Husserl has actually formulated a new
philosophy must remain an open question. He has at
least offered a method, that of clarifying our conceptions
by getting back to the essence of the datum of consciousness. An examination of the phenomenon as he under-

stands it should at least afford a view of the limits within which, so to speak, reality must operate, a view of that on which our thought must build. An attempt to attain such a view is made by Scheler, whose work is all the more noteworthy because it does not have the exclusive interest in formalistic considerations which characterizes Husserl's procedure. Scheler is as able as Husserl to carry through a subtle logical analysis but he is also able to allow his imagination to roam widely over man's spiritual environment and to return with significant data for man's spiritual life. The phenomenological method in his hands is made a means to a series of important suggestions for a theory of knowledge, value, and religion.

It is the use of the phenomenological method, claims Scheler in one of his later essays, the ability to get at the essence of the subject in hand, which distinguishes man from all lower orders of being. This it is which marks off *Geist* from mere *Leben,* the truly spiritual from the neutral life-process. It also separates spirit from mere intelligence.[2] Intelligence asks with regard to such a subject as pain how it came into being and how it can be cured. But the phenomenological question is: What is pain in itself, independently of the fact of my having it? What is pain in essence? This ability to distinguish between *Dasein* and *Wesen,* between existence and essence, gives man a window through which he can peer into the realm of the absolute. Plato meant this when he distinguished the universal from the particular. Buddha had it in the back of his mind when he asked not merely about the ailment of the sick man whom he saw, but about the nature of a world in which such suffering was possible. The sense of the *existence* of an object is present to the lowest forms of animal consciousness. It is merely a result of the resistance presented by the environment to the blind, struggling life-process itself. The *essence,* however, is found only by that higher form of conscious-

---

[2] Professor Whitehead makes a similar distinction between Plato and Ulysses. "The one shares Reason with the Gods, the other shares it with the foxes." *The Function of Reason* (Princeton University Press), p. 7.

ness which can say "no" to the obvious and to that which unguided life confronts. The process is not so much, as Husserl thought, that of suspending the judgment of existence as it is that of protesting against all existence which has a merely here-and-now character. Man is the eternal Faust, never satisfied with the present, ever intent to break the bonds of the immediately given. By this denial of the world and refusal to accept the limitations of the present environment man puts himself outside of nature and finds his own center as well as that of the world in a realm which is open only to spiritual discernment.

Scheler is not always so poetic, however, as he is in the later essays. In his monumental book entitled *Der Formalismus in der Ethik und die Materiale Wertethik,* the most systematic work he produced, he developed in detail and in ordered fashion a theory of values in general and ethical values in particular. The book is written against a Kantian background so that he is led into a somewhat prolonged discussion of logical and epistemological issues before his ethical philosophy comes clearly into view. He calls his own position that of "ethical absolutism or objectivism" on the one hand, or "emotional intuitionism and material apriorism" on the other. Kant was right, he says, in claiming that an ethical system to be binding must be formal. Attempts since Kant to ground ethics in non-formal principles, such as "life" or "well-being" only serve to show the soundness of Kant's position in this respect. Yet to say that the final sanction of ethics must be independent of both historical and psychological considerations is not, Scheler holds, to assert that it cannot be concrete. We must have a formal principle, but it need not be so empty as the one Kant articulated. If we seize upon any special good as basic we fall at once into the error of all induction. Any empirical good, for example any good linked up with the welfare of a certain community, state, or church, rests back on the continuation of a special historical or psychological condition. With the changing of this condition, and history surely shows us enough of such changes, the

good and its authority disappear. No final criterion can
be derived from any such shifting scene. This method
affords us no standard drawn from outside the observed
world of goods by which this world can itself be judged,
and the soundness of its own development tested. Our
task, then, is that of finding values which lie outside of
changing empirical conditions or are "prior" to them.
Are there such values, and are they entirely non-material
as Kant held?

What are values? According to Scheler the names for
values are no more mere names for qualities of the things
we call goods than names for colors are simply names for
qualities of bodily objects. Red is more than a quality of
a table. In the spectroscope it is an extended thing, something apart from and independent of other substances.
Similarly values, like pleasant, charming, friendly, noble,
exist in their own right, and not merely as qualities of
things or men. Furthermore, autonomous divisions exist
among these values themselves. The pleasantness of the
taste of a cherry is qualitatively different from that of a
pear. Also, we should not think of æsthetic values, such
as lovely, noble, as mere common qualities exhibited in a
variety of bearers. We know what "lovely" means as
applied to flowers, and "noble" as applied to horses, yet
we know it as an individual objective thing rather than
a common quality. An essence (*Wesen*) need not be a
general characteristic in order to be an essence. You can
get at the innermost nature of a man by observing a
single act as well as by observing him constantly. Notice
also that we can speak of the essence of an individual
man as well as of man in general. Jesus' saying: "No
man is good save God" means not that no one has any
good qualities, but that the essence of goodness belongs
to the realm of values, and not to qualities which are supposed to "exhibit" this goodness. Values are *sui generis,*
self-sufficient, given immediately and seen intuitively as
existing in their own right.

This theme of the autonomy of the realm of value and
the impossibility of deriving it from the realm of being is

a recurrent one in Scheler and his illustrations of it are legion. A glance at a few more of those which deal with the lack of dependence of a value on its bearer may help to bring out his point. A man may be agreeable to us, Scheler claims, without our knowing wherein this agreeableness consists; a work of art may be beautiful, a room hospitable or inviting, without our being able to say why. Again, it may be a matter of indifference to us whether a man is more of an artist or more of a philosopher, without our being at all indifferent to his personal value. I can know now that a certain day last August was especially beautiful without realizing that on that day a dear friend visited me. The value often seems to stride before the object as the first herald of its special nature, sometimes appearing more clearly than the object itself. A comparison between two values can also often be made although the objects are not more than dimly present in consciousness. Notice further that values do not change with their objects. When a blue bullet turns red we do not say that the color blue has changed. Nourishment remains nourishment and toxicity harmful although the same thing can at the same time be one man's meat and another's poison. Friendship does not change because my friend betrays me.

Value and being are coördinate conceptions. They defy all attempts to derive one from the other. The dualism which appears on the objective side in the separation between value and being is on the subjective side that between feeling and knowing. We must remember that a theory which brings out the "intentional" nature of consciousness can admit such a dualism without reducing its world to chaos. For the assertion of the dualism is just another way of saying that since all consciousness is consciousness-of-something, the fact that there are different kinds of consciousness, *e.g.* knowing, feeling, points to different kinds of objects of consciousness. The knowing consciousness is directed toward the world of existence, the feeling consciousness toward the world of values. Thus to say that value is independent of "being"

(*Sein*) is not to put values into a fictitious world, or even to visualize an eternal rift in our environment, but rather to point, on the basis of the theory of intentional consciousness, to different kinds of objects of experience corresponding to differences in our experiences themselves. The word "being" is actually used here in the limited sense of "object of knowledge," and Scheler, in arguing for the independence and autonomy of value is really arguing for the right of the emotional factors in experience to a hearing, and for the impossibility of reaching a decision as to their claims on the basis of tests made by "knowing" or rational processes alone. In fact, for Scheler, emotional experiences have precedence. With Augustine and Lotze he believed that emotional experiences are not mere subjective activities, but reactions to that which is objective. In them the world, that is the objective world, reveals its true nature. Reason and knowledge are themselves founded on the emotional interest which we take in our world, and each increase in our knowledge springs from an increase in interest. Love precedes knowledge and activates it. The object of love may turn out to be identical with the object of knowledge. But reality as value is apprehended through love, while as being it is apprehended through knowledge. And the emotional apprehension exists in its own right. In other words, the good and the true are distinct as intentional objects of consciousness, as *entia intentionalia*. Although it is the same "real" object "intentionally," that is, as object of directed consciousness, absolute being is *"ens a se"* to metaphysics and *"summum bonum"* to religion. Thus emotion and intellect, religion and metaphysics, are independent of each other and underivable from each other, although the object with which they deal, apart from its character as "intentional" object, may be the same.

Scheler's view of the primacy of the emotions, especially that of love, must be noticed later. Here let us merely observe how constantly he draws upon such scholastic conceptions as the "intentional" view of consciousness rather than the more common Kantian ideas. How far his position is from idealism may be seen by comparing him with Kant here. For Kant the *a priori* laws of mental acts determine the objects. But Scheler's *a priori* laws which govern objects are not laws inherent in the constitution of a unified understanding, but laws which are discovered in the essences of objects as they present themselves. And we must notice that *a priori* laws are discoverable in the emotional as well as in the logical field. In fact, Scheler's main purpose in *Der Formalismus* is to show the existence of an emotional *a priori*, to develop an ethics based on an apriorism of loving and hating which is the foundation of all other apriorism, that of knowledge as well as that of will. An analysis of the emotions themselves will reveal, Scheler believes, laws of preference which hold for feeling experiences on the subjective side and which point on the objective side to a hierarchy of values absolute in their authority.

If we are to follow Scheler to this view, however, we must take account in more detail of his opposition to Kant. Scheler believes that Kant's empty formalism and denial of material values rests on his inability to see that material values, although they cannot be defined, can be felt. In the case of final values, definition in terms of other qualities than themselves is of course impossible. Where a final good or evil is concerned, we can only point to the content of immediate experience. We can, however, ask under what conditions final values become experienceable. We find, for example, that the ethical value "good" appears in the act of realizing that which is the highest. And from the highest or absolute value down to the lower grades of relative values there is a traceable order. The superiority of a value is indicated in our own acts of preference, which in turn is revealed in the direction which our will takes. But again the fact that this preference and the will itself must not be grounded on purely formal considerations, in Kant's sense, comes out in the circumstance that to do "good" merely for its own sake leads to a form of Pharisaism. A Pharisee is one who loves his neighbor merely in order to "do good." Also, we must not limit ourselves, in our inquiry as to that in which good consists, too exclusively to acts of will. Many acts which we must call ethically good are rather automatic than deliberately willed. For the truly ethical person a moral act may be completely involuntary. The superiority of a value comes not from its relation to the will, nor from the way in which the will orients itself to any formal law, but from the knowledge which is revealed in the act of preferring. At the same time, hedonism's claim that man is dominated by desire is completely false. Hedonism reduces all things, goods, and persons to a level of indifference to value, and makes good things mere stimulants of desire. But this supposed constant striving for objects of desire is actually rare, and more pathological than normal. Further, it is possible to have value without any striving at all. We may feel the values in the discriminations of another person without raising the question of striving after them.

It all comes back, then, to a question of how we know material goods and evils, and at this point phenomenology is ready with an answer. No ethical system, we have seen, can be built on an empirical foundation, be that foundation historical, psychological, or biological. Ethics raises the question not as to what society judges to be good or bad, not as to what has led to good or bad results, but as to what "good" and "bad" are in themselves. And the knowledge of what good and bad are requires the intuitions of phenomenology. Even hedonism and utilitarianism, when rightly understood, imply the existence of such intuitive evidence. On what basis can utilitarianism claim that usefulness is the highest good? Experience in the ordinary sense of the word could never reveal this insight, nor could judgments based on it. Even if it had never been judged so, murder would be an evil thing. Even if the good had never functioned well in history, it would remain the good. This is not, as Kant thought, because the formal *Sollen* cannot be derived

from the *Sein*. It follows rather from the autonomy of
experiences of value. Ethical sanctions must have *a priori*
validity. On this point Kant was right, though his view
as to how this validity is exhibited was wrong. The
"form" or presupposition which underlies experience
need not be empty, and need not be an arbitrary construction, if it is seen to be a datum of intuition (*Anschauung*).
Are there, then *a priori* ethical laws which are data for
intuition and which have material content though independent of observation and induction?

To answer this, let us first ask what *a priori* really
means. What is given *a priori* is given prior to experience. It is given, however, not as propositions or sentences or forms of judgment, but as data out of which
propositions may be constructed. The *a priori*, also, is
not a synthesizing agency but simply that which intuition
reveals. The *a priori* character lies not in the fact that a
datum expresses an axiomatic truth or is the product of
the synthesizing activity of the mind, but rather in the
fact that it is seen immediately and convincingly, in the
absolute evidence of the phenomenological intuition, to
be incontrovertibly true. The latter is an intuition of
essences (*Wesensschau*). It reveals the *Was*, the *So-sein*,
the "whatness" of the object. This *Wesen* or essence is
given completely or not at all. Also, it is neither general
nor particular. The essence "red" is present as much
and no more to the general conception red as to any particular grade.

The *a priori* nature of these essences becomes clear in
the fact that in order rightly to observe a thing we must
already have intuited its essence. The fact that we
arrange and order our observations shows that knowledge of the essence is presupposed.

Essences cannot be defined or deduced or proved, one
can only point to them. The phenomenological intuition,
as distinct from all other experience, points immediately
to the data themselves, without the use of symbols, signs,
or other intermediaries. Further, as distinct from all
other experience, where the observed content is tran-

scended, phenomenology is pure immanent experience, treating only that which is itself given, not what is imagined, supposed, or believed. Indeed the distinction between what is given and what is believed breaks down. Phenomenology deals with data of experience, not with the constructions of an arbitrary understanding. Whoever, says Scheler, wishes to call this empiricism is welcome to do so. It certainly is not rationalism. Yet the data here are given *a priori*. But notice that the contrast between *a posteriori* and *a priori* is not between what is given in and what is given outside of experience, nor between material and formal. The contrast is between two kinds of experience, that which is mediated through the physical organism of an existential experiencer, and that which is pure, immediate, true for consciousness in general. An *a priori* proposition may have material content, "material" here being understood to refer to data for intuition rather than sense. Of the two propositions, A is B and A is not B, one is false because of the phenomenological insight into the material datum that the being and non-being of the same thing at the same time are incompatible.

Trouble has been made, Scheler thinks, by the division drawn between sense experience on the one hand and the organizing power of the understanding on the other. We are prone to ask: What *can* be given? instead of raising the simple question: What *is* given? The former question leads to the view that where there is no sense organ it is impossible for anything to be given at all. And then in order to account for place, time, and value which cannot be given in sense experience, it becomes necessary to turn to some kind of subjective organizing activity. Right here phenomenology helps us by showing how the essence or "whatness" of a thing can be given without raising the question of sense channels or an intellectual synthesizing function. The latter are as irrelevant as the knowledge that the one who has the experience has also two legs and one lung. Even an act of perception will demonstrate this. When I see a cube the given thing is not a sense datum but is the cube as a whole. Through a series of later acts I know that certain visual elements in the cube correspond to certain points in my perspective, and that questions of visibility and the synthesis of qualities must be raised. We see only one side of a surface, yet in the act of seeing it the datum that the surface has another side is always given.

Notice also how this point of the many-sidedness of the original experience is brought out in the case of what we call "strength of will." The question is not, as empiricism would have it, that of the reaction of a personality to an object, with a well-defined dividing line between the two. Rather the stronger the will, the more is the person's individuality lost in its object. In the strongest individuals of history the consciousness of an outgoing will from an empirical ego was least developed. Cromwell called it grace, Calvin the will of God, Napoleon talked of Fate, Bismarck of a development-tendency. The weaker the personality, the greater the conscious effort of will. On the other hand, to limit the *a priori* to the realm of the rational is to forget the *a priori* laws resident in the emotions. Our entire spiritual being, not merely the knowing part of our nature, works according to laws that are independent of the vagaries of the individual human organism. In feeling, preferring, loving, hating, there is an *a priori* content not borrowed from thought. Pascal was correct in pointing to a *logique du cœur*.

The view that some sort of spiritually constructive activity is needed to weave chaotic sensations into knowledge, or chaotic impulses into a system of values was built by Kant on the basis of what he mistakenly derived from Hume and Hobbes. If nature is the chaos Hume thought it was, and if man is the self-centered, mechanical bundle of drives Hobbes thought he was, then there is cause for Kant's terror in the presence of the given, and for the Puritan's distrust of all nature including human. But the world is not this. As revealed in the phenomenological intuition it is a series of data which in the knowledge field are *a priori* true, and for the emotions are *a priori* valid. Our emotions are our response to the call of the inner life of the cosmos. In them, especially in the experience of preferring one thing to another, we see the inner order and relationship which essences have among themselves. Not that the understanding prescribes laws for nature, but that the intuition finds laws in nature as relations among the data of being and value. Kant's transcendentalism and his subjectivism are both unacceptable. The latter rests on a supposed necessity of judgment. But this necessity arises from relations between propositions, such as that of ground and consequence, and not, as phenomenology would have it, from relations between data of intuition. Further, it is a negative necessity, since what it really means is that the contradictory is impossible. Phenomenology thus has at least two advantages over the older logic. First, it is affirmative where logic is negative. It makes positive statements about data of intuition, where logic's assertions are based on the contradictory quality of the opposite. Second, as we have seen, it goes directly to the original data out of which logic builds its propositions. What logic affirms only indirectly and in propositional form, phenomenology affirms at first hand on the basis of an immediate view of the original materials. In the ethical field this means that the binding quality of values rests on insight into the values themselves and their *a priori* order, not on an abstract *Sollen* or *Pflicht*. Insight into the essence of good in itself can alone determine what is normative for belief and for conduct.

Scheler may thus be said to answer his question as to the existence of *a priori* laws which yield material rather than purely formal evidence by redefining "*a priori*" in a manner to suit himself. Yet his definition is not an arbitrary one. It grows out of the main tendencies in his philosophy and must be judged in the light of them. By following Scheler a little further along this line and seeing the kind of laws operative among things of value which Scheler discovers through the use of this intuitional method we may be better able to judge the acceptability of his views.

We can have insight into the good, Scheler claims, and we can also discover through intuition the relations between goods. These relations are grounded in the nature of the values themselves and are independent of differences among the bearers of values. Values are higher the more lasting they are, the less they depend on either corporeal substance or other values, the deeper the satisfaction they bring, and the less relative they are to their setting, as, for example, the "pleasant" is relative to sense experience. Opposed to such relative values are those which can be called "absolute" in that they exist for "pure" feeling, that is, for "pure" or abstract love and hate, a love or hate which is independent of sense experience and indeed of life itself in that it is not dependent on the experience of any living bearer. In some cases the absoluteness of values is given immediately. The values resident in knowledge of the truth or in the quiet beauty of a work of art afford us glimpses of that which is independent of a bodily condition and even of life. In love the worth of a person is revealed as independent of the ups and downs of emotional experience.[3] There is a secret depth, writes Scheler in the spirit of Augustine, which tells us when these experiences have the quality of absoluteness. Jesus' word "No one is good" shows a feeling of the absolute value which is found in God alone. Obviously a value is higher the more nearly absolute it is. Also, values of persons are higher than values of things, the foreign value and the act of its realization are higher than the one which comes more naturally to us, values of acts, such as knowing, feeling, willing, are higher than those of reactions, such as sympathy or revenge, and the values of "intentional" experiences, *i.e.* experiences directed toward objects, are higher than those dependent on sensuous and bodily conditions. Indeed, values of the spirit must be sharply distinguished from those which come to us from the life process. They

[3] Stavenhagen carries this further in his *Absolute Stellungnahman.*

appear in "spiritual" feeling, loving and hating, which
are different from and not to be traced back to the similarly named biological functions. They are: (1) æsthetic,
(2) values of justice and injustice, (3) truth, (4) the holy.
Their order is—lowest the pleasant, next the vital values,
then the spiritual, finally the holy. The value which we
call the holy appears only in objects which are given as
absolute objects in intentional acts of consciousness.
Holy here is not confined to the special forms which the
idea of the holy has taken in the history of religions. The
holy itself is *a priori* valid, whatever forms it has taken
in human imagination. The oath, for example, has functioned through its relations to the holy, whatever the ideas
of the holy in men's minds when they made oaths. As emotions in which the existence of this value is reflected we
have blessedness (*Seligkeit*) and despair (*Verzweiflung*)
which are entirely distinct from happiness and unhappiness. Specific attitudes taken toward the holy include
faith, disbelief, respect (*Ehrfurcht*), worship, and others.
The act in which the value of the holy is grasped is a specific kind of love.

This brief survey is enough to indicate that Scheler
protests first of all, on the basis of the phenomenological
analysis of intentional acts of consciousness, against any
form of naturalism. The realm of values is independent
of any and all natural processes and has its own *a priori*
validity. Scheler protests further against formalism.
Values are given *a priori,* but they are given as bearers
of content, not empty nor dependent upon the validity of
a merely formal principle of duty. Further Scheler protests against rationalism. Values must be experienced
in and for themselves. They are not constructions of a
synthetic activity of the understanding, nor deducible on
the basis of purely rational principles. But of course he
protests also against that form of empiricism which
would make all knowledge dependent in the first instance
on sense experience. Much is given before sense experience comes at all. Nonsensual and yet not created by the
understanding are relation, order, movement, form, the

unity of the self, the unity of the world, and values. These
things are immediately given, the essence of each is
accessible through the immanent inspection which phenomenology affords. Through different kinds of acts of
consciousness we can grasp these objects, including
values which exist as immanent in the conscious act. This
does not mean philosophical idealism, for the objects are
not dependent on a mind, nor, it seems, can we say that
they are dependent on mind in general for their being.
They exist as correlative parts of conscious acts, as what
must be thought if thinking is to take place at all, or what
must be experienced in the nature of the case. This is
their *a priori* nature. Their validity is that of the *Gelt-
ung* which Lotze described. Their necessity is the necessity of the thing seen, rather than the thing judged.

Also important to notice is the fact that differences in
acts of consciousness, *e.g.* thinking and feeling, correspond to essential differences in the objects toward which
these acts are directed. Being and value are distinct
realms. Thought and the emotions in which values are
grasped are similarly distinct. Values are not to be derived from anything outside themselves, not even from
judgments concerning Being. A person whose mental
activities were limited to perceiving and thinking would
have no conception of what values are like. Where values
are concerned, feelings come first and also last. In loving, hating, preferring, values shine forth for what they
are, and reveal the relations among themselves. And the
primary value of all is love. In love the world discloses
its inner nature.

This constant emphasis in Scheler on the autonomy of
the world of value leads continually to the question raised
previously as to whether Scheler is not losing values in a
realm of non-Being if he makes their separation from the
world of being so complete. We have observed before
that he does not necessarily do this if he treats being
merely as the object of knowing just as value is the object
of feeling. The problem is one which is common to all
discussions of phenomenology, not Scheler's alone. The

phenomenologist is talking about a realm of essences
which he maintains is independent of existence, yet is
there to be seen in intuition, dealt with, taken account of,
so it is sometimes difficult to know how far to accept seriously his own assertion of its independence of existence.
There are traces also in Scheler of the scholastic idea that
in absolute Being *esse* and *essentia* merge. Finally, if
one considers Scheler's statements in the light of the
main trends of his philosophy, one is driven to the view
that Scheler considered the emotional experiences of man,
preceding and dominating his intellectual life as they do,
as themselves revelations of the richness of the cosmos.
One cannot doubt that for Scheler the world of the spirit
was as "real," in the ordinary sense of the word, as the
life process itself. In fact, from the point of view of
values it represented for him a higher degree of reality
than is given in the biological struggle, and from the
point of view of influence on man's conduct it represented
a more powerful form of reality than any other known.
In this sense Scheler's philosophy can rightly be called a
religious realism. Indeed, his own term for it was "a
realistically directed phenomenology."

It may be worth noting also that Scheler contrasts his
own view as objective with what he considers the subjective leanings of other writers, especially those of the
Kantian tradition who have tried to make religious
objects of knowledge derivable from human capacities
for knowing and experiencing. Scheler claims emphatically that the study of the acts of consciousness which are
directed toward religious objects is not a study of subjective states. His phenomenology is a religious *Noëtic*,
not a religious psychology. The psychology of religion
is positivistic, an inheritance from Hume, a study of subjective experiences. But religion is "subjective" only
when it is in error. That is why modern psychology of
religion makes so much of the abnormal. There is no
psychological explanation when a man believes that two
plus two equals four, but there is if he thinks that the
answer is five. The description of the psychological

states of a man at prayer is as irrelevant as the study of
the gastric juices in the stomach of the mathematician.
Even the great Schleiermacher fell into the subjective pit
when he made religion into a feeling of dependence. The
unity of the religious experience is that of a specific form
of consciousness which is organized with reference to a
very definite and very real object. Simmel's subjectivism, for which God is an idea springing out of the stream
of life, is even worse than that of Schleiermacher. The
idea of God is a means to nothing beyond itself. It is the
Absolute Reality on which all else is grounded. Like the
realm of value, the realm of religion has its own autonomy. The religious act is not merely something common
to all men, but something essential to the nature of man
as such, or rather, to the nature of consciousness as such,
as constitutive of consciousness as thinking, judging, perceiving, or remembering. And since consciousness is "intentional," when we say that the religious act is a constitutive part of consciousness, we mean that it is so because
its object is constitutive of reality itself. We are arguing
not from man's empirical need for God, but from the fact
that an analysis of pure consciousness discloses Absolute
Reality on the one hand, and on the other the religious
act in which it is grasped. Consciousness is oriented
toward a reality which is "supernatural" in the sense
that with the natural empirical world it has nothing in
common. Again, the laws of the religious consciousness
are autonomous, self-sufficient, laws of a *noëtic* rather
than a psychological sort. The religious consciousness
can furnish data for other consciousnesses, such as the
logical or the æsthetic. But it does not draw from them
in turn. Religion finds its norm within, not outside, itself.
The unity of the religious act is that of the act directed
toward and organized with reference to the *summum
bonum*. It is a unity independent of empirical factors
and which no amount of empirical research could discover.

Let us now turn to Scheler's application of his method
to a few specific questions which arise in connection with

the religious theme, drawing our material from *Der Form-alismus in der Ethik,* from *Vom Ewigem im Menschen,* and from a few scattered essays. One of Scheler's main points here is that phenomenology carries further the "negative theology" of such a system as Neoplatonism. The latter in claiming that God cannot be described has hit upon a real phenomenological essence, a whatness or *Sosein.* The essence or inner nature of God is the basis of our conceptions of Him but of course cannot itself be conceptualized. The negations of the negative theology were meant simply as indications or pointings which should direct the course of spiritual intuition. Phenomenology, Scheler claims, tries to do this same thing. Rightly used they should both effectively point the way to the true religion and the true philosophy.

We have seen that in the religious act a unique content, which we can rightly call revelation, is grasped. The religious object, speaking in analogies and not descriptive concepts, may be called absolute and holy. The essence of the godly was one of the original data of human experience, present long before reasoning concerning the nature of God occurred. God is not an inference from experience but immediately known. The absolute is not implied by but shines through the relative. Further, the relation of Creator to creature is not based on the principle of causality. A single example does not illustrate a cause. From the action of litmus paper in one instance we cannot generalize. But one work of art is sufficient to show the spirit of the artist, one creature can show what the Creator is like. Again, corresponding to the absoluteness and holiness of God are man's feelings of humility and abasement. "Thou art all, I am nothing," is the primitive expression of religious experience. Secondarily comes the conviction of creaturehood. Absoluteness and holiness are revealed in any true religion, no matter how faulty the conceptions by which they are conveyed. The sun is the sun, no matter how much astronomers' notions concerning it may conflict, and holiness is holiness even though the primitive fetish or even the god Apollo may not adequately convey its meaning.

The question of the historical origin of religion is then as meaningless as that of the historical origin of speech or of reason. Speech and reason differentiate man from animals and prescribe the lines along which intellectual development can take place. Similarly the religious act with its revelation of the godly is constitutive for the religious nature of man. And notice that this religious or spiritual nature which man has comes not as a development out of earlier processes, but represents a complete break with what has preceded. With its advent an entirely new set of standards is revealed. Spiritual values simply do not fit into a process whose end is biological survival. They are a liability rather than an asset where the aim is the protection and propagation of life. If such a purpose be the final one, then indeed all culture is but a blind alley, a sickness of life, as Klages claims, a *faux pas* of Nature, as Nietzsche argued. Man is therefore a new revelation of the presence of the godly in the universe. He, the God-seeker, is the point at which the Kingdom of God with its ideals breaks through into the world of our common life. How meaningless, then, are all those views which see in the idea of God only an anthropomorphism! Rather is man himself a theomorphism, a revelation of what the nature of God must be. One has a right to use the word anthropomorphic at all only if he is in possession of some standard drawn from outside the human realm by which human ideals may themselves be measured. As the God-seeker man does transcend his own human ideas, and in this self-transcendence he finds his own fulfillment.[4]

Right here lies the failure of all "humanistic" attempts to describe man and his experiences in categories taken from biology. Spencer, for example, in attempting to derive man's spiritual activities from the process of adjustment to environment, took arbitrarily the natural

[4] A further analysis of what is implied in man's self-transcendence is given in Martin Heidegger's *Sein und Zeit* (Niemeyer, Halle, 1927).

world which man knows through intellectual instruments developed in the struggle for survival and made it normative for all life and thought. But if this natural environment fits such instruments then it cannot be normative. A set of mental categories which have developed in the service of a particular species, the human, cannot be relied on to make life as a whole intelligible. Man himself cannot be taken as the final goal, nor the values of Western Europe as the final criteria. But if we see man as the God-seeker we discover that which is normative for all possible experience, not merely the human. The laws which we discover in this case will be, as phenomenology claims, independent of all empirical considerations, not abstractions from historical or psychological circumstances but as necessarily being what they are.

If we ask, as the critic of phenomenology always must ask, whether this stripping-off of empirical considerations does not leave us with nothing that is intelligible, in religious as in other fields, Scheler counters by pointing to the kernel of truth which can be found among some chaff in the ontological proof. Whatever truth lies in Augustine's ontological proof comes from the very fact that it does not depend on empirical circumstances. Its validity is that of logic itself. And back even of the logic lies the revelation of God as existing not in the conclusion, but in the implicit premise of the syllogism. One defect of the ontological proof is that it makes value a predicate instead of itself a center for predication. The value of the godly, revealed in the intentional act of love toward God, is the starting point for all our ideas as to what God may be like. Pascal's cry: "I would not seek thee, hadst thou not already found me," expresses just this. God is found originally in the completion of the emotional act of love toward him. The seeking is the conceptual defining which takes place within the limits set by the original datum. The effect of these limits is always felt. Man *must* think of God as absolute, infinite, and holy, and of the world as dependent on God for its existence. However problematical the "that" of God may be, the "what" is given incontrovertibly. Yet with it all, only that part of God which is intelligible to us is revealed. Part of God is unknowable. Our feeling of awe is evidence of this transcendence. Metaphysics makes a naïve mistake in trying to define God's nature too closely. Even the uneducated person who is truly devout knows that his names for God, such as "Father" and "Lord," are pictures and symbols rather than descriptions.

God is spirit, we may say, and God is love. Yet both these affirmations involve difficulties. Man can only assert that God is spirit if he is himself partly spirit, and this means, if he is himself not dominated wholly by life and its rules, but draws on the higher world for part of his being. We have already affirmed, however, that man is himself the God-seeker and that in his search for God he transcends the biological realm. Man is himself spirit in so far as he is personality, which means in so far as he expresses that inner union of reason and will which underlies the variety of human experiences. He is a personality, that is to say, when he is not lost in the diversity of life but remains an individual with unity of purpose. This unity is, in Scheler's view, the unity of the completion of the acts in which the personality is interested, especially the act of experiencing value. Man's personality and God's alike are to be found in the completion of these experiences. Or, as Scheler expresses it elsewhere, God is the concrete union of Being (*Seinseinheit*) in which reason and will, knowledge of the true and experience of the good, find their consummation. As absolute he can be deduced metaphysically, but his nature as personal and as this union of qualities can be completely grasped only in that experience in which reason and will have their common roots, the experience of love.

What kind of love is this? Not subjective, selfish love, not desire of any sort, but the love which the Greeks described as a striving, a tendency toward completeness, a rising from the lower to the higher. We have seen that the existence of good ends and goals presupposes the existence of that which is good in itself, and that the latter elicits in us this striving toward itself. Scheler's theory of the primacy of value and of the emotions comes out again in his statement that God as love is what makes the union of subject and object possible. Love is the means, presupposition, and ground of knowledge. Because God is love, all that he has created is of love, and love is the means to the deepest comprehension of all that is. In love we are one with ourselves, with others, with God. In love, furthermore, the values of the spirit shine through into this world of human affairs and reveal themselves for what they are.

Toward the end of his life Scheler's interests underwent a change which can best be described as a shift from the theological to the anthropological. The breaking of his connection with the Roman Church is one indication of the change in his point of view, and an appreciable difference in the style as well as the subject matter of his published writings is another. In the later essays he is much less concerned with the nature of God, divine love, and divine personality, and more interested in making an analysis of man's place in the scheme of things. The problem of a philosophical anthropology is to-day the central issue of all thought, he says in one place, and in another he remarks that in the confusion of modern theories man no longer knows what he is, but knows only that he is ignorant of himself. Scheler reviews various theories of man's nature and destiny: the Jewish Christian view of man as tainted with sin, a view which has influenced Western attitudes more than we realize; the Greek idea that man is distinguished from the rest of creation by the possession of reason, a powerful theory but one which hardly does justice to the irrational in experience; the positivistic, naturalistic view of man as only a special form of animal life which denies to reason any ontological status and makes concepts instrumental, again a plausible view but one which glosses over the difference between the vital and the spiritual; the pessimistic theory of such writers as Theodor Lessing and Ludwig Klages which makes man into a degenerate ape, and

finds in the intellect only an inferior weapon in the biological struggle for existence; and finally the new atheism
of such a writer as Nikolai Hartmann, which, on the
grounds of man's moral responsibility and its necessary
conflict with the will of God postulates the nonexistence,
much as Kant postulated the existence of God.

Against all of these views Scheler sets his own, which
is a development of his position as phenomenologist.
Man's ability, in true phenomenological fashion, to gain
a vision of the essential nature of the objects of his
experience is what, in Scheler's opinion, marks him off
from the rest of the world of living things. An animal
can sense the presence of the *Dasein* or existent thing in
space and time. All that is needed for this is the experience of "coming up against" something, of discovering
that which resists one's will. But man does not treat the
objects of his environment merely as things which stand
over against him. Man is selective, rejecting parts of
his environment in favor of others. Man sees the *Sosein,*
the inner essence, quality, or nature of the objects with
which he deals. The animal not only fails to do this, but
he hardly recognizes objects as objects. He hears and
sees without knowing that he does so. Man on the other
hand is self-conscious, able to recognize the environment
as such, not limited by his instinctive drives, able to deal
with objects as things and substances, and to transcend
the immediacy of the present moment. But, and here is
the important point, if man can frame a picture which
is independent of the here-and-now, and of the demands
of the immediately present, then he must have found a
vantage point outside the present empirical world from
which his judgments as to that world can be formed.
This was the fundamental truth underlying Kant's view
of the transcendental unity of apperception as a nonempirical factor which is itself the condition of experience.

Now this pure subjectivity which, since it is pure act
or a self-completing series of acts, must be always subject and never object is just what we mean by spirit

(*Geist*). Spirit is not dependent as is life (*Leben*) on the interests provided by our instincts. For the mere life-process only that is given, only that presents itself, which makes some appeal to an instinctive urge which the life-process itself has. But spirit, so far from being bound by its physiological structure or even its physical environment lives in the world of essences and so is free to modify its world creatively. As contrasted then, first with the inorganic, whose only unity is that of its chemical relation to other bodies, secondly with the lower organisms whose unity is that of an individual existence in space and time, and finally with the higher animal which has a nervous system but no way of distinguishing qualities as such, man as spirit achieves a center of interest which transcends the opposition between organism and environment, and is able through its own creative activity both to aid the spiritual tendency in the cosmos to influence the empirical world and to aid that spiritual tendency to realize its own possibilities for itself.

Man, then, as spirit is the great "No-sayer" (*Nein-sagen-könner*). He is the eternal protestant against all merely empirical reality. By saying "No" to that which is merely concrete and setting out to modify his world in line with his ideal interests, he affirms the existence of his own spiritual center outside the world of life and in the world of timeless ideas. This, says Scheler, is the beginning both of the metaphysical attempt intellectually to grasp the absolute and of the religious attempt to relieve the foreignness of the world by discovering love implicit in it. Thus in man the struggle between life on the one hand and spirit on the other becomes acute. The two are utterly opposed. There can be no higher synthesis. The spirit prescribes other goals than those which obtain in the struggle for survival. Man in his capacity as God-seeker becomes in these last essays of Scheler a coworker with God, an instrument for the realization of the divine will and one on whom this will must depend for the carrying out of its purposes. God, as opposed to the view taken in the earlier works is thus limited by man's choice. Man becomes not only that which seeks God but that in which God himself finds his own completion.

The foregoing will be sufficient to furnish an indication of the wide-ranging quality, the aggressiveness and the acuteness of Scheler's thought. He has offered a new intuitional method which supersedes the older logic, a defense of the objectivity of values, a description of the concept of the holy as necessarily implicit in the religious consciousness, and a new philosophical anthropology which views man as the point where the world of spiritual ideals breaks through into the world of biological struggle. Scheler's promised book on metaphysics was never written, and his arguments have therefore never been developed to the extent which he intended, but he has left enough to show the vigor of his imaginative insight and the sharpness of his analytical power.

His religious realism effectively complements the realistic tendency which is evident among American philosophers of religion. This tendency has been influenced to some extent by the emphasis placed by William James on the reality of the religious Object and the authoritativeness for the one who has it of the religious experience. Such books as *The Varieties of Religious Experience* and *A Pluralistic Universe* did much to point the way to a philosophy which should show the legitimacy of belief in a religious Object which can be both known and experienced by humanity, but which is not dependent on humanity's thought or experience for its own existence. Such a realistic philosophy is being developed by American writers through an analysis of the content of the religious experience and a study of the laws of its occurrence. Scheler's work supplements this in that it also takes account of the autonomy of the religious experience but places it in a larger setting by making it one form of "intentional" consciousness and furnishes thereby a new means for subjecting it to analysis and criticism. Scheler differentiates the religious from other forms of consciousness by its "direction" or "intention." This makes it possible for him to analyze anew both the subjective emotions from which it springs and the objective content to which it refers. Furthermore, this allows the ascription to the religious consciousness of the same kind of assurance in its deliverances that other kinds possess. In this particular Scheler's views are in line with those of Rudolf Otto's *Das Heilige* where the "religious *a priori*" is put on the same level with the *a priori* of the knowing process. But again, Scheler's treatment is more complete than that of Otto since Scheler is concerned in detail with the relation of the religious consciousness to consciousness in general.

Whatever its defects, the advantages of the phenomenological method at this point for the study of what is implicit in the religious consciousness should be clear. Phenomenology in Scheler's hands takes for granted the right of the religious consciousness to a hearing. Finding it a part of human experience, not merely in the psychological sense but also in the sense of "pure" consciousness, it pushes forward its analysis as it would in any other field and reports its results with as much confidence here as elsewhere. This recognition of the naturalness and legitimacy of the religious consciousness is itself an important contribution to the philosophy of religion. And the worth of the contribution is increased by the fruitfulness of the method in Scheler's hands.

The chief question that arises is not so much as to the validity of this type of analysis for religion, but rather as to its pertinence to the larger field of consciousness in general. If phenomenology can once establish itself, that is to say, as an acceptable method of immanent inspection and a means to the solution of problems of epistemology in general, the main questions concerning its usefulness for religion will have been answered. And the most important issue here seems to be whether phenomenology or the view of "intentional" consciousness has a right so easily to bridge the gap between subject and object by talking of the two as merely correlative aspects of a single process. The answer will best be found by seeing the use to which this statement is put. If the structure built upon it is both internally and externally consistent on the one hand, and on the other helps to illumine our view of man and his world, it must be judged acceptable. And these tests do seem to have been met. Consciousness is always consciousness of objects, it is "intentional," and it does operate according to laws which in Scheler's sense are *a priori*. Furthermore, the specific results which Scheler reaches do in general commend themselves. His belief in the objectivity of values, his massive insistence on the reality of the realm of the spirit, his description of man as the God-seeker and of the religious attitude as the attitude toward the absolute and holy, and his view of the part played by love in personality both human and divine, all commend themselves as consistent with religious history and with our knowledge of religious experience at its best.

The strength and the weakness of the phenomenological method are alike to be found in its independence of empiricism. A distinction should be made here between the use of the word empirical by Scheler and by recent American works in the philosophy of religion. For Scheler empiricism means merely psychological or inductive procedure, dependence on the psychological processes or on the common testimony of experience, the testimony of the majority. For such a writer as James the term is broadened to include the appeal to man's emotions and spiritual insight as contrasted with his strictly rationalistic processes of attaining truth. Scheler's independence of the empirical instance, inductive probabilities, or the practical generalizations of science, and his appeal away from the here and now to that which in the nature of the case must be so, does give him a wholesome assurance which would otherwise be impossible. It also enables him, as he has himself observed, to keep from falling into the snare of so many psychologies of religion which identify the phenomena of religious experience with the pathological and abnormal. Scheler's work, like that of James, is not limited to the kind of empiricism which bases its conclusions upon psychological description. In common with James, Scheler admits the right of religious emotions to speak for themselves. But he also goes further than James in freeing himself from a certain relativism which must always attach to the view that religious experience is nonconceptual and not capable of being expressed in universal terms. Scheler treats the religious consciousness as having *a priori* laws of its own which are binding for it in all circumstances and whatever the empirical conditions.

On the other hand, the weakness implicit in this division between phenomenological truth and empirical conditions comes to view when we observe the difficulty which phenomenology has with the problem of solipsism. Once all extraneous considerations have been bracketed, so claims the phenomenologist, the data of intuition will shine forth as clearly evident. But supposing that they are evident to the phenomenologist and not to his neighbor, or to one phenomenologist and not another. Whose intuitions in this case are to be trusted? Is it possible for all to travel the same high *a priori* road, and if not, what of its much vaunted universality? How do we effect the transition from the world of pure consciousness to that of psychological experience in which our everyday life is lived? The phenomenologist would of course answer that there cannot be any essential contradiction between the two, and that if there appears to be it is simply because we have not sufficiently clarified the problem in our own minds. This seems to imply a belief in the fundamental consistency of our entire world of experience. The world as knowable and experienceable, as object of consciousness, must be one. As such it must appear the same to us if we get our intuitions clear. And these intuitions, nonempirical as they are, must not be thought of even by the phenomenologist, as entirely cut off from our various tests, scientific and other. The more science we have, the more completely do we see what must be true of the nature of things, and the better able we are to discover what is necessarily true. The world of ordinary experience, although deliberately ruled out by the phenomenologist, must to some extent condition his own ability to deal with the *a priori* at all.

Naturally the phenomenologist will not admit this expressly, but it seems again to be implicit in the way in which Scheler allows his interest in history, biology, and sociology to lead him into these fields in the search for data. It is almost as if he were trying to show by personal example how a final reliance on the *a priori* should not interfere with but rather encourage an interest in human experience wherever it is found. His protest is not so much against the empirical instance as against taking it as merely empirical. It is the essence that we are concerned with, and the essence is as clearly revealed in one instance as in many. So it is our eye for essences which must be developed. If science or art or the study of history will help to develop it, let us use them.

Yet while the tendency of phenomenology has been to widen the gap between pure consciousness and ordinary experience by making it difficult to return from the vision of the ideal to contact with the actual, it is also true that in emphasizing the connection between the subjective and objective poles of consciousness it has in its own way brought the two realms nearer together. If consciousness is always consciousness of objects there can be no essential contradiction between objects and subjective states. Scheler's work is particularly apt here since his view of the far-flung frontiers of consciousness and of the larger reaches of experience has helped to bring home the truths resident in experiences as wholes. It is in the experience as a whole that the meaning lies. The relations which bind it together are themselves objective and not provided by the subject. Here again Scheler proves himself truly a realist at heart. His interest is in what is given, once the mode of apprehending it has been made as sure as possible. This also helps to save Scheler from the solipsism which dogs Husserl's footsteps. Husserl is more subjective and has more in common with idealism than does Scheler. Husserl also works for a completely presuppositionless philosophy where Scheler is intent rather on the broadest possible sweep of vision as preliminary to the most acute analysis. Scheler is interested in treating the values discoverable in history and in human experience as objects revealing the presence of *a priori* laws among themselves. The real is thus the rational not in the sense that the real is mind, but in that it is a legitimate object of consciousness governed by intelligible laws.

The question whether Scheler's realism is thwarted by the fact that his assertion of the independence of the world of values seems to separate them from existence entirely and to place them in a realm of fantasy, we have already treated. Scheler clearly did not himself feel that this was the case. Where the intentional nature of consciousness is under discussion he uses the word "being" in a limited sense, making it the correlative term to "knowing." The constant claim of phenomenology that it has no interest in the world of existence means simply that the world of space and time cannot dictate the laws of the spiritual realm. Scheler's realism as a matter of fact goes so far as to make him, when discussing the antithesis of life and spirit, ascribe to spirit a kind of reality which gives it a right to recognition entirely apart from the claims of the life process itself. Again it is clear from the contrast he draws that while the world of life is real in the ordinary sense, for which mountains of granite exist while mountains of gold do not, the things of the spirit are real in what phenomenologists sometimes call the "ontisch" sense, that is, the sense in which there are three-cornered triangles, but no round squares. For this view values as objects of possible judgment or experience have an undeniable validity. We feel here as elsewhere the queer paradox contained in Scheler's professed interest in the abstract compared with his actual interest, as a writer on ethics and religion, in the concrete content of experience. It is evident also in his absorption on the one hand in the immanent inspection of consciousness and his sensitiveness on the other to the specific insights developed in the religious history of mankind. The resolution of the paradox seems to lie in his conviction that the formal need not be devoid of concrete content. The principles which regulate consciousness and reality are independent of both history and psychology but the data with which they deal are definite, objective, and discoverable. Space and time are objective, and so are relation, order, substantiality, form, movement, the unity of the self, the unity of the world, and values. Scheler's insistence on the automony of religion itself is again a case in point, his unwillingness, that is, to make it in any way dependent on either metaphysics or ethics. The act of love in which man grasps God is the primary act of consciousness. Through it the religious man has access to the sphere of the supersensual, the sphere of that which as absolute love and holiness has a higher reality than the life process itself.

The final dualism, that between "life" and "spirit" which is so prominent in Scheler's later work is also a source of difficulty. If life taken by itself is so completely indifferent to value and to the world of ideas, and if the aims of the spirit are so far removed from those of the biological struggle, how can spiritual objectives ever find expression in life at all? Hegel believed that the Idea had power to operate actively in the stream of history. But Scheler will have none of this. In his view the world of ideas has no power in itself. It provides merely a check and limitation on the instinctive drives of life. Two questions inevitably arise at this point. The first is whether a thing with no power in itself can ever act as a check on an alien power, and the second is the specific question whether aside from the question of its own power spirit can ever dominate life when the chasm between them is so far-reaching as Scheler makes it. The emphasis on the substantial quality of the spirit even in its powerlessness is added evidence of Scheler's realism, but it is not a help toward the solution of the problem.

If Scheler had lived to write his book on metaphysics perhaps this and the other paradoxes would have been resolved. That he postponed it so long, and gave himself instead to so many other interests, is, however, itself significant. Phenomenology is less concerned with formulating a metaphysical theory than it is with applying its method to special problems of logic, ethics, and æsthetics. Perhaps this is the reason for such success as it has had. By the freshness of its point of view it has brought new data into the philosophical arena. Old questions have been made to appear in a new light and significant insights have been gained into supposedly outworn problems. Frequently it must be said, these insights have been the property of the individual phenomenologist alone and have not been shared by the group. As we have seen, Scheler differs greatly from Husserl, busying himself with ethics and religion where Husserl is absorbed in logic, and making a realistic emphasis where Husserl seems to be becoming more of an idealist. Heidegger, furthermore, has little in common with either. Phenomenology is not a school, but a group of individuals bound by the use of a common method yet differing among themselves as to the results which the use of the method achieves.

Scheler's projected work on metaphysics might have helped, then, to clear up some of the difficulties in his own thought, but it could hardly be expected to provide a unified philosophy for the phenomenological movement at this stage in its development. The one thing upon which all phenomenologists to-day unite is a common opposition to the attempted domination of ethics and religion by science and to the effort to derive by inductive and psychologically empirical methods principles which shall be normative for knowledge and for conduct. They cling to a common faith in the existence of *a priori* truths discoverable by an intuitive process. And while this points to a unified body of data which needs only to be seen to be understood phenomenologists seem to be content for the present with the use of their method for the attainment of such insights, individualistic or otherwise, as may be possible. This apparent diversity may seem a weakness in phenomenology as a philosophical movement but it should not impair its usefulness for religion. The story of the prophets and mystics of all times is sufficient evidence that the intuitions of religion are not prevented from being important by the fact that they are incommunicable. Religion has always been a matter of individual insight into meaning and significance rather than of universal demonstration, more an affair of passionate vision than of logic. The most stimulating writers on religion are those who have been able to convey a sense of the richness of their own intuitional life. This Scheler has done, and this it is which makes his work of outstanding importance for contemporary religious thought. American religious realism with its interest in the independence of the Object of religious knowledge and experience may well pay heed to this stalwart defender of the autonomy of the religious consciousness. Max Scheler has made human emotions a guide to the mysteries of the transcendent world of the spirit, a means by which the universe itself unlocks its secret.

A list of the more important of Scheler's works is added:

Der Formalismus in der Ethik und die Materiale Wertethik
   3. Auflage. Niemeyer, Halle, 1927.
      Scheler's most systematic work. It develops his ethical theory.

Vom Ewigen im Menschen
   2. Auflage. Der Neue Geist Verlag, Leipzig, 1923.
      A series of essays on religion. The first division (which itself is published in two volumes in the second edition) is the only division to appear.

Wesen und Formen der Sympathie
   3. Auflage. Cohen, Bonn, 1926.
      A study of the emotions.

Vom Umsturz der Werte
   3. Auflage. Der Neue Geist Verlag, Leipzig, 1923.
      Essays on philosophical subjects.

Die Transzendentale und die Psychologische Methode
   2. Auflage. Meiner, Leipzig, 1922.
      On the relation of ethics to epistemology.

Philosophische Weltanschauung
   Cohen, Bonn, 1929.
      A group of essays posthumously published.

Die Stellung des Menschen in Kosmos
　　Reichl, Darmstadt, 1928.
　　Lectures delivered six months before his death at Keyser-
　　ling's "Schule der Weisheit."

Of criticisms of Scheler the following may be mentioned:

F. HEINEMANN: *Neue Wege der Philosophie.* Leipzig, Quelle
　　and Meyer, 1929. A skillful and sympathetic interpretation.
E. PRZYWARA: *Religions-Begründung.* Freiburg i. Br., Herder,
　　1923. A fine-spun analytical criticism.
―――― "Drei Richtungen der Phänomenologie." An article in
　　Stimmen der Zeit for July, 1928. Freiburg, Herder.
J. GEYSER: Max Scheler's *Phänomenologie der Religion.* Frei-
　　burg i. Br., Herder, 1924. A criticism from the Roman
　　Catholic point of view.
E. CASSIRER: "Geist und Leben in der Philosophie der Gegen-
　　wart." An article in *Die Neue Rundschau* for February,
　　1930. A criticism of Scheler's latest position.
A. MESSER: *Deutsche Wertphilosophie der Gegenwart.* Reinicke,
　　Leipzig, 1926. Statement and criticism of Scheler's theory
　　of values.

NOTE.—To the editor of the *Journal of Religion* I am indebted for permission to use here the description of Husserl's position which appeared
in my article on "German Phenomenology and Its Implications for Religion" published in that Journal, Vol. IX, No. 4, October, 1929.

IV

RELIGIOUS REALISM AND THE EMPIRICAL FACTS OF RELIGION

By
ALBAN G. WIDGERY

Professor of Philosophy
Duke University

RELIGIOUS REALISM AND THE EMPIRICAL
FACTS OF RELIGION

In the preface to his *Naturalism and Agnosticism*, the late James Ward wrote: "I take it for granted that till an idealistic (*i.e.* spiritualistic) view of the world can be sustained, any exposition of theism is but wasted labour." There is no adequate justification for taking this for granted. And it seems important to challenge the idea that religion, at least in its theistic forms, depends upon the truth of an idealistic philosophy. The acceptance of this idea leads to the bolstering up of discredited types of philosophy for the supposed sake of religion, or to the rejection of reasonable consideration of theistic religion on the ground that with the abandonment of idealistic philosophy it is ruled out as a possible attitude for the critical mind. It is a patent fact that theism has been adopted without any apparent incoherence of thought by persons who have rejected Idealism as a general theory of reality. Non-idealistic forms of philosophy have been associated with Christian and non-Christian theistic Scholasticisms.

This is not the place to discuss the instabilities of Ward's own system: but certain aspects of it may be considered with reference to our main contentions. His criticisms of Naturalistic Monism, of Pluralism, and Idealistic Singularism demand the attention of serious thinkers. Nevertheless the rise of a definite trend to Realism since the publication of his first Gifford Lectures [1]—even in Cambridge itself during his own lifetime —is evidence that his arguments for an idealistic theory of knowledge have in no small measure failed to convince. It is not apparent that the subjective acts of knowing affect the resulting knowledge so that the qualities ap-

[1] *Naturalism and Agnosticism*, 1899.

prehended need be considered as apprehended differently from what they are irrespective of the acts of knowing.

Ward's interpretation of nature as composed of, or as the manifestation of a multiplicity of spiritual monads [*] (largely a restatement of much of the philosophy of his teacher Lotze), can only be regarded as a speculative hypothesis for the purpose of presenting a view of the whole of existence as spiritual. In part it rests upon a view of so-called natural laws as generalizations of the nature of averages, with the assumption that there are characteristics of contingency in the ultimates of nature. That assumption may not be justifiable. The appearance of diversity may be due to inadequacies in our acquaintance with details, such that the more those inadequacies are overcome, the more stable the system of nature may be found to be. Our conduct as related with inanimate nature is pursued in what may be justly called a rational manner without such a spiritually monadistic hypothesis as he proposes. Our whole interaction with nature is essentially on the basis of its being a definite objective reality, experienced more directly than any form of animistic analogy such as spiritualistic monadism involves.

Ward's treatment of religion is even more unsatisfactory than his treatment of physical nature. What he does in the main in this direction is to show that certain traditional ideas of religion fit very well into his general scheme of thought. In taking over these ideas he fails to make the necessary acknowledgements that he has obtained them from the realm of religion in which they have their bases. Having to his own satisfaction shown the difficulties of Naturalistic Monism, Pluralism, and Singularistic Idealism, he turns to theism as the one remaining plausible alternative view. After all has been said, the idea of God remains for Ward a hypothesis. It is required to round off his spiritualistic system. He does not show how he arrives at the content which the idea has for him. Thus, both as regards the spiritualistic charac-

[*] *The Realm of Ends,* 1911.

ter of nature and the theistic view of the whole, he really
gives us no more than speculative hypotheses.

It is important to remind those who cling to Idealism
for its supposed support of theistic religion, that there
are Idealisms which are non-theistic. The philosophy of
one of Ward's own colleagues—McTaggart [3]—is a conspicuous example. It will be found that the relation of
other well-known forms of Idealism to religion is not so
close or sympathetic as often supposed. F. H. Bradley's
idealistic description [4] leads ultimately to the contention
that religion is self-contradictory. He sees that religion
involves a relation between men and God: of that there is
ample empirical evidence. According to the fundamental
principles of his Idealism the Absolute is devoid of relations: it follows therefore that God cannot be the Absolute. The Absolute is alone perfect: hence God cannot be
perfect. Man, however, worships God as perfect: as such
He should be the Absolute. Hence, religion involves a
radical contradiction: for God must be treated at one
and the same time as the Absolute and not the Absolute.

Many objections may be made to such a train of
thought. The chief concerns the notion of perfection. For
Bradley perfection can be affirmed of nothing but the
whole: the whole is the perfect: the perfect is the whole.
Nevertheless the use of the term perfect for the whole
enables him to suggest something from the more ordinary
meaning, according to which it signifies highest excellence. But though the Absolute must include the highest
excellences of all kinds, it is not evident, *a priori*, that it
includes nothing more than these; nor that as a whole it
is more excellent than it would be without what it may
include besides these excellences. The presence of other
factors may be detrimental.

While Bradley recognized that religion involves a relation between men and God, he failed to appreciate another important fact about empirical religion, namely,

[3] See for example his *Some Dogmas of Religion*, 1906.
[4] *Appearance and Reality*, 1893.

that it maintains and in large measure depends upon the contention that *all* is not good or perfect. Men have formed a conception of God as perfect *in His own nature*, in the sense of good, not as "beyond good and evil," the meaning of the term perfect in Bradley's view. God is represented as being in His own nature beyond the conflict of good and evil, because His own nature is regarded as entirely good. But existence as we know it is not an Absolute realm in which the conflict is transcended, in which good and evil are "transmuted." Existence as we know it—and this is the realm with which religion has to do—is a realm of conflict in which the evil is as real as the good.

An allied, but in some essential features different, form of Idealism is expounded by Professor C. C. J. Webb.[5] He writes that not to identify God with the Absolute is to make nonsense of religion. In that case much empirical religion is and apparently must remain nonsense. The charge does not appear justified. Bradley gave one good reason why the God of religion cannot be identified with the Absolute, and no more need be said on that score. Webb's exposition seems to depend on a confusion between the perfection of God (alleged to be required by advanced religious thought) and the perfection of the universe. But religion does not find the whole perfect in the sense that it describes God as perfect.

The confusion can be considered from another point of view. Not infrequently religion includes faith in an ultimate triumph of the good and the eradication of all evil. The condition of this stage of perfection is read back through the whole temporal process. Time is then taken as phenomenal: and it is urged that for religion the real is the eternal. Thus considered the universe is regarded as eternally perfect. If that means simply that the whole is eternally the whole, the implication does not merit discussion. But in any case it would seem that, whatever the nature of the temporal, the eternal must include it within

[5] *God and Personality*, 1918. *Problems in the Relation of God and Man*, 1911.

itself: the Absolute, whatever the nature of appearances, must include those within itself.

The fundamental reason for rejecting Absolute Idealism is not what it ultimately implies with reference to religion. It is rejected as a form of speculation in which there is no adequate recognition of the distinctions of truths and errors, of goods and evils, religion and irreligion. The Absolutist logic fails entirely in its treatment of error. For it, ultimately, error is nothing more than the absence of truth. It is self-evident that where there is an error, the relevant truth is absent. But an error is more than such absence: it is or implies some form of positive affirmation. An error as a proposition is just as real as a truth; and equally positive in its implication. For Idealistic ethics as expounded by Bradley and by A. E. Taylor in his earlier work[6] the distinction between moral good and evil is also mere appearance.

There have been forms of Idealism which have evaded some of the difficulties of Absolutism, but which have nevertheless failed to do justice to the nature of empirical religion. The Berkeleyan Idealism of Hastings Rashdall[7] has serious epistemological difficulties. Though God was for him a Universal mind implied in knowledge and a Universal Cause, it was in His being the objective ground of moral values that His chief significance was seen. Rashdall's writings manifest a conspicuous lack of appreciation of religion as anything other than morality having its source and sanction in God and seeming to imply immortality. He recognized no apprehension of the divine other than in the experience of moral values. God is virtually unknowable except as an idea based on moral values and certain epistemological inferences. Similarly for Professor W. R. Sorley[8] God appears to be known chiefly through an intellectual hypostatizing of the universals of moral values as objective to the individual knowing minds. For both Rashdall and Sorley

---

[6] *The Problem of Conduct,* 1901.
[7] *Philosophy and Religion,* 1909; *Theory of Good and Evil,* 1907, Vol. II., Book 3.
[8] *Moral Values and the Idea of God,* 1918.

God is primarily a speculative conceptual implication of ethics. Yet both insist that ethics iself is to be based on moral experience as *sui generis*. Unless it is to be asserted that religion is nothing more than morality, it is reasonable to maintain that the concepts associated with religion are likewise first to be understood with reference to religious experience as *sui generis,* whatever application may be made of these concepts thereafter with relation to morals.

Religious Realism is the application of the ideas and methods of a Realistic philosophy to the facts of religion. But there are different types of Realistic philosophy, some of which are not thoroughgoing: and some of which are too narrow. Some so-called Realists have not entirely emancipated themselves from subjectivist traits of Kantian and Idealist epistemologies. In one way or another, often especially with reference to values, they still ascribe to the function of knowing some features of the thing as known. It can hardly be expected that Realism will appeal to those whose thinking is so dominated by a Kantian or an Idealist epistemology that they can appreciate no answers to problems except such as fit those theories of knowledge. It may be maintained that only a "direct Realism" which is comprehensive in its range is a thoroughgoing Realism.

The chief defect of most modern Realisms is their narrowness. There are forms of Realism which are simply naturalistic: treating the physical as though the only reality. Others add to this some recognition of universal ideas. The thoroughgoing realist will be realistic in all directions, with regard to the æsthetic, the moral, the religious, as all else. The judgment, "This statue is beautiful," qualifies the object. It does not simply mean, on the part of the person making it, "I like this statue," which is a statement about the person himself. When I say: "Mr. Brown's benevolence is good," I am talking of a quality of Mr. Brown. The statement is not the same as: "I like the way Mr. Brown acts." As a matter of fact I may not like his benevolence, if it is giving him a social prestige greater than my own. Nevertheless I cannot but admit that his benevolence is good; and also that I like benevolence as such. I like it because it is good: it is not good because I like it. I discover benevolence as a reality of experience, just as I find beautiful objects: and I happen to like both. Ethical goods are real as such; beautiful objects are real as such. Realism involves a realistic ethics and a realistic æsthetics. It also entails a realistic philosophy of religion. In opposition to naturalistic Realism the contention here made is that if the realistic method is applied fully within human experience it is possible to give a metaphysically realistic recognition to religion. Indeed, not merely possible, but, considering the part religion has played and plays in human life, a necessary recognition. Naturalistic Realism has tended to look on religion as an emotionally colored mythological symbolism for social relationships. This attitude is the naturalistic counterpart of Ward's view that Theism depends upon Idealism; rejecting Idealism naturalistic Realists ignore or deny the essentials of theistic religion.

Realism starts out from what is called the standpoint of "common sense." At this level it should acknowledge (1) the individual's awareness of himself; (2) his awareness of nature or the physical world of which his body is a part; (3) his awareness of other selves, especially those constituting human society; (4) his awareness of a relation to somewhat Other, however described, in religion. It is not maintained that everybody is explicitly concerned with (4), but for the majority of those accepting religion (a number too great to be ignored) this has to be included as an experience of reality as definite as any other. Realism as a form of description is in essential harmony with the attitudes of common sense. It treats all realistically. The awareness of himself is for the individual an awareness of a reality; the awareness of nature is an apprehension of something no less real than himself; the awareness of other selves is an apprehension of realities as real as himself. Similarly for the religious the awareness of the Object of religion is an apprehension of a reality as real as any other form of reality.

Realism recognizes that all description must point ultimately to the immediately or directly experienced. Every philosophy has to acknowledge ultimates: facts behind and beyond which it cannot go. What is the full range of such ultimates? Realism finds itself unable to refer all experiences to one form of ultimate. It maintains that Idealisms have never actually been able to reach such. They have always arrived at some kind of duality, as of subject-object, appearance-and-reality. Natural science cannot be said to have reduced all, psychical and physical, to forms of the physical or to forms of the psychical. A term such as "neutral stuff" which is sometimes used to imply an ultimate form of reality beyond the distinction of physical-and-psychical, tells us nothing positive which could be treated as a genuine ultimate. In itself it is as barren as Spinoza's initial idea of substance as the self-existent. Realism does not seek for one homogeneous substance in all existence. It is more definitely concerned with the acknowledgement of the multiplicity of experiences and realities.

In so far as the Realist searches for unity he strives to comprehend relations between the multiple particulars. No adequate expression of the whole as a significant unity has yet been attained. Realism acknowledges different forms of unity. Seeing that realities are mostly (if not all) dynamic, it has to admit that there are processes toward unification of particulars. From the point of view of religion it may be believed as a simple act of faith that all particulars may eventually be related in a significant unity, but Realism has not yet any doctrine of such a unity. And, in fact, it is a feature of religion that it inspires men to strive toward higher and higher forms of unification.

The enumeration of immediacies and the statement of inferences which may be made concerning their relations constitutes the whole range of human knowledge. It is therefore possible here to do no more than refer to their types, except as concerns the religious, with which Religious Realism as the subject of this paper has to do. The knowledge of the physical world rests upon immediacies which for convenience may be called those of sense, and the relations between sense objects. There are other forms of immediacies of moral and æsthetic values—of qualities and relations. The religious life is also a realm of immediacies, a direct apprehension of qualities and of relations as ultimates.

Another aspect of philosophical Realism needs to be referred to briefly. Many forms of Idealism have directed attention to universal ideas. They have described these as immutable and eternal. Taking them as the essence of reality, reality has been regarded as ideal, fixed and eternal. In some sense or other (not generally clear) all else is described as appearance. Sometimes the expression "degrees of reality" has been introduced, but rarely with any significance except this: that what is described as of lower degree is a smaller part and that of higher degree a greater part of the Whole. Realism rejects the term "degrees of reality": if it refers to the Whole or to a greater or smaller part of it, it says just that.

For Realism all is equally real. Not identifying reality with immutable universals, it does not equate reality with the eternally persisting. A toothache which lasts for one hour is no less real than a tree which has been growing since the seed was planted ten years ago. The difference is not in their reality, but in their duration. There is no logically justifiable inference from the present reality of anything to its future or eternal persistence. The self of which one is aware is a changing self; the physical world of which one is aware is a changing world; the society of selves is a changing society; and it may be equally correct to affirm that the Other of religion is a changing reality. What thought tries to find is not immutability but consistency in change. It would be incorrect to say that it always finds consistency in the propositions used about realities. Realities may be more harmonious (or

less) than the forms of expressions which refer to them
are consistent. There may be contradictions in expressed
judgments about realities, but that may be because some
or all of the expressions are wrong, and not because there
is radical opposition between the realities of one moment,
or the reality of one moment and that of the next moment
continuous with it.

Reality as Realism describes it is not static. Some
earlier, narrowly naturalistic views (now, however, radically modified by changes in the attitudes of natural scientists) presented a realistic universe as a rigid mechanism, no less a "block universe" than that of Absolute
Idealism with its eternal immutable reality. Realism finds
it necessary to emphasize the dynamic character of reality. But the dynamic character is such that distinction
may be made between what is relatively more and what
is relatively less permanent. This is important for religion. Differences in the persistence of one reality and
another are significant. In certain respects though the
form of expression is not satisfactory (and none other
can be found), realities are carried along in their own
processes. The self which has had toothache may be considered for all its later duration to be different on account
of that, to however small an extent, from what it would
have been otherwise. In some manner the whole past is
carried on in the present, as the past and present are carried into the future. What seems fundamental as against
the stress Professor John Dewey places on the novel and
unique is that the extent to which the present differs from
the past (as remembered or otherwise inferred) is small
compared with the extent to which it is similar. The relatively enduring and persistent bulks far more in life and
attention than the novel. The value and importance of
recognizing the novel is indubitable; but it is brought
into a false perspective by the philosophy of Professor
Dewey. And one consequence of this is that fundamental
features of the task of philosophy and of the significance
of religion are ignored by him.

Our interaction with nature and other selves depends

to a very great degree upon their relative stability. And one may note, for example, the importance of the relative stability of language. It may reasonably be maintained by the religious that the religious experience also depends upon a relative stability of its Object. Dewey's exposition in rightly challenging the idea of absolute fixity has tended to exaggerate the opposite extreme. And that is equally open to criticism: in fact, if the relative proportion of the novel to the stable is gauged, his attitude appears less correct than the one he opposes. Realism insists that the novel arises in relation with what is, by comparison, known at the time of the appearance of the novel, as relatively more enduring.

Man is not occupied with merely non-conceptual immediacies: he has ideas. Ideas have or may have a relation to such immediacies. That relation is itself a form of immediacy, which is incapable of description or of definition. Realism must simply accept it. For the sake of social intercourse linguistic terms have come to be applied to immediacies whether qualitative or relational, and so also to ideas. In itself a linguistic term is as different from the idea to which it refers as the idea is from the immediacies with which it is related. The relation between an idea and the immediacy (or immediacies) to which it refers is itself referred to by a term, as for example, when it is said that an idea "represents" something other than itself. A term may be said to "stand for" an idea, or to indicate a particular immediacy, qualitative or relational. There are thus important distinctions between immediacies and ideas and their forms of linguistic expression. The expressions used by the same person at different times, or by different persons at the same time, though referring to the same or to similar ideas or immediacies may not be identical, may even be logically inconsistent. As language (that is, words which have come to be used in human history and not mere sounds or visual signs) refers to ideas, so ideas refer to immediacies, qualitative or relational. Ideas are often inadequate representations of immediacies: still more often language provides inadequate expressions of ideas. There have been important differences in capacity for forming ideas, as well as of linguistic capacity for expressing them. This has been more definitely the case with regard to the content of religion than with regard to physical nature. The task of philosophy is in part to search for accurate and adequate forms of expression, comprehensive enough to represent all the facts. Contradictory expressions include some error, which philosophy endeavors to rectify by a closer inspection of the ideas and immediacies to which the expressions refer.

The development of a Realistic treatment of religion may be considered on a parallel with the chief movements in ethics in the last fifty years. In the early part of that period the dominant philosophical view was that morality is bound up with an Idealist metaphysics. An example of this is found in the work of Thomas Hill Green whose influence was widespread. The only other vigorous attitude in competition with this was that of the thinkers who endeavored to extract from the biological theory of evolution the fundamentals of ethics. Later writers turned in the main to show the invalidity and the inadequacy of both of these movements. It is not possible to deduce the criteria or the contents of morality from the universals of Idealism or from the conceptions of biological evolution.

Constructive movements in ethics have proceeded on the principle that the study of morality is to be undertaken as the study of any branch or aspect of nature: by an empirical survey of the relevant facts. It has been found that the facts of morality have relation to ultimate moral judgments which rest in themselves upon a form of intuition. Moral intuitions are not of the kind supposed by the so-called Intuitionist of earlier times. They are not immediate apprehensions of the rightness or wrongness of particular acts. Judgments concerning rightness are seen to be secondary. Moral intuitions are immediate apprehensions of this or that quality of feeling, character, or action, as intrinsically good or bad. In

short, morality rests on its own basis of particular immediacies. These are ultimate, and are the data with reference to which a general view of morality is to be built up.
These immediacies are treated realistically: they are not
regarded as due to the merely subjective character of the
particular individual. They are found to be constituents
of an ever-evolving socially objective whole.

Ethics is not concerned with finding one conception or
principle present or underlying all moral values, but with
bringing into relief intrinsic goods and bads, and tracing
socially and historically an evolving organic whole or
unity of goods. The peculiarities of the individuals contribute elements of a comprehensive concrete whole,
which in the dynamic nature of life itself is in process of
growth. So, in like manner, Religious Realism rejects the
attitude which endeavors to deduce the nature of religion
from a pre-conceived metaphysic, such as Idealism, supposed to be independently justified on epistemological
grounds. It follows the same methods as the modern
movements in ethics. It insists that there are religious
immediacies as definite as moral immediacies. It sees
religion as a historical and social process in which the
contributions of individuals and groups help to build up
an ever-increasing whole of religion.

Religious Realism charges most of the Idealist descriptions of religion with being occupied too predominantly
with the *ideas* of religion. In contrast with this it presents religion as a complex of ideas, feelings, practical
attitudes and actions, having their roots in distinctive
immediacies. The Realist stresses the important fact that
no actual historical religion can dogmatically and *a priori*
be affirmed to contain all that religion is. Rather, different sects of the same religion, appear to be concerned
with or to emphasize particular aspects of religion. For
a fully Realistic view one object of the empirical study
of religions is to arrive at the most comprehensive description of religion with all its known constituents. The
comparative study of religions is not concerned with
finding a common denominator of religions (which might

be thought of as the essence of religion), but with arriving at a view of a more or less organic whole into which the various elements or aspects of different religions will fit. In the ultimate analysis, views implied in different religions or particular sects of a religion are opposed not so much (if at all) in what they justifiably affirm as in what they directly or implicitly deny.

The history of religion shows the religions emphasizing not simply particular ideas, but also particular emotions, rites and practices. Early Buddhism stressed the condition of mental equanimity associated with the practice of meditation; Islam the state of inner peace through an attitude of submission to God, cultivated by the regular practice of prayer. In many of the Christian Churches feelings of joyousness and of social fellowship have been promoted and continued by congregational hymn-singing. A realistic attitude toward religion admits the great variety of emotional states and the diverse forms of practices which have evolved in relation with them.

As an application of the general principles of Realism, Religious Realism recognizes that methods as well as starting points and results have to be considered realistically. Each field of activity has its own particular methods and types of training. The action of the individual is a continuous process: he acts upon and is reacted upon by the different realities. An individual has some self-determination or choice as regards the direction of his activities. He may concern himself predominantly with physical nature: the research chemist as chemist does that. The civil administrator, the teacher, the religious pastor, may turn their activities predominantly to other selves, to human society. The saints and mystics of the religions have turned their attention mainly to the Object of religion.

But Realism also insists that the activities of the chemist or of the farmer, to be successful, must be of their own types, for which some kind of training or "learning by experience" is necessary. So also effective interaction with the Object of religion involves particular types of attitude and of action, particular types of training on the part of the adept. In all spheres of action appropriate methods have been only gradually discovered and improved. The history of religious practices is a history of attempts to discover and to use methods for interaction of the self and the community with the religious Object. They have fallen into certain main types, most of which are to be found in the great religions, though with differing degrees of emphasis.

For Realism religion is very complex, involving a variety of relations between the human subjects and the divine Object. In this exposition the objective side will be considered first. And at the outset it is insisted that religion is concerned with God as a reality, and not simply with the idea of God. Religion in its historical social expression has never been an attitude or complex of attitudes adopted toward the idea of God as a hypothesis. It is a false residue of Absolutist epistemology to suppose that the idea of God is somehow metaphysically one with God, and that in religion the relation of men to God is simply a relation of other mental events to the mental event which is the idea of God. It seems more correct to maintain that the ideas concerning nature have been determined predominantly by the objective characteristics of nature itself; that the ideas of other selves have been determined predominantly by the characteristics of other selves; and also that our ideas of deity have been determined predominantly by God as a reality.

In this connection it may be possible to restate the position of Descartes. His explanation of the existence of the idea of God in the minds of men is a causal one. His account differs fundamentally from Anselm's ontological argument. Descartes' contention is that the idea of God implies qualities which cannot be arrived at by consideration of the world of external nature or of man, and that there can be no adequate ground of the idea except God Himself. Though there are objections to his mode of statement, Descartes' suggestion may be essentially correct. It is not necessary, in fact it is in conflict with what is known of the development of religion, to suppose that there is in each individual mind an innate idea of God. Rather the idea of God has been gradually developed through contact with the divine and as one result of the interaction between men and the divine.

For Realism, therefore, the divine is apprehended in religion as a reality. Different concepts of this reality and different expressions of these concepts are found in the history of religion. The existence of these differences is no ground for doubt as to the existence of the reality itself. The nature of the Object of religion and of its apprehension may be in part suggested by consideration of other selves and their apprehension. Formerly it was widely maintained that the only justification for belief in other selves is by a form of analogy. The apparent simplicity of this view has made a wide appeal, but its inadequacy has become more and more recognized. It is quite impossible to account for the association of infra-human animals in flocks and herds on the basis that the individuals go through forms of analogical inference prior to such association, or in fact at any stage in their association. In the human being the development of the consciousness of self and the growth of the concept of self go along with a similarly increasing consciousness of other selves and a growth of the concepts of other selves. This two-sided development occurs from the earliest stage of infancy. It is to be noted, however, that though infra-human animals most often associate with others of their own kind, they also act toward animals of a different kind in ways similar to their actions toward those of their own kind. A dog will fight and may also play with a cat; it will show fear of or friendship toward human beings.

Illustrations might be multiplied which suggest in this connection something other than mere physical perception on the basis of which some form of analogical inference is made. In his normal dealings with others the human person is not conscious of such analogical inference and there is no adequate ground for assuming it in infrahuman beings. Human persons appear to be attracted or repelled by other selves through some kind of immediate awareness of their qualities. In the immediate awareness of the qualities of these other selves is the immediate awareness of their reality.

It seems to be due chiefly to not having an adequate and close acquaintance with religion as it has actually existed, especially among the unsophisticated, that philosophers have rarely recognized that the knowledge of deity is of the same type as this consciousness of other human consciousnesses. As a human being has an awareness of another human being as other than a mere physical entity; as the dog has a consciousness of other dogs (though probably no concepts of them), as well as a consciousness of human beings (though again no concepts), man seems to have an apprehension of the consciousness or self of a superhuman order. In early stages he tended to locate this consciousness in a variety of objects and to form ideas of a plurality of beings, thus giving rise to polytheistic forms of expression. Becoming more aware of the character of this consciousness he has gradually recognized the inappropriateness of such localization and such polytheistic expression.

Sophisticated minds have elaborated networks of ideas, chiefly on the basis of sense experience, which have too often distracted their attention from other realms of reality. It may take as many ages for mankind to free itself from these entanglements as it has taken to build them up. Hence one need not be perturbed if in their present condition the sophisticated do not admit the apprehension of a superhuman consciousness. According to some forms of Hinduism, with their doctrine of transmigration, it may take a large number of lives before an individual genuinely attains direct awareness of divine consciousness. And further, as previously maintained, the experience depends in part at least on the attitude assumed by the individual and by appropriate methods and training.

It is by such considerations as those of the last few

paragraphs that the description of God as personal is
to be understood and justified. There are diverse concepts of personality, some of which are inapplicable to
the divine. Experience suggests that the least unsatisfactory use of the term implies kinship with the self-
consciousness of man, involving a capacity for entering
into at least some of the relationships that man as a
self-conscious being may enter. Viewed thus, personality
is a general term which may be used with limited application by the prefixing of particular adjectives as in the
expressions, infra-human, human, or superhuman personality. The particular adjective implies qualities which
may occur only within the class so described. Men treat
others as personalities because of the kinship with themselves of which they are directly aware. They have called
deity personal because of a similar kinship with themselves which they have felt in their relations with Him.
The apprehension of qualities in the divine which they
have not become aware of in human personalities has in
no way negated this apprehension of kinship. Whatever
intellectual reasons may be given in addition for the
acceptance of God as personal, this is the ultimate and
essential basis for that description.

Religious Realism in acknowledging this direct apprehension of personality by personality can admit variations in the concepts formed of divine personality. In
forming such concepts errors may arise. There has been
a development of such concepts, dependent on development in the religious apprehension of the divine, and in
the intellectual and linguistic capacity for expression. It
must, however, be remembered that the term personality
is comparatively modern and, it may also be said, occi-
dental. Nevertheless what it implies has been recognized
in past and present, East and West, in the attributes
ascribed to deity. The qualities attributed to God are
similar to or consistent with the kind seen in men's own
nature as conscious. It is not adequate to say that this
is because man has "made God in his own image." For
it is also apparent that he has apprehended in and has

ascribed to deity qualities not at the time so apprehended in himself. Rather it may be maintained that in large measure men have striven to realize and in part have realized in themselves qualities which, before they possessed them, they apprehended, even though vaguely, in the divine consciousness of which they have been aware. That has been initially in the experience of the saints and religious leaders of mankind.

The concepts of the qualities ascribed to deity have arisen from the apprehension of these qualities in man's relation with God. With regard to this it is necessary to reject a form of contention sometimes met with: that only like can know like. Such a view is often found at the basis of some forms of Idealism, it being assumed that reality other than the human mind must also be of the character of mind, or otherwise it would be unknowable. The contention does not seem justified. From the standpoint of Realism it is urged that the individual mind may be aware directly of the qualities red and green and the taste of sugar, though the individual mind cannot be taken as itself red and green and of the taste of sugar. The mind can apprehend what it is not in itself, what indeed is quite unlike itself. Thus it is not justifiable to maintain that in order to apprehend the qualities of the divine the mind must itself be of such qualities. This is important especially with reference to what is implied concerning the nature of the divine by such terms as eternal and infinite.

Reference has been made to the necessity of recognizing that different and apparently contradictory forms of expression may nevertheless refer to the same ultimate facts. As an example of the difference which the form of expression may make while the fundamental implication may be the same, certain aspects of the theory of Jainism may be considered, as bearing upon what has been called above the Object of religion. The charge of atheism has been made by non-Jains against Jainism. It has been keenly rebutted by some Jains, but not by all. There is need here to consider carefully what is admitted. In the first place the individual human being in this life experiences himself as a finite *jiva* or living reality with the characteristic of consciousness. In contrast with this, however, there is also acknowledged *jiva* with the characteristics of omniscience (*kevali jnana*), omnipotence, infinite bliss. The fundamental question concerns the relation between these. And it is here that the Jain form of expression may be at fault, while its recognition of both may be fundamentally correct. For the expressions used in Jainism imply that the *samsari jiva* (the apparently finite consciousness) is in essence one with the *mukta jiva* (the infinite consciousness). The alleged difference is that from the former point of view it is in bondage to *a-jiva,* the non-living, "karmic matter."

The Jains who reject the notion that Jainism is atheistic can point to the description of the infinite *jiva* as fundamentally identical with the usual description of deity in philosophically theistic systems. Jains variously answer the question whether there is a metaphysical identity of all *jivas* considered as infinite; that is, whether there is really only one such *jiva* or whether there is still a multiplicity such as is found of *samsari jivas.* If the former is the case then the one infinite *jiva* resembles the theistic deity and the question may be asked whether Jainism is correctly expressing the facts in identifying the finite *jiva* in any way with this. On the other hand it is difficult to understand how there could be a multiplicity of beings all of whom have the characteristics affirmed of the *mukta jiva.*

A similar question with regard to the forms of expression arises with reference to the application of these ideas to practice. It is strongly maintained by Jains that the redemption of *samsari jiva* is possible only by the effort of the *jiva* itself. All that any, even the great leaders of Jainism, can do for the redemption of others is to teach them the doctrine. Nevertheless the *jiva* is truly the infinite *jiva* and ultimately it is this which achieves its state of pure spirituality, freedom from bondage. As this infinite *jiva* has the characteristics of deity (as expressed in other religions) redemption through it is in essence similar to that implied in theistic religions. It is not maintained that interpreted along their own lines entire consistency or clarity can be found in these Jain expressions: on the contrary they appear from any point of view to be defective in many ways. It is suggested, however, that what underlies the expressions is similar if not absolutely identical with what is involved in a Realistic expression of certain aspects of the relation of the soul to God.

A similar method may be used in consideration of certain forms of expression in Buddhism. It might perhaps be maintained that, if one took the vast range of Buddhism in its different sects, ideas, and practices, most known aspects of religion could be found in it. The main lines of its later development in Mahayana schools might be said to represent the efforts to make Buddhism more adequate to experience. Early or original Buddhism may be looked upon as forms of theoretical and practical expression of certain fundamental sides of morality and religion, chiefly those of the individual subject of religion. Stress is placed on individual effort; on dealing with the problem of suffering from the standpoint of the relation of the mind to it. It includes a tendency toward an agnostic or aggressively negative attitude toward external rites and to metaphysical ideas of a reality objective to the individual. Nevertheless Buddhism itself formulated certain methods for the practice of meditation. And the later developments of thought and practice show its strivings for and the attainment of recognition of a universal reality, toward which definite attitudes might be assumed.

In a brief essay the whole range of religious development cannot be treated. Here, therefore, no reference will be made to the levels at which the divine was localized in a plurality of objects with corresponding polytheistic forms of expression. For brevity in this discussion the Object of religion is referred to simply as God.

Religions show a variety of types of relation between man and God. It is important to notice the character of these relations. There is worship or adoration, allied with reverence. This attitude implies an awareness of certain qualities of God. The concepts of these qualities were not arrived at through inferences from facts of another kind, *e.g.* physical facts. They grew out of and along with the direct awareness of the qualities themselves.

Other relations and other concepts have arisen with the awareness of other qualities. There is trust or confidence, upon which has depended the flight to God in times of evil. Upon that the practice of prayer is based. Men did not begin to pray to God because, and after they had reasoned themselves into the acceptance of the hypothesis of a divine being. Practices tend to intensify the apprehension of the quality or qualities upon which they are based. It is not likely that those who have become sophisticated will immediately have an experience of this trust and apprehension of the qualities of a being engendering it, simply by adopting the forms of prayer. The warp in a man's mental constitution is not straightened out so easily.

There is also fear of God. This has arisen not simply from an awareness of divine power. It has depended in part upon an apprehension of something in one's self discordant with the divine, just as two human individuals may feel uneasy in one another's presence; or as one may feel in the presence of another who does not himself feel antipathetic. Fear of God is more often felt (and is not mere awe aroused by divine power) when there is sin or the attitude of sin in the human consciousness. This fear has been called "the beginning of wisdom" for it may lead to change of mind, the giving up of sin.

There is what is called communion with God, or, more emotionally tinged, love of God. The fellowship of silence is known amongst men as a restful and refreshing experience, a communion of souls. Lovers may get an indescribable satisfaction in silent relationship; a state of peace different from the ecstasy of amative excitement. Communion with God is a similar condition. In it men have realized the "peace which passeth human understanding." Few have attained to the love of God in a highly ecstatic sense. That may be regarded as a condition continuous with what is dimly apprehended in communion with God: as the consummation of religious striving. Some of the great religious saints seem to have experienced it with considerable intensity. Love of God, communion with God cannot receive adequate recognition in accounts which do not describe God as real. This is the rock upon which so many theories of religion founder.

Though the order of their apprehension and expression has depended on religious development, the order in which the qualities are here considered is of no special importance. There is the concept of power. Even from early stages this has been apprehended as other than physical power. Undoubtedly it has often been associated with happenings in nature, but they have never been treated as though merely physical events. Such power is of the kind called by anthropologists *mana*, perceived for example in the "spirit," the "fire" of a great bull, in the "strength" of an impressive personality. The power of God is at least in part apprehended as of the same type as the last mentioned. It was only when philosophy began to influence religious expression that such a term as omnipotent came into use. The religious mind has felt simply that God is powerful, sufficiently powerful to aid him in distress.

The majesty of God is allied with the power of God, but it also signifies something other. It is difficult to distinguish majesty from glory. Both terms indicate an impressive excellence arousing adoration and an attitude of worship in the beholder. Such worship is joyous, as though the majesty and glory of God somehow inspire this type of response in the hearts of His worshipers. The distinctive timbre of this quality of deity is only to be apprehended: it cannot be adequately defined in other terms. The majesty of God is not just another name for the magnificent totality of physical existence, for this, if for no other reason, that there is so much in physical existence in conflict with the implication of the term. The difficulty of finding suitable expressions for divine qualities has always been and remains great. In consequence, at times different terms seem to refer to what may be taken as the same quality. Thus the majesty and glory of God have been associated with the term "light ineffable" suggested by physical light, but obviously implying something different in essence.

Religions often have references to the anger or wrath of God. In recent times not a few have sought to dispense with these terms. It ought, however, to be taken into consideration that in more advanced religions the term is regarded as signifying "righteous anger." The implication is that God is felt to be in opposition to those who initiate or coöperate in any disorder in the divine scheme or schemes. The term anger of God has an ethical and religious significance implying that if good is not done from one motive or another the wrath or opposition of the divine is to be expected.

Confusion has arisen concerning the term mercy, as referring to a quality of deity, on account of discussions which have contrasted it with the justice of God. The notion of justice as a sort of mathematical equivalence between virtue and joy, vice and misery, cannot be satisfactorily applied to existence as we know it. There may be no such equivalence. The mercy of God need not be regarded as involving opposition to what may not exist. The justice of God may mean nothing more than His consistent "pursuit" of His own scheme or schemes. The mercy of God appears to refer to a quality similar to tenderness and sympathy. Divine mercy has been depicted as a quality of divinity expressed as feminine, as the mother goddess, or as implied or symbolized in the veneration of Mary, the mother of Jesus, in Roman Catholicism. God's love is felt as an attitude on His part akin to the love felt from other human selves, but the apprehension of it is of something far more intense and elevating than any human love. "The love of God is broader than the measure of man's mind; and the heart of the eternal is most wonderfully kind."

Holiness has been regarded as in the first place a distinctive characteristic of deity. The attempts to express this quality have been various, often leading to misunderstanding. It is certainly not simply the "numinous" or powerful, however closely it is related with this attribute. It should be frankly recognized that the term refers to a quality impossible to define. Diverse symbols have been used for it in different periods of human history and all too often students of anthropology have mistaken the symbols for the quality itself. There is a human analogue in saintliness, a peculiar personal quality which it must be insisted has been attained chiefly through the practice of communion with God. Human saintliness seems to be acquired through contact with the holiness of deity.

It was not until a late date in human intellectual development that the term "infinite" came to be used. It would be interesting and worth while to investigate its earliest uses. Within later times it has figured both in mathematics and in philosophy. Attempts have been made to find for it a specific significance in mathematics, but none of these succeed in suggesting anything beyond a finite, the extent of which is left indefinite. All terms in which one might try to define "infinite" must either include the connotation of infinitude, or, not doing so, never go beyond the implication of finitude. In religion the term indicates a characteristic of deity incapable of precise definition. In a general way all that may be said is that it implies a vastness, a greatness (not as it were of size) which has called forth awe. This characteristic has been felt also in relation with other qualities of deity. Thus we have "infinite power," "infinite wisdom," and "infinite love," the implication being that these qualities of deity share the quality of His infinity. There is a contrast with the felt finitude of man. The apprehension of the infinity of deity and the finitude of man has been the awareness of a distinct contrast. Infinity which has an indefinable connotation for religion characterizes deity but does not characterize man, who nevertheless apprehends it. It is an instance in which the concept of deity has not been elaborated from the nature of man.

The term "eternal" could similarly arise only at a late stage in religious development. It has a real significance for religion even though theoretical philosophy may be unable to give any further elucidation of it. In implication it contrasts with certain aspects of the human experience of the temporal. The realistic contention should be that man apprehending his experience as temporal is also able to apprehend the eternal as something distinct from it. From the point of view of religion the eternal is not timelessness, but while present in the flow of time somehow transcends it. Systems of naturalism, naturalistic realisms, and so-called humanisms offered us to-day tend to ignore the term. Nevertheless having arisen in human language and its use having been continued so long, it is reasonable to maintain that it has a genuine significance. That significance we believe lies in its reference to an apprehended characteristic of the Other which is the Object of religion. It is the one term which suggests stability and persistence contrasting with the apparent limitations of duration of other factors of reality or experience.

The attribution of knowledge to the divine has gone through a long and varied development. It may be seen in some of its early stages as implied by widespread practices of divination. By these practices it was sought to discover some elements of the divine knowledge as relating to human affairs. Such practices do not seem to have grown up from any sort of rational reflection that the divinities or spirits as such must have knowledge which might be wrested from them by appropriate means. Divination seems to be in direct line with what has later been thought of under the term revelation. The whole course of thought in this direction has grown up out of a felt relation of kinship with the divine involving a transference of thought from both sides. In prayer man has acted as talking to God and in revelation has apprehended the transmission of thoughts from God to him. In the process of development the thought of God has been characterized as greater than the thought of man and eventually come to be described as perfect wisdom.

The Realistic account of religion may also give due acknowledgment to a dominating trend in the evolution of nature and the process of human history, while at the same time admitting elements of discord and lack of harmony. Though nature may be regarded as in the main a stable system it cannot be said to be entirely harmonious. So likewise in spite of the amount of stability in human development history is not a scene of simply harmonious activities. Realism may regard the dominant feature of order in nature and in human life as in the main due to the activity of an over-ruling Power. It is on such a basis that religion cultivates in its adherents a feeling of confidence in life.

Looked at closely empirical religions are in essence more optimistic than pessimistic. Even Oriental religions which appear at first sight pessimistic are found not really to be so. For though they insist that human satisfaction is not to be obtained in complete immersion in passing events they point to a condition of existence in which peace and bliss may be attained. They are more optimistic with regard to the transient than some accounts suggest. Thus, for example, Hinduism while it presents passing experiences as the realm of *maya* or illusion also recognizes that once the reality of the divine has been apprehended passing events may be enjoyed as *lila,* the sport or the joyous creation of deity. Again in some forms of Mahayana Buddhism it is insisted that *"samsara* is *nirvana,"* in other words that the peace and bliss of *nirvana* is to be experienced within the realm of the transient.

Religious Realism has also to acknowledge certain important features of man which come into view in religion. Some of these have already been incidentally referred to in considering man's relation to God. Religion has arisen in and reveals an inner life in man. The course of human development, and especially of religion, has included the evolution of man's knowledge of his own spiritual reality, which has eventually acquired independent denomination as soul or self. The religions have emphasized certain essential characteristics of the soul. They imply in each and every instance that the soul is able to exert itself in the manner they suggest. The soul is treated as distinct from the body over which it has at least some control. The activity of the soul is directed in part to the realization of moral values. In the realm of the moral, the soul has often appeared to itself to be in relation with a Power beyond, which impresses upon it an ideal, apprehended more or less clearly at different times and by different minds. Man has felt within himself power to coöperate with deity or to resist deity, even though he has been convinced that if He so willed deity could crush him.

Over and above its awareness of its own moral capacities the soul has felt an urge to enter into communion with the divine. It has come to know itself as capable of the highest bliss in religious communion with God, and of the profoundest unhappiness in alienation from God. It has become aware of the reality of regeneration and spiritual rebirth. It has appreciated qualities of itself expressed in reverence and adoration. In religion the soul has tended to conceive of itself as permanent: hence has arisen the conception of immortality. Though the forms of expression given to this conception have varied greatly in the different religions, from absorption in the divine to forms of personal continuance, these expressions may be regarded as based in all cases on essentially the same kind of underlying experience.

Religious practices, realistically considered, are the modes in which characteristics of the human soul have endeavored to express themselves and to find a satisfaction which the soul cannot give to itself but must be had through practical relation with something apprehended as higher than itself. That so many persons at the present time have ceased to perform religious practices may be taken as one of the reasons for the widespread sense of futility in existence and lack of spiritual satisfaction. In the revulsion against particular forms of religious practice, there has been a tendency to neglect religious practices altogether. History shows a development from crude to more refined forms of practice. This may be seen in the history of prayer. Prayer as supplication for physical welfare has often been abandoned for religious meditation and contemplation. Ritualistic aspects of sacramental meals have become more explicitly regarded as aids to the cultivation of collective communion with God. Art in its various forms has been drawn into the service of religion as means for the cultivation and expression of the joy which religion brings.

A realistic attitude to religious practices should lead to a survey of the practices of historical religions with the purpose of endeavoring to see in what form they may be included in the richest whole of religious expression. It may be supposed that religion can be vital and grow only if it expands in sympathy for different sides of religious life and recognizes an increasing variety of forms of expression. The different religions may have their contributions to make to religious expression in its practical forms. During the latter part of the nineteenth century and the beginning of the twentieth the interpretation of Christianity as almost solely a social ethic has tended to draw attention away from distinctively religious practice and the profounder emotions that go with it. The experience of history suggests that a merely social interpretation of religion is not adequate to the nature of man.

A Realist account of religion such as is here outlined need not and should not be divorced from the support which may be obtained from philosophical consideration of aspects of existence apart from religious experience. Taken in relation with what is learned from the latter, philosophical consideration of experience as a whole may lead to a theocentric view of existence. The fundamental characteristic of order in the world of physical nature, and the possibility of essentially rational relations between human conduct as mentally initiated and physical nature, suggest one influence or power dominating both. That human minds are sufficiently alike to make coöperation between them possible, and yet sufficiently different to make such coöperation profitable, similarly suggests some over-ruling principle in their origination. Thus, though Realism may be unable to give as yet any description of a systematic unity of realities, it may hold that there is much which points to a dominating principle or reality.

The attitude adopted in this discussion has been that Realism is a description of realities. It may, however, be maintained that Realism can be adopted as a form of speculative theory in contrast with naturalistic and idealistic forms of speculation. Even viewed as a form of speculation Realism challenges comparison with these other forms. It is claimed that it is closer than these to what is generally described as the attitude of "common sense," and so keeps a more intimate contact between philosophy and practical life.

V.

AN EMPIRICAL APPROACH TO A THEORY OF CHARACTER

By
HUGH HARTSHORNE

Research Associate in Religion
Yale University

AN EMPIRICAL APPROACH TO A THEORY OF CHARACTER

THE "good life," to-day, is inadequately motivated. Ancient religious sanctions have lost their power to convince or control. The meager universe of yesterday, with its patriarchal deity, is placarded "to let." We have moved out. But there seems to be some difficulty in locating another spiritual habitation, and indeed there is some doubt as to whether it is good for the soul to settle down anywhere, even if a suitable universe could be found to settle down in. There is a moody acquiescence abroad, which, no matter how attractively expressed, dulls our ambitions, and makes all adventure either laborious or quixotic. Security, after all, is too easily assured. Men want it, but despise it, once it is achieved. Nor will they forever pursue the ideal of disinterested devotion to the common weal unless they can undergird it with something more than the self-satisfaction of being called noble or sportsmanlike.

The discussion which is here set down makes no claim to have discovered a valid basis for the good life, but it does propose that such a basis should be sought in natural and human events. It recognizes that mere description of process, no matter how accurate, is not in itself either normative or even determinative of future events. It claims, rather, that such speculation concerning human conduct as is likely to provide either sound direction or adequate motivation must be based on the description of the way things actually happen rather than on the way men have thought they ought to happen.

The happenings or events to be considered are unavoidably selections from the totality of experience, and this very selection may result from and lead to prejudice of one sort or another. Moreover, we shall necessarily have to deal with generalizations resulting chiefly from the investigations of others, and these generalizations may be erroneously reported. In order to move forward at all, however, we shall have to risk missing the road.

Three types of fact will be presented: first the way the universe, or the environment, deals with individuals; second the way individuals deal with the environment; and third the way individual and environment behave in constituting a functioning whole. What these facts, or presumed facts, may mean for a theory of character will then be considered.

1. Contingency

So far as God operates through nature, he is best thought of as a condition rather than as an agent. The natural world seems to be so constructed and carried on as to provide abundant opportunity for the diversification and development of living organisms. There is no evidence, however, that these goods are made available for individual organisms by a selective process which takes any account of the wishes of the individual, save as these wishes are factors in the individual's response to the environment. Obviously individuals vary in the extent to which they take advantage of opportunity, but there is no reason for supposing that there is any relationship between opportunity and will or virtue other than appears in the actual event. So far as the individual is concerned, the fortunes and accidents of circumstance are distributed in accordance with the law of chance.

Whatever may have been the opinion of the ancients regarding the contingency of natural events for subhuman life, there was in the Jewish as distinct from other Semitic tradition a forensic element, which is well represented in the prophets, the psalms and the book of Job. To Job's friends it was inconceivable that he could have been so afflicted with misfortune and sickness unless he had done wrong, and they proceeded to subject him to an extended "bull session" which was a cross between the third degree and treatment by a psycho-analyst. But he protested his innocence and was convinced that whatever may have been God's purpose in thus afflicting him it was not to punish him for his sins. In his mind there was no relation between fortune and virtue. Things are provided. Things happen. Man takes his chance.

Job's objective view of natural events opened the way to a sheer fatalism, on the one hand, and to a genuinely scientific approach to nature on the other. There was either no law in the universe, or law which connected events without reference to human desires.

While there is no reason to suppose that Jesus viewed nature as would a modern scientist, he apparently took a definite position against the forensic view current in his day. Sun and rain are available for good and bad, just and unjust. Tares and wheat grow together; both have access to soil and air. There is no prejudice in heaven against the sinner. The affliction of the blind man could not be attributed to either his own or his parents' sins.

Furthermore, in anticipation of the findings of science, Jesus was convinced that there was an element of dependability in the natural world, as well as an element of impartiality. There is a natural order upon which one can count. The distribution of goods may ignore the individual, but the goods are there if the individual can and will make use of them. The house built on a rock will stand. A red sunrise signifies stormy weather. A man with even one talent may expect a return for his labor. But it is necessary to fulfill the conditions laid down in the order of things if one would profit by them.

This combination of views regarding the natural world is admirably illustrated by the practice of certain insurance companies. Their rates of insurance are based on existing death rates or average longevity. Just how many out of one thousand persons of any age will live to any specified age can be predicted with considerable accuracy. But just which of the one thousand will be found alive at the time indicated, no man can tell. But one can take advantage of what is known of the causes of death to increase the probability that he will be among the survivors. Should the entire one thousand take better care of themselves than people do now, the actuarial tables would be upset, and the insurance companies would profit by the change. Hence it is good business as well as good education for insurance companies to print advice about keeping well and avoiding accidents. They know that they can count upon the forces of the natural world to create and maintain health—and profits—if the conditions are discovered and met.

In speaking of God as a condition rather than an agent, it is clear that we have in mind these two aspects of the natural order in relation to individual organisms, viz., impartiality (or the chance distribution of favorable and unfavorable events) and dependability (or the predictability of events). If we may dip into the evolutionary process at the point where life begins we may say that these characteristics of environmental behavior represent a divine strategy, since it is by reacting to these conditions life has evolved.[1]

But in the development of higher forms of life there has come into operation a type of behavior which is not completely described by the terms impartiality and dependability and which, indeed, occurs independently of these other conditions. It is found most fully developed in mankind, and brings to logical fruition all previous evolution. It may be called the process of individualization. In contrast with the behavior of the nonhuman phases of the environment, this process is concerned primarily with the control of the distribution of goods and evils. Without realizing that he does so, man takes over this responsibility, and thus essentially changes the way in which the environment impinges upon the individual.

The operation of this type of control has mixed evil with good. Small groups have profited by it to help one another at the expense of other groups. Out of this situa-

---

[1] This does not rule out a teleological interpretation of ultimate reality. If the universe purposes personality, the provision of "conditions" is its method.

tion have come wars and class conflicts; for in administering the world's goods man has too often failed to observe and follow those other features of divine strategy which we have called impartiality and dependability.

2. Integration

Let us turn now to the second set of facts which underlie the development of our theory of character. How does the organism respond to the environment? What distinguishes its behavior from that of inorganic objects? Or better, by what is an organism to be distinguished from its environment? The word "organism" itself suggests the answer: An object which behaves organismically, that is, which develops and maintains a unified pattern of response to changing situations, is an organism. The distinction is functional rather than mechanical or chemical, since the organism, like the rock, is physically continuous with its environment. Unlike the rock, however, protoplasm—the basic substance of all organisms—possesses the capacity to rearrange itself in relation to environmental changes so as to avoid destruction. This requires energy. Hence food. Hence the power to capture and assimilate food. Since the environment is three-dimensional and the organism thus exposed on all sides, there must also be differentiation of function within the organism and the mobilizing of resources with reference to that point at which food or danger impinges. The protoplasmic structure which provides for this differentiation on the one hand and this integration of response on the other is called the gradient.[2] From the point of highest activity there are communicated mechanically or nervously such signals as will focus action at this point, or in relation to this point.

In the long run this tendency to differentiate functionally has been represented by the increasing complexity of physiological structure and the tendency to integrate has been represented by increasing complexity of the nervous system. Life has proliferated and integrated

[2] See C. M. Child, *Physiological Foundations of Behavior* (Holt, 1924).

and has thus been able to meet environmental changes not only by adapted organs but by coördinated acts.

Integration is thus seen to be valuable not in itself but because by means of it the organism conserves its identity—resists absorption into the environment while maintaining equilibrium with it.

Mental activity shows the same tendency to differentiate in a changing environment. Serving on the one hand as a means for extending the scope of the organism's activity both in space and time, the mind proceeds beyond this point to develop interests which are of no service to the organism, which may even destroy it, but, in these superorganic activities in relation to what we may call a mental environment, it still maintains its identity as an individual mind distinct from other minds by its functional pattern or integration.

In an unchanging environment, the processes of differentiation and integration subside, life slows down and finally ceases. Complete adaptation to a static environment would be equivalent to death. Change is the source of action. Differentiation is the condition of life, the occasion for integration. If the universe is to offer endless creative opportunity to its creatures it must do so by providing endless differentiation, and hence with this principle of progressive differentiation one may well associate the concept of God.[3] Logically, this is the

---

[3] This is not intended to be a contradiction of H. N. Wieman's proposal that God is the principle of progressive integration. It rather suggests a more explicit consideration of a primary factor, whether called God or not. It might be better to include both processes in the concept of God. On the other hand, if we follow through the concept of God as condition rather than as agent in connection with the suggestion that differentiation precedes integration, then we must either exclude God from the processes of nature, or deny that his activity is purposeful (originally integrated). Since neither alternative is satisfactory, we may attribute the "condition," that is, the entire framework of nature, to a purpose of which it is the expression, or conceive of God as a mode of response to this condition, in which case the principle of progressive integration would seem to be the most useful type of hypothesis—a principle most clearly represented in organismic activity, particularly on the mental level. But for the individual, such activity is a part of the environing condition in response to which he achieves selfhood, so that, apart from any ultimate explanation, the practical basis of personality is a condition to which he may freely respond rather than an integrative process of which he is the inevitable outcome.

ultimate principle, for the integration of a totality would
be meaningless. Progressive integration implies progressive differentiation as its condition.

Once again, human beings in their dealings with one
another have failed to profit by an examination of the
way things happen. They have attempted to induce in
themselves and in those under their tutelage a type of
integrative action which defeats its own object.

Integration in subhuman animals takes place automatically. It consists of the marshalling of all the animal's resources to meet each emergency as it arises. For
each emergency a fairly stereotyped procedure is available and is brought into active play.

In contrast with this relatively simple behavior, it has
been supposed that children should be taught to organize
their responses around some ethical ideal, such as honesty, meeting even the most diverse and complex situations with conduct which would conform to the standard
in question. At the same time, children have been placed
in groups, the family, the school, the club, the gang, to
each of which they are compelled to make satisfactory
personal adjustments comparable to those which an animal makes to its physical and human environment. The
result is, for the average child, an *impasse*. If he adjusts
to his several groups, he falls down on his ideals. If he
sticks to his ideals, he gets into trouble with his groups.
When his ultimates are conceived in static terms while
his real world offers variety and challenge, he tends to
let the static ideal go, or else in attempting to conform
to a static ideal, he retires from active participation
with his groups.

These anomalies are well illustrated by the results of
the Character Education Inquiry.[4] In testing the consistency of children with reference to the standard of
honesty it was found that the average child was no better
integrated in terms of this ethical ideal than if he had
never heard of it, yet it had presumably been harped

[4] Hartshorne, May, *et al., Studies in the Nature of Character* (Macmillan, 1928, 1929, 1930).

upon in school and at home for years. Experience gained between his ninth and fourteenth years increases neither his honesty nor his consistency. But he does tend to behave the way his class group does, whether this behavior be high or low on the scale. Comparison of his behavior with his measured comprehension of ethical standards reveals practically no relation that is not accounted for either by his intelligence or by his responsiveness to his group. In other words, those who are most honest are not consistently those who are most clear as to the standard of honesty, or those who offer lip service to this ideal. Such integration as the average child possesses is of the same sort as characterizes his own pet animals. It is such as has made use of wit to seek a reasonably peaceful and complacent adjustment to social demands. It is not such as has involved those mental or spiritual aspects of the environment in response to which man may come to the full measure of an integrated personality. How these aspects of the environment may be conceived and brought to bear on the individual seeking adjustment to his world is the problem of the next two sections.

3. Cosmic Functioning

For purposes of analysis we have considered separately the conditions offered by the universe for individual stimulus and growth, on the one hand, and the integrative character of organismic response on the other. The concrete reality is a process incorporating both. We shall use the term "function" to signify this inclusive process.

Functioning occurs at different levels, or with differing degrees of completeness. Mechanical functioning may be illustrated by the activity of water in wearing down the hills. The hills are there and the water is there. The process of wearing includes both. The result of the interaction defines the function. A more complex type of mechanical functioning is found in man-made machines, in which the function of a part is defined by a result which is *intended*. The function of a carburetor is the *purpose* it serves in the operation of the automobile. Remove it from its context and it is just so much junk. It is from the successful activity of the entire mechanism that it derives its meaning.

Some would doubtless claim that biological functioning is essentially mechanical in nature. The function of a hand or an eye is understood in terms of the contribution it makes to the life and purposes of the organism. We are justified, however, in distinguishing organismic from mechanical activity, in view of the integrative character of the former. In order to be assimilated to this level of functioning, the parts of a machine must be viewed as parts of a *tool* which in turn is used by some organism as a means to an end.

On a still higher level we find biological functioning merging into primitive social functioning, as observed in an ant hill or bee hive. Here we see parts of wholes which are themselves complete biological entities but which can be understood only in terms of the contribution they make to the life of the social unit to which they belong. Thus among certain ants we find freight carriers, soldiers, egg layers and valets.[*] Each is an individual in the ordinary sense, yet each must fit into the work of the colony or cease to exist.

Much human activity is at this level. Industry is largely organized like an ant hill. The "hands" are identified by their jobs, so many to a job. Hardly more than the ant does the individual worker understand the meaning of the whole process. The management supplies for him the direction which the ant derives from "instinct." So with an army. The soldier does not know and is not supposed to discuss the plans of the staff. His job is defined for him. His duty is to obey orders.

For most individuals custom serves to define and control action whenever authority fails to specify details. Indeed authority itself is mediated largely through conventional standards and modes, without which the task

[*] See William Beebe, *Edge of the Jungle* (Holt, 1921), pp. 58-59.

of coercing large numbers of human beings would be almost insuperable. An ethic which views morality as conformity to convention is a mere verbalization of the behavior of ants and armies.

Military and conventional types of organization are the actual successors of primitive tribal arrangements which date back to man's early history. But few would claim that man is limited to these primitive modes of social action. Through other types of experience he has developed capacities and interests which are genuinely "social" and "personal." As generations have passed he has found increasing opportunity to use his own intelligence in the guidance of his conduct and in the determination of his goals. We find such opportunity best illustrated in democratic forms of social organization, such as a well conducted committee meeting, an old-fashioned New England town meeting, a wisely managed family, a student council, a modern classroom, the free play of children. Each member of such a group is contributing his intelligence and will as well as his skill and strength to the enterprise upon which the group is engaged. Together the members work out their purposes and the means for carrying them out, and together they decide how the work may best be divided. Each one understands not only his final responsibility but also its meaning for the entire enterprise. This type of experience we shall call true social functioning.

The levels of functioning may be roughly pictured by a series of concentric circles. At the center is that type of activity we have called mechanical functioning. It is fundamental to all the rest and occurs within all higher levels. Next we draw a circle which represents the level of biological functioning. This too is basic in all organic activity. Another circle stands for primitive social functioning of the ant-hill type. There is much of this in human life and probably a great part of social conduct will be of this nature for a long time to come. Finally we draw a circle which represents true social functioning, at which level the individual has come into his own as a coöperating whole, interacting freely with his group and discovering the meaning of his life in terms of the purposes of the group. Personality as we know it to-day is a product of such activity. It comes into being and grows through true social functioning. Each level represents a larger effective environment, a bigger whole to which the organism is sensitive. The functions of the individual are the functionings of this larger whole, and his behavior may be regarded as the functionings of this totality. The criteria by which one may judge whether or not an individual is thus assuming his full share in the creative group process are joy, skill in the processes involved, effective sharing in the formation and fulfillment of purposes, and the spirit of respect, goodwill and coöperation.

Thus we see that the type of integration one achieves depends upon the type of environment to which he must adjust. A crowd, to be successful, must be composed of individuals who can be readily stampeded. A gang demands and produces a gang personality. An autocratic group requires subjects as components and develops persons only to the ant level. A democratic group affords an opportunity for the growth of genuine selves.

In the preceding discussion we have confined our attention to the social aspects of the environment. This oversimplifies the picture. It would have been possible to define function in terms of the mutual needs and adjustments of organisms and the world of nature. The bee exists for the flower and the flower for the bee. They are dependent on each other, the one for reproduction and the other for its own nourishment and the nourishment of its offspring. The hive may be thought of as a device for producing the means for the cross fertilization of certain plants. The hive exists for the bee as much as the bee for the hive and the bee is an instrument of the flower.

Similarly, a man must produce goods in order to live and the goods he produces must therefore be required for the satisfaction of some need. Industry, like the hive, is a device for facilitating such production. Nor can we stop here, for even the democratic group exists not for its own sake but for some purpose which alone justifies its existence and its activity, and therefore the activity of its members.

What is this larger environment in relation to which true social function becomes meaningful? We might claim, on the one hand, that the physical universe exists for the sake of producing persons and derives its meaning from the values achieved by man, or we might claim that man has some contribution to make to a reality which transcends himself. If we accept the former view, then man, being the measure of all things, is left without guidance other than his individual fancy, or his joint agreements. If we accept the latter, we leave open the possibility of either discovering or creating some meaning for life as a whole in terms of which the activities of groups and of individuals may be appraised. It should be recognized, however, that "function" at this point becomes an interpretative rather than a descriptive term and it is with this understanding that its use is extended so as to include what we shall call religious function. Beyond the circle enclosing true social function we need another, which shall remain undrawn to suggest that there is no definite area to be included. From here on, we are impinging on all reality. The environment which conditions our conduct is mental, visionary, if you please. So far as any possible ultimates may influence us, they influence us at this level through the medium of our own ideas, our own values and hopes. Here we deal with a reality within which the essentially personal factors of our experience subsist. It stands for the vast perspectives of time and space and for the timeless values to which the human mind is responsive. To this mental world adjustments are actually made, just as they are to the immediate physical environment or to the demands of the appetites. From the standpoint of an infinite observer, the life of the individual may be interpreted in terms of his functioning as a part of a realm of final values in terms of which all else is judged as worthy or unworthy.

It is not proposed, however, that this world of ideas by which we hypothecate reality is or can be absolute and complete. Such a completed whole could have no definable functional relation to ourselves as there would be no inclusive environment with which it might itself interact. The logic of a functional analysis implies an infinite series of environments as a correlative of enlarging meanings. These meanings, however, are not already achieved by reality, and waiting for our discovery. They come into being in the course of that type of interaction between conscious organisms and their environment which we have called religious functioning. Ethics at this level of activity is a description not of obligations, but of functions, and ethical thinking is inductive discovery of the conditions of personal growth.

It is to be noted that functioning on the religious level is not separate from functioning at the lower levels. Each level includes those beneath it. A single complete unit of experience would be described as a wedge-shaped figure piercing to the center and reaching out to the circumference. A comprehensive description of human activity would consist of a complete set of such wedges, and each wedge would be a major human interest. Thus we should list health and safety, reproduction, justice, play, and education as these find expression in industry and hygiene, the family, government, facilities for study and art, and schools through which the young are introduced to these several areas of life. Men organize themselves in groups and institutions to provide the conditions of health and safety, and thus grows up an entire industrial civilization in all its ramifications. They organize themselves in families partly for their own happiness and partly to provide continuity within the institutions they create. They organize governments to keep the peace and to perform jointly many activities which will assist in the joint distribution of goods and the equalizing of burdens. They organize societies and institutions to promote the creative interests for which all the rest is but the physical underpinning. They organize schools to transmit this social heritage to the young and enable them to take up their activities at the point where they drop them, and carry them forward to new levels of efficiency.

But in all these activities, men seek for themselves that type of self-realization which we have called true social function. Most of our work is still on lower levels and as such it not only fails to develop personality but actually stunts and distorts it. With this situation, men are not contented. They are seeking to transform all human behavior so that through it they may truly function as human beings. For this interest, as for each of the others, they tend to organize themselves. The interest is religion and its characteristic institution is the Church. To this activity, when it is free from the drag of mere convention or the sanctions of external authority, we have given the name cosmic functioning.

4. Implications for a Theory of Character

As a first step in developing a theory of character from the type of data referred to in the previous sections of this discussion, it is necessary to consider how the self comes into being as one term of an experience of mutuality.

Consciousness and the self. When an organism is integrated so as to react to an object it is proper to say that it means the object and is conscious of it. But higher organisms can adjust also to their own processes of adjustment, to their own meanings, and thus be conscious of their own consciousness. This is taken to be the nature of self-consciousness. It is what being a self means. The objects to which a self adjusts are adjusted to as a stream of events having continuity of which the organism is aware, and at the same time the organism is conscious of itself as continuing in these adjustments.

This view is distinguished from that which identifies the ''self'' with the organism as a whole, in that it reserves the word self for an organism which is conscious of itself as continuing.[6]

Experience. The flow of events apart from any consciousness of events is not experience. Piecemeal adjustments with such relatively unrelated data as they involve is not experience in the full sense. This probably characterizes much of the subhuman world. But if successive events are reacted to in such a way that a record is left upon the reacting organism by means of which it can react to the stream as a whole—that is, if representing the stream of events there is a stream of data that is conscious of its own continuity, there is experience. Experience is the consciousness of the continuity of events. The self has already been so described. An experiencing organism is a self, is consciously organizing its data. These may or may not be true pictures of what takes place in the environment.

Ontogenesis of the self. The child is equipped with a structure which when subjected to certain types of stimuli develops into a self. These essential stimuli are contributed by other previously developed selves. The effective stimulus seems to be a mixture or alternation of emotion-stirring obstruction and appeasing coöperation through which the child's organism learns to adjust itself to a world of selves.

Many things contribute to the gradual distinction between the self and the not-self with language as a main factor, for by communication the area of conflict and coöperation is enlarged, the experiences of selves can be compared, and common experiences identified and consciously shared. From the earliest months this sharing of experience is taken to be the chief evidence of the true nature of reality, though reflection subsequently adds other modes of verification.

Other selves as well as objects are included in this shared experience only when selves are mutually meant

---

[6] Compare G. A. Coe's definition of a person as a reactor that is conscious of that to which it reacts, of the direction of its reaction and of its success or failure.

or pointed to not only as objects meant but also as objects *meaning,* and as the necessary witnesses, or even participating creators, of both our world of things and of our very selves. If one met with no response from others when he tried to communicate with them he would have no means of knowing whether he was awake or sane.

Phylogenesis of the self and the god. The pre-personal or pre-self modes of conscious response were probably pervasively emotional, the projicient system being rather exclusively used as means to the satisfaction of biological necessities as represented in the cravings and satisfactions of the autonomic. The friendly or useful or hostile or appetite-satisfying qualities of objects, projected into them by reason of the autonomic responses aroused by these objects, were more significant than their color or shape, save as these latter characteristics were signs of danger or utility. Reversion to this type of response is illustrated in the action of a man who kicks his shins against a chair in the dark. He apostrophizes the chair, and for the moment the chair is alive as was the entire world of his more primitive ancestors. Things as such, as not having attitudinal qualities, were only slowly differentiated from persons.

The pervasive aliveness of the pre-personal world was expressed by such terms as Wakonda, Mana, and this aliveness was experienced in some things more than in others and in some events more than in others. Probably, as some hold, the group experience, with its conflicts and coöperations, was a primary source of the sense of mysterious power. But as time went on the power was associated with fewer and fewer objects and events, such as storms, seasons, birth, death, sex, catastrophe, great men, etc. These experiences continued largely emotional. As selves became better organized, these things that behaved as selves were taken to be selves, and the world was peopled with demons, ghosts, spirits, gods and goddesses without number.

Further experience made emotional responses to many of these things and events increasingly inappropriate and they became mere things, mere events, with no personal connotations except by way of poetic description. Men and gods have become organized selves together, and the increasing unification of the human self has carried with it the complementary values experienced by the self—a conservative and conserving force when institutionalized; a radical and reconstructing force when free.

Science, being interested in the world of things as viewed unemotionally, tends to back the personal responses off the stage, and, so far as it is occupied with objects and their events, succeeds well in this, so well that unless it directs its attention to the study of persons, it is likely to end in a nonpersonal world of primitive appetites fed by exteroceptors and controls enormously expanded by the scientific command of material forces. A taste of this was experienced in the World War and is the daily lot of multitudes caught in the cogs of our industrial machine.

A higher self. It was noted that the self is an integration of data into experience. Similarly the coinciding experiences of two selves, which in the raw are just two streams of experience, may through a better integrated adjustment to their common environment become, at least temporarily, one experience in which each shares. The two selves are not merged; they overlap; but the overlapping constitutes a true higher self for each, though different, probably, for each. The most common basis is the sharing of an emotional experience as in a mob. A higher form is in the realization that a common experience is being shared. This may of course be an illusion. Or one may be conscious of the fictional character of the other self. In any case, the selves, or experiences, come together, fuse, or what not, in the consciousness of the individual. Communion is with what one self *takes the other to be*. One may think of the process of interrelation among such selves as gradually evolving a unified self inclusive of all the lesser selves of one's experience.

God and the self. Historically the God self has functioned as one of such contributing selves, the value of the communion depending on the relative development of the two selves concerned and the nature of the communion. In the long run this God self depends on what one chooses to make final in one's experience, just as our friends are what we prefer to think them to be, in spite of themselves. So God is a reservoir for ideals and serves as a foil for the development of the self toward its ideal.

The higher self, to which we alluded a moment ago, which emerges from our social experience and embodies both one's own and the common will, may be as much a discovery as a creation. God may be thus revealing himself to us, and at the same time he may thus be growing through interaction with human selves.[7]

Mutuality and the contingent universe. The attitude of science toward events, far from being hostile to religion, is the very foundation of faith in the possibility of genuine personality. As already noted, Jesus accepted probability as the basic law of the natural world, regarding it as a strategic device of creative significance. Instead of emphasizing, as a pessimist might, that ill fortune comes upon the good man without desert, he pointed out the equally significant fact that good fortune comes upon the wicked man without desert. Men do not "earn" good fortune. The last man in the vineyard was paid as much as the first. What Jesus did was to adopt God's strategy as his own, applying it to the treatment of individuals as the natural world applies it to the race. God provides for all. Man must provide for each, but in such a way as to conserve his freedom and make possible his growth. The goods are here. Man must take charge of their just distribution. Only as we include man in our view of the universe do we begin to envisage how God deals with the individual. And quite naturally: It is only through social experience of the sort just now described

---

[7] Compare the portrayal of the growth of God in *Green Pastures*. In this play, the Lord is represented as changing in character in response to the changing character of men. The character of God is a function of the imagination of the preacher who tells the Biblical story to a class of children in the prologue to the play. We are proposing here to omit the prologue.

that the self comes into being at all. The love of God for the individual, in the nature of the case, can be mediated solely through the love of man for man. But the man who would thus act for God must follow the rules of the game —no partiality, no judging, but rather going the second mile, giving the cloak as well as the coat, loving enemies as well as friends, bearing others' burdens. The fact that Jesus succeeded in doing all these things, and thus demonstrated the success of this method in dealing with man, is for those who have confidence in it a pivotal point in the history of civilization, for here the growth of persons is linked up with the fundamental creative activity of the universe itself.

We may illustrate what we have called divine strategy by an imaginary incident. Your son wants to cross a brook. He calls to you when you sit on the hillside watching him, and asks you to help him over. You do not reply. He begins to fret and fuss because he sees no way across and calls again. Still, no reply. He gets angry and shouts for help. You remain unmoved. Finally he calms down and begins to look around. Presently he discovers some stones, which you had placed there long before, and gets across dry shod. He comes running up the hill to where you sit, and begins to ask questions. "Say, Dad, did you know those stones were there?" "What do you think, Son?" "Well, I don't know. At first I was pretty mad about your not helping me, but now I begin to think that maybe you put those stones there yourself and just wanted me to find them for myself so I wouldn't always be a baby, but would learn how to take care of myself. Jiminy! That's a good idea. Next time I have Brother up here, I'll let him hunt the way I did, but I won't let him fall in the brook, Dad." The boy looks up at you and smiles. You and he understand each other now.

This is what is meant by mutuality—it is the supreme moment when another's self is discovered to us, opened to us, in that joint recognition of sympathy, affection and profound respect which the Christian calls love.

This is the great hypothesis. In terms of this creative

and cohesive social principle men may deal with a contingent world so as to achieve both inner integration and dynamic adjustment.

Character. We bring to the concept of character the whole range of meaning which we have passed in review. Character is the art of living. It is achieved through the experience of social and religious functioning, *i.e.* as men perform the activities of daily life with a sense of their significance for the largest totality of which they can conceive. The man of character is thus one who functions well as a human being, who adopts as his own the divine strategy, achieving self-integration through that denial of self by means of which he becomes for others the condition of their growth, supported in this adventure by his faith that in so doing he is acting in accordance with the nature of an overshadowing reality in which he lives and moves and has his perpetual being. The man of character is at home in the universe.

VI

GOD AND VALUE

By
HENRY NELSON WIEMAN
Professor of the Philosophy of Religion
The University of Chicago

GOD AND VALUE

Love uses glowing words; but accurate thinking demands cold, abstract terms. Our present effort must be a striving for the latter. So we shall discuss God in terms of structure and process. Everything intelligible is a structure. What is purely ideal and does not exist, is structure only. What exists is some process having a structure, unless it be chaos. If God in terms of structure and process awakens no response in the loving heart, we can only plead that there is a time for love and a time for clear thinking. Both are important and each can promote the other, but words appropriate to one are not appropriate to the other. We fear religion has suffered much from failure to make this distinction between the verbal needs of these two interests.

God is that structure which sustains, promotes and constitutes supreme value. It may be infinite. This structure characterizes the process of existence to some degree, otherwise it could not enter into our experience at all; and we can discuss only such structures as enter into our experience. In so far as this structure of supreme value enters into existence, we can speak of God as a process. But it extends far beyond existence, into the realm of possibility. And the whole of existence is by no means conformant to this structure of God. The terrible magnitude of evil makes this plain. In so far as this structure is bare possibility, it cannot exercise control over existence. But in so far as it is a process, it does exercise control. For nothing is causally efficacious save a process of some sort.

What must be the nature of this structure of supreme value? Some things about it we can discover by making an analysis of value. However we may define value in its elementary form, it would seem that supreme value

155

must be some system or structure which brings lesser values into relations of maximum mutual support and mutual enhancement. It might be claimed that such a system would have only instrumental or extrinsic value. Such a claim, we believe, is not valid. A system which brought lesser values into such relation that each derived maximum value from all the others, would be one in which each served and promoted all the others. Then the value of each would be its meaning for the system as a whole, *i.e.* its functional activity in sustaining and improving the total system. Thus the system as a whole would endow each activity with maximum meaning and value, and each activity would give value to the whole. Hence it would be only a matter of viewpoint which was called means, and which end. From one standpoint the system would be means, and the subordinate activity end; from another viewpoint the reverse would be true.

Such a system of maximum value is achieved in so far as all intelligent, self-conscious, goal-seeking activities of men, and as much of the rest of nature as possible, are brought into a single structure in which each sustains, liberates and magnifies every other to the highest degree. This mutual support and enhancement must be not only between contemporaries but also between successive generations, ages, and cultures. Such a structure we call the structure of integration; and the process by which it is achieved we call the process of progressive integration.

This structure as bare possibility is not causally efficacious. But to the degree that it is the structure of actual existence, that is to say, to the degree that it is a process, it does promote is own fuller embodiment in nature. To claim that all of nature is dominated by such a structure and process, is to fly in the face of all observable evidence. But to deny that there is any manifestation of this process anywhere in nature, is equally to run counter to what can be observed. To say that there is a process in the world which operates to increase the structure of value, and to that degree is the embodiment of this structure, does not necessarily imply that the process is teleological in the ordinary human sense of that word. Of course, so far as human beings recognize the value of this structure and strive for it, we have that much human teleology operative. But over and above human effort and intelligence, a certain degree of structure in society, human mentality and elsewhere, would seem to increase the probability of further increase of such structure. The mere fact that it exists and so operates in the form of a process, does not make its increase inevitable, but it does increase the probability that it will increase. The dice of contingency are loaded in its favor by the mere fact that it exists in the form of process.

Is God Process or Possibility

We have said that God must be a process, not merely a principle, and have indicated the reason. We have also asserted that that to which all human life should be dedicated by reason of its supreme value is not merely some possibility or system of possibilities but is rather the process which carries these possibilities. We must show reason why we make this claim, for many hold the opposite view. Many claim that the most important reality which can concern human life is not anything that exists but rather some non-existent possibility. Not what is but what ought to be, is the matter of supreme concern, they say. Not what is but the best that ever can be, should command our highest allegiance. Therefore, if we are going to use the word God at all we should apply it to these possibilities which are more precious than anything that exists.

This is an issue of the first importance: Should we give our supreme devotion to some process of existence because it carries the highest possibilities of value? Or should we focus our attention upon these possibilities as being more important than the process which makes them to be possibilities? We believe there can be only one right answer to this question and that is that the process cannot be considered of any less importance or

of any less value, than the highest possibilities which
it carries.

When we cut off the possibility from the process which
makes it a possibility, and prize the possibility as more
important than the process that carries it, we are assuming a self-defeating and self-contradictory attitude. The
possibility of highest value is not a possibility except by
virtue of the process which makes it such. To say that
the process is mere means and therefore of less value
than the possibility which is the end, is to set up a
wholly vicious dichotomy between means and end. The
highest possibilities of value can never be attained except
by way of the process which leads to them. Until we
can find in the process the identical value of the highest
possibilities which it carries, we cannot ever find the
highest possibilities of value, for the greatest value requires precisely this integration of means and end. Therefore, the object of supreme devotion, since it should be
the greatest value, must be not only the highest possibilities but also the process which carries these possibilities.

Still another objection should be considered which is
sometimes raised against this identification of process
and possibility as being the rightful object of supreme
devotion. Some hold that the best is not a possibility
at all, but an impossibility. Therefore, if we are to be
faithful to the best, we must not supinely yield to the
vulgarity of existence, either actual or possible, but
must give our highest devotion to that non-existent impossibility that never can be. R. B. Perry, Bertrand
Russell, Herman Randall, Joseph Wood Krutch, George
Santayana, many an æsthete and lover of art, and others,
have been eloquent on this point.

But he who adores the impossible, implies that his
adoring of it is of great value. Indeed he exhorts, and
insists, that the most important thing in human life is to
give our adoration to this impossibility or these impossibilities. But this adoring is itself a process of existence
because he who adores is an existing personality. Therefore the most important thing in human life for him and

for all mankind is to attain and to maintain that state of existence in which due esteem and appreciation can be given to this impossible best. Thus here also some process of existence is inextricably involved in the highest value and one cannot be faithful to the one, nor highly appreciate the one, without like faithfulness and appreciation of the other. That process of existence which lifts us to the level where we can appreciate this impossible best is, along with the impossibility itself, the most important reality which can enter into human life.

Here, then, are the two reasons why God cannot be identified with value apart from some process of existence. First, if the value be a value because it is a possibility of existence, it cannot be a possibility and hence cannot be a value apart from some process. Second, if the value be a value even when impossible of existence, then that process of existence which enables us to value it as such, cannot be ignored or excluded from the high esteem we give to the impossibility itself. Thus in any case some process of existence must be combined with some possibility (or impossibility) to make up the object of our supreme devotion. Since God is the name we give to such an object, God must be identified with that process of existence which carries the possibilities of greatest value, or which lifts us to the level where we can appreciate and adore the impossible best, which impossible best then becomes the characterizing value of the process which is God.

Henceforth when we speak of the process of greatest value we shall correlate it with the highest possibilities but shall not introduce the further complication of impossibilities. We shall do this partly to avoid a very confusing complexity in statement, and partly because we believe that when the so-called impossibility becomes appreciated and adored by existing persons, it thereby becomes involved in existence and, as a value, is no longer an impossibility. But we shall not further pursue the subtleties of the problem involved in value when it is conceived as a non-existent impossibility.

Is the Best One or Many?

When we inquire concerning what is the most important thing in all the universe, to which we have given
the name of God without regard to what further specifications may accrue to it, we are faced with a further
misunderstanding. It appears in the guise of an objection which assumes some such form as this: You cannot
exalt any one process as supremely important. What is
most important for one person at one time is not most
important for the same person at another time and much
less so for some other persons. What is most important
in one situation is not so in another. What is most important for one age, race or civilization, cannot be most
important for every other. Hence the most important,
meaning that which carries highest value, is not one but
many. Indeed it is an unknown and unpredictable multiplicity.

Unquestionably there are many different values,
whether by value one means a state of consciousness
or an existing thing or an indefinable quality or a
kind of relation between certain existent things or however one may define value. But when there are several
different values it would seem obvious that an organization of them, into a system of such sort that they
sustain and promote one another, is better than those
same values disorganized in such a way that they
obstruct, exclude and destroy one another. This would
seem to be so manifest that it scarcely requires an
argument. It applies not only to the values which an
individual may experience from time to time but also
to the values experienced by different individuals.
For example, a certain kind of music heard by an
untutored ear gives me ecstasy but palls upon me the
more I hear it. Furthermore, others do not enjoy it and
so my own enjoyment cannot be deepened and my sensitivity quickened by that inevitable modification produced
by social interaction. Also, it is not the kind of music
which can be cherished by successive generations and
thus acquire a tradition by which the individual can be

trained and sensitized to fuller enjoyment of it. Contrast such music with the opposite kind which does not pall but leads me to deeper enjoyment the more I hear it; which is enjoyed by others and so through social interaction the enjoyment of each is magnified and his powers of appreciation increased; which is enjoyed by successive generations and thus acquires a traditional sentiment and shapes the customs of a people so that the individual can be cultivated and refined by the culture of that people to find the greater enjoyment of this music. Certainly the second kind of music has greater value than the first.

What has been said about music can be said about all values. Some experienced values can be organized into a system wherein they mutually support and mutually enhance one another. The satisfactions found in truthfulness can be organized into such a system along with many other enjoyments, while the satisfactions found in lying cannot be so organized or at any rate not into such an inclusive system of mutual support and mutual enhancement. The enjoyment we get from rejoicing in the good fortune of other people lends itself to a most inclusive system of mutual support of enjoyments, while the satisfaction derived from vindictively overthrowing the fortune of others out of malice and envy cannot be so organized. So likewise there are gustatory delights, erotic delights, the enjoyment of power and all sorts of enjoyments which can be distinguished by reason of the fact that some of them lend themselves to the kind of organization of which we have spoken and others do not. Some can be progressively magnified by entering into such a system and some cannot. Plainly it would seem that they which do lend themselves to such increase and stability are better than they which do not.

What, then, might conceivably be called the greatest possible value? Would it not be some system which includes the greatest number and diversity of enjoyments but adjusts them to one another in such a way that they (1) support one another and so make each more secure,

(2) magnify one another by reason of the increasing sensitivity which the system produces in the individuals who participate in it, (3) enable each individual to find in his experiences not only immediate satisfaction but also the satisfaction, which is often much greater, of fulfilling a function in sustaining and promoting the system as a whole which may be carried down through history indefinitely, (4) a system which is not static but creative inasmuch as it enables one individual to integrate his enjoyment, idea, insight, technique with that of others and out of this integration to bring forth new and different enjoyments, ideas, insights, techniques to further enrich the system.

Now the sort of system we have described does actually occur more or less in human history. Indeed such a system is what constitutes a culture in the noblest sense of that word. Such systems of culture grow and then decline. But however much such a system may undergo transformation it never wholly passes out of existence unless the race which carries it, together with every record of that race and all other races which have had any contact with it, also pass out of existence. Even when such total extinction does occur, supposing it ever does, there is always the likelihood that the record of that perished culture will be unearthed and thus the system again become a living contribution to the historic enrichment of the experience of the race. Indeed we might say that this rediscovery and conservation of the cultural riches of the past is one of the very important functions of that process by which values may be increased.

We have tried to indicate what might constitute the highest possibility of value. It would be a system in which enjoyments are organized, not statically, but creatively inasmuch as the organization would bring into existence many enjoyments which could not otherwise occur and would make many experiences enjoyable which would not otherwise be enjoyable at all. Ideally it would make all experience enjoyable even when painful because of the recognized function which such painful experience might have in sustaining a total system of value. How nearly such an ideal system can be approximated we do not know, but that systems do occur which approximate such an ideal however remotely, would seem to be apparent.

If the highest possibility of value be of the sort we have indicated, what is the process which sustains and promotes such possibility? It would be that process by which values are organized in the way mentioned. This process might be called progressive integration. However, it would be a great mistake to think that any sort of increasing organization produces the kind of system we have described as constituting greatest value. On the contrary it would seem that only that kind of organized interaction between individuals can yield greatest value which elicits the most complete self-expression on the part of each individual member and promotes greatest mutual understanding. Such a process cannot be called the social process because social process means every sort of interaction between individuals and groups, and the greater part of such interaction is not of this sort at all. In fact, we do not think the adjective "social" has any merit at all for, while the process of organizing satisfactions which we here have in mind certainly includes interaction between human individuals and groups, it is by no means identical with all such interactions; and it includes, furthermore, interaction between human individuals and their non-human physical environment as well as interaction between these non-human factors.

But we cannot pause here to describe any more fully what we believe to be the nature of this process which carries highest possibilities of value. We do not know much about it; perhaps no one does. But certain features of it would seem to be rather obvious. However, our chief purpose in this section has been to refute the objection that the highest possibility of value is different for each individual, and for different ages of culture. We claim, on the contrary, that the highest possibility of value is the attainment of a kind of unity, namely a system in which all these values experienced by different individuals and in different times are organized so far as possible in such a way as mutually to sustain, enhance and creatively interact on one another; while all satisfactions which cannot be so organized must be pronounced disvalue if they are obstructive to this organization, and if not obstructive they are relatively very trivial. Thus, the very nature of highest value shows that it must be unitary since it requires the unification of otherwise separate values.

GOD AND THE UNKNOWN

There is another objection which we must consider. It is the claim that we are very ignorant, that we are encompassed with mystery, and therefore it is only naïve presumption which can claim to know or even attempt to inquire concerning what process in all the universe carries highest possibilities of value.

Our ignorance we would admit, and furthermore, would strongly emphasize. Whatever increase in knowledge has been achieved by the advancing sciences has only enabled us to discern more clearly how vast and dark is the mystery that enshrouds us. Just a little section here and a little region there and a portion yonder have been brought within the wavering light of a partial knowledge; but of all the rest we are quite ignorant.

Immediately this acknowledgment is made certain philistines raise a protest that runs like this: How can we give our supreme devotion to a process and possibilities of existence about which we know so little? Or if we can do it psychologically, what is the use of it? Isn't religion far better if it gives its attention to matters about which we have most specific and reliable knowledge? If religion insists on giving attention to what is so little known, then let us discard religion. Why concern ourselves with matters which lie beyond the reach of assured knowledge and efficient control?

We shall endeavor to show that the supreme importance of religion lies precisely in the fact that it does give highest allegiance to matters about which we have very little knowledge and no great control. This is true not because it is desirable that we should have little knowledge about the most important matters. It would doubtless be far better if we had the most complete and accurate knowledge about them. But the hard fact is that we do not have such knowledge. It is precisely the most important things in life about which our knowledge is least complete and least accurate. Yet men have often claimed to have accurate and full knowledge of these matters of greatest importance. They have been led to make this wild assumption and dogmatically insist upon it, because their need of such knowledge has been so dire. When we most urgently need anything, we frequently resort to the device of making ourselves think we already have it. It has been the folly of many religionists—and many non-religionists—to claim they had more knowledge about God, that is, about the process and possibilities of highest value, than they really had.

But the fact that our knowledge about such matters is very limited does not make them any the less important. To ignore them for the sake of lesser matters about which we have most specific knowledge and efficient control, is folly just as great as to claim a knowledge we do not have.

DEVOTION TO THE UNKNOWN

We submit that the most distinctive characteristic of the human, that which has enabled him to become more than a beast, is precisely the fact that he is able to, and actually does, focus his interest and efforts upon the unknown. The unknown does not mean the unknowable. Pure science, for example, is almost exclusively devoted to searching out the unknown, the unattained and even the unimagined processes and possibilities of existence. As soon as anything becomes known, that is, as soon as a clearly formulated and well-articulated concept has been achieved and tested concerning any matter, pure science has no use for it except to use this concept as a means to explore still further regions of existence and possibility which are not yet known or attained and, in great part, not even imagined.

Some will say that the unknown which science explores is always imagined at least in the sense of having an hypothesis concerning it. But that is only half the truth. While there must always be a hypothesis for use in investigating a specific problem, the specific problem is not likely to be investigated unless it is believed that it will lead on to still other problems and these to still others which are as yet not even imagined. As soon as the scientific investigator begins to suspect that his specific problem is a blind alley, that is, that it does not thus open out into regions as yet unknown and in great part unimagined, he is not likely to have much interest in it. Therefore, we say, this devotion to the unknown, the unattained and the unimagined, is the very breath of life to science.

But this interest is not only the breath of life to science. We have mentioned science first not because it illustrates the matter any better than many other branches of human life, but because it happens to be the assumed bulwark and standing ground of those who object to this interest in the unknown and unpredictable. Pure science is interested in trying to extend the accuracy and scope of our powers of prediction. That means that it is almost exclusively interested in those regions where we have not yet learned to predict with accuracy or with scope or at all. The supreme lure of pure science is the unknown and the unpredictable because its whole reason for existence is to transform the unknown into the known and the unpredictable into the predictable.

But this dominating concern with the unknown (or, if one wishes to express it, the little known) and with the unpredictable, is not limited to science. It is, we claim, the source of all that is distinctively human as over against the subhuman. Take the simple matter of conversation or discussion. The zest and joy of discussion lies in the fact that they who enter into it may hope to find emerging out of the discussion new insights and new perspectives that were wholly unpredictable, unimaginable and unattainable to the individuals before they engaged in such intercourse.

Of course, conversation does not always issue in any such high fulfillment. Most commonly it does not. Perhaps most commonly it is just a kind of gabble, a kind of automatic response which individuals make to one another when they meet, not unlike the sniffs, squawks, and cries which the lower animals display toward one another. But when conversation becomes distinctively and peculiarly human, as over against the subhuman, it does show creative character. Doubtless there are some people who never engage in a conversation without a preconceived notion of just how it should proceed and who refuse to follow it when it begins to open up unexpected and unimagined vistas.

Science and discussion are not the only ways in which this distinctively human interest shows itself. All fine art is of this sort. He who attempts to produce a work of art in the form of music or prose or poetry or any other form, by simply reproducing some established and well-known pattern without bringing forth anything which was previously unknown and unimagined, is not an artist at all. The same is true of human love. The glamour and romance of love lies in the anticipation of unknown and unpredictable experiences arising out of the intimate and profound communication of two personalities. And this is precisely what occurs in genuine love. He who would try to make all the communal experiences of love conform to a rigid preëstablished pattern, would stifle love and make it a routine way of adapting two personalities to one another with least fuss and with minimum attention given to one another. Still again social reconstruction and innovation is a further way of seeking for higher values than any thus far achieved in our established institutions. So also is the gathering up and conserving of the social heritage from the past and adding to it our own experiences and out of this assimilation of the old and the new achieving new insights and bringing further possibilities of value to light. This might be called creative education.

But these unknown, unimaginable and unpredictable possibilities of value which are explored and actualized by way of science, discussion, art, love, social reconstruction, education and conservation of social heritage, are not six separate realms of possibility. They are six different ways of exploring and actualizing the unknown possibilities of value which lure men on and make the human way of living worth while.

THE FUNCTION OF RELIGION

To be religious after the manner we here propose is to be sensitized to the process and possibilities of highest value while these are still very obscurely known, and to be sensitized to them not merely as possibilities to be explored by some one special art or science, but as that total system of highest value, sometimes called the Kingdom of God, to which all the arts and sciences and the whole of human life should be dedicated. Such dedication is religion of the sort we wish to advocate.

Always the chief function of a worthy religion is to quicken to the maximum this interest in the process and possibilities of greatest value which necessarily, in great part, exceed the reach of our present knowledge and control. If they are infinite, as they may well be, they will always not only exceed, but infinitely exceed, the scope of our knowledge and control. The reason why it is supremely important to have this interest quickened to the maximum has already been made plain. Without it there can be no science, no art, no love, no creative education, no progressive increase of a social heritage which brings forth ever new possibilities of value, no progressive reorganization of society to achieve further values, in a word, no life that is distinctively human. For the distinctively human life is the life of aspiration.

But, it may be asked, if man already has interest in unknown possibilities by way of the special arts and sci-

ences, what is the use of religion? Before these specialized activities arose, religion may have served a useful
function in that it represented man's interest in unex-
plored possibilities of value. But now that we have these
efficient techniques and specialized interests, each of
which opens out into its own reach of possibility, what
is the use of religion?

The answer to this is threefold. In the first place, any
interest which is pursued in disregard of other interests
interdependently connected with it, becomes an evil in
respect to these others, because it interferes with them.
But all the different arts and sciences are more or less
interdependent. Hence the unreligious pursuit of any art
or science, meaning the prosecution of it without regard
to the total system of good to which it belongs, becomes
an evil. In the second place, the supreme good, as we
have seen, is an inclusive system in which each constituent interest takes on maximum value by virtue of its
function in sustaining and promoting the whole system.
Therefore, if the several arts and sciences are cultivated
without religion, that is, without regard to the contribution they can make to the total system in which they all
achieve greatest mutual enhancement, we cannot hope to
serve the supreme good. In the third place, the conscious
and social existence of man requires a very complex and
delicately balanced system of innumerable components
in order to endure at all. The more highly developed and
specialized become the various arts and sciences without
religion, religion being devotion to this most inclusive
system upon which we depend for all experience of value,
is a dangerous evil. It threatens the very existence of
man as a conscious and social individual.

This structure upon which we are dependent for all
experience of value and all increase of value is not the
universe as a whole, but it is a certain structure in the
universe. This structure we call God because it alone is
worthy of the supreme devotion of all men in all ages.
No single art or science is sufficient to explore it or adjust

man to it. That is the task which requires the coöperation and conjunction of all the arts and sciences. Hence the increasing specialization of the arts and sciences, instead of making religion less needful, makes it more and more important for human living. It becomes increasingly urgent that we do not allow any lesser loyalty to usurp the place of this supreme loyalty, which is to God.

He who prosecutes any art or science should do so religiously, which means that he should pursue it not for its own sake alone, but for the sake of the important contribution it may make to unveiling, or adjusting man to, that total structure of value which is God. It is not true that religion can ever be superseded by the arts and sciences. Rather religion becomes increasingly important and ever more urgently needed as the arts and sciences become more specialized.

It is always necessary to distinguish between religion and philosophy in respect to the function just mentioned. Philosophy attempts to formulate a theory concerning that structure of existence and possibility which constitutes value. Religion, on the other hand, is devotion to it, devotion meaning practical effort and emotional appreciation, as well as intellectual inquiry concerning it. Religion means to take this structure of existence and possibility which constitutes value and make it the sovereign allegiance of our lives. Furthermore, a religion which is worthy does not take the philosophical theory as object of devotion. Of course, an intelligent religion will use the philosophical theory. But as soon as any theory or belief is set up as the ultimate object of supreme devotion it becomes a great evil, for our theories are never completely and adequately true. Therefore, a worthy religion will recognize the fallibility of every philosophic theory, indeed it will recognize that such theories are even more infected with error than most products of the human mind, and therefore will give its devotion not to the theory but to the structure of process and possibility at which the theory is aimed.

EVIL RELIGION

Religion cannot achieve knowledge or do any practical work except by way of quickening human interest in the process and possibilities of highest value to such a pitch that men will strive more earnestly and zealously in the various arts and sciences to achieve fuller knowledge and to further actualize these values. Therefore, since religion, apart from the arts and sciences, has no way of gaining knowledge or doing work, it is very easy for it to cultivate enthusiasm for the unknown and unattained values without directing this enthusiasm into any practical endeavor or intellectual search. Then we have what we call fatuous mysticism. Then the enthusiasm exhausts itself in gloating over the fact that there is something of supreme importance, but doing nothing more about it beyond going into convulsions of ecstasy and adoration. To keep the gaze of men lifted up toward values which lie beyond the controlled and predictable possibilities of life, is the supreme function of religion. Nothing could be more important. But if men merely gaze and gloat without striving to increase the knowledge and actualization of these possibilities by the best methods available, religion may become a liability instead of an asset.

But a greater evil frequently befalls religion. It consists in turning away from these unknown and unattained possibilities of value, ceasing to quicken human interest in them, and giving attention only to the attainment of goods that are already known and specified objects of human desire, such as more food to eat, better clothes to wear, more herds, more productive land, more money to spend. Of course, food, clothes, herds, land, money are indispensable tools to use in seeking further possibilities of value. We cannot seek unknown goods except by using known goods. Any religion which quickens interest in unknown possibilities of value in such a way as to make men disregard the known goods, is falling into the fatuous mysticism just mentioned. But we are now speaking of another and opposite evil which sometimes arises out of revulsion against fatuous mysticism. It is that of turning away from search after the highest good, because we know so little about it, and giving attention exclusively to known goods and particular specific problems. But when religion ceases to lift the aspiration of men toward the highest, however unknown this highest may be, it ceases to serve its own proper function and becomes merely a superfluous competitor with the arts and sciences, trying to divert the energies of men from these to itself. We must give our attention to particular, specific problems and known goods. But that is the work of the special sciences and the practical arts. If making religion "scientific" means to make it try to do this work which is properly the work of the special arts and sciences, religion becomes a blundering anachronism, always thrusting its inefficient efforts into the work of specialized interests to interfere and mess things generally and making an intolerable nuisance of itself. The aspiration which religion represents must always find expression in the efficient techniques and in the pursuit of known and controllable goods, but it must always treat these as tools and instruments and trails leading on. There is a function of life which is more important than any efficient techniques of life because it is the source from which the arts and sciences spring and the constant inspiration of their existence. It is the function of keeping the flare of human aspiration blazing high. A religion which does not do this becomes a pest. Religion must fire men with the realization of God, that is, with the sense of the process which carries highest possibilities, but with full recognition that we have much yet to learn about it.

But suppose, an objector might say, suppose this process is something we already know, something as familiar to us as our children's faces. And suppose the highest possibilities of value that ever can be attained are already attained and there is nothing higher that can ever be reached. What then becomes of all this talk about devotion to the unknown and unattained? Our answer is that if this speculative suggestion should be true, it still holds that we do not know with certainty that the process as familiar as our children's faces carries highest possibilities, and we do not know that this which we already have is the best that ever can be. Therefore, we cannot give our unmeasured love and loyalty to it. Therefore it still holds good that, if we are to be intelligent, we must give supreme allegiance to what is not fully and certainly known. We know with certainty that the supreme good is. But what it is, we do not know, even though it should turn out to be something very close at hand and fully in the light of consciousness.

Religion must not be scientific if by that one means to identify it with the techniques, conclusions and theories of the sciences at any stage of their development. Religion must not be social if by that one means to identify it with the hopes, strivings and ideals for a better social order which may happen to prevail at any given time in our history. Religion can and should serve the sciences and the social strivings of men but it can do so not by identifying itself with them and so losing its own unique identity. It can serve them only by fulfilling its own unique and indispensable function, which is to renew the courage and striving of man by quickening him with a sense of the best that is and ever can be, even when he cannot claim to know with certainty or completeness what it is. He can know that God is, without knowing specifically what God is. And he can know that there are highest possibilities without knowing specifically what they are. He can know this for much the same reason that he can know that what he does now will have some bearing on what happens to-morrow, even though he does not know just what will happen to-morrow and does not know just what doing of to-day will have the most important bearing upon it.

Religion that functions in this way has enormous saving power if by "saving" one means enabling a man to rise up out of any sort of disaster or disillusionment and go his way with unabated zest and hope. Indeed, the hour of most bitter disappointment and overwhelming defeat is just the time when his sense of God, that is, his sense of the unspecified process and possibilities of highest value, becomes most vivid, because a man has at that time no cherished ideas and projects to give him the illusion of having attained or conceptually grasped the highest good. We are so constituted that whenever we are moving successfully toward some specific and highly prized objective we constantly fall into the illusion that this particular goal is the most important thing in the world. But these special ends of endeavor never do constitute the greatest value, however important they may be as constituent elements in the total structure of greatest value, and often they are not even constituents. Therefore, the hour of disillusionment, of failure, disappointment or other disaster, which sends the man without this kind of religion to despair, cynicism, suicide or insanity, is just the time in which the man with this kind of religion experiences a marvelous rejuvenation because of his revivified sense of the structure of supreme value.

If in the hour of such bafflement a man projects some specific picture of this supreme good and identifies his picture with the reality, he is displaying that compensatory functioning of the mind with which the psychiatrists have made us familiar. But if he does not do this, if he fully acknowledges his ignorance, but recovers with acute vividness and power the apprehension of the unquestionable fact that there is this supreme good and dedicates himself to it, not knowing specifically what it is, nor claiming to know, nor even cherishing the conviction that he himself must be delivered from his troubles, but finding his release and exuberance in seeking to serve and find the good, then he is doing nothing that is pathological but is living in the most intelligent manner.

Imaginative representations of God may well occur if they are used simply as symbols. We must have symbols to think at all. Intelligence is impossible without symbols because thinking is impossible without them. But to treat the symbol only as a symbol, and to remember our ignorance, is to save ourselves from that subjectivism which is a persistent curse.

Professor Montague has rather wistfully expressed the hope that what we cherish most should not be dependent on what we cherish least. We believe this is a wrong approach. If highest value is to be found in meaning—and we do not know where else to seek it—then whatever sustains, promotes and leads to what is dearest, has this dearest as its meaning, and therefore has in itself all the value of this dearest. Hence it is our fault, not the fault of the nature of things, if what we cherish most is dependent on what we cherish least. We must learn to cherish the latter as much as the former. If we do not, it is because we are unregenerate. We must learn to appreciate the kind of value which consists in meaning. God is not necessarily what we cherish most, but is rather what we must learn to cherish most. The natural bent of the human heart is by no means a reliable guide to the supreme good. One does not love God until he is converted. To be converted, in this context, means to be so changed that one prizes most highly that upon which we are dependent for the greatest values. That is God.

God is not merely an abstract order that does nothing. Neither is he the process of nature that does everything regardless of value. But he is the structure of supreme value viewed as possibility of existence, and also that kind of process in nature which most nearly approximates this order of supreme value and promotes further approximation to it. Thus God is both the most beneficent actuality and the supreme ideal.

Some may jump to the conclusion that human life is that in the universe which meets the two requirements which we have said are the essential characteristics of God. But that is a great mistake. Most of human life does nothing of the sort. Some few rare activities of man do conform to these requirements. But some of the activities of every man, and most of the activities of all men taken collectively, are about as far removed from the kind of process which sustains, promotes and constitutes greatest value as anything you can imagine. The deification of humanity is the most pitiable absurdity man has ever perpetrated. But individuals and groups can participate more or less in that ordered process which is God; and to participate in it is the one high calling of man.

VII

A REALISTIC VIEW OF DEATH

By
GEORGE ALBERT COE

Formerly Professor of Religious Education
Teachers College, Columbia University

A REALISTIC VIEW OF DEATH

THE mortality of man has received from the religions of the world more elaborate attention than has any other single phase of our existence. Ceremonial, myth, creed, theology, philosophy—all are occupied with it. Yet the fact of death is more nearly a surd for thought, and for thought-directed conduct, than is any other universal experience. To the biographer it denotes empty time taking the place of filled time. To the priest it is a signal to seek compensations in imagination for a loss that is actual and not in imagination. To the mourner it is a wound that is to be healed by time and by attention to something else. The only event in the career of each of us that can be predicted with complete certainty is the one that we are most reluctant to think about. William James was substantially right when he said that scarcely any of us ever think definitely for even a few minutes at a time concerning our own departure.

Christians, no doubt, like to believe that they are different, and they do aver that the ending of life is no interruption, no blank time, no meaningless event. Yet, would not an unprejudiced observer say that they, like others, are scant of speech with respect to the nature of the event; that they do not practice reflection with respect to this aspect of their own future, and that their conduct, when a neighbor passes away, is what it would be if the dead were regarded as, in every practical sense, "done for"? Apart from accumulating property, insuring one's life, and making a will, what specific act weaves death into any design of ours? Who treats his own coming change as an opportunity, or as a resource, or as an event of which he can be in any sense or degree the master?

Those who do make death serve their purposes by giving their lives for a cause receive our awed praises. Even life-risking adventurers and seekers after "records" awaken in us half-puzzled admiration. Yet the possibility of a like deliberate choice of the place that death shall have in our less dramatic careers rarely occurs to any of us. We have no stomach for dying; our utmost quality is the negative one of not whimpering. This is called "accepting the inevitable."

The ethics of "accepting the inevitable" requires scrutiny. Stoicism accepted deprivation, pain, and death, not because they are inevitable, but because they were believed to be parts of a universe that is fundamentally rational. "I will what thou willest," was the spirit. This was no mere refraining from whining; it was a positive incorporation into one's character of the difficulties that other men shun as mere loss. For the Stoic the processes of nature, both within his own mortal frame and within the environment, were brought thus under an ethical conception. We moderns, helped by the natural sciences, have taken a few steps in the same general direction, for we have incorporated into our conception of goodness not a few sanitary and hygienic controls of the "inevitable" processes of nutrition, elimination, and the like. But the equally natural process of dying, which is equally a process of and in us, has not been included in this ethical conception of the natural life. Moreover, though there is a growing conviction that procreation should be deliberately controlled for ethical ends, no one appears to have noticed that the will to procreate remains half blind until it frankly takes up into itself the imposing of death upon those upon whom it imposes life.

The traditional Christian belief in a life after death, even if it is not mistaken as to its facts, does not solve this ethical problem. To Paul, death was not to be assimilated into the good life; rather, it was an enemy to be escaped. Accordingly, the doctrine of "the resurrection of the body" looks upon the natural process as tolerable only because a supernatural process supervenes upon it. According to this tradition we are to be rescued from the natural; we are not to master, assimilate, or utilize it. It is not necessary to dwell here upon the fact that the Pauline tradition risks everything upon a proposition concerning Jesus that is not tenable as history; nor need we pass judgment upon the truth of the Christian doctrine of life after death. For, whatever its truth or error, it does not assign any ethical significance whatever to the experience of dying. Religious fancy has not pictured angels, demons, or divine beings as hovering about the deathbed because at this particular point one achieves a moral success, or fails in a moral endeavor; it is non-ethical emotion that makes death appear so significant.

The Christian current, moreover, has been deflected. Angels and demons are becoming figures of speech; graveyards are ceasing to be uncanny; and the thought of the last judgment, with its gaping alternatives, no longer robs believers of any sleep. On the whole, however, dying is losing its old meanings without acquiring new ones; it is becoming more and more a blank for thought. This is true, though we are more and more burdened by the external paraphernalia of decaying beliefs. The cost of funerals is a case in point; so are our rapidly spreading cemeteries. The cemetery is, of course, a hangover from ancient beliefs, now abandoned, concerning the future of the dead body. We rationalize old burial customs by saying that they manifest our respect for the departed. Yet our graveyards are not beautiful; rather, they are a conventional and dull expression of grief and of a pointless thought of death. Moreover, they have become a serious economic burden. As our cities of the living have grown, so have our cities of the dead, appropriating, supposably in perpetuity, ever more and more of the surface of the earth. They do not serve the dead, and as for the living, cemeteries are both a costly and an inappropriate expression of sentiment.

What would happen if, instead of dodging the fact of death, steeling ourselves against the thought of it, or floating in an eddy of tradition, we faced it squarely, endeavoring to determine for ourselves what place it shall

have in a planned career? Suppose we were as objective
toward it, and as purposeful, as we are in the presence
and the prospect of thunder and lightning. How would
our views change, and our conduct? Could we here obtain
any light upon "religious realism"?

The aspect of religious realism that is here in mind is
the nature of its assumptions and its method of justify-
ing them. Whatever else a realistic philosophy of religion
may be, it at least assumes that the distinction between
"good and evil" is not merely an aspect of our desires
but also an aspect of the world-power within which we
have our being; and it maintains that, in a general way,
we are able progressively to apprehend what, from the
standpoint of this world-power, is good and what evil.
This increasing apprehension comes by way of our own
endeavors to increase good and decrease evil. These endeavors bring us in sight of new facts. We get acquainted
with ourselves and with what we really want, we discover
the causes of weal and of woe, and we uncover fresh resources for the good will. This gives to religion an
experimental aspect in a twofold sense: Through the
active testing of hypotheses we increase our foresight
and control, and at the same time we learn whether what
is deepest in us can coöperate with the more-than-us that
has us in its power. If it can, then here is the basic fact of
what religion calls fellowship with God.

Is death, then, mere frustration? Is there any better
way to deal with it than resorting to consoling fancies?
Or relapsing into silence, and refusing to think? Could
we perhaps deal with it, to even a slight extent, experimentally? If a fact in universal experience that is so
prominent and troublesome proves to be ethically unmanageable and meaningless, only a much qualified religious realism will be possible. On the other hand, if positive values can be found in death itself and not merely in
compensations for it, and if by foresighted management
we can increase these values; if we can make even a slight
beginning of a life-structure that includes dying within
our ethical purposing, then the basic assumption of reli-

gious realism receives thus much, however little, justification from this specific area of human experience.

That it is possible to find such values, and to make such a beginning, I shall now endeavor to show. A mere beginning only, for no complete solution of the problem is in sight; no unqualified ethical approval of death can be drawn from known facts. No objection is here made to going beyond these facts into constructs of imagination or of speculative thought; they are merely not within the purview of the present discussion. We are to ask, rather, what is observable; how much of it is manageable; what results follow a given policy, and whether there are signs that this or that policy accords with the nature of things —rather, the final question will be, What does the world-order seem like when it is viewed from this corner of our experience with good and evil?

That death often has value as a palliative is widely recognized, though it is mentioned, for the most part, under one's breath. If one's frame is tortured by unrelievable agony; or if one has irretrievably lost one's use of the organs that are essential to self-guided social living; or if the years have imposed such mental decay that one helplessly reverts to childish whims, petulance, and selfishness, all parties concerned, the individual and his fellows alike, have good reason to desire the end. Most of us, probably, have encountered among our own acquaintances instances in which the death of such a victim of life was desired by those who most loved him— desired because they loved him. The question why there should be suffering and decay is not answered, of course, by saying that the snapping of the thread is in these cases a blessing; yet, granted a world in which these misfortunes occur, death really does moderate the evil.

Many persons who see that this is so, however, shrink from acting upon their convictions. They confess that death is here an ethically desirable good, yet they postpone it as long as possible. Here is an individual (a recent instance) who is smitten with an incurable disease the last stage of which is an indefinitely long period of agony. The physician said, "The best that I can do for a life that is brimming with unrelievable torture is to refrain from prolonging it. Society will not yet tolerate an act of positive help." The patient's conscience forbade him to help himself to an overdose of morphine, though he and his friends longed for the end. Here, then, an ancient tradition, sanctified by religion, blocked the way to the ethical action that the situation required. There are signs, fortunately, that the tradition is weakening. In the United States refusal to prolong a life devoid of meaning, and in Great Britain and France positive help in terminating unrelievable suffering have met with a degree of tolerance that is significant. If such misfortunes are to occur, then death is to this extent an asset of which ultimately we shall take possession and control.

Let us consider, next, certain wider values that accrue by reason of the general setting of old age within the biological and the social order. The downward slope of the life-curve after middle age may or may not have a net value for the race; conceivably we may yet handle it so that it will increase the general weal in a manner not otherwise possible. This would make old age desirable, and the terminus of life would be a goal worth the winning. Be this as it may, there are aspects of long life that make the death of the old genuinely desirable to many, and on the whole a genuine asset to society. For instance, advancing years commonly entail loss of productive economic power. Now, the load that this places upon the shoulders of the more vigorous producers is mercifully limited by the invariable death of the aged. To many persons this will sound heartless. The vigorous producers will say that they gladly accept the burden, and moralists will aver that it is good for the character. But age itself should be heard from. Old people who have to be carried by others are thankful that willing hands and hearts are there, but there is deep and unrelieved pathos in the necessity of being carried without being able to do some carrying in return. Were it not for the certainty of approaching death, this pathos would naturally turn into resentment toward life itself. Moreover, at every point the ethics of the relation between old-age weakness and middle-age strength depends upon the positive value of death. The moral value of willingness to labor for the support of nonproducers would be effaced if there were no limitation upon the number of the nonproducers—the number must be small enough to make support possible without exhausting the source of support. On the other hand, from the standpoint of age it must be said that never-ending dependency would be an ethical monstrosity. Hence, the economic relief that accrues from the death of the old carries with it an ethical gain.

The decline of mental plasticity in old age is another pertinent fact, and it has ethical as well as psychological significance. Probably this decline is less a fated infliction of nature than we have supposed, and more a consequence of mental habits formed in youth and confirmed in middle life. Yet considerable shrinkage of interests, and considerable decrease in capacity to enjoy changes and to initiate them appear to be inevitable. A world managed by old men would be sluggish, at least, and it might break up because of inability to handle the spontaneous factors in man and his environment. Elimination of the used-up mental tissue of society is therefore an ethical desideratum. Aggressive minds are thankful, and properly so, when reactionary old men are rendered powerless by being removed from the scene.

Perhaps this also sounds cruel or at least inconsiderate. The old, particularly, may resent it. There is a tradition, dear to them, to the effect that years bring wisdom, that the accumulated values of racial experience are in the custody of age, and that only the steadying hand of those past middle life can protect society from the radicalism of youth. What is the evidence for this theory of the procession of the generations? Apparently it is pure assertion without evidence. Even G. Stanley Hall, who idealizes old age, maintaining that it has a distinctive capacity for perspective, synthesis, far-sightedness, and objective judgment, confesses that, as yet, the old have not risen to this, their proper function.[1] Age is usually contrasted with youth, whereas it should be compared with both youth and middle life. An impartial assessment of the habits of all three will show that youth is far more imitative and conventional, and far less given to radicalism, than old men suppose; that in respect to sensitiveness to differences, and in respect to range of perspective, middle age excels old age; and that the decline in elasticity that comes with advancing years often, if not commonly, has the effect of rashness. What, for example, is more incautious and precipitate than the political commitments that characterize the statecraft of old men?

If any old person, resolving not to think of himself more highly than he ought to think, will calmly survey the disabilities that the years have brought, he will realize that wisdom will not die with him and his cronies, but be saved by his death and theirs. It is simply not true that long experience brings superior insight. What brings insight, whether earlier or later in life, is the use of sound method within a sufficient range of facts. It is simply not true that objectivity, balance, unselfishness, or anything else that is requisite for the moral health of society characterizes the old. Moreover, though social health depends upon the presence of a conservative factor, it depends also upon limitation of this factor. It is death, chiefly, that does limit it. Therefore any realistically minded old person may well rejoice that he can make a final contribution to humanity by, so to say, resigning his office.

He who accustoms himself to such literal and straightforward contemplation of his own departure finds his world, and himself, enlarged and ennobled in the prospect. There is no longer any question of his accepting the dark inevitable, for he moves within a light and toward a light. Nor is his complacency that of the Epicurean who was indifferent to dying because where death is we are not and where we are death is not. No, the wise old

[1] *Senescence*, New York, 1923. Cf. pp. 417-428 with pp. ix and 430-432.

person accepts death because it positively fulfills his own will.

But the Reaper does not always wait for the grain to ripen. Some succumb whom, on ethical grounds, we should most desire to keep alive.

Here the value of a palliative is not discoverable, as it is in the termination of old age. *Prima facie,* the removal of a strong, ethically productive individual entails sheer loss both to himself and to society. How, then, can it be possible to weave such an event into the fabric of purposeful living? How can one who is in his most productive years contemplate the possible nearness of a fatal accident or disease with anything except either moral protest or the dumbness of moral vacuity? How can his friends or society see in his going anything but an ethical vacancy in the power that has us in its grasp? Is not the ethical fabric torn irretrievably?

But perhaps the rent is not so large as we suppose. Our estimates of it are made, as a rule, while the emotions of grief and disappointment still suffuse our judgment. When steady objectivity and a long perspective become possible, how often do we perceive that the lost worker or leader had already accomplished his distinctive task, had made himself dispensable. Further, the loss of a significant man often makes his meaning more clear and convincing than further life could have made it.

Of course, this does not dispel the darkness that surrounds the death of the young, who as yet have only prospects of productivity, nor does it approximate a complete solution for even one part of our main problem. Yet it does greatly reduce the apparent ground for looking upon death as the Great Enemy. Further, it points the way toward an ethical appropriation of the uncertainty of one's own life. For the ethically successful, life is not to be conceived, after the manner of the economic life, in terms of accumulation, but in terms of quality. One good picture is sufficient to proclaim the painter an artist. To give effect to a vital idea; to make what is important seem important; to make goodness attractive; to add a significant item to our knowledge; to help others to be worth while to themselves and to their fellows; to attain to a distinctive personality that gives richness to friendship or love—this is to have arrived. Death does not change the fact that here finality has been achieved.

By the quality of one's living, then, one can actually reduce one's vulnerability to the shafts of the Destroyer. This is not the same as saying that one's influence survives, nor is it the same as accepting, as compensation for the loss of faith in personal immortality, the thin and watery decoction from it called "the immortality of influence." The point is, rather, that the unqualified "No" that is our first and spontaneous greeting to Death at his worst is subject to modification into a qualified "No," the qualification being ethical and susceptible of being incorporated into a plan of life.

Can this qualified "No" develop, by a rational process, into a qualified "Yes"? I have in mind two persons who in their productive years watched the certain approach of dissolution. At first both met the onset of "the inevitable" with shrinking and dismay; but both achieved poise and mastery; they assimilated death instead of being assimilated by it; the final attitude was "Yes," and it was thoughtfully and ethically grounded, being the utterance of neither emotional excitement nor emotional exhaustion. In one of these cases a metaphysical conclusion, won by intellectual wrestling, played a part, but in the other case no formulated support of this kind was in evidence. One noteworthy feature, however, they had in common—active good-will or ethical love was the very atmosphere that both these persons breathed right through the crisis that overwhelmed them. It was love, obviously so, that cast out fear. Moreover, though the thwarting of justifiable ambitions was involved (not merely the vague "will to live"), *the will to love,* which is positive, a "Yes" attitude, gave its specific character to the whole situation.

One of these cases, that of a kindergartner and university teacher of kindergartners, is especially illuminating.

She was suddenly found to be in an advanced stage of a malady that unequivocally promised a period of awful suffering and then death. She was professionally successful and socially adjusted; she loved life; new conditions that permitted the realization of expansive wishes were opening; the shock was devastating. Her friends hastened to her with consolation, but behold! instead of giving, they received. From her they derived strength for their part in the ordeal. The marvel and the mystery of this relation became the topic of their conversation with one another. One of them, upon asking her what was the secret of her reposeful mastery, received this ultra-simple answer: "Oh, I don't see that I've done anything but just face the whole situation." Then she added, musingly, "From childhood I never was able to be religious in the same way as the people about me. I couldn't pray as they did; it seemed unreal. But when I saw one of the tots in my kindergarten take a difficult step toward a fine personality, there, for me, was prayer; and when I saw one of my university students struggle with a point and finally master it, again this was prayer." This was her whole account of her victory, in this life, over death. The glory of having a part in ethical creation was so great that even death could not change its "Yes" into "No." "Love," said an old seer, "never fails."

Here are two items, each of them of first-class significance for our problem, namely, "just facing the whole situation," and the consciousness of being an ethical creator. Each of them deserves a more extended study than the present occasion permits; but even a brief word may indicate the advisability of more experimenting than has yet been done with the life-death antithesis.

Psychiatrists know that mental evasions are the starting point for many of the most serious tangles within the personality. Flinching a disagreeable situation often makes us victims when by facing it we might be masters. Even a dentist's drill hurts less if, by relaxing, one avoids wincing. Moreover, flinching the disagreeable is the starting point for many a misinterpretation of our environment. The common practice of turning our face away from dying instead of toward it results, we may be sure, in a common error with respect to the place of death within the world order. A surmise is allowable (because it is based upon strictly objective grounds) that when we think of death as "the Great Enemy," or as the "*summum malum*" (as one writer calls it), we are in the thralldom of an illusion. Just how great is the illusion, and what the whole truth is, I do not pretend to say; we must find out by experiment. What can now be asserted is that this is a field for experiment; that the religious beliefs that have come down to us are not a proper substitute for the realism of this experimental approach; and that sporadic instances in which the two factors, facing the whole situation, and creative good-will, are present, enhance the significance of personality in the cosmos.

The realistic handling of one's own dying requires to be supplemented, of course, by a realistic treatment of bereavement. That self-pity is a prominent ingredient of grief is well known, though it is not popularly recognized or allowed for. Now, self-pity is self-entanglement. Often it comes little short of self-worship; always it bolsters up self-will; and self-will inherently and in advance negates the organization of oneself into any objective whole, social or other. A bereaved person simply cannot know where nor how much he is hurt, nor what hurts him, nor how his hurt should be handled, until, resisting self-pity, he "just faces the whole situation." This objectivity of mind requires no quenching of affection; rather, it rescues one from the danger of mistaking love of self for love of another. Indeed, objectivity is necessary if affection is to have luminous and unobstructed expression.

To the extent that such open-eyed affection is or contains the creative good-will that we have seen working wonders in those marked for death, it brings to the survivors' attention whatever in the lost one was or is ethically valid. In the contemplation of it sorrow justifies itself, and yet finds consolation and partial healing. The bereaved spirit comes back from wandering in vacancy;

sits down at its own fireside; lives, now, with finalities of a positive sort that have permament meaning and fertility.

When these two attitudes are achieved—unflinching facing of the situation, and release of one's capacity for good-will—then bereavement is no longer a mere "No." It becomes, rather, a heightened consciousness of that to which one can most whole-heartedly say "Yes." Hence, healing begins when we most deeply immerse ourselves in the objective actuality of the situation. Where the universe appears to be least regardful of values, even there an objective mind that maintains ethical interest and poise experiences something other than ethical vacuity; one is not a mere victim of fate. There arises, at least, vaguely and gropingly, gratitude toward the universe for producing beings worthy of profound affection, even though this affection makes us susceptible to profound woe.

We have now sketchily contemplated the conduct of the great not-us at the point where, to ordinary apprehension, it seems to be least regardful of values. We have found that conventional attitudes toward this conduct of the not-us lack certain conditions for the recognition of present values, and for free addition to them through our own conduct. When these conditions are supplied, it begins to appear that death, taken in the most empirical and realistic way, cannot be interpreted as a manifestation of ethical vacuity. It has positive value, and sporadic experiments with it add a mite of evidence to the hypothesis, or the faith, that valuers—persons—occupy a unique place in the stream of events. Change, where it seems most like an absolute, is not quite absolute, for to some slight extent we can use it for our own purposes. To what extent it may be plastic to our purposes; how far dying may yet become ethical coöperation between the universe and ourselves—this we can learn only by further experimentation.

VIII

PLATO AS RELIGIOUS REALIST

By
ROBERT LOWRY CALHOUN
Assistant Professor of Historical Theology
Yale University

PLATO AS RELIGIOUS REALIST

A PHRASE like "religious realism" has, in an obvious sense, both one meaning and many. It is usable in this book, indeed, just because it sets a theme to be played with variations. But a theme, however subtle or intricate, must be definite and the variations relevant, else there is babel, not music. So Plato would have said—did say, concerning both art and nature, again and again, with logical and metaphysical detail. That, in fact, was a major theme of his own: the need to recognize dominant *motifs* through all the flux of actual events—significant patterns or forms by virtue of which the flux is, in its measure, understandable and real; to search out the ways in which the *motifs* are related one to another, and each to its variations; to estimate justly the places of mind and form and brute fact in the whole; and to live by the insights attained in this search, carried on with persistence and with hope.

Both in temper and in doctrine Plato was a religious realist of first-rate importance for modern thought, a thesis which, I presume, needs explaining as well as defending. We shall use the term "realism," then, to indicate on the one hand a general attitude of mind, on the other a philosophical conviction of either of two main sorts. (1) In the more general sense, realism stands for the temper of one who is critical and level-headed, rather than wishful and heedless or visionary in his dealings with life; accustomed to distinguish between fact and fancy, and seeking to be guided, as far as possible, by disciplined inference from fact, though into actual human living, however hard-headed, fancy too must and does enter, avowed or ignored, and a realist worth the name will recognize it and use it deliberately. (2) Philosophic "realism" of a sort first so called in the Middle Ages, opposes "nominalism" on the respective status of particular facts and general forms. "Nominalism" holds that particular things and events perceptible by the senses alone are real, whereas general terms, or universals, are merely convenient names or notions that refer to groups of such particulars. Man is merely a collective name for particular men taken as a group. Contrariwise, "realism" holds that the general or universal term refers not primarily to the particulars as such, but to a form which they genuinely have somehow in common. It may hold that this common form is structurally present in and exemplified by actual particulars (as a theme in its successive developments), though distinguishable from them and independent of them in the sense that other particulars than these might exemplify it equally well, and that no actual group of particulars exemplifies it exhaustively—a version of the theory sometimes called "moderate realism." Or it may hold, on the other hand, that the general or universal terms refer to entities (Man, Equality, Justice) which have transcendent reality, independent of and prior to all particulars whatever—a version often called "extreme realism." (3) Realistic theories of another main type, opposed to "subjectivism" or to "idealism," overlap those just described in various ways; so that a given thinker may be a philosophic realist in both main categories or only in one. As against views which dwell on the self-sufficiency of mind, realism of this third sort affirms an obdurate environment by which mind is in some degree conditioned or negated. It may be content simply to emphasize the presence, over against a given mind, of stubborn facts, whose ultimate nature is left unspecified—a view opposed to "subjectivism" but not necessarily excluding "pampsychism," "personalism," and other versions of idealistic (spiritualistic) theory. Or it may affirm that, confronting, encroaching upon, or completely excluding what is commonly meant by mind and mental life, there is specifically nonmental stuff of some sort: physical or quasi-physical matter, as in "naturalism" and various dualisms, or else neutral entities, neither physical nor mental, as in "neorealism" and kindred views—by all of which metaphysical idealism as such is denied.

So much for the general term. For the special term "religious realism," it is enough at the moment to note three senses which correspond to the chief meanings of realism just distinguished. (a) In a general sense, religious realism may stand for the temper of one who subjects religious beliefs, hopes, and experiences to critical scrutiny, searching and persistent; and who seeks to be guided in his own dealings with religion by disciplined inference from facts of all relevant sorts, rather than by undisciplined wishes and fancies. One who maintains this attitude toward religion may, of course, or may not be himself a religious person. (b) There is, secondly, a sort of religious antinominalism which, whatever it may say about God, has much to say about the objectivity of values or of Value. It treats beauty, justice, truth, and the like, as established in the permanent order of things and worthy of unconditional devotion; either because the world is conceived as functioning persistently in ways which these terms suggest, or because Beauty and Truth and the like are, as such, independently and supernally real. (c) Finally, religious realism may denote the conviction that over against the minds of all men is an other, one or many, of such nature that it may suitably be called the divine, or God. The nature of this Other, and its relations to man, may be specified vaguely or with much effort at precision. In any event, for religious realism it is no human construct, but an obdurate environmental factor having ways of its own that condition, sustain, and, in part, set at naught the wishes and ways of men. The phrase may, of course, be used in other senses also, but these are enough for our purpose.

It is evident that one may be a realist, religious or otherwise, in one of these main senses and not in another; less evident that one view may combine them all, speculative realism and critical common sense alike. But this last is what original Platonism does. Hence its special claim to careful reëxamination by the tougher minds of our time, to whom just now it is most likely to be anathema.

To many this must seem a silly paradox. We have been taught all too well to think of Plato as dreamer, poet, mystic, preoccupied with stiff logical and moral absolutes, or with myths and vague, splendid visionings, about equally remote from the homely realm of fact. Not only orthodox medievals, but also many modern interpreters —philosophers, historians, men of letters, and writers, readers, and users of text-books—have concurred in ascribing to him as a chief doctrine that "extreme realism" which it is hard for most moderns not to brand forthwith as extreme unrealism. But I venture to think it has been made evident, by the ablest recent Platonic studies,[1] that this view needs drastic revision. The sentimentalized "son of Apollo" is fast being eclipsed by a far more significant Plato, founder and head of a long-lived

[1] I can make no pretension to more than a beginner's acquaintance with the field, and little of what follows is new, as any one familiar with the matter will see at once. One can find most of it said or suggested in books well known among students of Plato, though naturally I have formed my own judgments as well as I could. The works to which I am conscious of especial indebtedness include C. Ritter: *Platon* (vol. I, 1910; II, 1922), A. E. Taylor: *Plato, the Man and His Work* (1927), U. von Wilamowitz-Moellendorff: *Platon* (2 vols., 1920), J. Burnet: *Greek Philosophy, Part I: Thales to Plato* (1914), Paul Shorey: *The Unity of Plato's Thought* (1903), and Hans Raeder: *Platons philosophische Entwicklung* (1905); together with Lewis Campbell's editions of the *Theaetetus* (2d ed., 1883) and the *Sophist* and *Politicus* (1867), Jowett and Campbell's ed. of the *Republic* (3 vols., 1894), R. G. Bury's ed. of the *Philebus* (1897), and A. E. Taylor's commentary on the *Timaeus* (1927). G. C. Field's judicious essay, *Plato and his Contemporaries* (1930), came into my hands after this paper was begun, and clarified, corrected, and reinforced my own notions at various points.

With the foregoing works may be compared, for widely divergent points of view, G. Grote: *Plato and the Other Companions of Socrates* (4 vols., 1885); H. Jackson, "Plato's Later Theory of Ideas," in *Jour. of Philology*, X-XV (1882-6); E. Zeller: *Philosophie der Griechen*, Bd. II, Teil 1 (4th ed., 1889); W. Lutoslawski: *The Origin and Growth of Plato's Logic* (1897); and Paul Natorp: *Platos Ideenlehre* (1921).

I have used Burnet's text of the dialogues and letters of Plato (Oxford, 1899-1906 and later), along with Jowett's version; and W. D. Ross's ed. of the *Metaphysics* of Aristotle (2 vols., 1924), for Aristotle's comments on Platonism. The bits of home-made translation scattered through the paper, to help make plainer what I have understood Plato to say, may well need correcting.

scientific school, logician and mathematical philosopher, penetrating critic of contemporary affairs, and champion of a "high religion" against a variety of shams. This Plato is no less crucial for the growth of Western religious thought than the more familiar visionary idealist so long fought over by assailants and defenders of embattled orthodoxy. But he has something very different to say to the modern mind. He is a "religious realist" in a complex but a definite sense: hard-headed, sharp-tongued, critical, concerned both with stubborn facts and with equally unevadable minds and forms; tentative and exploratory, albeit an enthusiast with persistent convictions and a sense of direction; a seeker after good, conceived as somehow both real and ideal, here and yonder, under the sovereignty of a living God.'

I. As Devotee and Critic of Religion

In judging current religious life and in the shaping of his own, Plato as a true successor of Socrates shared both his teacher's capacity for intense devotion and his robust critical habit. In both men these were correlates of a deep distaste for self-satisfied ignorance, mental and moral laziness, superficiality and sham.

Plato presents to us a Socrates, now familiar to everybody, whose critical habit almost inevitably appears in the forefront of any discussion of his thought. Such unreflective skill as competent empirics—artisans, pilots, poets, statesmen—may have in their own fields he had been ready to praise, though as a guide to living it is always inferior to knowledge.' But pretentious ignorance he had pilloried without mercy. Among the more flagrant offenders, it would seem, were some of the new success-teachers (rhetors and sophists) of the smaller sorts, who are said to have accepted praise and pay for showy rubbish. Mountebank logic-choppers and word-splitters like

---

² See Appended Note, below, pp. 248-251.
³ *Gorg.* 511c-512d, *Meno* 97c-99d, Cf. *Apol.* 22, *Protag.* 319a-320b, *Gorg.* 455b sqq. I shall not raise here the vexed question whether and how far the Socrates of these and other dialogues correctly represents the real Socrates, for I am nowhere near a view that seems to me satisfactory.

Euthydemus and Dionysodorus, with their claque; brash young professors of "diplasiology and gnomology and eikonology" like Polus; noisy, innocuous devil's advocates like Thrasymachus—shallow intellectuals all:[4] these are, as Plato portrays them, among the most ludicrous and least estimable of the master inquisitor's opponents. Even the really able men, like Gorgias and Protagoras, are much too sure of themselves, and Socrates, though treating them with respect, is unable to endorse claims for them as teachers of the good life. But none of these, be it noted, are disapproved because they propose what is new—Socrates himself is a disturbing innovator; nor because they are too critical—Socrates, not they, is the "gadfly" who at length provokes the authorities past endurance. They are disapproved, one and all, because they are not critical enough:[5] they are content to rest in a half-thought-out skepticism, relativism, or opportunist conformity, and to exploit the admiration of folk who are merely less informed than they. And these uncritical admirers—or equally uncritical despisers —of the new teachers are guilty of the same fault. If unintelligence is most unbecoming in those who profess to teach, it is only less so in those who profess to practice; and soldiers, poets, statesmen, and plain folk[6] come in for their share of the gadfly's stinging until they put him

---

[4] *Euthyd., passim; Gorg.* 461b-481b (cf. *Phaedr.* 267c); *Repub.* 336a-354c. It seems to me an unanswerable question how far Plato's accounts here are trustworthy in detail. The basic facts, however, *viz.* Socrates' ironical attitude toward the new teachers and the dislike which some of them had toward him, seem sufficiently attested by *Apol.* 19d-20c, and 23e. It is significant also that a generation later, even Isocrates is scornful of the itinerant members of his own profession; see *Orat.* xiii ("Against the Sophists"), and the vitriolic defense thereof in the *Antidosis, e.g.* 197, 215, 221-2, etc. Grote and Gomperz seem to me both to have taken too little account of the distinctions between sophists of different grades which Plato himself draws; and to have built up a wholesale defense on too slender grounds. Cf. Eduard Meyer: *Gesch. d. Altertums* (2te Aufl., 1912) IV. 253-272.

[5] See, *e.g.,* the convenient summary in *Phaedr.* 266b-279b, which although in a comparatively late dialogue, well beyond the "Socratic" group, reflects with essential accuracy the basic attitude of Socrates in the earlier discussions, though it goes further in formulating it.

[6] *Apol.* 21b-22c; cf. 23e. Also *Laches; Ion; Gorg.* 481b-527e; *Meno* 89e-94e; etc.

to death as a doer of evil, a corrupter of the young, and an impious man.

But the very vigor and persistence of this Socratic criticism arises in part from intense moral and religious conviction, rooted deeply in the life and tradition of his own people. The sophists are clever cosmopolites, men of the world, emancipated from old rootings and old loyalties. Socrates has lived all his life in Athens, and like one of the greater Hebrew prophets—like Jeremiah, for instance, or like Jesus—he speaks as one who is striving to speak at once for the best in a tradition that is old and for a new that is yet to be.[7] It is notable, in view of his formal conviction for impiety, that he is nowhere represented as satirizing the recognized religion of Athens, nor, except in the *Republic,* as criticizing it adversely.[8] On the contrary, besides his special loyalties to "the Delphian god" and the "divine something" (θειόν τι καὶ δαιμόνιον) that is his inner monitor,[9] he believes generally in the gods of his city, cherishes its laws, and shares in its pious customs. And if he goes far beyond his fellows in persistent, uncompromising inquiry concerning all that he and they hold valuable, even this manifests, in a way, a familiar and genuine Attic strain, the characteristic striving for clarity that marks the best work of the Periclean artists;[10] and this very attack on obscurancy is maintained by Socrates as a mission from the universally recognized god of Delphi. His ruthless dialectic is itself an expression of his piety.

There is, indeed, one sort of religiousness which he

[7] Cf. Ritter: *Platon* I. 69, and the emphatic judgment of E. Meyer: *Gesch. d. Altertums* IV. 451-2, 461-2.

[8] See below, p. 219, n. 65. Evidence for Socrates' place "within the pale of Athenian orthodoxy" (Grote, I. 413) comes chiefly from the *Apology* of Plato, almost certainly the nearest to Socrates of all the Platonic writings, and from the *Memorabilia* of Xenophon, who, as is well known, represents him as a devout conformist (*Mem.* I. i. 2-20; iii. 1-4; iv. 16; etc.); but also from such passages as *Phaedo* 60c-61b, 118a, and the fervent expression of lifelong patriotism in *Crito* 52a-53a. *Gorg.* 523a-527a, with its reiterated affirmation of belief (523a, 524a, esp. 526d), is apparently a (presumably Orphic) venture beyond popular theology, quite possibly shared by Socrates.

[9] *Apol.* 28e-30a, etc.; 31c-d, 40a-c; cf. *Euthyph.* 3b; *Repub.* 496c.

[10] E. Meyer: *op. cit.* IV. 453-457.

riddles with ironic questions: that of the bigoted soothsayer and catharist Euthyphro, whose scriptures are the
old bloody and mysterious tales in Hesiod's *Theogony,*
"and others still more wonderful, not generally known";
who takes the notion of tabu so gravely that, in order to
free his house from "defilement" and the peril of ghostly
visitation, he has come in to the city to prosecute his own
father for murder, because through negligence he has
occasioned a man's death.[11] This archaic, self-righteous,
passionately earnest piety had won for Euthyphro more
than once the ridicule of city-bred Athenians who followed
more urbane cults. Being, therefore, himself a religious
outcaste, he sympathizes at once on hearing of the indictment of Socrates, whom he supposes—because of the
well-known dæmonic prompter—to be an exponent of
some such pious irrationalism as his own. He is soon
undeceived; for the terrible innocent, as always in need
of enlightenment, quickly has him circling helplessly
among old phrases and new ideas, unable not only to tell
what "piety" is, but even rightly to understand the question. His religion was one in which reflective, critical
thinking had never figured, whereas for Socrates, critical
thought is of the essence of religion, and irrationalism
akin to impiety.

It is clear, in short, that the grievance of Athenians
against Socrates was not that, like Euthyphro, he followed strange gods and mysteries, old or new: far better
if it had been that, for then they might have laughed at
him also as a harmless fanatic.[12] What he had done was
much worse. He had shared their own beliefs in the
accepted virtues and in the reality of recognized gods and
their concern for human conduct, and had proceeded
critically to explore and to act on these beliefs with a
single-mindedness and daring that was intolerable. "Men

---

[11] For a brief account of the *"mantische und kathartische Bewegung"*
to which Euthyphro plainly belonged, see E. Rohde: *Psyche* (7te und 8te
Aufl., 1921), II. 89-90, and the detailed material cited in the same, 62-89
and 90-99. Here the special sort of problem with which Eu. was trying
to cope is discussed on pages 72-78.

[12] *Euthyph.* 3c-e; cf. Xenophon: *Mem.* I. i. 1.

of Athens, I hail you as friends, and I love you; but I shall obey the god rather than you, and as long as I live and am able, I shall never stop seeking wisdom, and exhorting you and besieging, after my fashion, any of you I may meet. For I am a believer, men of Athens, beyond any among my accusers."[13] There was the trouble: not theological vagary, a recourse of inferior minds, but that which was much more difficult and disturbing—an intrepid orthodoxy which persisted in dragging to light and exploring without mercy its own basic principles and their consequences for conduct, and forcing these on the attention of others who professed also to hold them, on whose lips justice, temperance, courage, wisdom, and piety were familiar words, but who had not seriously inquired what these words meant and what they demanded of those who professed to live by them. His crime, in short, was being at once too devoted and too intelligent. Jeremiah and Jesus also, one recalls, were condemned as heretics.

Plato's religious outlook, if I understand it rightly, was in essential accord with that of Socrates, but went a good way beyond it in both speculative theory and explicit censure of common beliefs and practices. We shall examine here Plato's own practical religious attitude: the convictions that moved and guided him, and his reaction to positions which seemed to him unsatisfactory. Some details of his speculative theory will appear in later sections.

First, then, as to his own basic religious experience, which involved devotion both to Socrates and to Athens, devotion to "the good," and confidence in the goodness and the sovereignty of a living God: this complex whole subjected till near the end of his long life to the restless fire of a trenchant intelligence, and marked to the very end by severe intellectual effort. The same loyalty to

[13] *Apol.* 29d, 35d. 6-7. See also *Apol.* 26b-e, 28a-30c, 33b-c; *Gorg.* 526d-527a (cf. below, p. 241, n. 128); and cf. the significant exchange in *Euthyph.* 3c. 7-d. 4.

"the city, which is to say her laws," combined with the same urgency of criticism, that we found in Socrates characterizes also the more cosmopolitan Plato. No other document gives it so emphatic expression as his seventh letter, written near the end of his life to throw light upon his relationships with Dion and Dionysius II. of Syracuse. In it he tells of his own early hopes and political enthusiasms, his bitter disillusionment over the treatment of Socrates by oligarchs and democrats alike, and his abandonment, after the death of Socrates, of the ambitions which thitherto had guided his career.[14] Devotion to his friend and teacher and devotion to his fatherland had pulled sharply asunder. His dissatisfaction, however, as he sees it in long perspective, was with conditions existing not only in Athens—then sick on the fruits of frustrated imperialism and factional rivalries—but in "all the cities of the time." Conditions abroad, indeed, as he discovered later on visiting Greek cities of Italy and Sicily, seemed to be much worse than at home. Ready as he was and unsparing, then, in his own strictures upon Athenian affairs, let a foreigner speak slurringly of Athens (as many did when Dion was murdered by an Athenian) and he was quick and vigorous in her defense. For always discernible in and through the shifting details of the current situation, in his view, were distinctive social patterns and tendencies that defined Athens as she uniquely was in essence, perhaps had been in actuality in the distant past, and might come actually to be again. It was loyalty to these, along with his loyalty to Socrates, that helped to condition his religious attitude.

In the same period from which this letter comes, that is in the closing years of his life, he was working on the

---

[14] *Ep.* vii. 324c-326b. This is a long open letter written after the death of Dion in 353 B.C., when Plato was well past seventy. It is one of two such letters (vii and viii) "which seem to be accepted as genuine by every one now" (Burnet: *Platonism* 80. For discussion of the point, which has been in hot dispute, see R. G. Hackforth: *The Authorship of the Platonic Epistles;* U. von Wilamowitz-Moellendorff: *Platon* II. 278-305; C. Ritter: *Neue Untersuchungen über Platon* 404-415; or, for a brief statement, G. C. Field: *op. cit.* Appendix I). The remaining material in *Ep.* vii alluded to in the text includes 326b-e and 332b-336d.

Laws, concerned with this very matter of the basic constitution of a state, his longest work and perhaps the one
most directly practical in intent. Here his loyalty to
Athens and Athenian institutions, and in particular his
concurrence in recognized religious customs, appears
again and again, side by side nevertheless with biting
criticisms of things as at present they are. The unique
distinction of Athens, he makes a Spartan neighbor say,
is that proverbially her good men are good not merely
under compulsion, but genuinely and by nature (αὐτο-
φυῶς)—or by the grace of God (θείᾳ μοιρᾳ).¹⁵ And in the
ordering of life in the new Cretan colony (transparent
disguise for a new Athens) for which the aged Athenian
Stranger is suggesting a constitution, both the familiar
laws and the familiar temples and gods and ceremonies
of old Athens are everywhere.¹⁶ Yet the proposed constitution really is meant to be new, aiming at the development of the good life as a whole, not merely at some part
of it; reserving political authority for those alone who
are "wise," in the Socratic sense; and freely censuring
familiar aspects of contemporary life, both political and
religious.¹⁷

Nor is this effort to blend old and new, devotion and
criticism, merely an old man's weakness. Thirty years
earlier, when Plato in his prime had founded the Academy
as the first endowed school of advanced scientific and
philosophical research in Hellas, to become a home of
radical inquiry in ethics, politics and religion, he seems
to have founded it also as a religious association (θίασος)
for the worship of the Muses, and presumably of Apollo
their leader, the Delphian god in whose service Socrates
had lived and died. To them a shrine was erected in its

¹⁵ *Laws* 642c-d—though even this, to be sure, is a second best; cf.
Meno 99e-100b.
¹⁶ The general principle that a sensible legislator will give due regard
to antiquity in these matters is stated in *Laws* 738b-d, and a psychological
basis for it suggested in 797d-798d. As instances of its observance may be
noted 717a-b, 745b, 759c-d, 766a-b, 828a-e, 848c-d, 914a, 936e, 950e, etc.
¹⁷ "Much of what we have been saying is contrary to the custom of
states"—805b; and cf. 637d-638c; 630d-632d, 688a-d, 705d-706a; 689a-e;
714a, 715a-d, 805a, 800c-e, etc.

grounds, common meals were celebrated, and under their tutelage its life was to go forward during the nine hundred and odd years until Justinian closed the school and confiscated its property as dedicated to a proscribed worship.[18] From one point of view such dedication was a legal formality, bringing the school as a new organization into a recognized category—a measure in which other schools, including the "godless" Epicureans, concurred.[19] But the establishment of the Academy as a θίασος Μουσῶν almost certainly was more than a formal device; for in the sustained spiritual elevation and eloquence of the *Symposium, Phaedo, Republic,* and *Phaedrus,* rising at times to religious enthusiasm, we have in all likelihood a vivid reflection of Plato's mind during the very years in which the Academy was being conceived and brought into being.[20] The religious conviction which in the *Laws* has settled to a steady and graying glow, burns here at something like white heat. It seems, indeed, as though here, midway in Plato's life, after the sharp check to his youthful hopes, his loyalty to Athens and her venerable *mores* is genuinely fused with his competing loyalty to the proscribed, questing genius of Socrates, and transfigured in a consuming devotion to "the good." In no other way than this, as it seems to me, could his earlier loyalties have been reconciled, and his own life unified.

[18] Wilamowitz-Moellendorff: *Antigonos von Karystos* (in *Philolog. Untersuchungen,* IV), 46, 65, and Excurs 2, 279-283. Similar information about the Peripatetic organization is much more detailed, thanks to the extant wills of Aristotle's successors, Theophrastus, Strato, and Lycon (*ibid.* 264-272), but Wilamowitz believes the facts about the Academy sufficiently well established; cf. the same author's *Platon* I. 271-272. For a general description of θίασοι and their legal status, see P. Foucart: *Des associations réligieuses chez les Grecs* (1873), 1-53. By no means all of them were edificatory (*ibid.* 153 sqq.).

[19] Wilamowitz-Moellendorff: *Antigonos* 288 sqq. H. Diels would trace this sort of organization back to the very beginnings of Greek philosophy, bringing in the Ionians also ("Ueber die ältesten Philosophenschulen der Griechen," 243, in *Philosoph. Aufsätze,* 1887, dedicated to E. Zeller).

[20] Of the dates at which the Platonic dialogues were composed, not one is certainly known. Ritter's view as to the four named (see *Platon* I. 106 and notes), with which Peipers, Wilamowitz, Lutoslawski, Raeder, and, with unessential differences, Taylor and Gomperz agree, puts these four together as successive compositions of the period between 388, when Plato returned to Athens from his first visit to Syracuse, and 367 or thereabouts, when he left Athens for Syracuse on his second visit. It was in this same period, almost certainly, though no one knows just when, that the Academy was founded.

The concept of the good [21] as a lodestar and unifier of human thought and action was itself a heritage from Socrates, which Plato now develops [22] in a theory that seeks to embrace not personal conduct merely, but the commonwealth (πολιτεία) and the whole world as well. Our concern at the moment is not primarily with the nature of the good and its place in the world: these will be considered later. [23] Our present concern is with Plato's attitude thereto, as a second constituent factor in his religious attitude as a whole. In describing his relation to Athens, we have used the words devotion and criticism. The same terms are in place here. Plato's own words are love and logic (ἔρως, τὸ διαλέγεσθαι): love rising to the pitch of madness, logic like a skilled dissector's blade! [24] Moreover, these two are not antithetic but correlative, in the philosopher's life. He is properly to be called a lover, not in spite of but just because of his eager and ruthless search after knowledge, that may begin with delight in this or that thing of beauty, but must go on through recognition of the ways in which beautiful things are related, and through study not only of bodies but of minds and of social institutions, through a crescendo of "the sciences" culminating in the one universal science (to wit, logic) through which the vision of "beauty everywhere"—the absolute beauty of intelligible order, which is the ground of absolute truth also—is at length revealed. [25] "The beautiful" of the lover; "the true" of the scientist; "the good" of artist, moralist, mystic, and all plain men—these, declares Plato, are terms that have

---

[21] *Apol.* 21d. 4, and the "Socratic" dialogues generally.

[22] Very likely under the stimulus of contact with Archytas and the other Pythagoreans in Tarentum, which he had visited before arriving in Syracuse when he was "about forty" (*Ep.* vii. 324a. 5-6); cf. Wilamowitz-Moellendorff: *Platon* I. 246-252.

[23] Below, pp. 232 sqq.

[24] *Phaedr.* 244a sqq., 265a-b: "There are two forms of madness, the one occasioned by human infirmities, the other by divine alteration of commonplace routines," etc., with which cf. *Repub.* 518a-b, and *Theaet.* 174a sqq.; for the other side, *Phaedr.* 265e sqq.

[25] *Sympos.* 210a-212a, with which must be correlated the fuller statement in *Repub.* 517a-534e (note esp. 533a-e); and cf. *Phaedr.* 247a-257b, and the whole discourse of Diotima, *Sympos.* 202d-212a. These passages are all, esp. those of *Sympos.* and *Phaedr.*, pitched in keys of exaltation, and must be read with that fact clearly in view, and with due attention to the more sober dialectical passages in the same and in later dialogues.

relevance ultimately to one and the same reality,[26] cosmic order, discoverable if at all only by precise and comprehensive inquiry. "I cannot indeed be confident that this is the exact truth," Socrates is made to say, "but that something like this is the truth I am confident."[27]

Little further need be said, I think, concerning the intense desire (ἔρως, μανία) with which the lover of wisdom must seek this clear, illuminating vision. Without such single-minded devotion, indeed, he will hardly struggle through the laborious studies that lead up, stage after stage, toward that comprehension, which is on no account to be had, like a poet's rapture, by some casual breath of inspiration. The μανία of the lover, unlike that of the soothsayer, bacchant, or poet,[28] is not itself productive, so to say, of its own appropriate, satisfying end. The "madness" of these others is like a flood that pours in upon them, making them prophesy, exult, or sing out of the fullness of the inspiration itself;[29] it brings its own fulfillment. But the madness of the lover—and the philosopher, the truth-lover, is such a one—is a drought, an intense desire for something which is not fully given in the experience itself.[30] "Every one who desires, desires that which is not already his, and which is not present, and which he has not, and is not, and of which he is in want." A true lover (not a narcissist) is perforce a realist. The desired object is beyond him, and its attainment calls for further effort,[31] no matter how intense and

---

[26] Cf. *Phileb.* 65a.

[27] *Repub.* 533a. 5-6 (Jowett's tr.); cf. the whole passage, 532a-533e, and the half-serious, half-humorous portrait of the philosopher in *Theaet.* 173c-176a, absorbedly laying his measuring stick on the invisibles of the heavens and the earth and the waters under the earth.

[28] *Phaedr.* 265b.

[29] *Ion* 533c-534e.

[30] *Sympos.* 203b-204c, 205d, esp. the brief dialectical passage, 199c-201c.

[31] *Sympos.* 200e. 2-4. It is worth pointing out that these passages are understandable only as presupposing a mature and normal "sense of reality." They simply cannot be interpreted successfully in terms of the "egocentric" and capricious subjectivism that characterizes immature or impaired mental activity. For comparison with *Phaedr.* 265d-266b, a theme to which Plato returns again and again (*e.g. Polit.* 262a-263a, 284e. 11-285b. 8, 286d. 8-9, *Phileb.* 16c. 5-17a. 5), one may notice what Pierre Janet regards as the criterion *par excellence* of mental activity at its best: "In a word, it seems to me that two essential factors characterize the

how worthy the desire. And the effort required of the seeker after truth (or beauty, or the good—they go ultimately together) includes laborious, critical study, severe and untiring.

This is the side of Plato's thought that I desire, for the moment, to stress most strongly. So much kid-glove æstheticism has been extolled, and so many patrician finalities announced in his name that it seems right to insist with all vigor upon his own account of the way toward the discovery of the good. Putting aside indications in earlier dialogues, the first detailed statement is the proposed curriculum for the "guardians" in the *Republic,* picked men and women on whom the maintenance of the commonwealth mainly rests, from among whom "rulers" are chosen on the basis of proved fitness to rule. These clearly must have their eyes turned toward the good if they are to lead others toward it. How are they to be trained?

Not as at present, says Socrates. The usual way in which men of affairs are trained now is to cram in, it may be, a little hard thinking in early youth, if at all; speedily to submerge it in practical affairs with which philosophy is thought to have nothing to do; and later to return to it only as a polite pastime, out of all relation to everyday life. But men really fit to rule can be developed only by a continuous, all-round physical and mental education of steadily increasing difficulty, in which theory and practice, the study of the sciences and the performance of civil and military duties, proceed together.[32] Only those who sustain with honor this discipline of both mind and body, in practical achievement and in theoretical inquiry, may aspire to be rulers.[33] "Philosopher kings" in any gen-

---

highest levels (*les premiers degrés*) of this hierarchy: (1) unification, concentration, especially important when it is *new* and amounts to mental synthesis; (2) the number or mass of psychological phenomena that enter into this synthesis. The conjunction of these two factors, a new synthesis or strong concentration, and very numerous facts of consciousness, constitutes a character indispensable in psychology, which one may agree to call *psychological tension.*" (Janet: *Les obsessions et la psychasthénie,* I. 495).

[32] *Repub.* 497e-498c.   [33] 503a, e.

uine Platonic sense are neither benignant demigods nor armchair Utopians: they are vigorous, intelligent men and women, trained to think straight and to act with judgment, fit in body and mind to be leaders in the difficult business of living.[34] How then are these to be educated to find their own way and guide others toward the good?

The answer in a word is: by the hardest sort of scientific study, along with increasingly responsible participation in the actual conduct of civic life. Theirs is a "longer and more circuitous road" than that of civilians, not excepting skilled artists and professional men, because theirs is the most complex and difficult art of all. Even in childhood and youth, besides the traditional course of gymnastic and music (including literature), they will be introduced to the several branches of the more exact sciences—arithmetic, plane and solid geometry, astronomy, and harmonics (the one part of physics then being studied with any systematic effort at quantitative precision)—at first "in the guise of play."[35] The years from seventeen or eighteen to twenty are spent, as usual in Athens, in active military and athletic training, with theoretical work laid aside, for "sleep and strenuous exercise are unfavorable to study." At twenty the best of both sexes are selected for more advanced work.

From twenty to thirty this selected group, besides engaging in the civil and military duties that pertain to citizenship, resume their theoretical studies, which include now a more systematic presentation of the sciences, so that *the correlation* of these "with one another and with reality" can be made out. Discovery of this correlation by the student leads him directly to the threshold of philosophy, and is, moreover, the best criterion of his fitness therefor, since only one capable of this sort of synthesis is capable of the rigorous analysis and syn-

[34] Plato expressly disavows any intentional mystery-mongering here. He professes, at least, to be talking sober sense (499b-c).

[35] *Repub.* 504a-541b contains all the data for this account of the education of the guardians. The passage is too well known to require citation point by point, the sections most pertinent in detail being 536d-541b, and 521c-534e.

thesis of dialectic.[36] At the end of these ten years of practical and theoretical maturing, under patient surveillance, those young people who have shown themselves in all respects best qualified for training as "rulers" are segregated as a still more select group, for trial in places of authority. For five years they work intensively at philosophy proper—a postgraduate course, suitable only for students of relative maturity—and then at thirty-five they go back for another fifteen-year probation in practical affairs; only that now, instead of being enlisted men and simple citizens, as they had been from twenty to thirty, they are placed in responsible military and civil offices, both to gain executive experience and to prove still further their fitness or lack of it, under the stress of actual responsibility. Finally, at fifty, the few of outstanding theoretic and practical attainments are chosen as rulers—proved experts in living. Their concern thenceforth is to order "both city and citizens and themselves" with a view to achieving the greatest possible good. Much of their time will be spent in research and theoretic inquiry, but they take their turns also in administrative work, "toiling at politics," governing the city, and guiding the education of their successors. It is thus, says Plato, by this "longer and more roundabout road" through practical experience and theoretical research, that one may come to apprehend "the good" as universal goal.[37]

If there were need, it would be easy to show in detail how basic to Plato's whole outlook is this emphasis of laborious research. That the program of exact scientific and dialectical education is no transient enthusiasm is shown beyond cavil by its reappearance in abridged but essentially similar form in the *Laws*,[38] where once more it is associated with the need for guardians and rulers

[36] 537c: ὁ μὲν γὰρ συνοπτικὸς διαλεκτικός, ὁ δὲ μὴ οὔ; cf. above p. 208, n. 31. The point is worth stressing that philosophy is not concerned with some remote, esoteric realm, but with the correlation and criticism of the most exact knowledge attainable, for the sake of the most farsighted possible direction of life, in the world in which men actually live.

[37] 504b. 2, c. 9-d. 3, 532a. 1-b. 2; cf. *Sympos.* 210a-212a; etc.

[38] 817e-822d, 961a-968a; cf. 687e-688d, etc., and *Epinomis,* if it be regarded as genuine, adds emphatic reinforcement to these passages.

able to see the good as many-in-one,[39] and, more explicitly
than in the *Republic,* with the need for right knowledge
and worship of the gods. That Plato, moreover, put these
principles into practice is guaranteed both by the character of his own work during the intervening years,[40] and
by the work of his associates, done partly under his express direction.[41] But his zeal for mathematics and logic
is, after all, too generally recognized now to need further
proof. What is more commonly doubted is his right to be
regarded as a really critical thinker, "realistic" in the
most ordinary sense, and not as an oracular dogmatist.
This must be considered briefly.

Grote's judgment that "the relation which Plato bears
to philosophy is more that of a searcher, tester, and
impugner, than that of an expositor and dogmatist—
though he undertakes both the two functions"[42] will, I

[39] 966a. 5, 965b. 7-10, and the whole passage 963a-968a; cf. *Epin.* 991b-
992e, *et passim.* On the authenticity of the latter, see H. Raeder: *Platons
philos. Entwicklung* 413 sq.; A. E. Taylor: *Plato* 497 sq.

[40] As shown in such dialogues as *Parm., Theaet., Soph., Polit., Phileb.,
Tim., (Epin.)*; in the testimony of Aristotle concerning his oral teaching
in the Academy (see below, 250-251); and in Plato's own account of his
disappointing experience with Dionysius II., *Ep.* vii. 340b-344d, in which
recurs the familiar picture of the long, hard mental labor that alone can
issue in sudden insight, when "the mind, straining to the limit of human
capacity, catches fire" (344b. 7-c. 1; cf. 341c. 5-d. 2).

[41] These included, as is well known, Theaetetus and Eudoxus, the most
eminent mathematicians of their day, besides Speusippus, Xenocrates,
Heraclides, and numerous lesser men; while the older Pythagorean master
Archytas, mentioned often in *Ep.* vii, was long one of Plato's cherished
friends (see above, p. 207, n. 22). That Plato was accustomed to set a
difficult astronomical problem for research in the Academy is expressly
affirmed by Simplicius, in his often-quoted comment on Aristotle: *De
caelo* (Simpl.: *In Lib. de Caelo Comm.* 219a. 37-44; 221a. 20-34); and Aristotle's own anti-mathematical polemics (*Metaph.* A, M and N) are good
evidence of the preponderant interest in these matters among many members of the Academy. On the significance of these various names, see the
entries in G. Sarton: *An Introd. to the History of Science,* vol. I.

[42] *Plato* I. 366. Further, on the "Dialogues of Search": "Philosophy
is conceived as the search for truth still unknown; not as an explanation
of truth by one who knows it, to others who do not know it." "The sentiment of authority, instead of being invoked and worked up, as is generally done in philosophy, is formally disavowed and practically set aside."
As a modern parallel: "There are cases in which two chemists have carried
on joint researches, under many failures and disappointments, perhaps
at last without success. If a record were preserved of their parley during
the investigation, the grounds for testing and rejecting one conjecture,
and for selecting what should be tried after it—this would be in many
points a parallel to the Platonic process." The entire passage, 366-406, is
valuable, though parts of it seem to me greatly overstated.

think, seem fair, to any one who goes attentively through the dialogues, rather than simply through selected passages or a secondary account, however excellent. He will find in them a mind fundamentally serious, beyond doubt, but moving with irony and humor—if also on occasion with vehemence and bitterness—among problems both practical and theoretical.[43] He will find a fully conscious, technical use of hypothesis, and clear though partial expositions of its varying significance in the sciences and in philosophy.[44] He will find everywhere persistent effort to test various hypotheses, including the "theory of Ideas" itself, by destructive dialectical analysis;[45] balanced and supplemented by a "keen sense of reality" which very diverse critics have noticed.[46] And not least important, he will find careful and customary distinction among various grades of cognition, among which purely logical apprehension of terms and relations is ranked first in respect of clarity, precision, and certitude, though not necessarily in practical importance;[47] whereas both

[43] The irony and humor of Socrates are, of course, shared by Plato, else they would have faded out of the Platonic, as they so largely have out of the Xenophontic Socrates. But beyond that, the verve and finesse of Plato himself appear in an artistry that ranges all the way from broad farce in *Euthyd.*, half-mad, half-profound extravaganza in *Crat.*, and elaborate jokes like the midwife joke in *Theaet.* or the angler joke in *Soph.*, to the subtle character drawing of *Protag., Gorg., Sympos.*, and *Repub.*, and the intricate logical virtuosity of *Parm.* 137-166, or of *Soph.* 250a-260e.

[44] *Parm.* 135e sqq.; *Meno* 86d sqq.; *Phaedo* 100a-102a; *Repub.* 510c-511d, 533b-e. This usage has both likenesses to and differences from the familiar usage of to-day; cf. Burnet: *Greek Phil., Pt. I*, 162-4, 228-230.

[45] *Parm., Theaet., Soph., Phileb.*, etc.; and cf. n. 42 above.

[46] "Platons scharfer Wirklichkeitssinn"—Ritter: *Platon II.* xii, 421 sqq.; "common sense"—Jowett, introd. to *Soph.*; so Campbell: *Sophistes and Politicus*, xiv, etc.; "practicable working logic"—Shorey: *The Unity of Plato's Thought*, 7, 38, 51-53, etc.; and cf. above, p. 208, n. 31.

[47] *Phileb.* 58c. This whole passage, 55c-62d, is in many respects more accurate and more instructive in its discussion of the point than the better known passages in *Repub.* 476a-480b, 509e-511d, from which it differs in drawing its basic line not between "science" or "knowledge" (ἐπιστήμη = scientia), on the one hand, and "opinion" and "imagination" (δόξα, εἰκασία), on the other; but between logical and alogical factors in the various "sciences" (ἐπιστήμαι), of which many sorts, practical and theoretical (55d), are recognized and their human value affirmed (62b-d). The earlier analysis, however, seems to underlie *Tim.* 29b-d, 51d-e. The two are, in a sense, only verbally incompatible; but the analysis in *Phileb.* is both simpler and more fundamental, and seems to represent Plato's mature thought best.

by directly affirming the relative value of "true belief" and of "sciences" other than logic,[48] and also by freely using "myths" or "likely tales" in his own exposition where dialectical analysis is not feasible, yet without ever willingly permitting confusion of either methods or results,[49] Plato displays a nicer critical insight than either the Ionian dogmatists with their overconfident affirmations, or the Eleatic and Megaric logicians with their sweeping rejection of the alogical in every form. The clear impression I get from the dialogues, in short, is that of a thinker not only skilled in logic and scrupulous in method, but having a sensitiveness to gradations in both method and subject matter that is, so far as I know, the best safeguard against various sorts of verbalistic unrealism.

That Plato held, then, sound critical principles and a genuinely critical attitude seems to me clear. That he had a fully adequate conception of scientific procedure, or that he was always true to his own principles seems to me not so. He certainly gives evidence of a quite inadequate appreciation of the importance of systematic experiment[50] (as contrasted with simple observation and measurement, which he apparently rated at something like their true value); his appreciation of the complexity of the physical world and of the human mind was necessarily limited; and, perhaps on that account, he talks at times as though having reached final conclusions upon what now seem far too slender grounds.[51] But these strictures having been affirmed clearly and strongly, it is necessary at once to add caveats against two common misunderstandings, which do real violence to his thought. The first is that he was what is commonly called a "pure

[48] Cf. besides *Phileb.* 61e-62c, the passages cited above, n. 3.
[49] *E.g. Phaedo* 101d. 3-e. 3; *Theaet.* 209d-210d.
[50] *Repub.* 530e-531d; cf. Field's general comment, *op. cit.*, 40-43, in which, however, the phrase "mere game or recreation" must be taken with salt, even though Plato uses similar language.
[51] *E.g.* the condemnation of poetry and the plastic arts, *Repub.* 595a-608a; the assertion of the divinity of the heavenly bodies, *Laws* 899a-b, (*Epin.* 983b-984a); or the often cited religious censorship in *Laws* 907d-910e.

rationalist" in philosophy, in the sense that he conceived it the philosopher's task to derive by ratiocination all that is real from pure logical forms, which themselves are all derivable from one form, such as the good. There is, so far as I know, not a sentence in the dialogues that gives voice to any such notion of the philosopher's task;[52] there are numerous statements that exclude it; and it surely is time to stop fathering on Plato a mode of thought from which he expressly dissociated himself[53] and which he could not have held without abandoning his own distinctive position. How he did conceive the philosopher's task we have seen from one point of view.[54] From another, this task may be described as tracing out numerical and logical relationships in the actual, pushing such analysis as far as possible before letting the account end in the inevitable *et cetera* that signalizes the ultimate opacity of the actual to logical illumination.[55] So far is Plato from being a pure rationalist that he expressly affirms that actuality is *not* wholly amenable to logical analysis, and certainly not, therefore, derivable from pure logical principles.

A second misleading assertion often made is that in the late dialogues, in which the Platonic theology is most fully set forth, the author has ceased to be critical and has become a dogmatist. It is perfectly true that in the *Republic* and later writings, there is a larger proportion of positive—though still largely tentative—assertion, instead of mere question and refutation; a not unnatural phenomenon if it be true, as I think it is, that Plato was

---

[52] *Repub.* 511b-c describes the process of logical deduction, *not* as a sole method in philosophy, but as a logical complement to the converse process by which the "first principle" has antecedently been arrived at. Induction, in this passage, precedes deduction, and the mind must employ both. Moreover, the passage referring to pure deduction is expressly dealing with a limited field, not with metaphysics in general: it "ends in ideas" (511c. 2), and ideas are far from being the whole of reality. The same comment applies, so far as I can see, to *Crat.* 436d-e, which should be compared with *Phaedo* 107b, and the caution there indicated.

[53] *Soph.* 242c-249e, in which Parmenides and the "friends of the forms" represent different versions of such "pure rationalism."

[54] Above, notes 25, 31, 36, and the related text.

[55] *Phileb.* 16c-17a; cf. *Polit.* 285a-b; *Repub.* 602c-d; *Phaedr.* 265e-266c, 270b-272b; etc.

actually getting some problems solved. It is true also that in the *Laws*, especially, a really unwelcome rigidity and asperity is noticeable: partly, one suspects, a mark of advancing age—"Why should not Plato also have grown old?"[56] But even this needs to be kept in due perspective; and the numerous passages must not be overlooked in which the aged Athenian Stranger himself warns against premature finality.[57] Plato does not cease to be critically awake, even at fourscore years.

There is general agreement nowadays that a thinker's methods and viewpoint are not less important than his results; and that the value of his results, indeed, is inseparable from the ways in which he has arrived at them. If Plato's thoughts concerning God and man, therefore, were those of an irresponsible visionary, a feeling-philosopher, a wishful enthusiast, however noble, they could be of no more than literary interest now, such methods and viewpoints being properly suspect. But if, as I have sought to show, his enthusiasm was that of a genuinely critical, "realistic" mind, then the major drift of his thought—whatever changes be needed in detail— may well have lasting significance. The stature of his genius is not seriously questioned on other grounds, and his opportunity for hard thinking about first principles, during a long lifetime, surrounded by the best scientists of his day, untrammeled by censorship, yet closely in touch with the baffling problems of personal, social, and political life, was a rare one. This critical Plato, keen, humorous, ironic, and clear-headed with all his enthusiasm, is the "religious realist" we are considering.

Along with his acute devotion to Socrates and Athens, and to "the good," his religious experience included a clearly stated confidence in the sovereignty and the goodness of a living God. Speculative details will be examined later; for the moment I am content to stress the origi-

---

[56] H. Raeder: *op. cit.*, 419.
[57] The most notable passage is 769a-771a (so *Polit.* 294a-299e); and cf. 641d, 644e, 705e, 744a, 746a-c, etc.

nality, the philosophic importance, and the practical bearing of this strain in his religious thought. Its originality
can be judged best against the background of earlier
Greek thought. Before Thales and his hard-headed
Milesian associates, naïve anthropomorphism was general in Greece as elsewhere. Natural phenomena were
ascribed, without critical misgivings, to manlike agents,
gods and dæmons, whose doings were recounted in myths
taken more or less literally as statements of fact. From
all this the Ionian physicists broke free, substituting
physical stuffs and forces, and challenging once for all
man's right to read his own image *en bloc* into the world
about him. Excepting certain Pythagoreans and Socrates,
who used the ideas rather as matter of faith than as
reasoned theory, no trained thinker thenceforth until
Plato talked, as philosopher, about God and the soul
except in some Pickwickian sense.[58] It is Plato who, for
the first time, seriously follows up the suggestion of the
notorious freethinker, Anaxagoras, that Νοῦς (Mind) is
sovereign in the world,[59] and develops it as the basis of a
philosophical theology. His theory differs from the fables
which the physicists had scrapped, in its painstaking
definition of terms and relations, and its effort toward
dialectically tested grounding of the concepts employed;
and from the earlier philosophies, whether materialistic
or formalistic, in drawing an explicit distinction between
mind, which he thinks can be empirically identified as a
vera causa (αἰτία), and bodies, which empirically are
rather coöperant or conditioning factors (συναίτια), and
deliberately referring phenomena—all phenomena—ultimately to the former.[60] This is a new departure, both in
religion and in philosophy: a serious effort to analyze,

---

[58] See, *e.g.* Burnet: *Early Greek Philosophy,* index s. vv. θεός, θεοί,
god, etc.

[59] *Phaedo* 97b. 8 sqq.

[60] This statement needs to be qualified thus far: that, as we shall see,
minds (νόες) are but one class of *souls* (ψυχαί), to which latter "all
phenomena" are ultimately traceable; some phenomena being initiated
by nonrational souls which are not truly minds. This will be made clear
later. Besides *Phaedo* 96a-99e, see *Phaedr.* 245c-246a, *Tim.* 46c-e, *Laws*
888e-899d, *Phileb.* 26e-30d, *Soph.* 246d-249d, 265b-266e; and Section III,
below.

ground, and employ critically the concept of a living, intelligent God.

Not only is it new: it is integral to the metaphysic, combining logical, mathematical, physical, and psychological factors, that Plato is trying to work out; and it has importance also for the practical conduct of life—for morality and morale. As to the former point, what has been said and what is still to be said in Sections II and III must answer. As to the latter, it is perhaps enough to say that Plato, like Socrates but more systematically, rounds out his conception of the duty of man by conceiving it possible and obligatory for man to coöperate with God, who is good and the author of good, and in definite ways to be like him.[61] It is perhaps not far-fetched to see in this development Plato's restatement of the sense of divine mission so consistently affirmed and exemplified by Socrates, so tantalizingly skimmed over in the dialectic of the *Euthyphro,* and withal left so much in need of vindication and development.[62] For Socrates, the "gadfly," for Plato, the scientist and the self-devoted governor and every wise and temperate and just man: these are colaborers and imitators of God, not in addition to but just in and by doing faithfully their own proper parts. Morality merges in religion, not as merely extraneous, added sanction, but as integral fulfillment.

This account of Plato's religious attitude may close with a glance at his novel and vehement onslaught on "impiety." No other judgment is more emphatically voiced as his own than this: once in the *Republic* through the lips of his elder brother, Adimantus, and again in the *Laws* through those of the aged Athenian Stranger, who by common consent is Plato himself. The latter of these statements is in the discursive style typical of the *Laws,*

[61] *Repub.* 500c-501e, 613a, 379a-383b; *Phaedr.* 248a-253b; *Theaet.* 176a-177b; *Polit.* 268c-276e; cf. 294a-297d (correlation of divine and human rulership); *Tim.* 47a-e, 90a-d; *Laws* 715e-716d; (*Epin.* 976e-977a, 991b-992e). (The metaphor of the puppets, *Laws* 644e sqq., is obviously whimsy.)
[62] *Apol.* 28e sqq., etc.; *Euthyph.* 12a-14b.

and methodically distinguishes three kinds of impious
belief: that there are no gods; that there are gods, but
they are not concerned about human conduct; that there
are gods, concerned about human conduct, but they can
be bribed with gifts:—three views which, taken in that
order, are condemned with increasing heat.[63] Now condemnation and punishment, even capital punishment, for
impiety is, of course, nothing new. What is new is the
conception of what constitutes the crime. For in Plato's
judgment, the worst kind of impiety, worse than atheism
or indifferentism, is just that vulgar religionism which,
in the city that banished Anaxagoras and killed Socrates,
is so common as to pass unnoticed. This is the burden
of Adimantus' indignant protest in the *Republic*: the
familiar divorcement of religion from morality, and the
vulgarization of both.[64] Be pious and decent, say conventional parents and teachers, because it pays, either in this
world or in the next. Be pious anyway, whether you find
it convenient to be decent or not, coax salvation-monger-
ing Orphic mendicants, who promise for a fee to cajole
the gods with sacrifices and mysteries. The basic fault
here, of course, is the degrading of virtue itself into mere
venal gentility: be decent because it pays. To the rebuttal
of this Philistinism and the establishment of a better
view the rest of the dialogue is ostensibly devoted. But
the special debasing of religion is important enough to
call for a lengthy and forthright notice. The reply of
Socrates (which seems to me plainly Plato's)[65] lays down
two basic "articles of belief" (τύποι περὶ θεολογίας) : that
God is the author only of good to men, not of evil; and

---

[63] *Laws* 888c sqq.; 899d sqq.; 907e-909a.

[64] All three views discussed in the *Laws* are noticed here also, 365d.
7-e. 6; but the third is the one which here, as in the *Laws*, is most
unsparingly condemned, 362d-367e.

[65] 378a-391d. It ties up closely with the clearly Platonic speeches of
Adimantus and of the Athenian Stranger, already referred to; and it
goes beyond anything attributed to Socrates in the *Apology*, the earlier
dialogues, and the Xenophontic literature, in its strictures upon conventional religion. I surmise that here, even more plainly than in the
Euthyphro, we have Plato's verdict on the smug, second-rate religionism
that divorced piety from rational morality, coddled charlatans, and stoned
the prophets.

that God neither changes nor deceives. Demoralizing tales of vengefulness, greed, and caprice of gods or heroes, and of the fearsomeness of death and the life after death—all popular misconceptions[00]—must go, though they come from Homer himself; and with them, by inescapable inference, goes all ground for irrational fear and hope of buyable favor, and all the furtive or open bargaining that such fear and hope suggest.

The religion of Plato, in fine, while definitely theistic, is a "high religion" of vigorous rational inquiry and reconstruction, in which man is thought to collaborate with God by seeking to discover and to make socially effective a "rational good," the way to which is to be found by exploring the structure and working of the actual world. No conception of God or of man that contravenes this is Platonic: no pietism, no prophet ecstasies, no vague, noble ideality, and no finalitarian dogma, whether high or low, moral, æsthetic, Humanistic, classicistic, or other. Not bright visions but hard thinking is the greater part of authentic Platonism; and vision, which comes only with effort, is insight by which one must push on, with sense of direction renewed.

II. As Antinominalist: The Theory of Forms, and the Good

Having given thus much space to description of Plato's total religious attitude, we must examine some details of two of his most important speculative doctrines: his theory of forms, and the good; and his theory of souls, of which the chief is God.

In considering the theory of forms, we shall start from the *Theaetetus* and *Parmenides,* now commonly regarded as the earliest of the "dialectical dialogues." These together comprise, on the one hand a searching criticism, on the other an indirect vindication of the view held in the earlier dialogues that "the presence or communion"

---

[00] "As the many assert"—379c. 3; cf. 381c-d, 391d-e. This indictment of the poets and popular thought is much faded in *Laws* 886.

(εἴτε παρουσία εἴτε κοινωνία) [67] of specific common factors,
viz. definite and stable "forms" or "ideas" (εἴδη, ἰδέαι),
in the fluid and multiplex world of human experience is
indispensable to the forthcoming of knowledge.[68] In
Parmenides 128e-135b, this theory is subjected to criticism more searching than most thinkers have ever ven-
tured to apply to their own views, and its difficulties are
honestly and unsparingly brought to light; yet when all
is said, Parmenides himself concludes that to deny the
reality of stable, common forms "would destroy utterly
the possibility of reasoning" (τοῦ διαλέγεσθαι). This
conclusion is strongly reinforced by detailed analysis in
Theaetetus 152a-183c of a well-developed and well-de-
fended theory, credited jointly to Protagoras and the
Heracliteans, that does thus deny the reality of forms,
affirming instead a radical sense-relativism and fluxional
phenomenalism. On such terms, it turns out, no knowledge is possible, but only a welter of opinion in which
false cannot be told from true, so that the truth even of
the proposed theory itself cannot be maintained against
any one who may choose to call it false (161c-e, 170a sqq.).
The logical ground, then, of Plato's theory that forms are
real and stable[69] is that without them, knowledge is
impossible.

[67] *Phaedo* 100d. 5-6 (language used earlier in similar but not identical
fashion in *Euthyd.* 301a. 4, *Gorg.* 497e. 1-3, 498d. 2-e. 2). In this discussion
of the theory of forms, I am especially indebted to Prof. Ritter, to whose
detailed analysis I may refer as a whole (*Platon* I. 564-586; II. 3-320;
Neue Untersuchungen über Platon 228-326), though I have diverged from
it fairly often. Prof. Lutoslawski's discussion also is very illuminating,
though often extreme and to be used with caution.

[68] The clearest possible statement of this thesis is in *Crat.* 439e-440d,
where it is left as a problem for further cogitation; cf. *Repub.* 476a-480b,
602a-603b, and Aristotle: *Met.* 987a. 32-35; 1078b. 12-16. To the ultimate
question whether in fact knowledge *is* attainable, the only ultimate
answer seems to be that of Socrates in *Meno* 86b. 6-c. 2: "Some of these
things, indeed, I should not insist on too strongly. But that we should
be better and bolder and less lumpish in supposing we ought to search
out what is not known, than if we suppose the things we do not know
cannot be found and should not be sought—this I should maintain
aggressively, if need be, by word and by deed." An assertive skepticism
can be met by reasoned rebuttal, as in *Theaet.* 170e-171c; but the only
answer to shrugging agnosticism is robust "animal faith."

[69] This says nothing, be it noted, about its historical or psychological
origins, with which we are not here concerned.

But what are these "forms"? And how are they related to sensible things, and to one another? Primarily, as the foregoing argument implies, they are just *that* in a thing which renders a judgment about it true so far as it is true, or false so far as it is false: the factors which at once make this thing what it describably is, and are the ground for specifying its relationships with other things—for classifying, analyzing, defining it, and thus coming to know it as far as it is knowable. Now taken in the most obvious, "safe and untutored" sense, this must mean at least that if a thing is correctly judged as twofold, warm, or beautiful, then twoness, warmth, or beauty "as such" (αὐτό) must be veritably "present in" it, as the ground for such attribution.[70] This ground, moreover, considered "in itself" (αὐτὸ καθ᾽ αὐτό), must be invariably just what it is—twoness, beauty, and so on—else knowledge, again, were impossible.[71] A form as thus far defined, then, is not a thing, but a factor "present in" a thing. Neither is it simply an observable trait, in the sense of what-appears-to-this-or-that-observer—a shifty somewhat, as is well known; but a stable character whose real presence justifies the attribution to the thing "in" which it is present of just that single character itself. It

[70] *Phaedo* 100c-102e, 105b-c; cf. *Soph.* 247a. The precise meaning of "presence" (παρουσία) as used here, and of the other terms similarly employed, "communion" (κοινωνία), "participation" (μέθεξις, μετάσχεσις, etc.), and the like, is nowhere analyzed—neither by Plato, nor, so far as I know, by any other thinker. Pure logic can evade the issue by treating predication simply as classification; but metaphysic has to ask about the real basis of classification of real things (or phenomena, or events, or whatever is actual), and that basis evidently must be sought in significant likenesses and differences among things, which in turn involve the characterization of things by characteristics, which is precisely what is difficult to explain. Plato's metaphors seem as good as any, and his treatment of the point has the merit of not supposing a metaphor to be an explanation: all this being set forth, says Socrates, "naïvely and artlessly, not to say simple mindedly."—*Phaedo* 100d. 3-4.

[71] *Phaedo* 78d. 5-6, 100b, etc.; *Parm.* 130b; etc. If the meanings of predicables changed from moment to moment, no significant difference between true and false propositions could be maintained in logic; and if the real characters which are the ontal (real) counterparts to logical predicables turned chameleon, no significant difference between true and false judgments could be maintained in metaphysics—or in everyday life. A white *thing* may become black, and no harm done, to logic, science, or common sense; but if white "as such" should become black now and then, all three would be stultified.

is a "noumenon" in the proper sense,[72] a veritable, essential character comprehensible not by the senses but only by rational mind and thought (νοῦς, νόησις). Its distinction from a thing is underscored by two further considerations: that one form may be "present in" many things, which are then said to "participate" (μετασχεῖν, μεταλαμβάνειν, etc.) in it; and that some forms, at least, are not fully (perfectly, exhaustively) exemplified either by one thing or by any group of things such as are apprehended through sense perception.[73]

Thus far we have referred only to what Plato himself regarded as the most obvious part of the doctrine: that if a certain single character can be correctly attributed to a thing or a group of things, then that character "as such" must be veritably "present in" those things. It is a more difficult question whether there are not only attributive forms of the simple sort described, but also complex unitary substantive forms, "of man or of fire or of water," "hair and mud and dirt."[74] Yet difficult or not, the case is no less cogent for these, as Parmenides intimates, than for the others: if the judgment, "This (perceived thing) is a man" be significant, and either true or false, then a definite complex of characters connoted by the term man must be veritably either present in or absent from the thing thus judged.[75] And of these substantive forms, much the same account must be given as of the simple attributive forms. Each must be immutably just what it is, if considered "in itself"—man, ox, or whatever it be;[76] each may be present in many things; and some, at least, are not perfectly exemplified by any thing or group of things in which they are thus present.[77] The greater difficulty in clearly conceiving

[72] Not a *Ding-an-sich*, let alone an unknowable one. Kant or his interpreters have here a sad confusion to answer for.
[73] *Phaedo* 74a-75c.   [75] *Crat.* 385a-386e; cf. *Parm.* 130e. 1-4.
[74] *Parm.* 130c.   [76] *Phileb.* 15a.
[77] This last statement is to be inferred from what Aristotle says, *Met.* 987b. 14-18, etc., about Plato's drawing a distinction between the objects of mathematical study (τὰ μαθηματικά), and on the one hand sensible things, on the other true forms. Among the latter, it seems fairly clear, were accounted the circle "as such," the triangle "as such," and so on; cf. Ross's note *ad loc.*

substantive forms is due in part to their greater complexity, which makes it less easy to conceive them as unitary and immutable; in part to their closer proximity to the elusive boundary between the essential (abstractible, logically manipulable, universal) and the actual (*de facto*, individual, fully concrete), with the consequent danger of ascribing to them an equivocal or a false ontological status.[78] But if substantive forms cannot be dispensed with, their reality also must perforce be admitted, and the difficulties accepted as problems to be solved; and this is the course Plato followed, from first to last.[79]

Meanwhile, we notice one other point: that among the forms, numbers have an especially significant place. It is well known that Aristotle represents the doctrine of forms current in the Academy in his day as shaped predominantly in terms of numbers, and that he attributes the origin of the doctrine in this guise to Plato, whose thought was "in many respects," he says, "in accord with" (ἀκολουθοῦσα) that of the Pythagoreans[80]— though with very important differences, of which we are by no means sure Aristotle has given us an accurate account. If Plato came at length to hold that *all* forms are numbers, as the latter rather plainly suggests,[81] that goes

[78] My statement of the case, not Plato's, as regards the latter point, but I think not a wholly groundless conjecture in view of what he does say: namely, that the reality of attributive forms is the most obvious (*Phaedo* 100c-e, 101b-e, 105b-c, *Parm.* 130b-d). Incidentally, the familiar dictum that his forms are just "hypostatized abstractions" receives no support from this sort of remark. It is precisely the substantive forms— man, ox, and the like—that lend themselves most readily to hypostatization, and that were in fact so treated by later "extreme realists." Plato's express statements that one can more easily be sure of the reality of attributive forms, then, seems to imply that it was not "hypostatic" reality he intended to ascribe to them.

[79] Thus, *Meno* 74a-75a; *Crat.* 386d-e, 389a-d; *Repub.* 596a sqq.; *Phileb.* 15a; *Tim.* 28a sqq., 31a-b, 51a sqq., etc.

[80] *Met.* 987a. 29-988a. 1, besides the intricate polemical passages of books M and N, in which Plato's views are criticized along with those of Speusippus, Xenocrates, and the Pythagoreans. For a full marshaling of the relevant material from Aristotle and the Greek commentators, see L. Robin: *La théorie platonicienne des idées et des nombres après Aristote.* For brief discussions, see W. D. Ross: *Aristotle's Metaphysics*, I. li-lxxvi, and notes on 987a. 29-988a. 1, 991b. 1-992b. 20, etc.; and A. E. Taylor: *Plato* 503-516, and his article "Forms and Numbers" in *Mind*, N. S. 35: 419-440; 36: 12-33. [81] *Met.* 987b. 18-25.

beyond anything that is said in the dialogues. But that *some* forms are numbers is plainly taken for granted in the *Phaedo;*[82] and that "the elements of the forms are the elements of all things," that these "elements" are none other than those which constitute numbers, and that numbers, therefore, have a rôle of capital importance in the theory, seems quite in line with the description of the character and functions of "the indeterminate" and "the limit," in the *Philebus,*[83] with the familiar declaration that the insight of the dialectician is to be attained by carrying further the processes involved in the mathematical sciences,[84] and with the repeated association of cosmic order on the one hand with numerical relationships,[85] as on the other with the forms and with the good.[86] We cannot now go further into this very difficult and imperfectly explored part of Plato's thought. But it seems safe to say that if he assimilated forms to numbers, logic to mathematics, in his later thinking, he also assimilated mathematics to logic, "destroying the hypotheses" of the quasi-physical, atomistic Pythagorean arithmetic and geometry, and seeking to define both the number series and the geometrical quantities—line, surface, solid—as aggregates whose "first principles" (ἄρχαι, αἰτίαι, στοιχεία) are more properly subjects for logical than for mathematical discussion.[87]

[82] 104d (cf. 101b-c, 104a).

[83] 25a-26b, which seems to me, in accordance with some (not all) of Mr. Bury's comments (*The Philebus of Plato*, lxiv-lxxiv, etc.), and in divergence from those of Prof. Ross (*Aristotle's Metaph.*, I. lxix, 165, 171), to be in fact what it purports to be: an effort at further clarification of the familiar problem of the nature of forms, and their relations with things and with one another. The problem is announced in well-worn language in 15a-c; and then restated in 16c-18e in such fashion as to bring into relief numerical aspects of what is still a logical and metaphysical problem.

[84] *Repub.* 531d-533e.

[85] *E.g.* in *Gorg.* 507e-508a, *Repub.* 602d-e, *Tim.* 35a-37d, etc., *Laws* 817e-822d, 897c-899d.

[86] As in *Phaedo* 99a-c, *Gorg.* 507e-508a, *Sympos.* 210a-e, *Repub.* 508e-509c, *Tim.* 27e-31b, etc., *Laws* 903a-904e, 967a (a final echo of *Phaedo* 97b-99d, the true keynote in Plato's cosmology).

[87] This is to be inferred from such statements of Aristotle as *Met.* 992a. 19-22; 1083a. 31-35, as well as 987b. 18-988a. 1, already cited; although in his criticisms (*e.g.* 991b. 31 sq.; 992a. 2-10; 1080b. 37-1083a. 19) he is anything but careful to keep what he has indicated as Plato's thought clearly in view. See Ross's notes.

Quite as important as the question concerning the nature of forms, and certainly not less difficult, are questions concerning their relations to things, and to one another. A partial answer to one of these further questions has already been indicated: that the forms are "present in" though distinguishable from particular things, which "participate in" them, that is, have such definite characters as they do have in virtue of the "presence" of the forms. If one could read these statements in their original contexts without preconception, I venture to think he would get the impression of clear logical differentiation and close ontological association between forms and things. But since all of us are compelled to read Plato after Aristotle has told us (through various mediating interpreters) what to find there, it is not easy to trust our own eyes and Plato's own words. It is chiefly for that reason, I think, that we have so regularly read them as teaching not only a logical distinction but an ontological disjunction of forms from things, such that the forms are, so to say, a second order of things existing separately,[88] whose relation to sensible things would indeed pose intractable problems for logic and for common sense alike. Since it is obviously impossible to argue the matter out here, I may be permitted instead to outline what seems to me a sound procedure for discovering what Plato meant: (1) Use Aristotle's statements, even nonpolemical ones, with the strictest critical caution. Since it is fairly clear that he "badly misunderstood or misrepresented" Plato on various other related points,[89] there is more than a little likelihood that he has missed the mark here also. (2) Give due weight to these facts:

[88] Aristotle: *Met.* 1078b. 30-1079a. 4; 990a. 33-991b. 9; etc.
[89] The phrase is Prof. Ross's, *op. cit.*, I. 167. Instances of such inaccuracy on Aristotle's part are his equation of μίμησις ("imitation") with μέθεξις ("participation"), 987b. 10-13; his repeated confusion of the "indefinite dyad" with the number "two," 987b. 33-35; 990b. 19-22; 991b. 31-992a. 1; his similar confusion of "the one" (the principle of unity) with the integer "one," 992a. 2-10; his misunderstanding of the doctrine that the natural numbers are not composed of units and are not addible, 1080a. 15-b. 4; his statement that Plato says that a plurality of things result from a single impress of form upon matter, 988a. 2; his denial that Plato recognized "efficient" and "final" causes, 988a. 8-9; b. 11-14; etc.

that the statements which seem most readily interpretable as implying separate, transcendent existence of the forms [90] are found mainly in the group of dialogues now assignable with some confidence to a period in Plato's philosophical career when his theories were shaping themselves in broad, vivid strokes rather than in careful detail, and when he passed easily from the language of logic to that of enthusiasm; [91] that they appear, moreover, in passages that are plainly metaphorical or even mythical in character; and that even so, in many instances a continuity of the forms with sensible things is indicated by the introduction of some doctrine either of abstraction, of "recollection," or of creation. (3) Accept as normative for an interpretation of Plato's mature thought on this question: (a) negatively, the unanswerable demonstrations, in *Parmenides* 133b-134e and *Sophist* 248a-249d, of the unknowability and hence the uselessness of forms sharply and completely isolated from perceptible things and events, and especially from change, apart from the last of which human knowledge—nay, mind itself, cannot exist; [92] and (b) positively the partial and various analyses of knowledge and of reality in *Theaetetus, Sophist, Politicus,* and *Philebus,* in which Plato is working out by laborious inquiry, from diverse but related

[90] *E.g. Meno* 81c; *Sympos.* 210e-212a; *Phaedr.* 247c-e; *Phaedo* 75a-d; *Repub.* 508e-509d, 514d-516b; 597b-d; *Tim.* 28a, 31a, 51c.

[91] "This is the poetical mode of conceiving of the ideas, in which Plato embodied the feelings of wonder and delight with which he contemplated the first real inquiry which the world had seen. The object and end of that inquiry appeared to him surrounded with a mystic halo. . . . But Plato was far from resting in this as a final theory of knowledge." (Campbell: *Soph. and Polit.,* lxvi. The whole passage is in point.) Cf. also the succinct comment in Jowett's introd. to the *Parmenides.*

[92] Of the passage in *Soph.* Campbell plausibly surmises (lxxv) "that Plato at a late period of his course directs this argument against those amongst his disciples in the Academy who, resting in their imperfect realization of an earlier phase of his own teaching and reverting to Pythagorean and Eleatic elements, held the doctrine of ideas in the form in which it is often controverted by Aristotle. That Aristotle should not have observed this divergence between the master and the school may be inexplicable, but not more so than his silence about the *Parmenides"*— which, as is well known, he ignores in all his extant polemics against the theory of forms, although in that dialogue his own most telling criticisms had already been indicated; cf. with Campbell's suggestion the substantially similar one of C. Ritter: *Neue Untersuchungen,* 30-33.

points of view, both logical and metaphysical ramifications of his theory.

Since these dialogues are both later and more precise in composition than those of the middle period, they have obvious general claims to precedence.[93] But as to the particular question now at issue, it is not infrequently held that they are not really concerned with the theory of forms as we know it from the earlier dialogues, but with a new set of problems, treated by means of concepts that are foreign to the *Phaedo,* the *Republic,* and the *Phaedrus,* on which they cannot therefore be regarded as throwing light. This manifestly is a point not to be settled offhand. If similarity of language, in respect of such familiar terms as εἶδος, ἰδέα, κοινωνία, μέθεξις, and the like were conclusive,[94] there could be no argument; for these words recur again and again. But similarity of language is one thing, continuity of thought another, and the latter needs to be shown on more comprehensive grounds. A single example must suffice. The *Philebus* is, perhaps, the one of these later dialogues concerning which it can most plausibly be said that "Plato is working out a new analysis of reality without troubling himself about its relation to his old analysis,"[95] yet even here I venture to think that the new analysis is related in the most intimate way and with the clearest intent to a line of inquiry, involving the theory of forms, on which Plato had been working at least when he wrote the *Phaedrus* and perhaps earlier.

The *Philebus* is now generally regarded as written after—quite possibly next after—the *Sophist* and *Politicus.* In *Politicus* 262a-263a, in a brief digression, a problem of great importance, already noticed in earlier dialogues and basic to Plato's conception of metaphysical inquiry, is stated more accurately than hitherto and then expressly earmarked for discussion at a later time: the

[93] See below, pp. 248-250.

[94] As Bonitz, for example, held it to be: *Platonische Studien,* (3te Aufl.) 193-194; but cf. Ritter: *Neue Untersuchungen,* 47-49, and more generally, 228-326, and the detailed table opp. 323.

[95] Ross: *op. cit.,* I. 165.

problem, namely, of defining more clearly the grounds
underlying the method of "division according to essential forms" (κατ' εἴδη),⁹⁶ rather than according to superficial, incomplete, and arbitrarily imposed schemata.
Now it is this problem, stated in just this way, that is
announced in *Philebus* 16b-17a for discussion, and that
seems to me in point of fact the main theme of that
dialogue.⁹⁷ Moreover, the key to the analysis which follows is to be found in *Politicus* 283c-287a, in which it is
pointed out, as a fact of great moment (284d. 1-2), that
"the great and the small" or "more and less" can be
measured either relatively, by mere comparison with each
other, or absolutely, by comparison with a standard, "the
just adequate" (τὸ μέτριον), which is at once mathematical and axiological or evaluative (283e. 5-6, 284b. 1-2,
e. 6-8, 287a). That the problem is, in Plato's mind, directly pertinent to the theory of forms is made plain
beyond serious doubt, I think, by the occurrence of the
terms εἶδος and ἰδέα in *Politicus* 262a-263b, 283c-287a, no
fewer than thirteen times, and five times in the corresponding passages in *Philebus* 16c-17a, 23c-27b;⁹⁸ and
especially by the recurrence of the technical phrase "to
divide according to essential forms" or "along natural
lines" (κατ' εἴδη), in *Politicus* 262d, 285a, 286d, *Philebus*
23d. That the forms do not play in the rest of the *Philebus* a rôle such as they played in the *Phaedo* and the
Republic does not mean that they have been either forgotten or abandoned, any more than the critical pas-

⁹⁶ *Polit.* 286d. 9; cf. *Phaedr.* 265d-266b; *Crat.* 386d-387a, d.

⁹⁷ The accepted view is, of course, that the dialogue is primarily ethical,
with the admittedly original and important metaphysical passages brought
in incidentally. I am convinced, for reasons which cannot be developed
here, that this view puts the emphasis in the wrong place. Both the
Philebus itself, which on the usual view lacks basic unity, and its relations to other dialogues both proximate and remote, gain very much in
clarity if the dispute over pleasure, in spite of its intrinsic interest and
importance, be regarded as subordinate and illustrative, as the pursuit
of the Sophist and the characterization of the Statesman are in the
dialogues of those names. Cf. *Polit.* 285d. 3-7, 286d. 8-9.

⁹⁸ Even Ritter, for all his caution on this point, regards five (perhaps
nine) of these occurrences in *Polit.* and one in *Phileb.* as having the
distinctive sense described above, 222 sqq., *viz.* "veritable basic character"
(*Grundbestimmtheit, Begriffsrealität*): *Neue Untersuchungen,* table opp.
323.

sages in *Parmenides* 128e-135b and *Sophist* 248a-249e
mean that. It seems to me rather that Plato is here
simply carrying a step further his examination of the
far-reaching thesis which he had sought to demonstrate
in the *Sophist* and to illustrate in the *Politicus*—that
there is diverse and definite interrelation (κοινωνία)
among forms, as well as between forms and things."
This further step requires, not the *use* of the forms as
hitherto, for the solution of problems into which they
enter as quasi-ultimate factors; but a more penetrating
analysis than any hitherto attempted, to which the forms
themselves apparently are subjected, to explain why it is
that they, as well as things, can display complex interrelations. The "hypothesis" of the reality of the forms
as ultimates, in fine, put forth in the *Phaedo*,[100] and
tested, in the manner there prescribed, by employment in
the succeeding dialogues, is now itself to be "destroyed"
in order that its measure of truth may be "established,"[101] by an analysis that brings to light factors still
more ultimate than the forms, by which forms and things
alike are constituted. It is these more ultimate factors
whose nature is indicated in *Philebus* 16c-19a, 23c-27b,
and whose workings are illustrated in the rest of the
dialogue. But although this further analysis, which
indicates factors of "determination" and of "indeterminacy" and the work of an active "cause" in forms as
well as in things, does indeed go deeper than the earlier
discussions, it is none the less clearly continuous with
them; seeking to establish on firmer ground than before
the conception of dialectical inquiry as a metaphysical
method already set forth in *Phaedrus* 265d-266b, 270a-
272b, not to speak of both earlier and later examples.

The view of the relation between forms and things

---

[99] Cf. *Phileb.* 15a-c.

[100] *Phaedo* 100a-e, 101b-e; though in 104a-105c it is already declared
to be too simple; cf. below, p. 231.

[101] "Therefore, said I, the dialectical method, and that alone, proceeds thus to the underlying principle (ἐπ' αὐτὴν τὴν ἀρχήν), destroying
the hypotheses in order to establish them"—*i.e.* destroying their ostensible,
ad hoc finality and referring so much of their content as can be so referred
to a more ultimate principle (*Repub.* 533c).

which emerges from examination of these "dialectical dialogues" is in one respect, at least, unequivocal: there are not two separate worlds, realms, substantial orders, one of intelligible or noumenal things, the other of perceptible or phenomenal things, standing over against each other in reciprocal isolation. Forms and things are present together in one world, in which each is logically distinguishable from the other; in which there are complex, systematic interrelations among things, among forms, and between forms and things; and in which more ultimate factors than either things or forms are discoverable by systematic analysis, which tests every ostensible ultimate, and seeks to press ever further its search for "the natural lines of cleavage" and of unification [102] in the actual world.

We have already anticipated the answer to the question how forms are related to one another: they are interrelated in definite series and groupings that need to be discovered by detailed systematic inquiry. This is first intimated in the *Phaedo* itself, [103] and implied in the *Republic* in the account of "the form of the good"; noted as a nice problem in *Parmenides* 129b-e; at length demonstrated in *Sophist* 250a-260e, explored in detail in that dialogue and in the *Politicus,* and finally, as I think, further substantiated in the *Philebus* by a further analysis of the nature of forms themselves.

[102] *Phaedr.* 265e, d. This conception, restated more exactly in *Polit.* 262a-e, presupposed and exemplified throughout *Soph., Polit.,* and *Phileb.,* and no less integral to *Sympos.* and *Repub.,* on the one hand, *Tim.* and *Laws* on the other, effectually rules out any conceptualistic or neo-Kantian interpretation of Plato's thought; as perhaps, indeed, *Crat.* 386d sqq., and *Parm.* 132b-c might be thought to do with sufficient clarity. It is things-as-they-are, not things-as-we-suppose-them-to-be, that Plato professes to be concerned about. Unlike proponents of "the critical philosophy" in Kant's sense, he recognizes some (not all) of the difficulties in the way of achieving knowledge of noumenal reality, but refuses to give it up as impossible. For better, for worse, he is a realist at this point, not a phenomenalist.

[103] *Phaedo* 104a-105b—a passage not compatible with Prof. Burnet's view that the *Phaedo* presents pure Socratic thought, and yet that Socrates did not hold the κοινωνία of forms with one another (*Greek Phil., Part I,* 165 n. 1, though cf. 169-170). Prof. Taylor, who holds a like view, notices the passage (*Plato* 205), but does not take account of it in his later comment on the κοινωνία of forms (388). See also *Repub.* 476a. 4-8, and cf. Shorey: *op. cit.* 36, n. 244.

The "form of the good" calls for special notice, though it must be too brief and dogmatic to be at all satisfactory. We have already seen that the concept of "the good" as a unifying goal of human endeavor was for Plato a legacy from Socrates. The recognized virtues, that seem many and are indeed distinguishable, are yet also one: they are all embraced in knowledge of the good —not knowledge in the sense of specialized information nor technical skill, but insight into the nature and needs of man and the promises and requirements of each situation he confronts. This is the well-known burden of the early, "Socratic" dialogues—*Charmides, Laches, Lysis* —that culminate in the *Protagoras* in a comprehensive rebuttal of the opposing view. To develop and generalize this notion of the good as goal is a task which Plato keeps in sight throughout his philosophic career. Not only is it treated as a sovereign ethical and political principle in all the dialogues that deal systematically with these matters.[104] It becomes, besides, in the *Phaedo* a cosmological hypothesis, never thenceforth abandoned nor "destroyed," though later significantly developed and modified. This hypothesis, given effective rhetorical stress in the *Symposium* and the *Republic*—almost too effective, in view of the attention the passages have distracted from more sober ones—is restated in the *Philebus* in a form more precise though still by no means fully worked out; and finally receives, in the *Timaeus* and the *Laws* (and *Epinomis*), its most elaborate cosmological application.[105]

The theme announced in the *Phaedo* and developed in all these later variations is that the world is to be understood, if possible, on the supposition that the actual arrangement of things and events is the best that could be: "that in truth the good and ought bind and hold together" the world as it is. This is language which, out

---

[104] *E.g. Gorg., Repub., Polit., Phileb., Laws.*
[105] *Phaedo* 97c-99c (already foreshadowed in *Gorg.* 507e-508a); *Sympos.* 201c-212a; *Repub.* 508e-509c; *Phileb.* 28c-30e (cf. 25e-26b and *Polit.* 283c-284a sqq.); *Tim.* 28e-32c, etc.; *Laws* 715e-716d, 896e-898c sqq., 903a-904e, 967a; (*Epin.* 982a-c).

of its context, can make and has made for strange
doctrine. Read with its context, however, it has a meaning at least simple, familiar, and straightforward. The
complete hypothesis is that the world is ordered *by Mind*
(as Anaxagoras said, but scarcely half believed), *to the
end* that the good of every being therein shall be most
fully realized. It is in this sense only that "the good and
ought" is that "cause" of the world order which
Socrates would like to find: it is final cause, in Aristotle's
idiom, but it is in no sense efficient cause. *That* is Mind.

I have found no cogent reason to take the less prosaic
statements in the *Symposium* and the *Republic* in any
other sense, though the weight of competent opinion is
overwhelmingly on the other side. I find myself constrained to read the celebrated passage in the *Republic*,
concluding: "The good is not essence (οὐσία), but soars
even beyond essence in dignity and power," as a bit of
good oratory. That seems to be how Plato takes it. Says
Glaucon at once, "very comically, 'Gad! what a glorious
flight!' " [106] But supposing the whole passage to be read
as an exact, though metaphorical, statement of theory,
everything it says can, I think, be understood in the
terms which the *Phaedo* provides: If the world is so
ordered that all things in it work together for good, which
is the universal goal, then whatever in the world is understandable must be understood (γιγνωσθῆναι) in relation
to that goal, since everything is as it is, because it is good
that it should be so. The essence (οὐσία) of each thing, of
course, is what it is descriptively—treehood, manhood,
and so on—but over and above this descriptive or definable character is the locus of the thing in the cosmos,
without which it would not *be* (εἶναι) at all. The good,
then, as goal of the cosmic order, a goal which cannot be
adequately described but only appreciated or "seen"
(517c), and talked about, if at all, in metaphors, is in

[106] 509b. 9-c. 2. The irreverent pun (ὑπερέχοντος, ὑπερβολῆς) seems
unmistakable, though it comes over clumsily into English. It is evident,
at least, that Plato was not hypnotized by his own eloquence. (Jowett's
translation of this whole passage, with its recurrent personifying term
"author," and its "ludicrous earnestness," is very misleading.)

this sense "beyond essence," that on it the intelligibility, essence, and being (γιγνωσθῆναι, οὐσία, εἶναι) of things depend. But all this, still, is because Mind is the orderer.[107]

In the *Politicus* and *Philebus,* this vague if lofty concept is supplemented in a most important way, already suggested in earlier dialogues. In *Gorgias* 560d-e, 507e-508a, for example, it had been affirmed on the one hand that excellence (ἀρετή) is always associated with orderly arrangement, that the final cause, so to say, is inseparable from an appropriate formal cause; and that in the world as a whole, the formal order that issues in good may be viewed both as moral and as "geometrical." To this concept *Politicus* 283c sqq. returns. Both in weaving and the other arts, and in human conduct, it is necessary to recognize two sorts of measurement: (1) a purely relative and quantitative sort, as when threads in the loom, or speeches in discussion, are compared one with another and it is seen merely that this is longer or shorter than that; and (2) a teleological and evaluative sort, as when the comparison is made with a standard, "the just adequate" (τὸ μέτριον—"the mean" in the sense not of "average" but of "due proportion"), which is manifestly, as we have already noted, at once quantitative and normative in its significance. A fine fabric or a fine man is distinguished from its contrary chiefly through exemplifying or approaching this nice balance between excess and defect of the manifold variables that enter into its composition.[108] It is, then, with some precise adjustment in structural form that good is associated as

---

[107] Though that is not said here, it is said in other major passages that deal with the point, including that in the *Phaedo* which is earlier; there is nothing here to contradict it; and since the primary interest of this passage is in sound logical and ethical education, rather than in cosmology as such, there is plausible reason for its omission here.

[108] It is unnecessary to point out the basic identity of this principle with the Pythagorean concept of the just blend (κρᾶσις), and its kinship with the still older bits of folk wisdom carved at Delphi. It is not so much a Platonic as a Hellenic concept. What seems to be new here is its systematic identification, in the Socratic manner, as the work of reason: "For 'Know thyself!' and 'Be normal!' (Σωφρόνει) are indeed the same thing." (*Charm.* 164e. 7 sq.)

outcome. And to effect such an adjustment, and thus to bring into being the good that can be achieved in a given situation, is the work of intelligence at once scientific (ἐπιστήμων) and artistic (τεχνικός, productive or administrative)—the mind of a master weaver, or of a statesman-king, who with or without fixed rules but always in accord with clearly apprehended principles, intertwines diverse threads or human lives to achieve a result that is good.

This conception is sufficiently important to demand one or two further comments. First, it is clear that the good retains here both its status as end, or final cause, and its character as something to be recognized, appreciated, and denoted, rather than measured, analyzed, and defined: it is still in this sense "beyond essence." What has been added to the earlier statements is the express assertion that good as goal of the arts is invariably associated with a "formal cause" that *can* be measured, analyzed, clearly defined, and directly aimed at by a mind that has the requisite knowledge, *viz.* a certain optimum proportioning or adjustment of the variable factors in a composition. When that is achieved or closely enough approached, in a given case, good is achieved. Secondly —a point often ignored—this μέτριον, this optimum adjustment of specified variables, though perfectly definite in any given situation, cannot be simply generalized therefrom into a stereotype to be applied indiscriminately; rather, the μέτριον in each situation must be determined with reference to the chief result sought in *that* situation, and the accuracy of such determinations must be judged by their practical outcome.[109] Hence the superiority of a trained mind dealing with problems not by

[109] *Polit.* 286d-287a, 293a-296a, *et sqq.* Thus, the right length for a discussion is such as will actually subserve the specific end sought, whether pleasure in talking, or swift arrival at a conclusion, or improvement in dialectical power. So too the physician may use, in given cases, any modes of treatment that his knowledge suggests, and his technique will be approved if it *heals the patients.* "In this [sc., the end and outcome] and in nothing else, I take it, we shall find the only true criterion of a medical principle, or of any other"—(τοῦτον ὅρον ὀρθόν referring back to 292c. 5, etc.) Thus and thus far, on this as at other points, Plato and Peirce join hands.

rote nor by fixed rules, but by insight into principles, and acquaintance with facts. Just as the pilot or physician of superior skill "makes his art his law,"[110] so must the genuine statesman—and, by implication, every one who aspires to live the good life at its best, for that also is an art. And therefore not anarchic. With all the complexity and variability of their materials and of their specific goals, the arts could not exist but for the fact that in each situation a μέτριον, a "just adequate" adjustment of diverse variables, can be approached or achieved; and to achieve or to approach it is the artist's task. Hence, as now appears more clearly, the pertinence of such intensive and far-reaching studies as those prescribed in the *Republic*. Though they do not "teach goodness" directly, as the Sophists professed to do, they provide the basis for insight into the sort of intricate adjustments, mathematically and logically determinable, with which in one form or another good in the actual world is invariably associated.

Now it is this view which in the *Philebus* and later dialogues is elaborately worked into Plato's cosmological theory, a step perhaps already intimated in *Politicus* 234b-d. Human arts and artistry are inconceivable without standards of the sort we have been discussing, and such standards are not arbitrarily set up by whims or desires of the artist:[111] they are somehow intrinsic to the actual situation in which he is working, and in which of course his own actual nature and activity are a part. The case here, in short, is reminiscent of that already discussed, in which the scientist faces the problem of finding and following in his analyses the "natural lines

[110] *Polit.* 297e. 10-11, 297a. 2.
[111] *Polit.* 284a-b. Although his desires play their parts in determining the end sought, the conditions through fulfillment of which the desired end may be achieved are determined by other factors in the situation, involve "real difficulty," and need to be mastered by systematic inquiry. It is just for this reason that in Plato's view, real artists (*i.e.* builders, navigators, physicians, statesmen—not mere "imitators" such as rhapsodes, poets, and painters!) need to be scientists. The "standard" of which we have been talking—if the point is not already obvious—is *not* an æsthetic standard, a matter of taste: what constitutes a ship or a bridge good is not conformity to a standard of taste, but embodiment of sound engineering principles.

of cleavage" in the actual world;[112] and it is, in fact, in close conjunction with that problem that Plato now treats this one. Having noted[113] that there seem to be four essentially distinguishable kinds (γένη, εἴδη, ἰδέαι) of factors in the familiar range of human experience—"indeterminates" or variables (τὸ ἄπειρον), "limits" such as definite numerical ratios (τὸ πέρας), "compounds" of variables with limits (τὸ μεικτόν), and "causes" of such combinations (ἡ τῆς συμμείξεως αἰτία)—he makes bold to generalize this analysis, and to suggest that in the world at large these same kinds of factors are to be postulated.[114] τὸ μέτριον, as one would expect, is assigned to "the family of the limit" in the general account,[115] and there is no reason to suppose it holds any other place in the cosmological projection of that account. Indeed it alone fulfills completely the description of "the limit kind" (τὸ περατοειδές) as that which "estops opposites from discord, and by introducing number makes them symmetrical and harmonious."[116] It is with this sort of formal factor in human art, as we have seen, that excellence is associated; and it is evident from 30a. 9-c. 7, doubly reinforced by such later passages as 61b. 4-9, 64c. 5-65a. 5, that the same is taken to be true of the universe.[117] But no less evident is it that in the universe, as in a weaving room or a shipyard, the limitation of opposing variables by measure and the resultant achievement of good is the work of mind.

We are still, therefore, upon common ground with the *Phaedo*. It is still conceived that good is the goal of mind at work in the universe. But it is clearer now, after a serious start has been made upon the sort of exact inquiries which the *Republic* and *Phaedrus* had declared necessary, that the achievement of good is inseparable

[112] See above, p. 231, n. 102, and the discussion of the forms *passim*.
[113] *Phileb.* 23c sqq. The passage teems with complications and difficulties that require minute examination; cf., *e.g.* Bury: *The Philebus of Plato*, xxxix-lii, and App. A and D.
[114] 30c; and the whole passage, 28c-30d.
[115] 24c. 7; cf. 25b. 1.
[116] 25d. 11-e. 2, *et sqq.*
[117] The entire passage, 55d. 1 to the end of the dialogue (cf. above, p. 213, n. 47) bears more or less directly on the point.

from the fulfillment of conditions that involve "real difficulty,"[118] if the argument from human experience holds
good at this point. And Plato believes that it does, as
we shall see in the concluding section.

Meanwhile, this running comment on the good and its
place in Platonic cosmology may be concluded, without
too great violence to the facts, by saying that the lines of
interpretation opened up in the *Politicus* and *Philebus*
are followed without essential change in the *Timaeus* and
the *Laws*. "The maker and father of the whole," the
divine "craftsman," "God" (ὁ θεός) of the *Timaeus*,[119]
is good, and desires that "as far as possible, all things
shall be good and nothing bad."[120] To this end he
brought "all that is visible . . . out of disorder into
order," and that largely in just the way we have been
considering: through the introduction of complex and
exact quantitative ratios, to the specification of which in
great detail the dialogue is in large part devoted.
Similarly in the *Laws*, the very orderliness of movement
in the heavenly bodies is the best evidence that they are
actuated by God, who is rational and good; and the sort
of study that fits men to follow God and to lead their
fellows is study that gives much attention to mathematical and logical disciplines, by which alone insight into
the nature of the world and of man, and achievement of
the good life is made possible.[121]

Thus we proceed still in the development of the cosmological theme of *Phaedo* 97c-99c. *Good* is the end in
the light of which all things are as far as possible to be
understood, but which can itself only be recognized and
appreciated, not analytically defined. *Order,* largely
geometrical and numerical, is the formal condition basic
to the realization of good, both on the small scale and on
the large; and this does lend itself, by its very nature, to
exact and comprehensive measurement and analysis,
through mathematical and logical inquiry. *Mind,* finally,

[118] *Polit.* 284a. 9.
[119] 28c. 2, a. 6, 30a. 2, etc.
[120] 30a. 2-3; cf. *Repub.* 379b-380c.
[121] *Laws* 897b sqq., 966e-967e, 818a-822d, 715e-716d, etc.

is the agent by whose activity order is comprehended, and discovered or effected among the variables that are the apprehensible but not ultimately intelligible stuff of actuality, the good being thereby progressively achieved.

We are dealing, in short, from beginning to end, with a teleological theory which, whatever its degree of validity, is at least straightforward and coherent. If there be an important emendation in the later statements, it is I think a growing emphasis of the *alogical* factors without reference to which the actual world cannot readily be described. But this recognition of aspects of reality that are opaque to logic is far from making Plato a misologist, either skeptical or pietistic. Rather, the intricacy and penetration of his own analyses, and his stress upon the need for a ceaseless pushing forward of exact inquiry, are most marked precisely in these later dialogues. On the other hand, if it be true that his lectures "On the Good" were full of bewildering mathematical discussion,[122] the most natural supposition is not that he lost himself at length in number-mysticism and defined the good itself as number,[123] but that in the manner of the dialogues from the *Republic* onward, he continued to urge, it may well be with a zeal incomprehensible to less strenuous or less mathematical minds, the need of insight into quantitative order as a formal basis or vehicle of good, which itself remains ultimate and undefined.

III. As Theist: The Theory of Mind, Souls, and God

The foregoing section has laid heavy stress on the basic importance of νοῦς, mind or intelligence, in Plato's cosmology. What remains to be said can be developed directly and briefly from that point, giving proof, on the one hand, that Plato himself conceived the place of mind so, and on the other hand indicating the manner in which he elaborated this belief into a critical theism. We

[122] As Aristoxenus reports, *Harm.* 30. 16-31. 3, on the authority of Aristotle.
[123] Though Aristotle comes very close to saying just that, *Met.* 1091b. 13-15; cf. 988a. 14.

ascribed to him at the outset, as a religious conviction, confidence in the goodness and the sovereignty of a living God. To the philosophical versions of this conviction as he worked them out we now finally turn.

A central passage and the most convenient from which to start is *Philebus* 28c. 1-31a. 10, concerned overtly with the question to which of the four classes of entities just enumerated νοῦς belongs. The answer is clear: "that νοῦς is 'head of the family' of the said cause of everything,"[124] an efficient cause, not the only sort, indeed, as we shall see, but the most important sort. For intelligence is "king of heaven and earth," "ordering and arranging years and seasons and months," as "all the wise agree—magnifying, indeed, themselves."[125]

By way of reasons for this belief, one suggestion is offered in the passage we are considering, and others are developed elsewhere. But before turning to these, we must notice another essential point: that intelligence is inseparable from soul (ψυχή), being inseparable from life (ζωή), of which soul is the ground.[126] Here once more, as in the cases of εἶδος and νοῦς, we touch upon a concept that figures indispensably in every stage of Plato's developing thought. It had been constantly in the mind and often on the lips of Socrates,[127] inasmuch as he had considered the proper training and care of the soul (comparable with the training and care of the body) to be

---

[124] 30d. 10-e. 1—reading, with T and the scholiasts, νοῦς ἐστὶ γενούστης τοῦ πάντων αἰτίου λεχθέντος, taking γενούστης in the sense of γεννήτης (not as "progenitor" but as "chief member," "head of the house"), and regarding it with Stallbaum and Apelt as a *facetia;* cf. Bury's note *ad loc.* It seems to me that 31a. 1-3 and 30c. 5-7 clearly require a reading that definitely classifies νοῦς as cause, not merely as "closely related to the *genus* Cause" (Bury, xli), which would leave it not definitely classified at all. Bury, I think, makes too much of σχεδόν in 31a. 8 (see also lxxii), but he himself elsewhere (xliv sq.) treats Reason without qualification as "the efficient, or shaping and ordering, cause of the world as an intelligible Cosmos."

[125] 28c. 6-8, 30c. 5-6—the glint of irony again keeping in true perspective, without obscuring or retracting, a bold speculative affirmation; cf. above, p. 233 and n. 106.

[126] 30c. 9-10; *Soph.* 249a. 4-7; cf. *Phaedo* 105 c-d.

[127] *Apol.* 30a. 5-b. 2; cf. 40c-41c, *Lach.* 185e, 190b, *Charm.* 160a-b, 175d-e, *Protag.* 313a-314b, *Crito* 47c-48a (though the word ψυχή is here avoided), *Lysis* 218b, 220c, 222a, etc.

man's chief concern. It appears in mythical and imaginative passages in such borderland dialogues as the *Gorgias, Meno,* and *Cratylus,*[128] which foreshadow more detailed and systematic development later. And when in due course, in the *Phaedo,* the provisional outlines of a full-length metaphysic first appear, it is in a dialogue which Plato himself refers to later as "the discourse on the soul."[129] In it for the first time soul is dealt with as a metaphysical, not merely a religious, moral, or mythical concept. The arguments assigned to Socrates are acutely criticized by two former associates of the Pythagorean teacher Philolaus, and a number of results emerge which, though they are stated here as in varying degrees falling short of certainty,[130] are for the most part maintained and used by Plato in later discussions. Thus, the soul is held to be a substantial entity, capable of influencing bodily behavior, and not an epiphenomenon;[131] having life as an intrinsic and ineradicable character, and for that reason immortal and imperishable;[132] able to live independently of the body, both before birth and after death; and able, whether with or without the body, to apprehend the intelligible forms or essences, with which when wise it shows itself closely kin.[133] To these notes of the soul we must add one more, already implied in the foregoing account, but in the *Phaedrus* and the *Laws* made explicit and declared to be *par excellence* "the essence and definition of the soul": soul is self-mov-

[128] *Gorg.* 523a-524e *et sqq., Meno* 81a-e, *Crat.* 399d-400b, etc. In these passages, Orphic-Pythagorean influence seems plain. Whether or not we are still dealing with views held by Socrates is another question. I incline, with Taylor and others, to think we are. Rohde says no: *Psyche* I. 310 sq., II. 263 sqq.; but his view as a whole involves, *inter alia,* a conception of the *Republic* which as Ritter shows (*Platon* II. 487n., I. 273-8) is pretty certainly untenable, and his whole case is weakened thereby.

[129] *Ep.* xiii. 363a. 7—not quite, as Prof. Taylor has it (*Plato* 177), "the discourse of Socrates about the soul." How much here is Socrates and how much Plato is still far from clear.

[130] *Phaedo* 107a. 8-b. 9 may serve, since it closes the inquiry, to indicate the critical temper of the whole.

[131] 85e-86d, 91c-95a. I borrow Prof. Taylor's apt reference to the familiar theory of Huxley, *Plato* 194, 196 sqq.

[132] 105c-106e, together with the whole passage 100b sqq.

[133] 72e-80a, etc.

ing, and the source (ἀρχή, πηγή) of all motion or change.[134]

We are ready now to examine Plato's reasons for believing that νοῦς ἔμψυχος—intelligent soul or living mind —is sovereign in the universe. Three will serve as typical. (1) The presumption of continuity, both structural and functional, between man and his environment.[135] At the physical level this continuity is evident. On the one hand, the physical constituents of living bodies are derived from and sustained by great stores of such constituents in the universe; on the other, bodies as unified structures derive from and are sustained by the physical world which is itself a unified structure, a body. Since living bodies, moreover, have souls which also, presumably, are derivative, it seems necessary to suppose that the physical cosmos, greater and finer than our bodies in other respects, has soul also, whence ours are derived. When, further, examining not merely the composition of the human animal, but also the ways in which it functions, we recognize that the productive "cause" that effects our animation, coördinated behavior, recuperation, and in general the complex organization and correction of our living, "acts with all manner of wisdom,"[136] it must seem to us unreasonable to deny that the far more impressive order of the cosmos is effected by such a cause also, "quite rightly called wisdom and mind." And finally, since "wisdom and mind would never occur in isolation from soul," the inference is that gods as well

[134] *Phaedr.* 245c. 5-246a. 2 (a curiously concise bit of argument in the midst of exuberant rhetoric); *Laws* 894b-896b. Since our interest here is somewhat narrowly metaphysical, we omit reference to the numerous psychological passages which fill out the concept of soul with concrete detail; for which see Ritter: *Platon* II. 428-496. That the self-moving mover of *Laws* 896a, etc., is no attenuated abstraction but the concrete psyche of psychology is proved by 896e-897b.

[135] *Phileb.* 29a-30c.

[136] 30a. 9-b. 7—taking ἐπικαλεῖσθαι as mid., not pass.: "calls upon" (for help), "calls into play"—in which I venture to differ, perhaps mistakenly, from the commentators consulted. The whole passage is difficult, but the main point—the attribution of wisdom or intelligence to the "cause," *or* the identification of the "cause" with wisdom—seems clear, in view of the speeches next following.

as men are living minds, minds ensouled—King Zeus himself, and others with their respective attributes—"through the power of the cause." Thus we agree with "those who long since declared that mind is ground of the whole." [137]

But is this supreme νοῦς itself really ensouled? Is it *living* mind, or merely rational order, form, law—perhaps the "Idea of the Good"? Equivocal phrases—equivocal for us, if not for Plato's first readers—in *Philebus* 30d. 2-3, b. 4, and c. 6 leave the latter interpretation not impossible, though I think the former is intended. The argument next examined puts the answer beyond doubt.

(2) The impossibility of conceiving true being or reality (οὐσία, τὰ ὄντα) without reference to power, life, and mind.[138] Against over-zealous materialists and transcendentalists alike, a tenable notion of οὐσία must be defended. The former, "naïvely laying hold of rocks and oaks"—like Dr. Johnson's great stone—"insist that only the tangible is real, defining οὐσία as identical with body." The latter, in reaction against these stubborn folk, "contend that true οὐσία is certain intelligible and incorporeal forms," wholly immutable, inactive and impassible, sharply separated from body, which is mere "becoming."[139] Now the very assertiveness of both parties opens the way to their confutation. Each party claims correctness for its own view, while in the same breath "eliminating science, or thinking, or mind," one by excluding from the scope of reality what is incorporeal, the other by excluding "motion and the moved"; not realizing that in either case any valid assertion, including its own, would be impossible. Both clearly are wrong. It must be held, against the former, that there are incorporeal realities, or factors in reality, to wit, forms (not to

---

[137] 30d. 8: ὡς ἀεὶ τοῦ παντὸς νοῦς ἄρχει = *Phaedo* 97c. 1-2: ὡς ἄρα νοῦς ἐστιν ὁ διακοσμῶν τε καὶ πάντων αἴτιος—the Anaxagorean-(Socratic?)-Platonic hypothesis so often referred to, which only Plato seriously tries to establish.

[138] *Soph.* 246a-249e; cf. for the use of δύναμις, *Phaedr.* 270d.

[139] Cf. above, p. 227, n. 92.

speak of souls), the presence or absence of which makes significant differential judgments possible; against the latter that inasmuch as reality itself is known, it is acted upon and so far "is moved," and cannot therefore be described, in any case, as consisting of inactive, impassible forms. But that which thus "moves" the reality known is mind, certainly then not less real than that which is known by it; and mind is inseparable from life, from soul, from motion, though it requires stability too, as we have seen. Indeed, both stability and change, bodies and forms, souls and minds—all come within the scope of reality, which may best be defined in terms of *power*: "I suggest, then, that whatever has power either to affect any other thing whatsoever, or to be affected in the slightest degree by the most trivial cause, even if only a single time, genuinely *is*. For I believe that the criterion of the real is nothing other than just power." And of this the strategic center, as the argument shows, is living mind.

(3) The marks of intelligent craftsmanship and control in the world as we find it.[140] What is familiarly known as "the argument from design," which even Kant found impressive though not conclusive, is Plato's by right of discovery and settlement, though accumulating knowledge about the world has expanded and altered it greatly—as he would have desired.[141] The notion of a divine Designer-Creator recurs again and again in the dialogues from the *Republic* onward,[142] and evidence bearing upon it is interspersed in many parts of the discussions. But the compact argument in *Laws* X is fairly representative. Soul, being alone self-moving, is the ultimate source of all movement, *i.e.* of all change: it is coextensive, in other words, with the class of the efficient cause.[143] But souls may be either rational or irrational,

---

[140] *E.g. Laws* 894b-898c. I know no more clean-cut and lucid exposition of this passage than Prof. Taylor's, *Plato* 490-493.

[141] *Laws* 769a-770a, 821a.

[142] *E.g. Repub.* 596a-597e, echoed in *Soph.* 265a sqq.; *Polit.* 260a, 273a sqq., and the whole myth; the passages in *Phileb.* already examined; *Tim.* 28a sqq., 30a sqq., etc.; *Laws* 715e sqq., etc.

[143] Cf. above, p. 217, n. 60, p. 242, n. 134, and p. 240, n. 124.

in varying degrees. Which sort of soul, then, is the
source of change in the actual world? Souls of
both sorts, since there are both regular and irregular
changes. But the most impressive instance of observable motion, the most extensive and inclusive, is precisely the most regular of all: the movement of the stars,
which is the nearest physical counterpart to the
movement of mind—though the latter cannot be
directly observed by "mortal eyes" nor adequately comprehended by human wit. The heavens, then, declare
the sovereignty of Living Mind, νοῦς ἔμψυχος; "the best
soul," *i.e.* the most rational, is indicated as the chief of
all efficient causes; "astronomy and the other exact
sciences" which, when but faultily understood, "gave rise
to much irreligion and confusion," now are opening the
way to a far sounder, because a more rational, religious
outlook.[144] For if Living Mind at its best be really
dominant in the universe, then the hope of the *Phaedo*
and the exultant proclamation of the *Republic,* that good
is the supreme end of all, are not without rational foundation.

One obvious difficulty stands in the way of such optimism: the actual prevalence of evil. Plato faced this problem fairly enough, though his answer was never concisely
formulated. His first step in dealing with it is to disso-
ciate the causes of evil, whatever they be, from God, who
is good. This is the first of his "articles of belief," as we
have seen.[145] The nature of these other causes comes out
in the later dialogues. They are, roughly, of two sorts:
refractoriness of working conditions (συναίτια), and irra-
tionality of agents (αἰτίαι), which always are souls. (1)
On the one hand, there is the sort of obstacle found by
every artist in the conditions of his task. Neither the
unformed material nor the μέτριον is bad—both are indispensable; but the task of embodying the μέτριον in the
material to effect that symmetry of harmonious propor-

---

[144] *Laws* 966e. 4-968a. 1.
[145] *Repub.* 379a-380c; cf. above, p. 219.

tion that issues in good, involves being always on guard
against "excess and defect from the norm, not as an
imaginary but as a real difficulty in the work."[146] If the
effort fails, and the result falls short of its proper and
intended excellence, *that*—the faulty result—is evil, so
far as it is at fault, though good in the degree that it does
realize the desired end. Evil and good are both teleological concepts, applicable not to beginnings as such,
but to ends and to stages in their realization. There is
no ultimate impersonal factor (such as "matter" or
"chance") which is either evil or the root of all evil. Yet
it is true that one factor contributory to evil is to be
sought in the very neutrality of such impersonal constituent factors as do appear in things: to wit, "the indefinite" or variable, and "limit." The distinctive character
of "the indefinite" is just "indeterminacy" (ἀπειρία);
that of "the limit" is just "limitativeness" (πέρας)—the
limiting definiteness of an exact quantity, an exact ratio,
or the like. Both are indispensable "instrumental conditions" (συναίτια) for getting productive work done; but
neither gives the slightest active help or guidance to the
doing of such work. There is obviously no guidance in
the indefinitely variable; while an exact quantity or ratio
may be exactly wrong for the purpose in hand. Each
exact quantity or ratio excludes all others from that part
of the situation in which it obtains; and yet among all the
possible adjustments, each thus excluding all the others,
the one "right adjustment"[147] must be achieved or
closely approached, else evil will be the outcome. One
source of evil, then, is, so to say, the difficulty of finding
the right way of combining factors which are themselves
intrinsically neutral and noncoöperant. Only intelligence
can deal hopefully with such a problem.

(2) But some souls that try to deal with it are unintelligent. And these are the true "causes" (αἰτίαι) of evil.
The "difficulty" intrinsic in the conditions for productive

---

[146] *Polit.* 284a. 8-10; cf. above, pp. 236, 238.
[147] *Phileb.* 25e; cf. *Polit.* 283e, etc.

work makes evil possible; the blundering of more or less
unintelligent souls makes it actual.[148]

For neither the original difficulty nor the blundering is
God responsible. As to the latter, the general plan and
government of the world is his, but "the formation of
individual character he has left to our individual wills.
For according to his desires and the nature of his soul,
each of us, nearly always and for the most part, comes to
be what he is."[149] As to the former, God himself has not
been wholly free from the limitations involved in productive work as such; so that the world is not, even basically,
perfect, but "as like himself as possible."[150] So long, on
the one hand, as unresolved indeterminacy is a factor in
all actual situations, actuality is not wholly amenable
even to divine intelligence;[151] and that such indeterminacy is taken to be ineradicable, so long at least as
creative work is in question, seems indicated by the alternative epithets "necessity" (ἀνάγκη) and "random
cause" (πλανωμένη αἰτία) by which Timaeus apparently
refers to it. Likewise in the intricate inflexibilities of
quantity and ratio, there is another ἀνάγκη with which
even God must contend.[152] He has made and is making
the world as good as a genesic world like this can be, but
it lacks much of being perfect.

Still, the dominance of intelligence and the ascendancy
of good are not therefore to be despaired of. On the one
hand, the world is so far ordered that irrational living
punishes itself, and leads to its own correction, or subordination.[153] On the other, though it be true that chance
also figures in the course of the world's affairs, it does
not follow that science is nullified. Not chance alone, but
"God, and with God chance and contingency, govern

[148] *Laws* 896d-e, etc.
[149] *Laws* 904b. 8-c. 4. I translate freely, trying to make the sense clear
without the context.
[150] *Tim.* 29e. 2; cf. 30a. 1-2, and Taylor's note *ad loc.*
[151] Cf. above, p. 215, and notes 55 and 47.
[152] *Tim.* 47e. 3-48a, 7, etc. (see Taylor's note on 47e. 4-5); *Laws*
818a-b.
[153] *Laws* 903e-905c; cf. 715e sqq.

human affairs as a whole. It is surely reasonable to concede thirdly that scientific skill (τέχνη, applied science) should go with these; as, in the contingency of stormy weather, I for one should conceive it a great advantage to understand navigation."[154]

No thinker of Plato's dimensions can be presented fairly in a sketch of post-card size, even if the knowledge and skill of the expositor were far greater than mine. The only way to judge whether he speaks as a realist to realistic minds is to read what he had to say: to read it if possible in his own words, and if not, then in the sharpest translations available. Like many another old master, he has suffered from protective coats of varnish, and his colors are dimmed and glozed. But the colors are there, laid on with a bold and subtle hand, in a gallery of canvases full of verve and sensitiveness and humor and toil and vision, and the fierce loyalties and honest questionings of healthy living.

APPENDED NOTE
(See above, p. 199.)

The grounds for the general viewpoint assumed in this paper can be indicated simply enough, though proving their soundness requires intricate argument. (1) The most influential critics of the last century, preëminently Zeller, regarded the great dramatic dialogues—*Symposium, Phaedo, Republic*—as presenting the definitive statement of Plato's philosophy, with the "theory of Ideas" as central. The critical or "dialectical dialogues" —*Parmenides, Theaetetus, Sophist,* and *Statesman*— were taken to be mere preliminary inquiries leading up to the dramatic and eloquent statements of the theory in the *Phaedo* and in the *Republic,* V-VII. A more attentive study of these dialectical dialogues has shown, however, that for various reasons it seems necessary to regard

[154] *Laws* 709b. 7-c. 3.

them as later, not earlier, than the more dramatic dialogues, and as of capital importance for the right understanding of Plato.[155] For once it is recognized that the acute examinations of the theory of Ideas and immediately related problems, in the *Parmenides, Theaetetus, Sophist,* and *Politicus,* together with the fresh analysis of reality in the *Philebus,* are subsequent, not preliminary, to the dramatic statements of the theory, it is plain that the dramatic statements are not in fact the definitive presentation of his thought. Moreover, in the light of the later analyses, these earlier passages themselves appear to require a different interpretation from that frequently put upon them. For whether the dialogues together reflect a relatively coherent though developing philosophy, or two incompatible theories, an earlier and a later, or even divergent theories of two different men,[156] it is clearly necessary to give precedence, in seeking to understand

[155] Stylistic and other tests connect them with the latest dialogues, the *Timaeus* and *Laws.* The argument is summarized clearly and with restraint by Ritter: *Platon* I. 199-280, and by Raeder: *Platons phil. Entwicklung,* 1-88; and in very simple terms by Field: *Plato and his Contemporaries,* 64-76. The groundwork of the main position, *i.e.* the dating of the dialectical dialogues after the *Phaedo* and *Republic* instead of before, was laid in Campbell's *The Sophistes and Politicus of Plato* in 1867; but it has gained general recognition chiefly within the present century, since the publication of Lutoslawski's *The Origin and Growth of Plato's Logic* in 1897.

[156] Ritter, for example, without asserting a finished and unchanging Platonic *Weltanschauung,* maintains that a pervasive consistency in viewpoint is discernible through both earlier and later dialogues. There is development and qualification, but not abandonment of one position for another. H. Jackson, on the contrary, urges ("Plato's Later Theory of Ideas," in *Jour. of Philology,* X-XV, 1882-86) that the theory in the *Phaedo* and *Republic* undergoes a change so drastic as to amount to its virtual abrogation in the later dialogues; and Lutoslawski similarly presses what he takes to be numerous irreconcilable differences between earlier and later stages in Plato's thought. Finally, Burnet (commentary on the *Phaedo, Greek Phil.: Part I,* and *Platonism*) and, more circumspectly, Taylor (*Varia Socratica, Plato: the Man and his Work,* etc.) hold that the "theory of Ideas" put forth in the dialogues up to and including the *Republic* was not properly Plato's theory at all but that of Socrates, from which Plato's own view, adumbrated in certain of the later dialogues and referred to repeatedly by Aristotle, differs more or less sharply.

In general, it is a version of the first of these views that I prefer, though without anything like final certitude; but whatever the reader's judgment as to this particular point, the interpretative principle stated in the text is not substantially affected.

Plato's own maturest thought, to the later and more literal rather than to the earlier and more figurative discussions. Only a rejection of the later dialogues as not genuinely his—a desperate measure no longer in scholarly
repute—or a proof, now seemingly impossible, that
though genuine, they represent either immature or senile
and therefore relatively unimportant views, would
materially alter the case.

(2) A second ground for the position here taken has
been furnished by closer examination of the direct testimony of Aristotle to what Plato taught in the Academy.
It is generally agreed that the Platonic dialogues, like
the similar compositions of other philosophers,[157] were
intended, in many instances, for circulation among
readers with a layman's interest in philosophy; in some
instances, presumably, for perusal by members of his
own and of other philosophical schools;[158] but not primarily, if at all, for the instruction of Plato's students.
To this latter end discussions and lectures in the Academy were devoted; and in these lectures, judging from
Aristotle's testimony,[159] Plato taught some doctrines
which are not precisely identifiable in any of the dialogues, but which are most closely approximated in those
now recognized as late. It is likely, on more than one
score, that some, at least, of these teachings Plato himself never committed to writing, certainly not for publication.[160] The glimpses of this "unwritten doctrine,"
worked out through the living processes of inquiry and
instruction in the Academy, which we get from Aristotle
and the commentators show plainly that it was dominated

---

[157] For numerous examples, see Grote: *Plato* I. 111-112.
[158] Ritter: *Platon* I. 270-271 and note; cf. Field: *Plato,* etc., 60.
[159] See above, pp. 224 sq.
[160] Aristotle refers to them as ἄγραφα δόγματα (*e.g. Phys.* 209b. 15);
and Plato declares, *Ep.* vii. 341c-d, that one cannot learn philosophy
from books, and is represented as declaring further, *Ep.* ii. 314c, that
as to the central issues in philosophy, he himself has "never written of
these matters, and there neither is nor will be a writing of Plato's"; cf.
comments in Burnet: *Greek Phil.:* Part I, 220-222; Taylor: *Plato* 23 and
note.

by logical and mathematical interests.[161] Many of its details—how many we cannot tell—are lost, presumably beyond recovery, but the necessity for redressing the balance of emphasis in our interpretation of Plato is abundantly clear.

[161] See L. Robin: *La théorie platonicienne des idées et des nombres après Aristote* (1908), 254 sqq. I have tried to indicate above, p. 239, how I think this emphasis of mathematics is to be interpreted.

IX

CAN RELIGIOUS INTUITION GIVE KNOWLEDGE OF REALITY?

By
EUGENE WILLIAM LYMAN

Professor of the Philosophy of Religion
Union Theological Seminary

CAN RELIGIOUS INTUITION GIVE KNOWLEDGE
OF REALITY?[1]

It may facilitate the discussion of our theme if I begin
by indicating what is the present situation of thought,
as I understand it, in respect to the cognitive aspects of
religion. Aside from the authority view, which does not
admit the right of philosophizing at all except as it undertakes to guarantee established authority, there are, I
think, four fairly definite views of the matter which prevail in the field of religious thought.

First, there is the view of the idealistic philosophy.
This view regards knowledge in the religious field as
something wholly derivable from the nature of knowledge
in general. Study the nature of the knowing process as
such, this view says, and you will find God. You may even
find the laws governing the development of all religious
experience, as Hegel thought. Or you may find the essentials of the Christian way of salvation, as Royce taught
when he derived the doctrine of the Beloved Community
from the triadic process of perceiving, conceiving, and
interpreting, of which he found knowledge to consist.
This view, then, does not find in religious experience a
really independent source of knowledge, which we can
ignore only at the risk of being left with a world-view
that is needlessly curtailed and confused. But on the other
hand, it claims to buttress religious certainty with a far
stronger certainty from the non-religious realm.

Secondly, there is the view of the postulate philosophy.
It might, of course, be called the Ritschlian view, except
that Ritschl himself is not its most characteristic embodiment. We have to look for it, rather, among those Ritschlians who sought to rectify Ritschl's teaching by purging

[1] Reprinted from *The Journal of Religion*, Vol. IV, No. 2, March, 1924,
by permission of the University of Chicago Press.

it of its Lotzean elements and making it consistently Kantian. But we find it also outside the definitely Ritschlian group, for example, in the symbolo-fideism of Auguste Sabatier and Ménégoz, and in the *Religionsphilosophie* of the Dutch philosopher, Rauwenhoff. This view rests upon the doctrine of phenomenalism. Knowledge in the full sense of the term is limited to phenomena and has nothing really ontological about it. Neither in the realm of physical nature nor in the realm of mind can we know reality as such. Still, behind the screen of our phenomenal knowledge the ontological realm remains, and about this realm our moral and religious nature is free to make postulates. If these postulates are regulated by the moral categories, they acquire a rational standing as things that we have a right to believe. Thus, in the view of the postulate philosophy, our moral and religious experience together have an independent status alongside the system of organized knowledge, which ought to be recognized by all who are trying to form a worldview. But this independent status for moral and religious experience is acquired at the price of its being excluded from the realm of genuine knowledge.

In one important respect, however, this view of religious experience claims for it a superior status in regard to knowledge. Religious experience can be the source of value-judgments which make possible a more adequate understanding of the nature and meaning of man's inner life than a strictly scientific, psychological account of that inner life could be—more adequate, that is, from the standpoint of solving man's actual spiritual problems. But after all, these value-judgments, according to this philosophy, cannot transcend the phenomenal realm and give access to the ontological, except by the method of postulation already indicated.

Thirdly, there is the view of the immanence theology. This view has never admitted that the ontological realm was incapable of being genuinely known, as has the postulate philosophy. And at the same time it has not relied, for the knowing of that realm, primarily on the epistemological arguments of idealism. Its main procedure has been, under the pressure of advancing scientific knowledge, to transmute the idea of a Divine First Cause into that of a Divine World-Ground. Scientific knowledge, it holds, studies processes as exactly as possible, but the knowing to which this study leads is inherently a relative matter, and always leaves open the question as to the absolute Ground of the relations. Now, according to the immanence theology, the character of this absolute Ground is known in religious experience. A presupposition is involved here, the establishing of which is left to philosophy—the presupposition, namely, that the absolute Ground must be of the nature of spirit. Even so, however, the way in which religious experience has availed to give knowledge of this absolute Ground has been left vague and undefined. The strength of the position seems largely to have been derived from showing the unsatisfactoriness of agnosticism. If the view that the absolute Ground is unknowable is unsatisfactory and even contradictory, then the religious consciousness has seemed to fall into line as a grasping in experience of that which philosophy has already vindicated in the abstract —the reality of the absolute Ground.

Finally, there is the view of naturalistic humanism. This view recognizes the immense importance of religion in human life and seeks to interpret it so that it will have a large positive and permanent value. But since this view gets its cosmology by adding together the various physical sciences, and then adding on the human sciences, and finds no inevitable speculative problems involved in these various addings, it sets aside altogether the notion that the ideas and experiences of religion may possibly contribute to our knowledge of the universe or the deeper nature of reality. Accordingly, what the ideas and experiences of religion enable us to know are psychological and social processes and values. The naturalistic humanist must admit, to be sure, that the ideas and experiences of religion have almost universally intended to tell us something about reality and the cosmos, but from this rôle they now have been completely displaced by the physical and human sciences. Hence those who have the interests of religion at heart will seek to confine the meaning of its ideas and experiences wholly to the field of psychological and social processes and values. To avoid a too violent break, this view permits the retention of the old terms, which had the interpretation of reality and the cosmos as a part of their meaning, but it requires that they be regarded purely as symbols, which denote human processes and ideals exclusively.

Broadly speaking, then, these four views as to the cognitive side of religion may be said to hold the field to-day, and the recognition of them serves to define, in a comprehensive way, the scope of our problem. Now, the conception of the matter which I wish to present involves the hypothesis that the views which make religious experience an important and irreplaceable way of apprehending the deeper nature of things and of man's relation to them—namely, the second and third—are nearer to the truth than the other two. Into the inherent limitations of those other two views we have no time to enter. To do so with regard to the idealistic argument from the nature of knowledge would be largely threshing over old straw. To do so with regard to the view of naturalistic humanism is one of the most important tasks of the philosophy of religion to-day. But keeping to the hypothesis that the views which appeal to religious experience as an independent way of apprehending reality are more adequate than the other, what I wish first to urge is that, without reconstruction, these views are seriously handicapped for their task.

The difficulty is that both the view of the postulate philosophy and that of the immanence theology are based mainly on phenomenalism and derive their strength from transcending agnosticism. But phenomenalism and agnosticism seem to be pretty nearly extinct among philosophic thinkers at the present time—at least in England and America. No doubt with many special scientists to-day agnosticism is still a favorite attitude with respect to things theological or metaphysical. But our philosophers are all gnostics rather than agnostics. That is, they all hold that, at least with respect to important sections of reality, we can know things as they are. Idealists, monistic or personal; realists, new, naïve, or critical; pragmatists, supernaturalistic or naturalistic; naturalists, mechanistic or panpsychic; evolutionists, mechanistic or creative—all are ontological rather than phenomenological in their teachings.

The result for the postulate philosophy is that there is no marked-off realm into which postulates on the basis of morals and religion can be projected. The maker of postulates on the moral and religious basis has now to recognize that his postulates need to be about realities otherwise known. Hence he needs to consider what connection there may be between what he postulates with respect to these realities and what is known about them in non-religious ways. Or if, as a pluralist, he simply postulates additional realities, he must admit that his postulates are gratuitous, from any other point of view than his own. But such was not the case when the validity of phenomenalism was widely accepted.

The result for the immanence theology is that, with respect to its central doctrine of an absolute Ground underlying the relative processes known by science, there are many competing interpretations, and not simply one or two rivals of the religious view, such as agnosticism and materialism. Especially in view of the revival of pluralism, the immanence theology cannot so readily assume that there is a single world-Ground, which is either unknowable or else is knowable as a spiritual reality. There is need, then, from the standpoint of the immanence theology, of some more definite understanding of the contribution that religious experience is able to make toward interpreting the underlying and unifying aspects of the world.

And now, after this too long résumé of the present situation with respect to our problem, I can state the central thesis, as I conceive it, for this discussion. It is that *religious experience affords us intuitions of truth and of reality, which are important and irreplaceable contributions to the philosophic interpretation of reality and life as a whole.* In other words, religious experience does not result in postulates projected into the universe because we cannot know it, but it yields intuitions by the aid of which the universe may be genuinely known. And again, when we seek to know the underlying grounds of certain natural processes, religion may be of great value, because a part of its essential functions is the grasping of such underlying grounds in intuition.

1

The testing of any such thesis must be based first of all upon the facts. How far is intuition actually present in the experience of religion? And if present to any important degree, what kind of place does it occupy?

There are two aspects of religious experience in its fully developed forms which are pretty generally recognized as fundamental, namely, salvation and inspiration. This means that, if religious experience is vital at all, it is recuperating, healing, reconciling, unifying, liberating in its effect upon the person who has it; and it means also that such experience is kindling and elevating, bringing enthusiasm in the pursuit of the good, heightening and sustaining moral energy.

But there is a third aspect of religious experience which has no such uniformly recognized status as salvation and inspiration, but which may perchance be equally fundamental. This third aspect is illumination. This aspect, it is true, gains universal recognition so far as the prophets and founders of religion are concerned. Illumination from the divine side and vision from the human side are, as all doubtless would agree, parts of the prophet's experience as he himself understands it. And it may be generally admitted also that, in the case of men of genius like the prophets, this element of experience is somehow normal and inevitable. But aside from such outstanding exceptions, theology has been inclined to limit the phenomenon of illumination to the cult of mysticism. In other words it has not seen in illumination a generic, or even a widespread, trait of religious experience.

Now, the experience of illumination, which is felt to have its source in God, has as its counterpart the human attitude of intuition or vision, just as the counterpart of salvation is trust or surrender, and that of inspiration is fidelity. A certain place, then, among the phenomena of religious experience, intuition, as the counterpart of illumination, admittedly has. But is its place so exceptional that in the case of most religious persons the other two phases of religious experience, salvation and moral energizing, come to pass without it?

Let us consider for a moment the relation of the prophet to the movements that flow from him. The prophet himself, obviously, is not the philosopher or theologian. He is neither elaborating a tradition, nor speculating, nor building a system. His great, far-reaching convictions of truth can hardly have been gained in another than intuitive way. But what of his disciples and followers? Do they take their truth from him entirely at second hand, or have they gained from him some capacity for fresh intuition of truth? In the Christian movement the latter seems emphatically to have been the case. The Spirit was in the early Christians, not only giving joyous assurance of salvation and new moral energy but also as a power of discernment. The Spirit not only bore witness to the truth, but it was felt to be, especially under the interpretation of Paul, a source of free and independent apprehension of truth. This means that fresh intuition of the realities of religion was a vital part of the early Christian experience. And this is precisely the result that the work of Jesus was adapted to produce. He appealed to nothing else but direct insight, and he made no provision for substituting any other kind of appeal later.

Now, what is true of the early Christian movement is true, I believe, of the influence of the Old Testament prophets. One of the greatest achievements of Old Testament criticism is the discovery of how late the spirit of prophecy survived in Judaism. In diverse forms and in the face of adverse political and social conditions, the prophetic capacity for the intuitive apprehension of truth was kept alive till the Prophet of Nazareth came. If this be not so, that which is most essential to a historical understanding of the Prophet of Nazareth is lacking.

But broadly speaking, the like is true of all the movements that have sprung from the prophetic leaders in all religions. This is proved by the fact that all these movements tend to get out of hand, through their very excess of independent intuition and creative energy, and that it is only after such a period that tradition and authority begin to assert themselves strongly. For, undoubtedly, the element of independent intuition in religion has its dangers as well as its value. And the measure of any great religion may well be found in the kind of balance which it strikes between the claims of its characteristic tradition and its capacities for fresh insight. The Gospel of John, for example, is an impressive instance of the wise balance of these two factors which Christianity was early able to make, though not able steadily to preserve. There is, then, sufficient reason for recognizing intuition as a prevailing characteristic of all great religions during their early periods of rapid growth.

But after theologies have developed and ecclesiastical authorities have established themselves, these elements of illumination and intuition tend to become obscured, so that it is possible to regard them as not being abiding characteristics of religious experience. However, do the theologies and the institutions of religion effectually displace intuition and illumination? And when they apparently do so, do not the capacities of religion to bring salvation and moral inspiration decline? And further, in proportion as intuition and illumination become suppressed, do not they tend to reassert themselves, sometimes in one-sided and extreme ways, thereby proving that they are vital constituents of religion as a whole?

The most obvious evidence that such is the case, so far as our own religion is concerned, is the part that mysticism has played in the history of Christianity. In Christianity mysticism has been a persistently recurring phenomenon. It appears, of course, in the early church in the consciousness of the Spirit as a present power in the believer, to which we already have alluded. It continues, evidently, for at least so long as the function of prophecy is recognized and valued. It reappears in the writings of Dionysius the Areopagite and their influence. We are apt to say: Here is something foreign to Christianity introduced from neo-Platonism. But we also should ask: Why are these neo-Platonic ideas welcomed —just as Carlyle asks concerning Mohammed, when it is said that his power consisted in the sword, "Where did he get the sword?"

In the medieval period, mysticism must be reckoned with scholasticism as one of the two great modes in which Christianity expressed itself. It is, moreover, a very varied phenomenon. It is embodied in pantheistic mystics like Scotus Erigena, and in orthodox mystics like Bernard of Clairvaux; in practical mystics like St. Francis and speculative mystics like Eckhart; in intellectual mystics like Aquinas and antirational mystics like Ruysbroeck.

But medieval mysticism also flows on into the Reformation and the counter-Reformation. Concerning the Reformation in this respect let me quote from Windelband:

Luther's work of liberation owed its origin and its success not least to mysticism—not indeed to that sublime, spiritualized form of viewing the world to which the genius of Master Eckhart had given expression, but to the movement of deepest piety which, as "practical mysticism," had spread from the Rhine in the "League of the Friends of God," and in the "Brothers of the Common Life." For this mysticism, the disposition, purity of heart, and the imitation of Christ were the sole content of religion; assent to dogmas, the external works of holiness, the whole worldly organization of church life, appeared to be matters of indifference and even hindrances: the believing soul demands only the freedom of its own religious life—a demand that transcends all these outer works. This was the inner source of the Reformation.[2]

But the counter-Reformation, as a part of its effort to make an effective stand against Protestantism, developed its own type of mysticism, as is seen in the quietists.

But, again, in the post-Reformation period, mysticism continues to reassert itself. We see it in the form of pietism reacting against the ultra-confessionalism of the Lutheran churches. We see it in George Fox and the Society of Friends protesting against the deadness and formalism of the religion of their time in the name of the Inner Light. We see it in such a personality as that of William Law rising up to resist rationalism and worldliness. And the influence of William Law and of Moravian pietism were powerful in producing the evangelical revival in the Wesleyan movement.

Now this persistently recurring mysticism has various aspects and interests, but in its cognitive aspect it is always an experience of intuition and illumination. However we may interpret the matter for him, the mystic himself has the consciousness of immediate apprehension of truth and reality. Thus from the phenomenological standpoint, certainly intuition and illumination are seen to be among the characteristic data of religious experience.

Nor should we prejudge the question of the worth of these experiences as knowledge by classifying mysticism in wholesale fashion as an aberration and as fatally tending to the pathological. Pathological phenomena are frequent enough in mysticism, and where we have a highly developed cult of mysticism, that is, where mystical experience is made an all-controlling end-in-itself, we doubtless have an aberration from sound and fruitful religion. But we have seen that the tendency of mysticism to become a cult develops over against an equally exaggerated emphasis upon creeds, confessions, and ec-

[2] *History of Philosophy*, p. 365.

clesiastical authority, or upon mere rationalism, or over against a too tolerant acceptance of worldly culture. It would seem, then, that, so far from being inherently pathological, mysticism represents elements in religion which cannot be permanently stifled without extinguishing religion itself. And among such elements intuition justly claims a foremost place.

We have taken the early, prophetic phases of religion and mysticism as a recurrent phenomenon in Christianity, as our chief evidence that intuition is a fundamental characteristic of religious experience. But by rights we should go farther and ask whether intuition is not present by implication in many of the more theologically developed forms of religion. This, I believe, could be shown to be true to a noteworthy degree. In such a highly integrated conception of faith as we find in Paul, for example, the intuitive element seems unmistakable. Faith with Paul is not simply, as with the author of Hebrews, "the assurance of things hoped for, the proving of things not seen." It is a living communion with Christ as an indwelling divine Spirit whereby he has the mind of Christ and gains freedom in respect to the apprehension of truth as well as in moral action.

Again with Augustine, who has always been a fountainhead for theology both with Catholicism and with Protestantism, direct vision of things divine was central. This was true, not only in his own experience, but also, by reason of his neo-Platonism and his doctrine of divine grace, in his theological interpretation of religious experience. Says Windelband: "The knowledge of the intelligible world is for Augustine also, essentially, illumination, revelation." [3] The Reformers, too, when they began to realize that they must rebuild the structure of theology, coupled with the authority of the Bible, as Auguste Sabatier showed, an appeal to experience and to the *testimonium Spiritus sancti* which, so far forth, involves a recognition of an intuitive element in religion. So likewise, modern theology begins in Schleiermacher

[3] *Op. cit.,* p. 281.

with an interpretation of the Christian faith which rests back on intuition. The "Christian consciousness" of Schleiermacher's *Glaubenslehre,* while a specialized historical form of piety, rests back on the *Anschauung und Gefühl des Universums* which his Discourses declare to be that in which piety itself consists. Still further, in the teaching of Coleridge, which so influenced theology in England and America, and in New England transcendentalism, intuition had a place of central importance.

We cannot go farther than thus to indicate some of the historical reasons for recognizing that intuition is present, explicitly or by implication, in some of the more complex and highly integrated phases of the religious life, such as faith, revelation, the religious consciousness, or knowing through the heart or in personal experience. For further reinforcement of this point we must depend on what remains to be said upon the validity of religious intuition. But in the threefold appeal that has been made —to the prophetic phases of religion, to the recurrent mysticism of Christianity, and to the elements implied in vital religious belief—sufficient reason would seem to have been furnished for recognizing intuition as a fundamental characteristic of religious experience, coördinate with salvation and moral inspiration. If this view be true, we might expect that, when intuition is suppressed, salvation would tend to become formalized and inspiration would decline to routine fidelity. And this is what the dialectic of history appears to prove. But such being the case, the fact should be borne in mind by theology no less distinctly than the corresponding fact that, when the elements of intuition and vision in religion are unregulated by reason or tradition or social interests, the well-known dangers of mysticism will result.

2

If intuition is a fundamental characteristic of religious experience in its more vital forms it presumably is valuable, but the question still remains, is it valid? That is, does it give us what it purports to give—a knowledge of

reality? Conceivably, intuition might be valuable without
being valid as knowledge. At least, the naturalistic humanist would seem bound to think so, if he recognized
intuition as being an important phenomenon in religion
at all. He might say that it was valuable for building
moral sentiment or making social adjustments, but he
could hardly find it valid as a knowing of reality. But its
value is much less ambiguous if it can be found to be
valid. This then is the interpretation that we should test
first. Does religious intuition give us what it purports
to give—a valid knowing of reality?

We began by pointing out that the postulate philosophy
and the immanence theology had the advantage, as compared with idealism and naturalistic humanism, of giving
religious experience an independent status, with a contribution of its own to offer toward the making up of
a world-view. But we also noted that they were conditioned on phenomenalism, and that phenomenalism has
lost its force as a presupposition for the interpretation
of the moral and religious life.

With respect to the postulate philosophy, however, it
must be admitted that it has had the support of at least
one preëminent philosopher who was not a phenomenalist, namely, William James. Undoubtedly James's emphasis on the will to believe, over-beliefs, and postulates
has done much to reinforce the postulate philosophy and
its influence on liberal theology. But James in his *Varieties of Religious Experience* accepted as valid the testimony of faith, prayer, and mysticism to a "More," beyond our conscious and known selves, from which saving
experiences come. And in his *Pluralistic Universe* he
stretched out cordial hands of welcome to Bergson, accepting from his philosophy precisely those elements that
are conditioned on intuition. Here then is a line of development beyond phenomenalism, which may be of service in reconstructing the postulate philosophy and the
immanence theology.

Certainly one should not seek to evaluate the principle
of intuition without making use of the interpretation of

that principle by Bergson, the philosopher who to-day gives it the largest place in his thinking. Bergson in his well-known definition says: "By intuition is meant the kind of intellectual sympathy by which one places one-self within an object in order to coincide with what is unique in it and consequently inexpressible." [4] And by intuition he holds that we get beyond symbols to absolute reals. Thus we get the actual self, real time, other selves, real individuals in the evolutionary process, the new and creative in that process, and the ultimate cosmic principle.

But Bergson's conception of intuition has already had to run the gauntlet of criticism, and of some of these criticisms we should take account at once, for they may serve, not to abolish his conception, but to correct and supplement it. The most evident of these criticisms is that Bergson's conception involves a too radical opposition between intuition and intelligence. If intelligence has been an instrument of practical utility in the struggle for existence, as Bergson says, so has intuition, and whatever handicap that may involve belongs to both. Again, if there be such a sharp opposition between intuition and intelligence, why is Bergson so insistent that intuition needs all the attainable results of intelligence to which to apply itself? And, more simply, if intuition can know real wholes, why should not analysis know real parts?

But with reference to the meaning of intuition itself, as Bergson uses the term, questions must be raised. Is intuition precisely the same thing when applied to one's own self, and to other selves, and to long lines of evolution or the cosmos as a whole? Questions like these are raised by Höffding in his critique of Bergson's idea of intuition, and he points out that Bergson does not sufficiently distinguish between the intuition which is the first result of all psychical activity and the intuition which is "the summit and conclusion of the work of thought." The first, exemplified in sensation, memory,

[4] *Introduction to Metaphysics*, p. 7.

imagination, Höffding calls "concrete intuition." [*] The second, illustrated by the comprehensive glance by which a thought-totality is grasped, he calls "synthetic intuition." Similarly W. R. Sorley, in conjunction with a criticism of Bergson, emphasizes the importance of recognizing "the immediate knowledge which we have in sense-perception and in the consciousness of our own inner life," and also the "synoptic views of reality," as he prefers to call them, by which we get wholes like one's self, or other selves, or a world-view. These synoptic views, he says, "possess the wholeness of immediate intuition." [*]

Now let us accept the positive correlation of intuition and intelligence as a needed correction of Bergson's idea of intuition, and the distinction between perceptive intuition and synthetic intuition as a needed elaboration of that idea, and see what results for our problem. Let us test the matter first in a field that is not specifically religious, though one with which religion is always vitally concerned—the field of the knowledge of selves.

I would urge, then, that intuition, perceptive and synthetic, is valid because it makes possible a genuine knowledge of personal selves as metaphysically real and opens the way to the rediscovery of the soul. If we grant the validity of the perceptive intuition, we are able to find a unique principle of unity in the phenomena of personal life. And having gained such a principle of unity in personal consciousness, we may proceed to psychological analysis without losing the distinctive character of that with which our analysis starts out. Intuition gives us the advantage in understanding the self that possession of the seed of a plant gives us in understanding the plant. It gives us a living principle that can react to environment in characteristic ways and become something beautiful and fruitful. But if, in addition, we grant the cognitive significance of the synthetic intuition, based on the intuition of perception, the way is open to understanding

[*] *Modern Philosophers*, pp. 254-58.
[*] *Moral Values and the Idea of God*, pp. 260-70.

a personality as a whole in its individual quality. Assuredly, the more that is known of psychological processes and biographical facts in a given instance, the more accurate the synthetic intuition is likely to be. But without the intuitive synthesis the concrete individual, as he is for himself and as he acts in society, can hardly be said to be really known.

But when, by the aid of intuition, the self is thus known in its unity, there is no need of regarding it any longer as a phenomenon of something unknowable or as an epiphenomenon of the brain. Rather it presents itself as something metaphysically real, and we are put upon the way to the rediscovery of the soul. It was Kant's denial that the inner sense could afford an intuition of the soul, which completed the case for phenomenalism. If not here, then nowhere could reality be known as it is in itself. But no sooner had Kant exorcized the ego as a knowable soul from his system, and swept and garnished the place which it had occupied, than five other egos returned to the place left empty. For Kant tells us of the empirical ego, bound by the chains of causation; and of the ego as the transcendental unity of apperception, which is neither cause nor effect, neither substance nor attribute, but only a logical point of reference; and of the ego as a thing-in-itself, unknowable; and of the ego as a transcendental ideal, the goal of knowledge; and of the moral ego, which posits its own freedom. This is a real bedevilment of the situation. But if you recognize the inner sense as affording intuitions of reality, you have once more a single self restored to sanity, a rational soul.

But again, the validity of intuition in its two aspects is shown by the fact that by recognizing intuition as cognitive we can solve the problem of the relation of judgments of value in religion to judgments of existence. The Ritschlian teaching that religious knowledge moved wholly in the realm of value-judgments has been illuminating and yet ambiguous. It has been illuminating because it has served to bring out the practical, functional, and ethical aspects of religion. It has been ambiguous because it has left doubtful what was meant as to the relation between value-judgments and judgments of existence. There are three different meanings of the notion value-judgment which should be kept distinct, but they have not always been so kept. First, a value-judgment may be a definition of value in the abstract; second, it may express an experience of making values real—bringing them into existence; third, it may express an experience of discovering values to be already existent. Now the value-judgment as applied by the Ritschlians to the interpretation of Christian experience involves all three of these meanings. But logically if, as so many Ritschlians have done, one confines all judgments of existence to the field of phenomena as controlled by mechanical causation, there never can be value-judgments of the second and third kind as applied to religious matters. The human soul experiencing redemption by the power of God, and being set free by him to work for the Kingdom of God, and being made a member of a community of free beings which is devoted to that same end—these great conceptions of the Ritschlian interpretation of Christian experience are all incomprehensible on the basis of a doctrine of value-judgments that is coupled with phenomenalism. For they all imply that values are efficacious in the cosmos and in human life, and can be made increasingly so. But the judgments of existence that phenomenalism can recognize do not permit values thus to be efficacious in existence.

But when we recognize intuitions, perceptive and synthetic, as cognitive then we can understand the value-experience as a discovery of reality, or a making of reality, or both. A religious experience that is intuitively apprehended as both objective in source and good in quality can be accepted as having a prima facie claim to acceptance in both aspects equally, that is, both as good, and as coming from an objective source which makes for good. But if at the same time this perceptive intuition becomes the clue for a synthetic intuition of a comprehensive process or for one yielding a world-view, then both the objectivity and the moral worth of the religious experience are strengthened. For synthesis is one of the marks of objectivity.

This interpretation of religious value-judgments as involving intuitions of existence is different from the position to which some of the Ritschlians came, in order to defend themselves against the charge of offering only a religious positivism—namely, the position that judgments of existence may be based on judgments of value. For such judgments of existence are only postulates once more. But there are elements in Ritschl's own doctrine which pave the way for the interpretation which we have just given. Ritschl put the Lotzean theory of knowledge above the Kantian—indeed, his notion of the value-judgment is derived from Lotze—and in accord with Lotzean ideas he describes the soul as feeling and remembering its own abiding unity, as the cause, under stimulus, of its own experiences and as conscious of being an end-in-itself. And he insists that all philosophic world-views have a religious quality in that the "affirmation of a supreme law of existence . . . is a departure from the strict application of the philosophical method, and betrays itself as being quite as much an object of the intuitive imagination, as God and the world are for religious thought."' It would have been a gain if some disciples of Ritschl had undertaken to make him consistently Lotzean, as others sought to make him consistently Kantian. But whatever the outcome of such an enterprise might have been, it seems clear that a theory of intuition is needed to free the doctrine of religious value-judgments from entangling alliance with phenomenalism and make it adequate to the inherent meanings of religion.

The category of intuition would seem to have been sufficiently deduced or justified if it makes possible the rediscovery of the soul and affords a solution of the problem of judgments of value and judgments of existence in religion. But there is an added aspect of this

' *Justification and Reconciliation*, p. 207.

question of the validity of religious intuition which remains to be pointed out briefly. This can best be done in anticipation of an objection. It may be objected that intuition as it has been treated here is neither the self-sufficient intuition of many of the mystics which turns its back on reason nor the intuition of the axiomatic sort, which supplies us with something absolutely self-evidencing and infallible; but rather that it is simply a function in experience which contributes to knowledge. And if such be the case, does it not acquire a hypothetical character on account of which it after all cannot really be distinguished from the postulate?

A hypothetical quality does indeed attach to intuition as here interpreted. But between the intuition as here understood and the postulate there is all the difference that there is, in the doctrine of physical things, between the eject and the percept. The notion of ejects takes the subjectivity of our physical experience for granted and devises a scheme to account for its seeming objectivity. The notion of percepts takes the objectivity of the same experience for granted and simply calls for tests to eliminate illusions. Now the postulate is to the intuition in the spiritual realm what the eject is to the percept in the physical realm. The postulate only becomes objective by a *tour de force*. The intuition, on the other hand, bears the marks of objectivity upon it, and only needs to be tested. It would seem, then, that there is real superiority for the intuition over the postulate in interpreting our world—especially when the theory of percepts is triumphing over the theory of ejects in the physical realm.

But further, though intuitions be not absolutely self-validating, they may help to validate each other. That is, intuitions in the religious realm, as in other realms, may grow into an organized body of intuitive insight. This will not take place without reflection and criticism, nor without practical testing. And in this process many intuitions will be rejected, and those that remain will be modified and grow. Thus from this point of view, theological thinking has a constitutive place in religious experience no less truly than intuition has. But the more intuition becomes a coherent body of insight the more it has claim to objective significance, for, once more, the synthesis of judgments is one of the chief tokens of their objective worth. Religious intuitions, then, which meet the test of becoming parts of a coherent synthesis of such intuitions, have a real claim to be genuine and irreplaceable contributions to man's philosophy of the world and of life. Even in their systematized form they are subject, of course, to the further test of their congruity with our other systematized knowledge. But if we set them aside, or reduce them entirely to other phases of experience, we not only lose something indispensable to the understanding of religion, but also lose one of the principal resources of the human spirit in comprehending and reacting upon its world.

Religion, as we all know, but perhaps too often forget, has profound kinships with morality, with poetry, with philosophy, and yet it is to be identified with none of these but is something in and of itself, able to draw from each of the others and in turn to fructify them. And this uniqueness of religion, which indeed must be kept in vital relation with our other great interests, can hardly have justice done to it apart from the recognition of intuition as both valuable and valid.

X

AUTHORITY WITHOUT INFALLIBILITY

By
WALTER MARSHALL HORTON

Professor of Theology
Oberlin Graduate School of Theology

AUTHORITY WITHOUT INFALLIBILITY

THOUSANDS of inexperienced laymen are now being compelled, willy-nilly, to try their hand at building themselves a habitable structure of religious thought. The whole framework of their inherited faith, corroded and undermined by those "acids of modernity" of which Mr. Lippmann writes so feelingly, has collapsed about their ears; and they are under the necessity of replacing it somehow.

They are not getting on very well. No beginner gets on well, in any field of human endeavor, without a good deal of authoritative guidance, and the tragedy of our present situation lies in the fact that authoritative guidance in this peculiarly difficult field of religious thought is not now available.

To be sure, we still have with us the time-honored "infallible" authorities: the infallible authority of the Church of Rome and the infallible authority of Holy Writ, each alleged to be the veritable voice of divine omniscience, speaking clearly and confidently amid the confusion of human opinions. Many would willingly put their trust in one or the other of these authorities, if they could; but they have eaten of the fruit of the tree of modern knowledge, and the Eden of infallibility seems closed to them forever. The old authorities are powerless to help them; and they have found nothing to take their place.

The advocates of liberalism in religion (who might be expected to offer some assistance to these bewildered novices) seem to be prejudiced, by their own cardinal principles, against the idea of offering authoritative guidance to anybody. Ask them for it, and they will tell you that, in our emancipated age, it is necessary for every man to be his own authority. Religions of authority, they will aver, belong to the childhood of the race; now we have outgrown the need of tutelage, and can think for ourselves. Free thought has its perils and its agonies, no doubt; but after all, was not Lessing right when he preferred the endless, adventurous *pursuit* of truth to the *possession* of truth? "Rely upon your best judgment; trust the accent of the Holy Ghost, speaking to you directly in your own soul; there is no better rule."

All this sounds impressive—at first. The endless pursuit of religious truth *is* the most thrilling and rewarding of all adventures—provided one has nothing else to do, and no immediate social responsibilities to meet. But these inquiring laymen are not in that position. They are not professional religious thinkers, who can afford to retire from the world like Hindu holy men, and make the unraveling of the tangled skein of existence their lifelong business. They are busy men and women—parents perplexed about how to bring up their children, men of affairs perplexed about questions of public policy—and what they want is a religion that they can use *now*, immediately, as an aid in the defining and performing of their present duties, with some confidence that in yielding themselves to this religion they are not playing the fool. Such men and women soon grow weary of the pursuit of religious truth if it does not rapidly lead to definite and practically helpful conclusions; and since the religious quest is perhaps the most arduous and baffling of all human endeavors, they get but a dusty answer to their urgent questions. As matters stand, there are just two likely issues to such an adventure in private religious investigation: either the inquirer "comes out by the same door where in he went," cynical, disappointed, and skeptical of *all* religion; or, if he finds that he simply cannot do without a religion of some sort, he yields himself, in desperation, to the religious guidance of the first person who approaches him with an air of authority and certainty, proclaiming, "Here is the panacea; I have it, and there is no other."

It is hardly too much to say that unless liberal religion can assert its rational faith more clearly, aggressively and authoritatively than it does at present, the perplexed and bewildered populace is going to be driven back into the arms of the Church of Rome—or some other organization which claims infallible authority, and teaches with an air of certainty.[1] I met a young man recently who told me, with disarming frankness, the story of his conversion to the Roman Catholic faith. Becoming seriously concerned, for the first time in his life, about the meaning of this puzzling world, he had spent all one winter going from one Protestant church to another, looking for light and guidance. He summed up the results of his quest in an expressive gesture of complete bewilderment. Individually, the Protestant ministers seemed to him to be groping in the dark; collectively, they created by their combined dissensions a perfect Babel of confusion in his mind. Then, out of mere curiosity, he went to a retreat with a Catholic friend; and there, for the first time in his life, he heard clear, definite, authoritative religious teaching. That was what he had been craving; and because he found it first in the Catholic Church, he became a Catholic. It was his good fortune to fall into the hands of a venerable institution, the guardian of a great tradition; in his state of mind, the result would have been the same if he had met his authoritative teacher in the person of an astrologer, a spiritualistic medium, or an aggressive proponent of the Association for the Advancement of Atheism. In either case—whether he fell victim to religious conservatism or religious quackery—the blame could be laid at the door of liberal Protestantism which might have helped him to reach a reasonable certitude on matters pertaining to religion, if it had been willing to speak with more authority.

[1] If it be asked how one who has left the "Eden of infallibility" behind him can get back to it again, the answer is that he must take a circuitous route. Disillusioned Protestants, who cannot recover their faith in the infallibile Bible, find the infallible Church's voice quite seductive, because strange and unfamiliar. The one possibility that no disillusioned person considers, is the faith of his fathers; and yet secretly, by a devious path, he is trying to return to it.

At this point, a protest will have to be entered on behalf of the liberals. "Surely," they will say, "you cannot expect us to compete with Rome! We do not believe in any sort of infallibility; neither Bible, nor Church, nor Christ himself, so far as we can see, escapes the taint of human fallibility. How, then, can we lay claim to certitude in our convictions, or speak upon religious themes with an authority that is even remotely comparable with that to which the Church of Rome lays claim?"

Now it is of course beyond dispute that liberal Protestantism cannot conscientiously claim the right to speak with *infallible* authority upon religious matters, to settle all religious questions by a simple process of appeal to a Supreme Court; and yet I am ready to maintain that liberal Protestantism, without denying its own principles, can speak with an authority which will bear comparison with Rome's—an authority all the more effective and impressive because it recognizes the right of private judgment, and does not pretend to absolute certainty.

Authority without infallibility—is that not a contradiction in terms? Even Auguste Sabatier, the opponent of all "religions of authority," was inclined to think so; but I am convinced that he was mistaken. What the inquiring layman really hopes to find in his religious authority is not inerrancy, but the same kind of competence and reliability, based upon knowledge, skill, and experience, which he finds in his physician or his legal adviser. After all, no system of religious infallibility can be guaranteed to *work* infallibly; it has to be administered by admittedly fallible mortals. No chain is stronger than its weakest link; and it is impossible to link divine omniscience with human weakness without impairing the sense of absolute certainty at some point. The conservative Protestant may be sure that he has the infallible Word of God in his hands, but he cannot infallibly apply it to his own problems. The Catholic may be sure that the Church is divine, and cannot err; but he knows that the priests who interpret the Church's doctrine to him are human and fallible, like himself.

Actually, then, the most that the layman can reasonably demand of his religious authority is a certain amount of protection against his own inexperience, and against religious fraud and quackery. The liberal Protestant clergy can give this rather better, on the whole, than the Catholic priesthood; for in the back of the layman's mind there lurks the not altogether unfounded suspicion that the impressive unanimity of the Catholics is artificially secured, by the simple process of suppressing dissent; while one may be sure that if the liberal Protestants manage to agree on anything, the agreement has been freely arrived at, as a result of open discussion. Such a free consensus of opinion carries with it a weight of authority which does not properly belong to any consensus resulting from coercion or excommunication. It has something of the prestige which attaches to the pronouncements of a congress of scientists—a prestige based upon the known fact that every scientist is perfectly free to challenge and criticize whatever his colleagues may say.

At one point, to be sure, authority without infallibility would differ radically from the traditional type of authority: it would not make a blanket claim of certitude applying to all religious doctrines; rather, it would employ a graded scale of certitude, ranging from truisms and axioms at one end to hopes and over-beliefs at the other. This is an important difference. It was indeed a great comfort to our Protestant forebears to be able to believe that whatever the Bible said was true because the Bible said it; and that everything in the Bible was *equally certain,* whether it be a simple moral principle or a bit of detailed information concerning the future life. It was a great comfort, but it involved a great peril; for if all the affirmations of the Bible stand or fall together, then to cast doubt upon one is to cast doubt upon all. This is precisely what has happened. Our present acute attack of religious uncertainty is due to the fact that, doubt having been cast upon the more remote and speculative aspects of Christian doctrine, it has spread thence to the entire system.

I am convinced that a more modest and cautious type of religious authority will in the long run prove more reliable, and more helpful to the layman. Candidly admitting that it does not possess absolute truth, candidly distinguishing between what it knows, what it believes, and what it hopes, "authority without infallibility" will increasingly win men's trust; while "infallible" systems of authority, more imposing at first, collapse at last beneath the weight of their own pretensions. I believe that if liberal Protestants could once clearly perceive that an authoritative body of religious teaching is needed, to keep the inexperienced from floundering helplessly in the bog of religious skepticism, they could create such a body of teaching without in any way compromising the right of private judgment, and without excommunicating anyone for heresy. It would comprise three main divisions:

(1.) *Scientific theology*—a body of affirmations proved and tested, confirmed by all competent authorities, and to be disregarded at one's peril.

(2.) *Philosophic theology*—a body of reasoned convictions involving value judgments and hence not scientific, but supported by much evidence, and a great deal of authoritative opinion.

(3.) *Practical or empirical theology*—affirmations of religious faith and hope, based upon knowledge and reasoned convictions, but necessarily venturing out beyond the realm of the known into the realm of the possible and the conjectural. It would be the theologian's business to survey all such affirmations with a critical eye, and convert them if possible into affirmations of the first or second class; but the imperfections of human knowledge are such that it is by faith, not knowledge, that we must be guided in our most critical decisions.

In the remainder of this article, we shall endeavor to work out a set of rough specifications which will aid in the construction of our proposed edifice of religious doctrine. We shall begin, of course, with scientific theology and end with practical theology; for the cardinal principle on which our whole structure is to be based is this:

Distinguish carefully, in all your teaching and your thinking, between beliefs which can be empirically verified, and those which cannot. Reduce as many of your beliefs as possible to strictly scientific form, and build with them the foundations of your faith. What remains may do for the philosophical superstructure, or the religious turrets and battlements; but it should not be put into the corner stone.

Hereupon, of course, we encounter the immediate objection that there is no such thing, and can be no such thing, as a scientific theology; that it is inconceivable that theology should ever pass the severe entrance requirements which are still delaying the admittance of psychology and sociology into the aristocratic circle where physics, chemistry and biology hold court together. As to the fact that there is *as yet* no such thing as a scientific theology, there can be little dispute; but as to the impossibility of it—there, we protest! And we venture to predict that there will come a day when, psychology and sociology having long since been duly recognized as properly accredited sciences, theology will have advanced to such a stage that her application papers cannot be rejected with derision. A scientific theology may not be the whole of theology; but a scientific theology is both possible and needful as a basis for philosophical and practical theology. Let us therefore set down our caption boldly, in large type, and beneath it work out some provisional specifications for the establishment of this, the foundational part of our structure of doctrine.

1. Scientific Theology

It is necessary at the start to come to some understanding concerning the nature of science, and the meaning of the word "scientific." There is much confusion at this point. Certain exponents of the physical sciences (notably Professor Eddington) have lately been defining the "limitations of science" in terms that, while they greatly clarify the field of the physical sciences, seem to jeopardize the very existence of the social sciences. If the world of science is the world of quantity, the world of the precisely measurable, then psychology and sociology can never become more than pseudo-sciences; or at best they must confine themselves to the dreary and relatively unimportant business of taking mental measurements and compiling tables of social statistics. If such a definition of science tends to rule out the social sciences, it of course, *a fortiori,* tends to rule out the possibility of a scientific theology. It does not deny that a world of the qualitative exists, beyond the confines of the world of science; nor does it deny that knowledge, of a sort, may exist in this qualitative world; but it draws a sharp and well-nigh absolute distinction between all such merely empirical knowledge and true science.

Needless to say, the exponents of social science are not accepting this view without a struggle. Psychologists —whose position midway between the natural and social sciences makes them susceptible to influences from both quarters—are somewhat divided on the issue. Some of them, like the behaviorists, seem disposed to gain the favor of the old established sciences by conforming to their strictest and narrowest requirements, and eliminating all psychological concepts which have the taint of quality, value or purpose upon them. Others protest that such a procedure destroys psychology's status as a separate and distinctive science, with a field of its own, and reduces it to a mere branch of biology. Whatever attitude the psychologists may eventually take, it is clear that the sociologists have no choice in the matter. They *must* demand a broader definition of science, or give up their claim to be scientists. Their attitude is well expressed by Professor Ellwood, in his recent book, *Man's Social Destiny:*

Science [says Professor Ellwood] is the tested knowledge that comes from experience, by using any and all methods that will reduce to a minimum errors of judgment. It is experience tested, verified, and universalized. . . . The "orthodox" scientists, as we may call them, would apparently limit the field of science to the measurement of objective conditions and the formulation of laws in such relations. They would not recognize the subjective or the world of values as within the field of science. . . . The real question is, of course, not what meaning we should attach to the word "science," but whether we can get tested, verifiable knowledge in the world of our subjective and social experiences, and so in the world of values. Hardly any one would say that we do not have tested and verifiable knowledge as regards health, though health is obviously a value; and he would be very rash who would say to an economist that we have no tested knowledge as yet regarding wealth and economic values. Moreover, this tested knowledge does not consist always, or even in a majority of cases, of quantitative measurements.[a]

Professor Ellwood makes it plain that science, even in this broader sense, would have its limitations. Though it might *deal with* values, qualities, meanings and purposes *as aspects of human culture;* it could not *judge between* or *evaluate* them. That would be the task of social philosophy, as distinct from social science. But with this limitation once recognized, Professor Ellwood believes that the way would be open for the foundation of a series of new sciences, whose service to the cause of human culture would be of the greatest possible significance. "Thus," he says, "there would be pure sciences of government, of religion, of morals, and even of fine art and education, and supporting all would be sciences of human relations, of human group life, and of culture itself. These studies would be recognized as having the same scientific validity as the sciences of physical nature."

I believe that Professor Ellwood's protest against the narrowing of the definition of science is thoroughly justified. Wherever there is a well-marked group of phenomena to be studied, there a science is possible; and the methods of that science are not to be dictated by other sciences, but by the nature of the phenomena to be studied. The criterion of a science is not to be found in the employment of the method of precise mathematical

[a] *Op. cit.,* pp. 88, 94, 96.

measurement, or in any other method, but in the discovery, within a carefully circumscribed field, of a system of general laws applicable to all the phenomena in question.[*] No one disputes the existence of human society and culture; hence a science of sociology is possible and desirable, however difficult it may be. Physical science, biological science, social science: these three primary and general sciences,[*] with their auxiliary and subordinate branches, and with bio-chemistry and psychology as connecting links between them, form a recognizable body of actual and possible knowledge, to which the name "science" is clearly applicable. Any definition of science which does not apply to the whole of this body of knowledge is a poor definition.

But where shall we place scientific theology? Shall we follow Professor Ellwood's lead, and describe it as a branch of social science—the "pure science of religion," cognate with the pure sciences of government, morals and education? Or shall we locate theology somewhere beyond social science, and demand another expansion of the definition of science?

There is something tempting about Professor Ellwood's proposal. It would get theology into the body of the accepted sciences without a struggle or a qualm— just as sociology could get into the body of the natural sciences if it would treat society mathematically and mechanistically, and ignore the realm of values. From this point of view, theology would become the sociology of religion: the study of religion as a factor in human culture. The history of religion and the psychology of religion would be theology's closest auxiliaries; but all three of these sciences—the history, psychology and sociology of religion—would be conceived as mere accessories of

[*] Cf. E. Baudin, *Qu'est-ce que la Philosophie*, Chapter on "*La connaissance et l'esprit scientifique*," especially pp. 46-53.

[*] I am here following, in simplified form, Professor Baudin's admirable classification of the sciences, based on a revision of Comte's. Baudin makes the important distinction between *primary* sciences, which deal only with general *laws*, and *secondary* sciences (of which *history* is the great example), which deal with individual and concrete *facts*. (*Op. cit.*, Chap. IV, "*Objet et classification des sciences.*")

the general and primary science, sociology. Since the history and psychology of religion, and general sociology, already exist in at least partially scientific form, the founding of a scientific theology would on this plan be relatively simple.

Too simple, by far! For theology would be purchasing admission to the body of the sciences at too great a price. She would be sacrificing her claim to possess a subject matter peculiar to herself: the knowledge of God. To reduce the science of God to the science of religion would be very much like reducing physics to—well, let us say, the history of physical discovery, the psychology of eminent physicists, and the study of the social repercussions of mechanical inventions! It would rob theology of its characteristic *object,* and turn it into something as different from itself as a biography of Darwin or a history of the evolution controversy is different from the study of the "system of animate nature." No, it looks as though scientific theology could not properly establish itself without a struggle—without getting the scientific world to admit that *it is legitimate to postulate the existence of God as an actual fact, as indubitable as the existence of the physical world, the animate world, and the human world!*

Imagine the surprise and consternation, rapidly turning to indignation, which would greet such a statement, if it were made in the presence of a congress of scientific men! "To postulate the existence of God—what is that," they would protest, "but to beg the whole question of the truth of traditional Christian theology? What is it but to show that theology is, as we have always suspected, dogmatic and anti-scientific in its very essence?" But softly, softly! Our statement has been misunderstood. We are not claiming that it is legitimate for a scientific theology to postulate the existence of the Christian God, or the Mohammedan God, or to assume the correctness of any fully developed conception of God. We are only claiming that it is legitimate to assume that the word "God" points to something worthy of study, as do the

words "nature," "life," "mind," and "society." We
are claiming that it can safely be assumed that the relations of man with that "something" are as real and as
open to investigation as are his relations with stars and
atoms, animal species, and other human beings. We are
protesting against the view that sociology is the last of
the primary sciences, and we are asserting that there
is room for another primary science beyond sociology,
before we arrive at the line which divides science from
philosophy.

But what, precisely, would be the subject-matter of this
new science? How could "God" be defined, so as to make
his existence as certain as that of the earth? Just here,
we shall be obliged in all candor to recognize that we
are not "the first that ever burst" into this unknown
sea of scientific theology. Two thinkers in particular,
Professor Macintosh and Professor Wieman, have done
important pioneer work in the exploration and surveying
of this new territory; and each of them has offered several alternative "minimum concepts" of God which may
help to clarify our thought on this difficult and crucial
question. Professor Macintosh defines God as "the ultimate Object of religious dependence, or the Source of
religious deliverance"; or again, "that Factor in human
experience which produces, on occasion of man's continued right relation, a definite and qualitatively predictable
result."[5] Professor Wieman following the same general
line of approach, defines God as "that object, whatsoever its nature may be, which will yield maximum security and abundance to all human living, when right adjustment is made";[6] "that character of events to which man
must adjust himself in order to attain the greatest goods
and avoid the greatest ills";[7] "that upon which we are
dependent, that which sustains us in every breath we
breathe, that which shapes the cells of our bodies and the

---

[5] *Theology as an Empirical Science*, pp. 27, 97.
[6] *Religious Experience and Scientific Method*, p. 381.
[7] *The Wrestle of Religion with Truth*, p. 14.

impulses of our hearts according as we adjust to it in this way or that."[8]

All of these definitions, it will be seen, are quite non-committal with regard to the question of the precise *nature* of God. They define a field to be investigated; they do not tell what must be found in it. Therein, they are all well fitted to serve the purpose for which they are designed. Any criticism of such concepts, on the ground that they do not fully correspond with the meaning of the word "God" in highly developed religions like Christianity, is beside the mark. I believe, however, that there is one serious defect running through all of them: they are too utilitarian, too anthropocentric. To define God solely in terms of what he does for man is like defining electricity as a form of household convenience. If we begin with the general proposition (which both Professor Macintosh and Professor Wieman appear to accept) that the word "God," in its most general sense, refers to the Object to which religious experience points, then we must at once recognize the fact that there is a powerful non-utilitarian strain in religious experience, the world over. The gods are not merely sources of possible benefit to their worshipers; they are regarded as adorable in and of themselves; they are regarded as responsible for the goodness and beauty that is sown broadcast through the whole creation, and not merely for the little portion of blessing that chances to fall upon us men. When Professor Wieman comes to develop his concept of God and to state his own views concerning God's nature, he at once admits this. A God whose nature is expressed in Whitehead's "principle of concretion" or in the "holistic" principle of General Smuts, a God who is defined as a "value-making process" or "integrating process"[9] at work in the universe at large, is a God who is no mere human convenience. Would it not be desirable,

---

[8] *Methods of Private Religious Living*, pp. 22, 23.
[9] See *The Wrestle of Religion with Truth*, Chaps. VI-XIII, and more especially, the article entitled "A Workable Idea of God," in *Religious Education* for December, 1929.

however, to put the non-utilitarian element, if possible, into the original "minimum definition"? This might be accomplished by defining the divine Object as "that which humbles him who beholds it, and exalts him who reverently adjusts himself to it"; or again, "that which deserves supreme devotion, and repays such devotion with supreme fullness of life."

Just here, however, we meet with a formidable objection: "Is it not clear that all definitions of God, even the broadest and most non-committal, involve value-judgments, since the concept of God cannot be divorced from the concept of *the good?* If so, how can the idea of God possibly be treated as a scientific concept?" Let us examine this objection carefully. Its force is derived from the common belief that the realm of values is a purely subjective realm; that goodness and beauty are purely relative to human tastes and whims. The catch lies in the word *"purely."* Value, goodness and beauty cannot be defined without some reference to human interests and human emotions; they are relative to human desires and strivings; but they are not *purely* relative thereto. Indeed, if it be proper for a person unversed in mathematics to offer an opinion on the general bearing of the theory of relativity, I should like to venture the assertion that the final effect of Einstein's work will be to put an end to that era of illusionism and subjectivism which Immanuel Kant inaugurated. Kant insisted upon one kind of relativity: the distortion of reality which is due to its being known, appreciated, or valued by human minds. Hence arose the impression that whatever intelligibility, beauty or value is discovered in the world is not really *there,* but is "projected" into the world by the human mind—a tragic and paralyzing conception! But now that Einstein has made relativity universal, relativity has lost its sting. The relativity of things, events, and values to the human mind is only one aspect of the general relativity of everything to everything else. From this point of view, goodness and beauty inhere in the general structure of events, and depend not only upon human desire, but quite as truly and even more significantly upon their cosmic Source, Ground, or Determinant—which is what we mean by God.

Scientific theology does not presume to *judge* between values; that is the task of philosophical theology; but it does treat values, and their Source, as a real objective phenomenon, worthy of study. It presupposes a realistic theory of value. It presupposes that there is a real distinction, grounded in the nature of things, between what is valued and what is valuable, what is desired and what is desirable, what is worshiped and what is worthy. It assumes that there is a relatively stable structure of things, and process of events, by which all values are determined far more truly than they are determined by our momentary whims; and it is this cosmic structure and process which it proposes to study, as sociology studies the structure and process of society. God, for the scientific theologian, is an entity vastly more complex and vastly more difficult to investigate than society, or the mind, or the living organism, or inorganic matter, but just as real. Indeed, God is *more* real than the entities with which the physicist or the biologist deals, for these simple sciences owe their exactness to the fact that they have artificially isolated and abstracted certain of the more manageable aspects of reality from their concrete context; while the theologian is dealing with a vast network of concrete relationships, and takes his data from the most unitary and synthetic of all types of human experience.

Scientific theology has two main branches: pure theology, and applied theology.[10] Pure theology is concerned with the knowledge of God, for its own sake; applied theology is concerned with human welfare, as affected by man's relation with God. Universal religious experience—together with its constant allies, moral and

---

[10] The distinction here made is, I believe, a more careful and precise distinction than that which I attempted to make in *Theism and the Modern Mood*. What I called pure theology in that book, I now call scientific theology; what I then called applied theology, I now call philosophical and practical theology.

æsthetic experience—constitutes the main body of data for both pure and applied theology; but pure theology endeavors to isolate the *constant factor* in religious experience, which points to a dependable cosmic Ground, conditioning all religious men in all times and places; while applied theology endeavors to determine the *precise conditions* under which a successful religious adjustment ("salvation") takes place. All pure sciences which formulate the general laws of events—mathematics, physics, biology, sociology—are contributory to pure theology; all applied sciences which bear upon the problem of human welfare are contributory to applied theology—chief among them being that union of medical science, applied psychology and practical sociology which is coming to be known as *mental hygiene, or euthenics,* the "science of the good life."

The beginnings of both these branches of scientific theology might be discerned in those evangelical sects which have made much of "experimental religion" and the "experience meeting." Ideally speaking, a Methodist class meeting, in which a group of people relate to one another "what the Lord has done for them" in converting them from evil ways or in answering their daily prayers, might be compared to a group of scientists comparing notes on the results of their laboratory experiments. The Christian Scientists have this ideal consciously in mind, and go so far as to talk about "demonstrating" their conceptions in the laboratory of life. In both cases, however, it is to be feared that the desire to edify the brethren frequently prevails over the stern requirements of scientific objectivity; and it is therefore necessary to check and test the naïve pronouncements of religious experience by as many objective standards as possible. Here, the general history and psychology of religion, together with the attested results of all the other sciences, must be at the command of the scientific theologian. He must, very literally, "take all knowledge for his province." Small wonder that the birth pangs of our new science are protracted and severe!

2. Philosophical Theology

What has been said about the difficulties of scientific theology makes it evident that no great practical benefits can be derived from it for a long time to come. For the puzzled layman of the future—say a thousand years hence!—it will be a great bulwark of certitude; but for the puzzled layman of the present, it is hardly more than a tantalizing hope. For him, there is much more immediate comfort in a theology that is soundly *philosophical*.

By a soundly philosophical theology, I do not mean a purely speculative theology, detached from scientific knowledge and religious experience, and left free to roam in cloudlands of its own imagining. The ultimate court of appeal, for philosophy and science alike, is experimental verification. But neither do I mean to commend a type of philosophy so positivistic, agnostic and earthbound that it refuses to deal with questions concerning the ultimate nature and destiny of things. Metaphysical questions are not meaningless questions; in the long run, they are the only important questions; and it is foolish to try to dodge them, for when we refuse to think about them, we are unconsciously taking sides. A soundly philosophical theology will endeavor to reduce as many of its convictions as possible to an experimentally verifiable form; and it will give itself a broad and solid scientific foundation; but it will not fear to deal with those great ultimate questions on which men have always been divided, and to which, perhaps, no final and absolutely compelling answer will ever be given. If theology refuses to attempt a rational solution of these problems, men will accept some irrational solution of them—perhaps with disastrous results, for there are no errors more serious than those which affect one's fundamental philosophy of life.

But let us make our conception of philosophical theology more precise, by pointing out wherein it differs from scientific theology. John Dewey once said, epigrammatically, "The difference between science and philosophy is—ethics!" By this he meant, presumably, that a philosopher claims the right of making value-judgments, which is denied to the scientist, and is concerned with the bearing of truth upon the general art of living, as the pure scientist is not. As Baudin puts it, the philosopher combines and reconciles the scientist's disinterested quest of truth with the practical man's empirical quest of the good life. He reminds the scientist that knowledge is for the sake of life; and he reminds the common man that systematic thought is necessary if all knowledge and life are to be harmoniously organized. We may add that philosophy deals with a host of questions which—either because they involve judgments of value or because they involve the effort to pierce beneath phenomena to their ultimate cause or essence—cannot be settled on a purely factual basis. Every science rests upon a tissue of assumptions, and philosophy, in its endeavor to unify all knowledge, cannot avoid the task of examining and reconciling these assumptions. As to the methods of examination which are employed in philosophy, it is a bit difficult to generalize. Perhaps the following rule would roughly express the usual mode of procedure:

Lay out all the competing opinions upon a line, endeavoring to comprehend all possible logical alternatives between the two extremes. Then examine each of the competing opinions dialectically, probing them for internal inconsistencies and fallacies as Socrates used to probe the opinions of his contemporaries, and bringing to bear upon them the whole body of known facts and commonly accepted values. Use every possible method of examination upon them; twist and turn them; view them from every angle. To guard against bias, be particularly sympathetic to those opinions which are most opposed to your own; and endeavor to restate your own view in such a way as to incorporate every bit of solid truth and enduring value which you discover in other views. Eventually, narrow down the alternatives by this process of elimination, until all extreme and untenable views have been canceled out, and the pendulum of opinion, no longer

*fluctuating wildly from one end of the line to the other,
vibrates within a narrow range. There, within that narrow range, you may be pretty certain, the truth must lie.*

I think it will be the testimony of all who have studied
philosophy for any length of time that, while its initial
effect is profoundly disturbing to all provincial and
merely traditional opinions, its ultimate effect is to give
a sense of assurance. To have examined all conceivable
opinions upon a given question, and to have incorporated
in one's own view valid elements from all of them—
including the most violent and the most foolish—is to
feel solid ground beneath one's feet, even though the
final answer to the question at issue may forever prove
elusive. Philosophical certainty is not the same thing
as scientific certainty, but it is very real; and if theologians wish to speak with authority to the layman, they
must pay the price, and cultivate genuine philosophic
disinterestedness. Practical religious teachers, driven by
the urgency of immediate religious needs, cannot cultivate this sort of detachment, perhaps. They must be
content, as the authors of the great creeds of the Church
were content, to maintain a certain *balance* in their teaching, even though it lead to logical inconsistency. They
must affirm that both free will and determinism are
somehow simultaneously true, and Christ is somehow
both human and divine, and God is somehow both three
and one. But the philosophical theologian must not be
content to let these inconsistencies stand. He must be
forever going behind religious creeds and phrases, to
find the literal truth which reconciles the partial truths
which they reveal. And though his task may be an endless one, the concepts which he laboriously hews out are
solid building stones for the structure of religious certitude which we need to erect.

If it be asked precisely where theology is to be placed,
among the philosophical disciplines, the answer will depend upon the classification which we adopt. A convenient general division of the problems of philosophy is
to be found in the distinction between *critical* philosophy

and *metaphysical* philosophy. Critical philosophy judges and evaluates; metaphysical philosophy seeks to "go to the bottom" of things. Under critical philosophy are to be classified (1) the general theory of knowledge (epistemology) and of values (axiology); (2) the three great normative disciplines, logic, ethics, and æsthetics; and (3) all the specialized branches of critical philosophy, such as philosophy of education and political philosophy, whose function is to exercise rational guidance and control over some important human activity or interest. Under metaphysical philosophy are to be classified a host of problems which at once emerge when one seeks to define more precisely the nature of the entities which science and common sense take for granted; things like space, time, matter, life, mind, society, nature, God, Universe. The endeavor to get at the underlying structure and organization of these commonly accepted entities is often called *cosmology,* while the further examination of ultimate categories like Being and Becoming, the One and the Many, the Relative and the Absolute, which even cosmologists are disposed to take for granted, constitutes the most technical and abstruse branch of philosophy, sometimes called *ontology.* On this basis, theology will appear twice in the list of philosophical disciplines: once under critical philosophy, as *philosophy of religion,* and once under metaphysical philosophy, at the point where all cosmological problems converge.

As philosophy of religion, theology endeavors to make a critical evaluation of the rôle which religion has played in the life of the race, the validity of religious knowledge, the relation of religion to ethics, the relative merits of different religions, and the relative merits of different types and tendencies in the same religion. Then, planting itself within that religious tradition which seems on the whole truest and best, religious philosophy seeks to enrich it, and guide its further development, as educational philosophy seeks to guide the development of education. Obviously, the religious critic needs to be versed in the history of religion and the general history of thought and culture, and he needs to have a subtle and delicate capacity for appreciating religious values, somewhat similar to that kind of sensitive taste which one finds in the best literary and musical critics, or in critics of civilization like Carlyle, Ruskin and Tolstoy. Scientific theology, no matter how fast it may develop, can never eliminate the necessity of this kind of thinking.

As metaphysical philosophy, theology is not greatly concerned with the more abstruse problems of ontology; but it is deeply concerned with all those questions of the structure and organization of things which are comprehended under cosmology. God, Man and the World—the three pivotal concepts around which all systems of theology revolve—are all metaphysical concepts; and the greatest theologians have been thoroughly alive to the fact. Every revolution in metaphysics has its repercussions in theology, as every revolution in science has its repercussions in metaphysics. The chief difference between the philosophical theologian and other metaphysicians is that he can never quite overlook his practical responsibility for religious guidance. He knows that human destiny hangs trembling in the balance between salvation and destruction; and he therefore concentrates his attention upon those questions which have some clear bearing, direct or indirect, upon "the chief end of man." It is well that some should voyage about freely in the sea of metaphysics, impelled by pure curiosity; but such cannot be the mood of the philosophical theologian. He must maintain a delicate balance between that disinterestedness and open-mindedness which is required of him as a philosopher, and that concern for practical soundness, stability and balance which he shares with the pastor and the preacher. He cannot forget the inquiring layman, with his desire for certainty and authority; yet if, in the effort to be reassuring, he becomes dogmatic and unphilosophical, he forefeits his title and loses his authority.

3. Practical, Empirical, or Common-sense Theology

We now return to our expectant layman—not empty-handed, but not wholly successful in our quest. It is something to have acquired the assurance that scientific certitude may some day be reached concerning many of the fundamental problems of religion, and that philosophical certitude is already attainable concerning many others. That takes religion out of the realm of fairyland, and gives it standing in the realm of the knowable. Yet it must be confessed that if the theologian's authority and the layman's certitude depended on the possibility of reducing all religious convictions to strict scientific or philosophical form, the situation would be somewhat discouraging. There are no questions so momentous as religious questions, but there are none so inextricably involved in mystery and obscurity. Reason casts but a flickering candle flame; amid swirling mists, we must *feel* our way, rather than *see* our way, in matters of religion. He who would wait for full philosophical certitude, before embracing a religious credo, must wait forever.

What then? Are we condemned to resort to guesswork when scientific certitude and philosophic certitude are lacking? Is there nothing between reasoned philosophy and blind faith? To ask such a question is to be at once reminded that scientific and philosophic knowledge are not the only knowledge we have. Before science and philosophy existed, men had knowledge, of a sort; and the great bulk of the knowledge by which men live to-day does not rise to the scientific or philosophic level. Science and philosophy are only the highest and chilliest peaks in the great mountain range of human knowledge. What we call empirical knowledge, or common sense, forms the broad basis for all the more highly specialized forms of knowledge; and for practical purposes it is *superior* to science and philosophy.[11] Common sense lacks disinterestedness and objectivity, order and method, exactness and consistency; but it is apt to contain a certain native wit, a certain sense of proportion, a certain prac-

[11] Baudin, *op. cit.*, chapter on *"La connaissance et l'esprit empirique."*

tical insight which is all too rare among scientists and philosophers. Not only in religion but in every sphere of practical affairs, there are many things that are hidden from the wise and learned, and revealed unto babes!

Now, the general rules for the acquiring of practical religious certitude are not altogether different from those we have been laying down for the acquiring of scientific and philosophical certitude. Experimental verification is the supreme test for practical religion as it is for scientific theology. The weighing of logical alternatives is not a method confined to philosophical circles; Socrates put his questions to all comers, in the market place. It is possible for empirical thinking to have a great deal of the scientific or philosophic, even though it does not fully reach the scientific or philosophic level. Nevertheless, there is one great disturbing factor whose presence makes the whole atmosphere of practical religious thought quite different from that of science and philosophy: *the pressure of life.*

I need not repeat the argument of James's "Will to Believe"; his general contention, that there are certain "forced options" in matters of religious thought—and that the most central questions belong to this class—is too well known and too plainly true to need extended discussion. Now, the consequence of the doctrine of the forced option is, that a purely rational certitude, based upon complete philosophic detachment and complete scientific impersonality, is unattainable precisely where it is desirable! How great is the danger of self-deception when the question at issue is whether or not the soul is immortal, whether or not life is worth living, whether or not there is something in the universe which supports our highest aspirations and endeavors! Yet, twist and turn as we may, there is no escape from life's imperious demand that we make *some* assumption. Practical religious certitude is experimental; but the experiment is complicated by the fact that faith and hope, self-interest and generous desire—in short, the whole man, body and soul—is cast into the alembic. The fundamental canon

of practical religious thinking would read somewhat as
follows:

*Do not be a disinterested bystander; take sides. Do
not wait until all logical alternatives have been carefully
sifted out; the time is short. As soon as it becomes morally imperative to choose between religious attitudes, act
at once, though you have but the dimmest of intuitions as
your guide; and let the issue decide whether you were
right or wrong. Allow no hypocritical cleavage to appear
between your convictions and your actions; for a religious conviction merely entertained in the mind soon
fades back into the fog from which it emerged; while a
conviction acted upon provides for its own correction, and
grows at last into a practical certitude.*

There can be no doubt about the practical advisability
of these maxims. Religious autobiography is full of evidence for the proposition that decisive action is the surest
road to religious certitude. Detached philosophic reflection, apart from such action, leads to a paralyzing skepticism, which has no merely intellectual cure.[12] But is there
not a radical inconsistency between the maxims of practical religion and the maxims of rational theology? Is
there not a flat contradiction between the spirit of scientific tentativeness and philosophic open-mindedness, and
the spirit of partisanship, the spirit of decisive, venture-
some, passionate, loyal conviction which characterizes the
truly religious man? Are not *rational* certitude and *religious* certitude simply incompatible with one another?

That there is a real and serious problem here, it is
useless to deny. Practical religious teaching and rational
theology *are* contrary to one another in mood and method.

[12] I am personally acquainted with a man who suffered an almost
complete collapse of faith while engaged in the work of the ministry.
With the consent and sympathy of his church, he went back to first
principles, and for some time preached nothing but the one conviction
still left to him: that it was better to be honest than to be dishonest.
Living by his, he gradually found other convictions looming up out of
the fog—which he lived out and preached out as soon as they appeared.
He thus escaped, more rapidly than he at first believed possible, from a
paralysis which would surely have become permanent if he had confined
himself to rational reflection.

One is sometimes tempted to exclaim that the conflict between science and religion is as nothing when compared with the conflict between theology and religion! It is rare indeed that a man combines within himself the capacity for critical reflection and the religious genius's capacity for deep self-commitment.[13] In going from theology to religion, and back again, one's fundamental principles are turned topsy-turvy. For theology, reason precedes faith; and—as we said at the beginning of this discussion—it is necessary to reserve all mere over-beliefs for the turrets and pinnacles of one's structure of doctrine. For religion, on the other hand, faith precedes reason; and it is a cardinal principle that he who refuses to begin by believing something will never understand anything at all.[14] It is only the pure in heart who see God; there are moral preconditions of religious knowledge; and the first of these is, that one must become as a little child, receiving in faith many things that are mysterious and difficult to prove.

Unless this paradox can somehow be resolved, our whole investigation threatens to come to naught; for if there is such a radical contradiction as this between technical theology and practical theology, the continuity of our carefully graded series of certitudes is completely broken; and instead of leading up to a climax, we have been leading up to a *débâcle*. If there is a great gulf fixed between rational and religious certitude, then what we have said concerning the possibility of scientific and philosophic certitude in theology has no bearing on the layman's problem of authoritative religious guidance; and if religious experience is as partisan and irrational as we have described it, then it has no evidential value— and our layman is back where he started from, forced to choose his religion on a hit-or-miss basis.

[13] It is related in the *Acta Sanctorum* that St. Thomas Aquinas, near the end of a life devoted to theological analysis, had one day, as he stood at the altar saying Mass, a vision of religious Reality—and returning to his cell, put away forever the unfinished manuscript of the *Summa*, saying, "I have seen too much; I shall write no more."

[14] *Credo ut intelligam.*

The way out of our dilemma begins to appear when we note the fact that the pressure of life, which forces us to leap to conclusions on religious questions, is not absolutely uniform, but varies from moment to moment. We are not always at a crisis; between times, we may stop to recover our rational equilibrium; and if we are very cool-headed, we may examine (and even *alter*) the very foundations of our faith, when no special strain is being thrown upon them. It is psychologically impossible to be a saint and a theologian at one and the same time; but it is perfectly possible for a saint to be a theologian in his spare moments; and there are some rare souls who are able to alternate constantly between the two attitudes, to the enrichment of both.[15] Indeed it must be emphatically stated that no one is fit to be a theologian who does not know from experience the meaning of religious faith and religious insight; while, on the other hand, no religious genius deserves a following who is not ready to submit his intuitions to rational criticism and experimental testing. The career of men like Newman, Tolstoy, Keshub Chunder Sen, and other profoundly self-critical religious seekers is proof that genuine *discovery* is possible in the field of religion—discovery that may come, like the solution of a scientific riddle, only after long and painful groping, and many false scents. The authority which attaches to the findings of a man who has consecrated his whole life to the religious quest does not amount to infallibility; but it is very great—even if his findings, when viewed by an impartial observer, are seen to be largely negative. Consider then the far greater weight of authority which attaches to the findings of certain peoples, like the Hindus and the Hebrews, who have devoted practically their whole *history* to the religious quest, and who have thus woven upon the loom of time a vast fabric of religious experimentation, in which the consequences of different religious hypotheses

[15] St. Augustine actually had the faculty—observable throughout his *Confessions*—of catching himself up short in the midst of a prayer, making a theological observation, and then resuming the prayer with added fervor!

are to be traced in human blessedness and human tears.[16]

The practical upshot of these considerations is, that the theologian who wishes to achieve for himself a practical religious certitude, which will form legitimate basis for his work of authoritative religious guidance, must alternate between religious insight and rational reflection. Chronologically and psychologically, he must begin by becoming a religious seeker himself; he must be an amateur before he is fit to be a professional. He must, like everyone else, make the initial venture of faith that is involved in the assumption that there is something in religion; and he must realize for himself, by personal experience, enough of the richness of some specific religious tradition to give him confidence in its essential soundness. Then, turning to reflection, he must compare his heritage with other heritages, correcting and amplifying the tradition to which he has provisionally subscribed by all the scientific and philosophic tests at his command. Then, returning once more to the mood of appreciation, he must deepen his knowledge of the religious experience of his predecessors and contemporaries, and ask himself whether, in the process of rationalizing his faith, he has not needlessly sacrificed many things that are valid and precious in the faith of less sophisticated people. Remembering that empirical knowledge is superior to scientific knowledge for practical purposes, he must beware of taking too haughty an attitude toward the great religious teachers of the past, simply because their technical knowledge was defective; and he must listen with reverence to the objections which naïve religious experience is continually raising against his rational creed. Thus alternately going to school to the untaught religious genius, the scientist, and the philosopher, there is good prospect

[16] I mean to suggest—though it would take another article to develop the suggestion adequately—that practical religious experience has a logic of its own, different from the logic of science and philosophy, but equally valid in its own sphere. If we grant that all religions are seeking in various fashions to realize fullness of life, then the consequences of various religious hypotheses, as revealed in biography and history, give us the means of testing their validity.

that he may at length become precisely the sort of person for whom the hungry multitudes are eagerly looking to-day: a genuine *authority* in matters of religion. Given a group of such theologians, the dream of an authoritative *body of teaching* might not prove to be unrealizable.

Finally, it should be noted that religious authority, thus conceived, is not the destruction but the fulfillment of those time-honored systems of religious authority whose grip upon the populace has only recently begun to weaken. The authority of the Church—that is, the authority of the consensus of religious insight and opinion in the whole religious tradition which we inherit—is bound to be respected by any theologian who desires to correct the observations of his own limited experience and his own personal peculiarities. The authority of the Bible—that is, of that body of literature which represents the formative and creative period in the history of our religion—is bound to be respected by any theologian who recognizes the fact that every great religious tradition tends to become corrupted by extraneous influences, and needs from time to time to be recalled to its first principles. Leaning upon this vast body of objective religious teaching, the liberal theologian may regain for himself something of that sense of being the humble interpreter of a great body of accredited truth which gives confidence to the physician as he stands between his patient and the facts of medical science. But in leaning upon the authority of the past, he will never forget that there is nothing infallible, nothing final in the "deposit of faith"; and he will welcome criticism, correction and contradiction as necessary to the progress of religious discovery.

I have great hope that a theology which is at once scientific, philosophic and practical may soon be able to furnish authoritative guidance—not *less* but *more* effective than that which was offered by the old absolute authorities—to the multitudes of people who are now so pathetically disturbed and so hopelessly befuddled upon religious issues.

XI

EXPERIMENTAL REALISM IN RELIGION

By
DOUGLAS CLYDE MACINTOSH

Professor of Theology
Yale University

EXPERIMENTAL REALISM IN RELIGION

1. Phenomenological

Religion has a double taproot. It is deeply grounded in our consciousness of reality and our seeking of values.

First consciousness of reality, in the infant child and in the infancy of the race, was already, if not actually religious, potentially so. It is not merely that, as Professor Hocking suggests, the first dawning of consciousness involves a vague "idea-of-the-whole," that in coming into the world at all one comes into the presence of the Whole,[1] and so has a first dim apprehension of what some would call the Absolute; primitive reality-feeling is, or soon comes to be, something more specific. Wonder and awe; a vague sense of a "numinous" reality[2] or mysterious power, eliciting reactions now of fascinated attention and again of shuddering fear; a feeling of utter dependence with no language at first in which to express itself but a cry—these ways of reacting and feeling are at once so characteristic of infancy, so elemental in the experience of primitive man, and so persistent a feature of his religious life, as to suggest the view that man's first consciousness of cosmic reality was, if not a religious, at least a quasi-religious experience.

At the same time, it must be admitted, there is raised in the minds of some the question whether historically religion has not been simply the lingering but gradually disappearing remainder of primitive, prescientific, and even infantile modes of human behavior, feeling and thought. There is, however, another possibility. Perhaps the primitiveness of religion is an indication of its

[1] W. E. Hocking, *The Meaning of God in Human Experience,* 1912, pp. 97, 95; cf. p. 233.
[2] See R. Otto, *Das Heilige* (Eng. tr., *The Idea of the Holy*), *passim.*

307

universality and of its probable permanence as something essential to the life of man. May it be that the truth is not that religion is being or ever will be completely outgrown, but simply this, that primitive religion needs to grow up? It is notoriously true that religion needs to outgrow its infantile and primitive forms of thought and modes of expression; but this is no more than can be said of every phase of human life. The grown man must put away childish things.

It is a noteworthy fact that religion does not disappear with the passing of the generations; it develops. With the growth of man's knowledge of the world and at-homeness in it, the numinous sense becomes more specialized in its reactions. Not everything and everyone is any longer object of fascinated wonder and holy awe. Familiarity breeds irreverence and religious indifference, more or less. But there is still for the thoughtful and susceptible the mysteriousness of certain aspects of life and the environment, and especially of reality as a whole. There are the starry heavens above, for instance, to stir man's awe and wonder, and in spite of all his increasing competence and sophistication a lurking consciousness of a higher power, a mysteriously hidden and yet urgent and awe-inspiring object of ultimate dependence, as undeniable and unescapable a thing, and yet seeming often almost as unknown and unknowable, as "wholly other" to the cultivated modern as was the primitive *mana* to the untutored mind of the savage.

The other root of religion in the individual and in the race has been the appreciation and seeking of the various human values. A value is a quality which anything has by virtue of its relation to an end-directed process, that is, a process regarded as working toward an end, whether the end be consciously contemplated in the process, or not. This definition of value includes the truth of subjectivism, which insists that every object of every interest is a value; at the same time it would admit the main contention of objectivism, that there are values which are valid independently of whether they are subjectively appreciated or not. It covers not only the value which depends for its existence upon the consciousness which appreciates it, but also such values as those of food and shelter for the maintenance and development of unconscious life. Moreover, if it should appear that there are, in addition to all such finite transient values, others which, whether humanly appreciated or not, are really valid as having permanent and universal worth in relation to the spiritual development of human personality—such values, perchance, as those of ideal rationality in thought, ideal beauty, and ideal goodness of character—our definition of value would be found sufficiently broad and elastic to cover these also.

From the point of view of our definition values may be classified as instrumental, terminal, and (relatively) fundamental. In relation to any particular end-directed process itself the *terminus ad quem* has positive terminal value. Its *terminus a quo,* as that from which the directed process is moving away, has negative terminal value. Whatever promotes an end-seeking process has, relatively to it, positive instrumental value. What hinders or is an obstacle to it has negative instrumental value. The end-directed process to which the ends (positive and negative) and means (or obstacles) under consideration are relative, has of course in relation to itself a value which is positive and fundamental. But from the point of view of some other end-directed process there may be a transvaluation of values, the original fundamental process with its *terminus ad quem* and instruments coming to have in this new relation negative value, while its obstacles and *terminus a quo* have positive value. A further point of some importance is that while a value is primarily a *quality* of some object, valued *things* and *ends* of action are also commonly spoken of as "values."

The question as to whether, in view of the obvious relativity of values, there are any which may be reasonably believed to be absolute in the sense that they are universally and permanently valid for persons (whether recognized as universal and final, or not), is ultimately the question as to whether there are any *processes* the value of which ought to be (or can reasonably be) recognized and appreciated as having positive worth, always, everywhere and for all. Now in the general process of developing personality, individually and socially, are included certain constituent processes (for example, intellectual, æsthetic, social and moral development—in a word, spiritual development) which may be reasonably appreciated and believed in as universally and finally valid. Universal and permanent desirability in the value of processes implies a corresponding universal and permanent validity in the value of their positive ends (*termini ad quos*), considered not as static points in a future development but rather as flying goals of a future progress, the direction rather than the absolute location of which is indicated by such ideal terms as rationality and knowledge of the truth, culture and beauty of personality, righteousness and the good will, true friendship and unselfish love. Furthermore, universal and permanent validity in processes and ends imparts a similar ultimate significance and value to their most effective, and particularly to their indispensable means.

Religion as a phase of man's active, practical life is rooted, as we have suggested, in the appreciation and seeking of values. Human valuations set the ends for the sake of which, as we shall presently see, man cultivates the religious life. At first the values for the sake of which man is religious are the crudely physical and sensuous values in which the child mind and primitive men are principally interested. As man develops an interest in the more ideal values, these tend increasingly to take the place of material ends and interests, so that in some of the more advanced phases of religion attention may be said to be centered in the promotion of those values which are felt to be of the highest importance or even in some sense imperative, not only for the individual but for the social group.

It has always been with those values which have been felt to be most imperative that religious modes of con-

sciousness and behavior have been most closely associated. At first what seemed most imperative was either
what was deemed essential to survival—especially of
the group—in the struggle for existence, or what was imposed upon the individual by the group, often without
any clear indication of the genuine social reasons back
of the injunction, often with the substitution of some arbitrary and artificial reason. More and more, however,
with survival made reasonably secure for the time being,
interest came to be centered not in the struggle for
existence simply, but in the struggle for a better existence; and with the progressive emancipation of the
thoughtful individual from the arbitrary authority of the
social group, values which were genuinely and intrinsically imperative came to be substituted for the often
arbitrary and oppressive commands and prohibitions of
society. In particular, the values of individual conscien-
tiousness and good will and of the true well-being of
society have come to be, for the free, thoughtful and
generous, not merely conditionally imperative (that is,
imperative for the realizing of this or that particular
purpose), but imperative categorically or unconditionally
(that is, under any and every possible combination of
circumstances). Such absolutely imperative values naturally and rightly come to be appreciated as of central
importance for religion—so much so in fact that there
are some who would define religion as being in essence
neither more nor less than "a consciousness of the highest social values" (Ames), or the socially "shared quest
of a good life in a good world" (Haydon). This is surely
to give to "the moral law within" all, if not much more
than all, its true religious significance.

Such definitions, however, are manifestly one-sided.
Over against this social theory according to which religion is just the seeking of values, particularly the social
seeking of values and the seeking of social values, we
may place the almost equally one-sided view that religion is the mere consciousness of a mysterious reality
or power in the cosmic environment. However intimately

religion may be related to such phases of human experience as contemplation of the starry heavens above or of the moral law within, it is not, in its most characteristic development, to be identified either with the one or the other. *Potentially* religious the consciousness of mysterious cosmic power and the recognition of imperative spiritual and social values may be, but either without the other is not yet religion in its full or characteristic essence. Morality is not religion, even though it be potentially religious. Morality touched with emotion is morality still, even if it be the more potential of religion for that emotional touch. Mere devotion to ideals, however universally and eternally valid, can never be more than the content or a part of the content of religion without its form, just as wondering awe in the contemplation of reality, or even of a higher power, is, if there be no reference to ideal or human values, the mere empty form of religion without its vital content.

Neither is religion the simple aggregate of these two constituent elements of our interest and experience. Form *plus* content, reality-feeling *plus* value-appreciation do not necessarily amount to religion. Rooted in our awareness of reality and in our quest for values, *the distinctively religious interest is an interest in the relation of reality to values*. Not the relation of each and every reality to each and every value is that in which religion, as it develops, comes to be and remains specifically interested. The relation, rather, of reality viewed as a more or less unitary whole, and especially of reality in its more mysterious and still somewhat transcendent aspects, to all genuine human values, individual and social, and especially to such as are felt to be the most imperative—this it is that forms the focus of attention in all the more characteristic developments of the religious consciousness. May it not possibly be that social and moral values are somehow enforced by the mysterious awe-inspiring power upon which we feel that we are ultimately dependent? Is there not an extrahuman factor or cosmic power at work for the promotion of genuine human values? Will reality, or more specifically the mysterious higher power upon which we are in the last analysis absolutely dependent, assist us in the production of values, especially those values of moral character and social well-being which we feel to be absolutely imperative; and if so, under what conditions? And can we trust that higher power with which we and our values ultimately have to do, for the adequate conservation of our highest values over and above what man with his own unaided powers can accomplish? These are the specifically religious questions and matters of concern.

There has been a persistent tendency from very early times to interpret the relation of the mysterious cosmic power to the highest social values animistically, that is, in terms of the attitudes and activities of an essentially personal spirit or spirits. Recognized moral obligations to oneself and others are regarded as the law or will of a mysterious cosmic spirit, or personal power. At least some of the spirits, or more especially the supreme spirit, God, is believed to work providentially for the promotion of human well-being, and this beneficent activity of God, it has been commonly held, is facilitated by the establishment of the right relationship—whatever that may be—between the human being and his God. And finally, man has come to entrust his future well-being and the conservation of all his most cherished values to the benevolent care of this same divine person or spirit.

It is but natural that man should do this. Animism is the first philosophy of the mysterious—naturally so, for what can be more reasonable than that man should interpret the unknown by the known, the not-self by the self? And what more natural than that man should carry this animistic principle of explanation into his religious thinking and interpret the mysterious higher cosmic power in essentially personal terms? It will be a part of our task to inquire whether and to what extent, if at all, this principle of explanation which was so natural and reasonable for primitive thought can be regarded as essentially true and valid to-day.

With the widening of man's experience and the growth of his acquaintance with reality—or rather with particular realities and the various kinds of reality—his interest in the relation of reality to values tended to become increasingly a multiplicity of different interests, all having to do with the effectiveness of particular things and human persons as means for the production and conservation of the several values appreciated. More and more life tended to move in the round of these immediate practical interests as distinguished from the original religious interest. What was left of the religious interest now tended to become remote and vague, an interest in the relation of reality as a whole, or of the inveterately mysterious element or the supreme power in reality, to individual and social values. And so, with development in the direction of a scientific and socially ethical type of adjustment to things and persons, life tended to become in a sense secular rather than distinctly religious.

Secularism has generally been regarded as hostile to religion, but in the light of later developments it is perhaps not too much to say that some considerable measure of secularization was necessary, if the specific differentiation of religion from other phases of primitive life and its eventual higher development were to be made possible. Ordinary life had to become secular in the sense of man's learning to help himself by adjusting himself in matter-of-fact ways to the familiar objects of his everyday world. Man had to free himself to a considerable extent from the inhibiting feeling of awe which originally possessed him in the presence of the unfamiliar and mysterious. Only against the background of such a relatively secular life and in contrast with it could a specifically religious type of experience be recognized as such.

But of course it was not enough, for the developing of religion as specifically different from other phases of life and experience, that life should undergo this preliminary secularization. Something had to happen to show the inadequacy of the ordinary secular outlook and ways of living. Nor has life ever gone on for long without the occurrence of such events. In human experience definite *crises* frequently occur, in which, when imperative values are threatened, the familiar scientific and social adjustments fail to meet the situation with satisfaction to man's insistent needs. Once more there arises that primitive feeling of absolute dependence, that numinous sense of a mysterious and overpowering cosmic reality. Not only does the question of the fundamental relation of reality to human values become urgent once again; in the extremity of his need man feels that something must be done about it. In order to escape from his evil plight or to avert an impending disaster he feels impelled to take up toward the still mysterious and awe-inspiring higher power something like the experimental attitudes and adjustments which he has found so effective in dealing with the familiar things and persons of his ordinary life. "At their wit's end all men do pray." Man is but groping at first for the right adjustment, and as his experimentation is in the realm of his reawakened religious interest and directed toward the still mysterious and awe-inspiring power whose favorable attitude toward his threatened values he desires, it may be said that the adjustments he now makes are specifically religious adjustments, and that what he is seeking is a specifically religious experience of deliverance from experienced or threatened evil—that is, an experience of salvation—through the agency of the specifically religious object or reality (God) to which he is seeking to be rightly adjusted.

This turning, in a crisis, to God for salvation from evil is a perennial feature of vital religion. This is what the "theology of crisis" is trying to get us to appreciate once more in our day. Only in the extremity of his need does man tend to turn from man and material things, from science and self-help, to wait upon the still largely inscrutable higher power which he cannot choose but recognize and which he feels to be that upon which ultimately he and his values absolutely depend. Commonly,

however, man does not remain, as the theologians of crisis seem to teach that he ought to remain, in a relationship of mere passivity and agnostic helplessness toward the mysterious higher power; the attitude is usually one of active adjustment and expectant waiting for a response.[*]

This active experimental attitude in religion is given a certain direction by the interpretation of the religious object in animistic or personalistic terms. As a consequence of this interpretation prayer, praise and propitiatory offering enter largely into the attempt to fulfill the necessary religious adjustment. But like every other form of experimentation the process is at its best one of trial and error. Often the experimental adjustment fails; sometimes it succeeds or seems to succeed. At least the desired deliverance from actual or threatened evil sometimes occurs; and, when it does, there is a natural tendency to interpret this favorable event as due to the agency of the higher power (commonly thought of as spirit) to which in the first place religious adjustment was made. In other words, the satisfactory sequel to a certain religious adjustment is interpreted as involving discovery or "revelation" of the reality and favorable attitude of that which is the special object of religious interest and adjustment, the object to which, interpreted as spirit, the gifts were offered and the prayers and praises addressed.

In popular religion such conclusions are as a rule rather uncritically drawn; so much so that it may almost be said that it is the chief task of critical empirical religion to draw its conclusions as to verification in religious experience without committing the common fallacy of *post hoc ergo propter hoc*. In other words, what religion has to do in order to establish its case is to find, in

[*] It is true enough that in many instances, as Barth and his followers contend, the individual arrives at an impasse, even in his religious experimentation and seeking, until in some way he becomes subjectively convinced of the authenticity of some event or being as a veritable "Word" or manifestation of the purposive activity of God, and that then only does he find it possible to enter into a positive and expectant religious adjustment.

relation to its specific object, an adjustment which will prove to be *dependably* successful, that is, that will dependably condition progress in some definite and desirable direction. Only then can it be said that religious experimentation discovers something in reality which corresponds to its practically universal presupposition that a higher power favorable to human values really exists. Even when such verification of faith occurs, assuming that it does occur, questions as to whether the dependable reality is or is not spirit, and just what, more particularly, its characteristics are, remain as problems for further consideration and solution.

This view of religion, emphasizing as it does the place of experimental adjustment to reality for the promotion of values, favors what may be called the *experimental theory of the genesis of religion,* though not without recognizing elements of truth in other theories. The principal theories of the origin of religion may be grouped under the following six heads: nativism, naturism, collectivism, animism, mysticism, and experimentalism. By the term nativism may be meant either that religion is the expression of a simple, specifically religious instinct or that it is a special development of some particular instinct in more or less disguised or sublimated form, such as the herd instinct or the sex instinct. In its more scientific form it has this much truth in it, that into the emotional and expressional sides of religion there enter, either as sublimated or else in their crude original form, most of the impulsive elements of human nature, whether these be thought of as inherited or as specific tendencies or "drives" acquired during the infancy of the individual. Naturistic theories rightly call attention, although generally in a one-sided way, to the primitive feeling of awe and sense of dependence in the presence of the more stupendous and mysterious aspects of cosmic reality; but that this is one of the main roots of religion we have already pointed out. Collectivism, or the social value theory of the genesis of religion, rightly points out the other principal root of the religious consciousness, namely the value-seeking tendency; but, as commonly stated, the theory fails to take adequate account of the equally fundamental importance of the primitive consciousness of cosmic reality and power. Animistic views fix attention upon primitive man's natural tendency to interpret all reality in terms of what he knows about himself; but such theories commonly overlook the fact that there is much more in religion than a mere philosophy of nature, whether it be crudely primitive or scientifically sophisticated. The theory which would find the genesis of religion in mysticism has to meet the criticism that the mystical experience in which it claims to find the origin of all religion is either a religious mysticism in which, as a contemplation of the religious object, the previous existence of religion is presupposed, or else a non-religious mysticism, involving no consciousness of a specifically religious object but being simply a highly emotional contemplation of the natural environment, so that in neither case is any explanation given of the genesis of the specifically religious consciousness as such. Such criticism would hardly be fair to the theory, however, since an originally non-religious but more or less mystical contemplation of nature might conceivably, if combined with suggestions from animism, lead to experimental adjustments of a specifically religious sort, thus becoming a factor in the genesis of religion in the full sense of the word. But this would be no more than to say that, as in the case of each of the other theories, nativism, naturism, collectivism, and the animistic theory, so too in the case of the mystical theory what is set forth is only one of many factors which enter into a rather complex causal process.

What is needed is a synthetic view of the genesis of religion, and in effecting such a synthesis a prominent place may well be given to what may be called the experimental theory, or experimentalism. It is a view which has been too much neglected, perhaps in part because in the form in which up to the present it has been chiefly known —that given it by Sir James Frazer—it is inadequately stated and actually misleading. According to Frazer religion is a transitional stage between magic and science in man's experimental adjustment aiming at the control of natural powers in the interest of human values; and more particularly, it consists in the attempt to propitiate unseen spirits and persuade them to use their power to intervene in the natural world and control its forces on man's behalf. In criticism of this particular form of experimentalism it may be pointed out that religion is not necessarily bound up with the attempt to control external nature without the employment of natural means. It is no mere prescientific substitute for magic. It often happens that what the religious man is interested in, in seeking the aid of some superhuman spiritual reality, is not supernatural intervention in the external world to adjust it satisfactorily to human desires, but rather a change in the man himself, so that he may be better adjusted at one and the same time to the necessities of the natural order and to the demands of the spiritual ideal. Moreover, it has not been shown that man, in seeking inner spiritual aid in religious ways, must necessarily be unscientific. Indeed, if it be a fact that religion at its best is of real help toward a better way of living, the truth may well be that one cannot be completely scientific if he refuses to make any use whatever of the resources of experimental religion for the solution of his practical life-problems.

What we mean to say in advocating experimentalism as a theory of the genesis of religion is that religion is an integral part of man's experimental adjustment to reality for the promotion of values. Rooted in an awareness of a mysterious higher reality and in the appreciation and seeking of human values, and particularly interested in the relation of that power to these values, religion first becomes religion in the full sense of the word when it becomes a way of life, a way of promoting or at least seeking to promote appreciated values by means of an adjustment to a specifically religious object, regarded as not only a reality but a power.

When thus interpreted, experimentalism as a theory of the genesis of religion makes it possible to do full justice to the mystical theory. Mystical religion is closely related to primitive reality-feeling, but as specifically religious it contemplates its object as somehow embodying, or at least as being favorably related to, what has the highest value. Experimental religion begins in contemplation of mysterious cosmic reality as possibly favorable to man's highest and most imperative values, an attitude which includes the beginning of trust, the characteristic attitude of practical religion. And while experimental religion finds what is perhaps its most characteristic expression in the use of religious power as means to appreciated ends, it tends to pass over, under favorable conditions, into a satisfied contemplation, more or less mystical, of this same religious object (reality or power) as end. Alternation in the reverse direction, from contemplation as end to use as means, may also take place; but the use of objects as means very commonly precedes the highest appreciation of them as ends.

But to carry our experimentalist theory of religion further, not only is the differentiation of religion from other phases of life to be interpreted in terms of experimental adjustment to reality for the promotion of values; the same thing is to be said of the differentiation which in the course of history has taken place within religion itself, namely, its differentiation into certain regional groupings of religions, into the various national and founded or international religions, and into religious sects and individual religious formations. All such differentiation may be considered as religious experimentation on the part of the human race. This fundamental and rather obvious fact is in great danger of being overlooked by those historical and sociological students of religion who are primarily interested in pointing out the economic and other non-religious or not distinctly religious factors which have entered into these differentiations within religion. In practical experimental religion the other human interests are presupposed, the distinctively religious interest being centered in the question of how to find a dependably effective and satisfactory adjustment to a divine reality or power, whether as means to other ends, or as an end in itself. The many and wide differences which have developed within religion are often viewed cynically, but they were to have been expected and really have very great value for critical religion. What the individual can do in the way of experimentation in religion, where inner sincerity is all-important, is decidedly limited; but here in the history of religion one has before his eyes the results of the race's experiments. Like all experimentation, it has been a trial-and-error process, and here the amount of error, judged from any one point of view within the whole, is immense; still one may learn much even from the mistakes which others have made.

The results of experimentation in religion are to be seen not only in the differentiation of religions, but in religious progress as well. In the course of history religion has made progress not only by being influenced by the general advance of the race in knowledge and rationality, in æsthetic culture and in moral and social development, but also and especially by building up a gradually growing body of knowledge, based upon experience, of just what it is as well as what it is not that religion is good for, that is, knowledge of what religion can be depended upon, under specific conditions, to accomplish. In earlier times religion tended to be tried as a quasi-magical means of promoting any and every kind of appreciated value, including the most sensuous and material; but such religion was essentially prescientific, and much of its experimentation was bound to be discredited in time. Fortunately for the persistence of experimental religion, however, man often found that entering into religious adjustments for one purpose was, although disappointing so far as that particular purpose was concerned, of very great value from another and even more important point of view. Many times, praying for victory and

success by direct supernatural intervention in the immediate environment, he gained not that, but faith in the
reality of a friendly power sufficient for his imperative
need, and through this faith the courage, perseverance,
and such other spiritual qualities as were directly instrumental to the ends originally contemplated. As a result
of such experiences man has been learning what religion
is good for as well as what it is not good for; he has
been learning, slowly but surely, to depend upon divine
power in the special ways characteristic of religion, not
for such "answers to prayer" as would involve a sus-
pension of the laws of nature, but for such *effects* of
true prayer in the life of the spirit (and through that,
such other effects) as experience teaches him he may
expect to obtain on condition of a definite type of religious adjustment. From this point of view the verbal
expression of the prayer is not the prayer; the prayer
is the religious adjustment itself. Still, the verbal expression, the "prayers" which we "say" may have great
value; they may be found to work by way of auto-suggestion for the maintenance of that dependably effective
and therefore "right" religious adjustment in which
alone true prayer consists.

Thus as a result of experiment, observation and reflection, historical religion in its more progressive forms
has been tending to seek preparation for crises, deliverance from actual and threatened evil, and positive
achievement and success in life, less and less along lines
of direct intervention on the part of the mysterious power
in the external world, and more and more in the direction of inner readjustment and integration and the development of a good and efficient will. It is true that,
becoming more moral in his interest, man has come to
be more interested in the possibilities of promoting moral
values through religious experience; but, in this turning
from the outer physical world to the inner realm of the
spirit in his religious life, man has been fundamentally
influenced by the discovery that it is in the latter rather
than in the former sphere that he can reasonably look

for dependable results on condition of a specifically religious adjustment.

Thus progressive experimental religion has been becoming at once more rational and more moral, more spiritual and more scientific. This is not to say as yet that the religious man really does get, through religious experience, any scientific knowledge about an independently existing God; for the present I am satisfied to point out that, within the limits of his realistic religious presuppositions, the religious man, in becoming more critically empirical and logical, is becoming less unscientific and more scientific, and that certain results of his religious experience and logical thought naturally seem to him to yield genuinely verified knowledge of a really existent God. Man seems to have been finding out through experience what he can depend upon religion (or reality through religion) for, and how he must relate himself to reality in religion, if he is to be able to depend upon it for the results desired.

The specifically religious adjustment which, it is claimed, tends dependably toward a desirable experience of emancipation and achievement, primarily in the moral and spiritual realm, is a very specific adjustment or series of adjustments. It begins in aspiration toward an ideal of higher moral and spiritual attainment, not only as an ultimate end in itself but also as instrumental to the redemption and regeneration of society.[*] It culminates in self-surrender, appropriating faith and a habitual willed responsiveness toward an object regarded as at once ideal and real, friendly and accessible, efficient and for one's religious need sufficient. Such a religious adjustment, it is claimed, makes dependably toward the desired result.

It is important at this point, however, that one possible source of misunderstanding be removed. What is claimed for religious experience on condition of this

[*] A general attitude of good will (unselfish love and forgivingness) is an important means of facilitating the desired ethico-religious experience, which in religious adjustment at its best includes a higher achievement along lines of just that same active good will toward men.

"right religious adjustment" is not an exact, quantitatively predictable result. There may indeed be almost
no noticeable result unless the qualitatively right adjustment is maintained with a high degree of intensity (concentration of attention) and persistence. Otherwise the
desired result may be inhibited by any one of a number
of adverse factors, or by a combination of several or
all of them. Among such adverse factors are an unfavorable social environment, antagonistic instincts or
"drives," deeply ingrained contrary habits, ideas and
prejudices of an opposite tendency, repressed complexes
giving rise to hindering processes, an abnormal supply
of hormones from the "glands regulating personality,"
lack of energy through malnutrition, and pathological
conditions in general, whether physical, mental or social.
On the other hand the normal tendency of the "right
religious adjustment" may be rather suddenly reinforced by the release from the unconscious of the energy
and emotion associated with a long repressed but growing conviction as to truth or duty or a new religious life.
In some instances this reinforcement seems to have been
sufficient to overpower and submerge completely the impulses of depraved appetite and to nullify in large measure the influence of an unfavorable social environment.
But whether inhibited or accelerated in the particular
instance, there is, it is claimed, a dependable tendency
toward a universally desirable moral and spiritual result
on condition of an earnest and persistent maintenance
of the specific religious adjustment to which we have
referred.

It is essentially this religious adjustment which
emerges and conditions the result in the religious experience of moral conversion. In vital religion of moral redemption there tends to occur a spiritual or ethico-religious crisis, in which, if spiritual disaster is to be avoided,
an experience of regeneration or renovation of the moral
will seems imperative, and, as a necessary means to this
end, a whole-hearted decision and act of turning to God
in order the more effectively to be turned from recog-

nized evil and toward the true good. Presupposed in this
momentous decision and act is the thought of God as
great enough and favorable enough to man to be ready to
respond effectively to the right religious adjustment
along lines of man's imperative need. When, after a life
relatively irreligious (or wrongly religious) and characterized by moral failure, man in his spiritual crisis has
recourse to God, entering whole-heartedly into the religious adjustment described and persisting therein, he
eventually experiences a moral conversion of will and
spirit which he tends very naturally to interpret as being,
in its essentials, the work of the God to whom he adjusted
himself. At the same time he is led to feel that such
an experience is universally valid and imperative.

In so far, then, as what Barth, Brunner, and their associates are concerned to insist upon is the spiritual crisis
of conviction of sin and the revelation of God in the
experience of spiritual conversion, they may well be
heeded by those interested in the phenomenology of experimental religion and ultimately in the question of its
validity and truth. Moreover, in interpreting the emergence of the faith or religious adjustment which conditions the conversion experience as already involving, as
a factor, the gracious operation of God, they may be, so
far as we can yet say, well within their rights and within
the truth.[5] It may be suggested, however, that the value
of the service which these theologians are undoubtedly
rendering is seriously impaired by their reaction to that
predestinationism and those exaggerations of human im-
potence which were so characteristic of the theologians
of the Reformation, notably Calvin.

[5] Suggestive in this connection are these words of an individual psychologist and psychotherapist: "Character is not unchangeable, there is
a way out of all its difficulties. . . . By his own means and arts man cannot
force his way out of these difficulties of character. . . . The way out comes
as a creative act which we cannot force by our self-education or our
psychotherapy. . . . Our efforts remove the obstacles. If we do not
remove the obstacles we may make the creative act impossible. . . . The
practical experience of science agrees with Christianity: Conversion comes
by Grace. . . . But if we think we have cleared away all the obstacles,
and the recovery still does not set in, then our estimate was wrong."
God Helps Those . . . by Fritz Künkel, M.D., 1931. Pp. 268, 278.

We are now in a position to offer a definition of the essence or, more specifically, of the good essence of religion. By the essence of any historical or experienced reality we mean that in the actual which it is essential to retain in order to realize the true ideal—provided always that this "essence" can retain its existence and vitality when separated from all elements of the actual which it is essential to get rid of. From the point of view of this pragmatic but realistic definition of essence, the good essence of religion may be formulated as in the following definition: *Religion, presupposing and involving the pursuit of values regarded as of supreme importance, is essentially a conscious relation, not merely of inevitable dependence upon a higher power, but also and more especially a relation of active adjustment to the higher reality or power upon which man's highest values are believed ultimately to depend.* Furthermore, since our concept of essence does not require that the full essence of a reality developing in history be explicitly revealed in the earliest stages of that historical development, we may include within our definition the following addendum: *also, especially in its higher and more successful developments, an experience of deliverance or achievement, tending to be interpreted as due in significant measure to the agency of the higher power to which adjustment was made, and tending also to be followed by a grateful and in some cases a mystical contemplation of that religious object, and by an affirmative response to what are taken to be its requirements.*

What we have stated in the above definition is only the general *form* of religion. But in the preceding discussion something as to the essential *content* of religion was also suggested, at least tentatively. Ultimately the question of the content of essential religion is the question not merely of what values are worthy of being sought through religious adjustment, but of what the values are which experience shows to be capable of being promoted in dependable manner through appropriate religious adjustment. Naturally and apparently with good reason there come to be attributed to the divine power or reality religiously depended upon, the same values and qualities of character as have been found to be dependably promoted in man in and through this right, or dependably effective, religious adjustment which he has discovered. Furthermore, there is a reciprocal tendency to evaluate these qualities of character in turn as "divine," not only when they appear as a result of explicit religious adjustment, but more generally. This is on the principle that since a certain value-producing process is increased, accelerated, through a certain kind of adjustment to God, so that the *increased* value-production is naturally ascribed to God, we have in this circumstance a clew to the objective source of the *original* production of those values, and not to their subsequent increase (through religion) alone.

And so it is surmised and comes to be affirmed in the name of religion in its higher, more ethical and spiritual developments not only that the religious object, God, to whom adjustment is made, is spiritual, characterized by ideal moral goodness, spiritual beauty and rationality, and that he is the main objective source of spiritual progress in so far as this is manifested as a result of religious attitudes and experience, but that the spiritual everywhere is divine in quality, and this for the reason and in the sense that it is rooted in the being and nature of God. Thus a religious interpretation of the cosmic process in which these presumably divine values are produced is suggested. Not only is the divine object to which religion adjusts itself affirmed, on the basis of successful religious adjustment, as an existent reality and as being at work in man's spiritual progress through religious experience; it is also affirmed that God is immanent in all spiritual progress and reality. And this suggests in turn the idea of an intimate relation between the immanent spiritual reality called God and the laws and energy of the physical world—a relation which, it is felt, may be somewhat analogous to the relation between the human mind or spirit and the human body.

These various religious affirmations, made with varying degrees of assurance, call for critical examination in the light of philosophy. Up to the present point our discussion has fallen under the caption of the phenomenology of religion. We are not using the term "phenomenology" in quite the sense in which it is employed by Husserl and Scheler, who mean by it philosophy without *any* presuppositions as to existence, whether of world, self or God, and without (at first) choosing between subjective idealism and realism. In our procedure we have not questioned the ordinary "common sense" realism with regard to a single real physical world and a plurality of real human selves; but we have been careful to preserve the purely phenomenological point of view with regard to God. That is, we have made statements about what the term "God" means to the religious man, what God is from the point of view of religion, without assuming anything as to the metaphysical validity of the religious way of thinking. We have assumed neither that the God of which the religious speak is an existent reality, nor, after the manner of "psychologism," that God is a mere idea in the subjective religious consciousness. Our phenomenology of religion has been simply a historico-psychological study, without either ontological presuppositions with reference to God or epistemological presuppositions with reference to religious knowledge.

But the religious problem is too interesting and urgent for it to be desirable or even possible to remain for long on the neutral ground of phenomenology, between religious realism and a subjective or psychological idealism such as would see in God nothing but the subjective idea of God or the mere subjective content of the religious consciousness. Either God in some religiously acceptable sense of the term exists, or no such being exists; religion is either fundamentally valid or else, even at its best, illusory, false and essentially bad. We must press on beyond mere phenomenology into the paths of epistemology and ontology. Our second part will deal with the problem as to the possibility of verified religious knowledge and reasonable religious belief. Our third part, building on the foundation of the first and second parts, will attempt to state and to bring together into a more or less unified whole what we can know and what we can reasonably believe with reference to the object of religious interest and experience.

2. Epistemological

It has been intimated above that the observant and critically experimental religious man has been learning to employ, on the basis of his realistic religious presuppositions, the logical procedure of modern inductive science. Before inquiring particularly as to whether his underlying religious realism may or may not be a reasonably tenable philosophical position, let us look a little into the question of the logic of empirical religious thought.

Scientific method is, or claims to be, the universally valid way of proving the truth of true judgments about reality and of discrediting the claims of judgments which are not true. This presupposes the notion of truth, which, as everyone who has not been tampered with knows, is some sort of agreement or correspondence or identity between the idea and the reality or subject-matter about which it is predicated, judged to be true. But, as Bradley, among others, pointed out, and as the history of intellectualist attempts to frame a definition of truth abundantly shows, the moment we begin to ask what kind of identity or correspondence truth is, we get into a peck of trouble. If, for the judgment to be true, the identity between subject and predicate must be total, one is led to the conclusion that only a meaningless proposition, of the form a is a, can be strictly true. Any other judgment, being of the form a is b, does not state a total identity between subject and predicate, and so is not true but false. On strict intellectualist principles, then, according to which truth is identity, neither more nor less, between subject and predicate, all judgments must be either tautologous or false.

But we must not forget that in actual judging in everyday life the subject of the judgment is not the mere word which we use when we express the judgment in a spoken or written proposition. That is a mere symbol of the reality (actual, supposed or assumed) which is the subject-matter judged about. The subject-symbol is *assumed* to represent the subject-matter, and the predicate-symbol is *now declared* to represent it. But if the subject-matter is a concrete thing, how can any predicate be identical with it? Every predicate, as such, is a mere logical idea and not a concrete thing. The number of ideas that may be predicated of a concrete reality, if any may be, is unlimited. Only an infinite, omniscient mind could have an absolute or total identity between its idea (or ideas) of the reality and the reality itself. A true judgment about reality is not, according to the intellectualist definition of truth, a possibility for the human mind. No human judgment, strictly speaking, can be true—not even this one! Only an Absolute Mind could possibly judge truly about reality. But why should an Absolute Mind, having all knowledge already, make any judgment at all? On intellectualist principles, then, there seems to be no such thing as truth of judgments.

But judgments, even if never strictly true, so far as intellectualism can see, are made and for practical purposes must continue to be made, and they may at least be evaluated according to their practical working value in everyday life. May there not be some sort of practical value of judgments or of predicates which will serve as a criterion of truth, in the sense in which truth is really accessible to the human mind? We need not jump to the conclusion, so characteristic of recent pragmatism, that truth means no more than the practical value of ideas, their "working in the way in which they set out to work." If that were the case, truth might contradict truth and there could be no guarantee in the nature of truth that any judgment was true universally and permanently. Not even the pragmatic judgment about the nature of truth could be presented as true in the sense that it ought always to be recognized by all as the true notion of truth!

It can scarcely be denied, however, that judgments are actually made, that they claim to represent reality by an idea or predicate, and that in practical life judgments in which the predicate represents (corresponds with, is identical with) the subject-matter sufficiently for the practical purposes with which the judgments were made are *taken* as true. But not every judgment which is taken as true ought to be taken as true; there is a difference between apparent or nominal truth and real truth. May we not believe then that a judgment is really true if its predicate represents the subject-matter (that is, if the idea corresponds with, is identical with, the reality) sufficiently for whatever purposes *ought* to be considered in making the judgment, or in deciding between this judgment and its contradictory (one or the other of which must, of course, be true)?

Here we seem to have arrived at a definition of truth in which the general notion of truth (correspondence or identity of idea with reality) is taken from intellectualism and the criterion of truth (practical value) from pragmatism. More technically, intellectualism furnishes the proximate genus to which truth belongs, and pragmatism the differentia of the species. And the definition is stated in such a way as to make room for judgments which are accessible to the human mind and yet true in the sense that they are as objectively and permanently valid as is the duty of a given person in a given situation at a given time. For the moral consciousness, that is being objective and valid enough.

But when we come to apply our results to the actual judgments of everyday life, we may often fall into doubt as to whether they are really true in the sense in which we have defined truth. When can we be sure that we have taken into account all the purposes which ought to be considered in making the judgment? Many times we cannot be sure; but, in such cases, if we have the right to believe that we have considered all purposes that ought to be considered in making the judgment, and if the representation of reality by idea is sufficient for all the purposes considered, we have the right to believe that our judgment is true.

But can we never get beyond the mere moral right to believe in the truth of our judgments? Can we not attain to knowledge that our judgments are true? We can, and we often do. Many times what is affirmed more or less tentatively in a judgment or working hypothesis is discovered in immediate experience to have been a true judgment. For instance, if we judge that a certain object is in a certain room, and then enter the room, and discover the object there, we know that the judgment we tentatively made was a true judgment; our working hypothesis has worked *unto verification.* Acting upon the trial-predicate we have been led into an experience in which, in a complex of many sense-elements and re-vived images, we apprehend, perceive, empirically intuit as *presented,* that which in our idea was only *re-presented.* Such, at least, is the common sense way of stating the procedure of science.

We have been led to make a distinction between judgments which we have a moral right to believe to be true and judgments which we know to be true, and the difference is made by the fact that in the latter instance we have been able to employ the scientific method of verification. The recognized test of true representation is presentation; the test of the true hypothesis is perception, immediate experience. What we can experience we can know. If there is an independently existing physical world and if we can have genuine first-hand experience of it, so that what it is as a reality is at least partly presented within the field of our direct observation, we can know it, at least in part. The same statement may be made about the human self, and about the religious object, God. If there is a human self and we can have experience, an empirical intuition, of it, we can know it. If there is an independently existing religious object, or God, as religious realism maintains, and if we can have any direct experience of this divine reality, we can have some genuinely verified, or scientific, religious knowledge. Whether or not we can and do have to any extent, however limited, any such immediate experiential acquaintance with an independently existing divine reality is the central problem of religious epistemology. This problem we must again postpone until we shall have carried a little further our examination into scientific method, particularly in connection with religious thought.

Our immediate problem may be stated thus: assuming, for the moment, that immediate experience of independent reality (whether of world, of self, or of God) is to some extent possible and actual, how may we verify our general hypotheses or theories as to the divine action and nature, and how may we build up new generalizations about the reality in question in a logical or scientific way? There are two questions here; let us first take up the question of the verification of general hypotheses or theories. The first thing to be done is to deduce from the general theory in question, in connection with our relevant verified knowledge, some consequence or consequences which must follow if the theory be true. The next step is to examine the relevant facts, and compare them with the deduced consequences. If any logically deduced consequence is contradicted by observed fact, the general theory from which it was deduced is refuted (assuming that the rest of our supposed knowledge of reality involved in the deduction is really valid). If on the other hand a particular logically deduced consequence is found to agree with the relevant observed fact, all we can say is that reality, so far as observed, is *as if* the theory were true. And no matter how far the process may be carried, we never arrive at demonstrated knowledge that the general theory is true, but only that so far as we have examined its logical consequences in the light of the relevant facts, we have found it to be as it would be if it were true. As Professor Whitehead reminds us, ''No observation ever does exactly verify the law which it is presumed to support."[*] Einstein himself frankly admits that no amount of experimentation can ever prove his theories to be right, while a single experiment may at any time prove that they are wrong.

The point of importance here for our present purposes is that this logical limitation of scientific method applies no more and no less to the attempted verification of hypotheses concerning the religious object, God, than to general hypotheses concerning physical nature or the human self. Only what can be immediately experienced, perceived, empirically intuited in a crucial experiment, can be completely verified. The process of gradually approaching a goal which is never quite reached is nevertheless of great significance for practical guidance and reasonable belief, and this is equally true in relation to the world, to the self and to God. And, as a matter of fact, the approach to full verification often seems so close, that by common consent the general hypothesis is recognized as belonging for all practical purposes to the body of scientific fact.

The other phase of scientific method is the process of building up a generalization on the basis of particular observations of fact. This is what is known as induction in the more specific sense of the word. The whole of this inductive procedure is obviously based upon the never-to-be-completely-verified principle of the dependableness of reality, or "uniformity of nature," as it is generally called when applied to the physical world. The fact that this principle never has been and never can be fully verified by the finite mind has long been recognized as imparting a degree of theoretical uncertainty to the inductions based upon it; but it has generally been felt that this is not important from a practical point of view, at least in connection with the physical world, which has commonly been believed to be absolutely uniform, even if we can never verify the assumption of absolute uniformity completely. Believers in a genuine human freedom have held that there is an ultimate indeterminacy

[*] *The Function of Reason,* 1929, p. 67.

and absence of complete predetermination in connection with the activities of the human mind and will; but here again the belief was one never to be completely verified from a theoretical point of view.

Recently however the situation has been radically changed as a result of the investigations of Heisenberg and other physicists. It now appears that not only is it permissible to believe in a principle of indeterminacy in the human will in spite of a high degree of dependableness in human behavior taken in the mass, but that even in the physical world, in spite of the high degree of dependableness in the behavior of electrons taken in the mass, scientists have discovered an ultimate principle of indeterminacy with regard to the behavior of the individual electron under certain conditions. What seems to be true then is that, in spite of an ultimate indeterminacy and possible freedom both in the physical and in the mental realm, there is so much dependableness that laws of a statistical sort may be formulated with a high degree of certainty and over a very extensive area of fact. There may be, so far as we can tell, throughout the physical and psychical realms, some measure either of indetermination or of creative self-determination (or, in the physical, of creative determination by another), and yet there is habit, regularity, mechanization enough for scientific investigators to be justified in looking in both realms for still further illustrations of the "reign of law" beyond those which have already been discovered.

The point of particular interest for our present purposes in all this is that the principle of the dependableness of reality may be applied as a basis for scientific exploration and generalization in religious experience as truly as in experience of the world and of self. This does not exclude the possibility that there may be an element of creative self-determination (mere *in*determination is not the only alternative to complete predetermination from without) as well as a principle of law or habit in the operations of that God or divine reality which the religious man believes to exist as the objective cause of the dependable desirable results at which he claims to arrive in what he considers true religion, or religion at its best. He does not claim that his empirical religious knowledge of the responses of a divine factor can be formulated as mathematically exact laws of quantitative results applying to each and every individual instance; they are rather statistical laws, laws of tendency toward a certain result on certain conditions in the case of any given individual. But the same thing now seems to be true of all reality, psychical and physical, as well as of what is taken to be divine; the laws are not mathematically exact for the ultimate individual, but rather a statistical statement of a tendency or of an average result throughout the group.[7]

In building up generalizations inductively on the basis of particular observations of fact the general procedure is that indicated in Mill's five methods, except that in practice all that is ordinarily possible is to approximate the degree of certainty which would result under the ideal conditions suggested in Mill's formulations. There is, as critics have pointed out, the greatest difficulty in applying the best of the methods, particularly the Method of Difference and the Joint Method of Agreement and Difference. All the methods are really different phases of the single attempt to isolate the phenomenon to be explained and its conditioning cause. But, in all this, scientific method is in no worse case when employed for the gaining of religious knowledge than when used to discover the laws of the physical world or of the human mind. Unless it can be assumed that there is experience of the reality in question (the world, the self, or God), there can be no basis for scientific generalization; assuming that there is such experience of independently existing reality, the methods of inductive generalization with

[7] The principle of indeterminacy (with what it involves for the theoretical permissibility of belief in either a limited indetermination or a creative determination) which recent investigation has shown to have application even in physics, the former stronghold of determinism and mechanism, is no doubt applicable in biology and sociology as well as in psychology and empirical theology.

their difficulties in application are essentially the same in the various fields of interest.

It is sometimes maintained, alike by those who claim empirical religious knowledge and those who dispute the claim, that the characteristic method of empirical theology is the Method of Residues, the principle of which, as applied to the data of religion, might in their opinion be stated in some such way as this: Subduct from the phenomena of religious experience those features which are manifestly due to natural causes; the remaining features of the phenomena may be concluded to be due to a supernatural cause, presumably God.[8] This, I think, is a serious mistake. The Method of Residues is not radically different from the other methods. While valuable for suggesting new hypotheses, it is in itself the least conclusive of all the methods, and its use in connection with religious experience does not necessarily lead to any supernaturalist or metaphysical explanation at all. Like the Method of Difference, to which it is a halting and inconclusive approach, it may be applied on the basis of a purely psychological or phenomenalist point of view. Suppose, to be explicit, that we subduct from a religious experience (or "bracket") all those features which are obviously due to causes other than the specific religious adjustment (such as suggestion, social pressure, habits, complexes, sublimated impulses, instincts, drives acquired in infancy, racial libido, hormones, and in general, special conditions of physical and mental health and peculiarities of personality and native intelligence); it may be found that there is still in the religious experience a certain moral trend which it seems reasonably possible to explain as the effect of the specific religious adjustment, whether there be or be not any such objectively existing God as the adjustment itself presupposes. This use of the Method of Residues may suggest definite religious

[8] R. G. Milburn, in *The Theology of the Real*, 1925, says "a rigorous application of the Method of Residues should lead to the discovery . . . of facts which are intelligible only upon supernaturalist assumptions," pp. 26-7; cf. pp. 59, 95, etc. J. H. Leuba would restrict empirical theology to a similar use of this method, which, of course, he regards as invalid; see *A Psychological Study of Religion*, 1912, pp. 220-27.

experimentation, in connection with which the Method of Difference, the Method of Concomitant Variation, and the Joint Method of Agreement and Difference may be employed, still on the purely psychological or phenomenalistic basis. It is not the Method of Residues that leads to a metaphysically real, independently existing God, but a realistic religious epistemology as a philosophical interpretation of facts which as facts of religious experience, are describable in terms of the psychology of religion, whatever be their true philosophical interpretation. It is only when the psychological description is taken as a complete metaphysical interpretation (on the principle of subjective or psychological idealism) that the religious man and the philosopher have the right to object; and even then the objection is not properly made on the basis of the Method of Residues, but rather, as we have said, on the ground of the arguments for a realistic religious epistemology.

We must now turn to the problem of epistemology proper. Defining knowledge as adequate and adequately critical certitude of the presence of what is really present and of the truth of judgments which are really true, we have to ask whether knowledge of reality in general and of religious reality in particular is possible for the human mind. Historically, experimental religion has been, especially in its earlier phases, a naïve religious realism, but with further experience it has become more critical. Continuing to assume that there is a religious object or divine reality existing independently of man's consciousness of it, and that it ought to be possible to get some evidence of its reality and present activity in response to the right religious adjustment, if only that right religious adjustment can be found, the religious man persists in his experimentation and interprets the resulting experience in the light of his presuppositions. Assuming a critical direct realism, experimental religion arrives by an essentially scientific procedure at certain generalizations about the religious object and its activities, just as physical science and what has been called "self-psychology" on the basis of a similar critical direct realism in their respective fields arrive at certain generalizations with regard to the physical world and the psychical self. Is this increasingly critical and would-be scientific common-sense realism essentially valid, especially in the realm of religion? To this central problem of religious epistemology we must now, with whatever light we can derive from general epistemology, address ourselves.

From a preliminary survey of the problem a few things seem reasonably clear. We can have adequate certainty as to the immediate content of our own present consciousness. Furthermore, we cannot complain of the degree of our assurance as to the truth of certain mathematical and other logically necessary propositions, when we understand just what it is that is affirmed, and why. But all such mathematical or logical truth and certainty, while absolute enough, is merely hypothetical, supposititious. It is concerned not with actuality, but only with possibility and necessity. More explicitly, it undertakes to state, on the basis of rational reflection, not what the real world, the real self, or any other existent reality *is*, but what it *may be* (that is, what is theoretically possible) and what it *must be, if* some other things are (that is, what follows necessarily from the assumed premises). Now if the reality to be known be simply idea, either in the sense of the immediate content of (our own) consciousness or the mere abstract entities and relations of rational thought, or both of these together, it would seem that we can know reality. But is this all the reality we are interested in knowing, especially in religion? On the other hand, if the reality we would know be a concrete and independently existing reality, but one which never becomes content of our immediate human experience, how can we verify in experience our ideas about it, and without such verification, how can we know it? How indeed can we ever know the independently real? Can an independently existing concrete reality be immediately experienced in the conscious life of man? If what we are seeking be the same kind and degree of truth and certainty in our judgments about independently existing concrete reality as we have about the immediate contents of our own present consciousness and about the abstractions and hypothetical propositions of mathematics and logic, it may well be that we must remain skeptical. Such absolutely certain knowledge of the truth about independently existing reality would require valid certainty not only that our ideas (predicates) are true representations of the content of immediate experience, but also that what exists independently becomes, in perception, content of immediate experience. The former difficulty may be overcome by means of the definition of truth we have offered, but whether we can have not simply an immediate experience of independently existing reality, but also in this experience a mathematically demonstrative certainty that we are having such experience and knowledge of independent reality, may well remain a matter of skeptical doubt.

But we have reason to be skeptical of skepticism itself, at least as a final position. Whether or not we can attain to absolute truth and knowledge in our judgments about reality, we have to make such judgments, and when our judgments are made with adequately critical care we find that they work as if they were true. From a practical point of view at least, science has validity. If, however, the hypotheses which work unto verification in the scientific sense are to be regarded as real truth and real knowledge, must we not be able to hold to a direct intuition of independent reality in normal perceptual experience? Is such direct intuition of independent reality defensible in epistemology?

There are three main species of view in current epistemology, namely, idealism, dualistic realism, and direct or monistic realism, and each species exists in several varieties. We shall look into these in turn, giving some attention to their application to the physical world and to mind, as well as to the religious object. This may prove to be important, not only because the results of general epistemology may throw much light upon the problems of religious epistemology, but also for the reason that, if and in so far as the religious object is regarded as immanent in the world and in man, the evidence for the reality and experienceableness of God may be found to be bound up with the possibility of believing in the world and the self as *experienced* realities.

By idealism in epistemology is meant the view that the reality which we seek to know, whether the physical world, the self, or God, is essentially idea and therefore eminently knowable. We shall first consider epistemological idealism with reference to the physical. Finding that not everything which appears to sense can be reasonably regarded as belonging to an independently existing world, and desiring to avoid the view that physical reality is a wholly independent, unexperienceable and therefore unknowable world, many thinkers have been led to adopt a subjective or psychological idealism, according to which all physical objects are nothing but ideas in the psychological sense, contents of consciousness, appearances in the mind that is aware of them. Obviously from this point of view it could be claimed that experience and knowledge of the physical are not only possible but actual. Furthermore, it is frequently argued in behalf of the theory that it is a natural and reasonable interpretation of experience, for the reason that we are never able to perceive, remember, imagine, or be in any way aware of any object except one which is perceived, remembered, imagined, or in some way an object of awareness, that is, a content of consciousness; so that it would seem that we have no basis in experience for supposing that anything exists but contents of consciousness, ideas in the psychological sense of the term.

This argument from the "egocentric predicament," as it has been called, is not a very conclusive one. Even assuming physical realism, that is, the doctrine of a real physical world existing independently of the mind's consciousness of it, it would still be true that the mind could never perceive nor think it, except as something perceived or thought of. And being related to a conscious subject as object of awareness is not necessarily to be dependent upon that subject or that awareness for existence. For example, my existence, when I am object of your consciousness, does not depend upon your consciousness. Moreover, if the argument from the egocentric predicament proved anything, it would prove solipsism, the doctrine that only the self with its ideas or conscious contents exists.

The next problem for the idealist, then, is how to find some way of retaining the old common sense belief that we have knowledge of independently existing reality and the new psychological point of view according to which the object of experience depends for its existence upon the conscious subject. The desired unifying concept is found in the idea of consciousness in general, or other mind. The physical object depends, it is still held, upon consciousness, but not necessarily upon *my* consciousness; when not real in my mind it may continue to exist in some other mind or minds. This less subjective, more objective form of psychological idealism (still appropriately so called) interprets the object as idea in the psychological sense, namely as dependent content of *some* consciousness.

When psychological idealism is applied to the subject as well as to the object, that is, when the self to which objects are present is interpreted as mere idea or feeling or other content of consciousness, real only when and as consciously experienced, we have what is at once a more extreme and yet a disguised form of the doctrine. The subjectivism is disguised, for while the object is still regarded as essentially a content of experience, the existence of the object is no longer said to depend upon consciousness or upon the psychical subject. Both physical object and psychical subject are said to depend for their existence upon their being experienced. But this pure empiricism or disguised psychological idealism is a very unstable doctrine. When it is said that the conscious subject is real only when it is consciously experienced

as idea or content of consciousness, it being assumed
that sometimes experience is subjective (explicitly related to a subject) and sometimes not, it is impossible
to dodge for long the question as to whose experience it
is in which contents are experienced non-subjectively.
That this is no idle question is evident from the familiar
fact that we often recall experiences which we were not
explicitly thinking of as *our* experiences at the time we
were having them. The experiences were non-subjective
in the sense that there was no explicit self-consciousness
in them, and yet we are now aware that they were subjective in the sense that they were our experiences, else
how could we now recall them? It is difficult to deny the
common-sense personal realism which holds to a reality
of mind, over and above the *idea* of the self as a transient
content of the stream of consciousness.

When subjective or psychological idealism is applied
in the realm of religion the result is that God, the religious object, is held to be nothing but the idea of God in
the mind of man, or at most the immediate content of the
religious consciousness, wholly dependent upon that consciousness for whatever reality it has. Obviously this is
what is popularly known as atheism, and it is no more
likely to prove satisfactory to the practical religious interest than it would be for a hungry man to be told that
there is no food except the idea of food in the mind. To
assure him that the idea exists in other minds as well as
in his, would give him but little comfort. What is wanted
in real life is real food, a real world, real persons and
a real God, not mere ideas of these. And it does not appear that the argument for subjective idealism is any
more demonstrative in religion than it is when it is used
to prove that there is no physical world nor any personal
self except as an idea in the stream of consciousness.

It is an outstanding defect of psychological idealism
that it has no way of distinguishing between reality and
appearance. No reality is more than an appearance in consciousness and all appearances are similarly real in and
for consciousness. But in practical life the distinction be-

tween realities and mere appearances is very real and important. If idealism is to be retained it must seek to become an objective idealism; it must furnish a criterion of objective reality as distinguished from mere subjective appearance. There are in fact two main types of objective idealism. One of these is abstract, or, as we may call it, logical idealism, a view which seems to have arisen under the joint influence of mathematical sciences, such as geometry, and the process of finding logical definitions. As in a definition the concrete subject-matter is equated with an abstract predicate, as being *what* it is, so in logical idealism genuine reality as distinct from appearance is said to be the logical idea, the abstract universal, the universally valid definition, what rational mind would think, whether any mind is actually thinking it or not. And as in geometry the real point, straight line, and circle are the ideal point, ideally straight line and ideal circle respectively, rather than our crude attempts to represent them in the realm of appearance, so it is concluded, in logical idealism, that the true reality, as distinct from all appearances, is the perfect or rational ideal. It is the ideal world that is the real world, and the ideal self that is eternally real and the only real self. Similarly from this point of view the divine ideal is the only real God. As the eternally perfect Ideal, God is the final end of everything; but as having reality only as ideal, God cannot be the efficient cause of anything. Manifestly such a God cannot be made the object of trustful dependence, even if it may be made, in a sense, the object of adoration. It is an absolute validity, not an absolute reality. Logical idealism in religion, like the parallel doctrine regarding the physical world and the psychical self, is the result of taking predication too absolutely, as if the whole reality of the concrete subject-matter could be found in the abstract idea which is all that the predicate is, even in the most adequate definition. It is the result of overlooking the fact that the identity asserted in the judgment between subject and predicate is not an absolute, existential identity but a practical

identity, a functional equivalence for the purposes underlying the judgment.

Convinced that reality must somehow be something
more objective than the psychological idea, the mere dependent content of a stream or streams of consciousness
(which is all that it can be according to subjective idealism), and feeling at the same time that reality must be
something more concrete than the mere validity of an
abstract ideal, however universal and eternal (which
is all that it can be according to the abstract logical idealism which we have just examined), the modern idealist
has sought and claims to have discovered a higher synthesis of the two. Thus it seems to him unnecessary to
turn back from idealism to the realistic mode of thought.
Asking what must be true if psychological idealism, the
doctrine that reality is the concrete subjective idea, and
logical idealism, the doctrine that reality is the abstract
universal idea, are both true as far as they go, only not
the whole truth, the latter-day idealistic dialectic has
evolved the concept of reality as the concrete universal
idea, the logical idea within the psychological idea, the
concrete content of empirical consciousness in so far as
it fits into universal rational form.

This logical-psychological idealism, or objective idealism in its concrete form, is certainly a better practical
substitute for realism than is either of its component elements taken separately. It is more objective than psychological idealism (subjective idealism) alone, and more
concrete than logical idealism (abstract objective idealism) alone. It enables one to distinguish reality from
mere appearance on the one hand, and from mere rational possibility on the other. But it remains as yet
somewhat ambiguous. Is the other mind or consciousness
in which reality exists as rational idea, whether it appears to me or not, *one* mind, one consciousness, or is
it *many* minds? If we say it is a single, all-inclusive
rational consciousness, an Absolute Mind which experiences and comprehends everything, how shall we reconcile this with the fact that ignorance and error are real

in our human experience? As real they must be included, just as they are, in the experience of the *all-inclusive* mind, and yet of course there can be neither ignorance nor error in an *all-knowing* mind. Ignorance supplemented and error corrected would no longer be ignorance and error. Manifestly a single mind cannot be both absolutely rational and absolutely all-inclusive. If on the other hand it be suggested, as it has been by some, that each element of human experience must be modified, transmuted into something different by the mere fact of its being included in the same consciousness with everything else, then it must be recognized that according to this suggestion it is not really *my* experience which is included in the Absolute, but something different, something else. Thus it turns out that the supposedly all-inclusive Absolute is not really all-inclusive after all. This seems to amount to a self-refutation of logical-psychological idealism in its singularistic form, according to which reality is a single, all-inclusive Absolute Mind. The Absolute of absolute idealism, then, which some have been bold enough to offer to religion as a substitute for its God, simply does not exist. So be it; if the Absolute, as a single, all-inclusive mind or self, *were* a reality, it would be the only reality, and you and I as individual selves or minds could not be real at all. To accept the Absolute would be to gain a God at the cost of losing ourselves.

But what shall we say as to the pluralistic form of objective idealism, the view, namely, that the "other mind" in which reality exists whether I am conscious of it or not, is not a single, all-inclusive mind, but many minds which only collectively are inclusive of all reality. On the face of it pluralistic idealism has this to recommend it, that it would at least permit us to regard ourselves as real. But while singularistic idealism saved the idea of a single world or universe at the expense of reducing all minds or selves to one, pluralistic idealism, holding like all concrete idealism that the object depends upon the subject, manages to save the reality of the many minds only by positing as many totally distinct worlds, as many universes, in fact, as there are minds aware of a world. And if the universe of which I am aware is totally different, existentially and numerically, from the universe of which you are aware, it follows that I can never perceive or know any concrete thing which you or any other mind knows. Moreover, I can only act, presumably, within my own world or universe, and so never in the world of which another mind is conscious. Thus knowledge of common objects, mutual knowledge, intercommunication, and all other forms of interaction become alike inconceivable, logically impossible. In the light of such absurd logical consequences objective idealism in its pluralistic form must be judged self-refuting.

But it seems clear that if all reality is mind and its ideas, it must be either one all-inclusive mind and its ideas or many minds and their ideas. And yet each supposition has been found to lead to absurdity. The logical procedure would seem to be to confess frankly that concrete objective idealism in both of the two possible forms is absurd and must be given up. Several attempts have been made to carry the dialectic of idealism one step further and effect a "higher synthesis" of the singularistic and pluralistic forms of a doctrine apparently deemed too precious to be sacrificed under any consideration. The philosophy of the "personalists," according to which reality is a multiplicity of persons, that is, of free finite individual minds (with their ideas), all included in some way in a personal Absolute or World-Ground, leaves obscure the question as to whether the many are completely included in the One, or incompletely only. As a matter of fact both affirmations are made; there is no real synthesis. Mediation between singularistic and pluralistic idealism was also attempted by Royce, his proposed solution of the problem being that since every person is a community of persons (*e.g.* the trinity involved in the *self* interpreting the *self* to the *self*), and since every unified community of persons is in some sense of the word a person (even the law recognizing a corporation as a person), the Absolute can consequently be at once a single person and a community of persons. This is manifestly a purely verbal solution, hardly worthy of a great philosopher; the sense in which a person is a community is not the sense in which a community is a community, nor is the sense in which a community is a person the sense in which a person is a person. The humorous suggestion made by a pluralist (F. C. S. Schiller) that the single, all-inclusive consciousness, or Absolute Mind, must be "so badly dissociated as to be downright mad," a suggestion which, were it taken seriously, could only prove disconcerting to religion, is not, when carried through to its logical conclusion, essentially different from pluralism. If there were some reality besides persons, some world other than the merely dependent content of personal consciousness, then it might be held without contradiction that there are many persons and a single universe, or world; but if any real world must necessarily depend upon the personal subject which is conscious of it, either there must be only one person or else the universe cannot be a single world.

But why insist on going on with the idealistic dialectic with its stubborn attempt to unite real contradictories? Why not use the logic of common sense and take the self-contradiction to which logical-psychological idealism has been led as a *reductio ad absurdum* of something somewhere in the premises? Instead of pressing on at all hazards, why should we not turn back and examine our tracks to see just where it was that we went astray? We have already noted, indeed, that both psychological idealism and logical idealism were based upon very inconclusive and (in so far as they claimed to be demonstrative) fallacious arguments. And in so far as these two elemental forms of idealism were treated not as initial certainties but as working hypotheses, certainly one or the other has worked badly enough to be considered refuted.

We are ready, then, to turn definitely and, so far as we can predict the future course of our thought, definitively from idealism and to examine the tenability of its alternative, realism. Is it possible, not on a naïve unphilosophical basis alone, but critically and rationally, to hold to physical, personal and religious realism? Physical realism holds that a real physical world exists independently of all human consciousness of it. Personal realism holds, as a minimum statement of doctrine, that there is a real psychical self, distinct from ideas or feelings of a self and existing as the subject of consciousness even at times when there is no explicit self-consciousness. Many would go further and say that there is a reality of mind, not to be reduced to the purely physical, which persists even during the intervals between the times of such consciousness as we are able, if we wish, to introspect, or later to remember. Religious realism would hold that the religious object, usually called God, is an existent reality, not depending for its existence upon man's religious consciousness. This is a minimum statement, which may be interpreted in any one of three ways: either that the divine reality is discoverable as wholly immanent within the physical world and the lives of persons, or that it wholly transcends all such physical and human reality, or that it is both immanent in part and transcendent in part. But in all forms of religious realism God is something more objective than the mere idea of God or religious consciousness as such, and at the same time something more concrete than the rational or spiritual or divine ideal, as mere ideal. Even if religious consciousness and appreciation may be found to facilitate certain divine processes in human life, there is, from the point of view of religious realism, something divine which exists without being wholly dependent upon that religious consciousness and appreciation for its reality.

One form of realism which is common among scientists and philosophers is dualistic realism, or epistemological dualism, the doctrine that there is an independently existing reality but that it never comes within the field of man's direct experience and so remains forever beyond the range of human knowledge. Thus dualistic realism with reference to the physical world holds that there is an independently existing physical reality which is presumably the objective or external cause of our sensations. But the effect is not even necessarily like the cause, and for the dualist the world of our immediate sense-experience, being the joint product of these sensations and the forms of human understanding, is a mere phenomenon, a construct within experience which is existentially distinct from the independently existing reality and probably very different qualitatively from it.

Obviously, then, dualistic realism with reference to the physical leads logically to agnosticism. If we can never have the independent physical reality presented within the field of our experience, we can never compare our thories with the reality, and so we can neither refute nor verify them. Some avowedly dualistic realists claim to have scientific knowledge of the world quite as truly as those who, whether idealists or realists, repudiate the dualistic view. This claim may be allowed, but if the dualist is able to verify his ideas about the physical world, is it not probably just because his dualism is not a true account of the relation of his experience to reality? If his dualism were true he would have no experience of independent reality, and so, not being in a position to compare his thought of the reality with the reality itself, he could never establish the truth of his thought. May it not be that it is not the dualist's experience or his science that is at fault, but rather his philosophy, his theory of knowledge, according to which less than justice is done to what happens in perception?

Often the logically necessary agnosticism of a consistent dualistic realism is not acknowledged; but of late even the dualism of what is an essentially dualistic position has been so disguised by ambiguous language on the part of certain philosophers as to hide from the philosophers themselves the fundamental dualism and consequent agnosticism of their position. For example, it is said by some that though the existent physical thing never becomes a datum to the percipient, the sense-datum, not being an existent thing but a logical essence like the predicate of a judgment, may have more than one embodiment at the same time, and so may be both a content of direct experience and an essence of the independently existing and never directly experienced thing. Moreover, it is contended, *when perception is truthful,* the sense-datum not only may be, but *is* the essence of the existing physical thing. In knowing the essence of the thing, we know *what* it is; that is, we know it. But it seems a fatal admission on the part of those who hold this position, when they acknowledge that we do not know *that* the thing is; we simply *believe* that it is, in an act of animal faith whose only justification is that, generally speaking, it works well. So long as it is assumed that the existing thing never becomes a datum, never is directly experienced, we are left without any sufficient basis for the opinion that the essence which we apprehend really is the essence of the independent thing. From this point of view, strictly speaking, we know a *what* and we believe in a *that;* but we do not *know,* we only *suppose,* that what we know is what the thing is. The existent thing and its essence, naturally united in the datum of sense-perception, are here unnaturally disunited. In the end even the proponents of this view have to acknowledge that they do not really know that our perception ever is truthful. Obviously the escape from dualism and agnosticism here is only verbal at best. As for the divorce between the what and the that, the essence and the existent, the sense-datum and the physical thing, let us have none of it. What nature hath joined together in the perceived object let not epistemology put asunder.

Dualistic realism in the psychical realm is the doctrine that the metaphysically real subject of consciousness, the thinker, is forever inaccessible to introspection or to any other form of observation, and hence is, strictly speaking, unknowable. Similarly, dualistic realism in religion holds to the independent reality of a God of some sort, but maintains that that God remains forever completely transcendent, being never revealed within the realm of human observation or experience. Such a divine being would be strictly unknowable; all ideas about it would remain unverifiable. From such a dualistic point of view arguments aiming to prove the existence of God may be and have been devised; but all they can prove, in the absence of the conditions of empirical verification, is either the rational possibility of believing in the existence of God, or the rational necessity of concluding to his existence if we make certain assumptions, or the rational and practical necessity of believing in God for some particular purpose or other. To be rationally possible or permissible, a belief would have to be free from self-contradiction and not inconsistent with any known fact. But there is always needed some further consideration beyond mere rational possibility or permissibility to tip the scale of judgment in favor of belief in actuality. To be rationally necessary means to be necessarily, *i.e.* logically involved either in some assumed hypothesis or in some categorically imperative end. In the former case the necessity is only hypothetical, depending on the validity of what is assumed; moreover, in the absence of any empirically verified knowledge about the religious object it is always possible for the skeptic to refuse to adopt the proposed hypothesis. In the latter case, where the necessity seems categorical, it is possible for the cynic to deny the validity of the categorical imperative, or for the pessimist to suggest that what it is logically necessary to believe for the realization of a categorically imperative end is quite possibly a mere "indispensable fiction" and not true after all. It would seem desirable, then, not only in order that we may have verified religious *knowledge,* but possibly even for the steadying of religious *belief,* that at least some of our thoughts about the religious object should be verifiable somewhere in direct experience of divine reality.

Turning from dualistic realism, then, because of its incompatibility with the possibility of knowledge (verified truth) about reality, let us consider the tenability of a direct or monistic realism. According to monistic realism as applied to the physical, in normal sense-perception things are presented within the field of immediate experience and observation, so that direct acquaintance with the independently existing physical world is possible and actual. In the changing complex of sense-qualities we apprehend (intuit, perceive) physical things (configurations of energy) which are not the mere complexes of related sense-qualities. This theory is monistic in the purely epistemological sense of the term, according to which there can be affirmed (at least partially, *i.e.* to some extent) a numerical oneness, an existential identity, between the object as perceived (directly presented) and the object as independently real.

This view is the necessary alternative if we are to avoid both epistemological idealism and epistemological dualism. It holds that in veridical perception we apprehend the independently existing physical thing *in* its appearances. In discovering to some extent what it is, we learn that it is. The essence of the thing as given in our experience is not an abstract essence, it includes and involves the thing's existence. The appearance is the existing thing appearing, even if there may be more of the thing than just that which appears. Through direct perceptual experience we gain considerable knowledge about independently existing reality, as in the various branches of physical science, for example.

Monistic realism may be applied to the psychical as well as to the physical, with the result that in addition to our direct perceptual knowledge of physical things (inorganic and organic) it is maintained that we apprehend or intuit in complexes of sense-qualities, memory-images, ideas, and the like, various psychical processes such as sensing, perceiving, remembering, imagining, conceiving, judging, reasoning, willing, etc., and that in these complex processes we further apprehend (intuit, become aware of) our own mind or self, or conscious subject, as that which perceives, remembers, imagines, thinks, desires and wills. Using the term "perception" broadly, we may say that this self-knowledge is perception in an introspective complex. But we also apprehend the self in connection with various sorts of bodily behavior, as that which not only desires, intends and wills, but also causes certain kinds of bodily behavior. Self-knowledge is thus not perception in an introspective complex alone, but perception in a complex of bodily behavior as well.

From this same point of view other minds, whether human or belonging to less advanced types of animal life, we apprehend not in an introspective complex, but in the complex of bodily behavior and its products. But for an adequate apprehension of selves (our own and others') as persons, there seem to be needed, in addition to this relatively simple perceptual cognition, certain additional elements of interpretation and appreciation.

According to monistic realism in religion, in certain phases of human experience and particularly in religious experience at its best, divine reality is presented with sufficient immediacy to make possible a genuine acquaintance with it. We apprehend, intuit, perceive a divine factor, not exclusively but especially in religious experience at its best. In other words we make empirical discovery of a divine reality; a divine reality is revealed. In the light of such experience of a divine reality it is possible to test certain religious hypotheses with a view to their being either verified in an essentially scientific sense or refuted.

It may well be that monistic realism in the sense defined above will be found to be tenable in all three of the realms considered, the physical, the psychical, and the divine or religious. That remains to be seen, but at any rate the fact that such a view would make it possible to maintain that genuine knowledge is possible constitutes for the practical, common sense, non-pessimistic mind a reason for being disposed toward its favorable consideration. But it must be noted that there have been certain extreme developments of monistic realism which do not stand up well under critical examination. One such form of extreme monistic realism is the common prephilosophi-

cal view known as naïve or natural realism. This is not
so much a theory as a tendency rather uncritically to
accept experienced qualities "with natural piety" as
belonging to reality in its objectivity, with little or no
recognition of the subjective origin and nature of much
of what we experience in connection with the world, the
self and other selves, and God. It soon begins to show
signs of disintegration, however, under the influence of
critical reflection in face of the conflicting impressions
which different observers at the same time and the same
observer at different times get of the same physical
things, the same human persons, and what is presumably
the same religious object.

What was called at the time of its appearance some
twenty or more years ago "the new realism" undertook
to make the original natural monistic realism self-consistent and a satisfactory theory of knowledge by applying universally the principle that consciousness is an
"external relation" so far as the object is concerned,
that is, that being experienced or known or in any way
thought of makes no difference to the existence or qualities of the object of such awareness. Physical things
might pass into and out of any subject's consciousness
without any change in them except their becoming and
ceasing to be objects of that person's awareness. From
this point of view all qualities of things that might be
perceived under any conceivable condition must exist independently in the thing—waiting, as it were, to be perceived. This applies to colors and other sense-qualities,
as well as to such "primary qualities" as shape, quantity, location, and duration. Each thing, according to this
theory, is a practically infinite aggregate of independently real aspects, almost all of which never actually
appear to any finite percipient. It seems at best a very
extravagant view, violating the useful scientific principle
that, in making explanations, entities ought not to be
multiplied beyond necessity. But still more serious is
the objection that inasmuch as consciousness is held to
be an external relation so far as the object is concerned,

the objective content of illusion, hallucination, error, fantasy, contradictions, and the like, must be regarded as real independently of their being perceived or thought. From this point of view error is logically impossible, since whatever the person in error experiences or believes must be real independently of its being experienced or believed. For example, idealism, which must be regarded by the extreme monistic realists as erroneous because it contradicts their doctrine, ought also to be regarded by them as true for the reason that, as they say, consciousness can only be of what is in reality, whether anyone is conscious of it or not. This surely is a *reductio ad absurdum* of monistic realism in its extreme form. An attempt is made to gain a semblance of plausibility for the view by suggesting that in their original independent reality all things are neutral entities which merely subsist, like eternal ideas or possible objects of thought, and that they are physical or mental only by virtue of certain (external?) relations in which they are taken. We are not concerned to deny that many things which never could exist do in some sense *subsist* as possible objects of thought, but what we are fundamentally concerned with in epistemology is the possibility of knowing independently *existing* reality, and we know no existing thing which is neutral, *i.e.* neither physical nor mental. What seems to have suggested the doctrine is the fact that we know many contents of experience which are at the same time in the physical world and in the life-history of a mind.

Extreme monistic realism is also sometimes applied to mind. The attempt has frequently been made of late to show that mind, so far from being hidden, is a fully observable object with no transcendent aspects. Some maintain that consciousness is a relation of implication or meaning between physical objects; others hold that mind is that cross-section of the environment to which the organism is responding, or the behavior of the organism in response to such a cross-section, or both together, that is, the totality of the cross-section responded to and the responding behavior. Now it may be that we apprehend or intuit consciousness and mind to some extent in complexes of perceptual contents and in the complex processes of intelligent purposive behavior; but it does not follow that the complex of physical objects perceived or the complex physiological processes of behavior *are* the consciousness empirically intuited in and through them, still less that these are *all* that mind or consciousness is. The question whether any observed behavior is *accompanied by consciousness* is not a meaningless question, and its meaning is not, Is the observed *consciousness* accompanied by consciousness?

Extreme monistic realism is sometimes applied to the religious object, with rather remarkable results. Sometimes the outlook is confined to the individual himself or to himself and those who agree with him in some particular traditional religious faith, the entire objective content of religious experience being interpreted rather uncritically as verification of the faith, and all being interpreted as revelation of independent religious reality. This is extreme monistic realism in religion in its original naïve form. Sometimes an attempt is made to transcend the limits of a particular religion and to interpret as objective reality whatever is experienced in any genuinely religious experience. This is in the religious realm what "the new realism" was in the physical, and it leads to a similar doctrine of the objective reality of entities so mutually conflicting that to affirm the one is to deny the other. Indeed so pluralistically is reality conceived from this point of view as to lead logically not simply to polytheism but to both polytheism and the monotheism which contradicts it.

One other variety of extreme monistic realism is that which centers its attention upon mystical religious experience. Here not only is God, the object upon which the mystical consciousness is concentrated, regarded as independently real, but whatever God seems to be in the mystical experience, that he is said to be in his independent reality. More specifically, it having been assumed that whatever the mystic vividly experiences in his mystic state is thereby revealed as ultimate reality, and that what he does not thus experience is thereby shown to be ultimately unreal, *maya, an illusory appearance*; and, furthermore, it having been discovered that to the mystic in his state of extreme religious concentration time and space, physical objects, finite selves, and all things evil tend to lapse from consciousness, leaving God alone as that which seems to be real, it is accordingly declared that God is the one and only Reality, the ineffable One, that super-rational, super-beautiful, super-moral Being whose sole reality excludes from reality the whole spatial-temporal material world, the finite self, all evil and all becoming. The main criticism to be made of this is that it is so dogmatic and uncritical as virtually to deny the knowledge-value of all experience, whether religious or not specifically religious, except a very specialized type of religious experience, the psychological conditions of which strongly suggest that in large part it may be of the nature of hallucination under the influence of religious self-hypnosis.[*] At any rate, if a narrow dogmatism is to be avoided everything which seems so assured to the mystic on the basis of his mystical experience must be subjected to all the valid tests we know, the test of working in practical religion and practical life in general, and the theoretical test of consistency with all that has been learned about reality through human experience in general. When treated thus critically, it is likely

[*] Perceptual intuition of physical, psychical and religious objects may well prove to be the foundation of all our knowledge of reality, but we must not overlook the fact that perceptual intuition is not infallible. An extreme illustration of its fallibility may be found in the way in which a person reading while falling asleep sometimes reads words and even whole clauses which are not in the text at all, but have been supplied by associative apperception. This is but an exaggerated instance of what commonly occurs in proof-reading. The way to correct such mistaken perceptual intuition is to wake up and gain a truer perception through more alert attention. May it be that some of the features of extreme mystical intuition are false appearances due to the fact that the mystic is falling asleep, as it were, in passing into the trance, and that what he needs to do in order to correct the false impressions supplied by his own associative apperception is to wake up to the real world, the real self and the real God?

that mystical realism will have to give up, not necessarily its assurance of the reality, accessibility and religious sufficiency of God, but its dogma of the *sole* reality of God, with its corollaries, the unreality of the physical world, of space and time, of the finite self and of all evil.

Before turning finally from naïve and the "new" realism and their religious counterparts to see if we may be able to find some less dogmatic and more defensible form of direct or monistic realism on which to base the possibility of knowledge of reality in general and religious reality in particular, let us look at the view of Professor John Dewey and some of his followers—a view which he himself has called naïve realism and immediate empiricism, and which in a somewhat more developed and definite form Professor Arthur E. Murphy has called objective relativism. Professor Dewey claims to stand with the plain man and the empirical scientist in asserting that if we want to know what a thing is, we must go to immediate experience and find out what it is experienced as. Professor Murphy claims that we perceive and know independently existing realities, but always only relatively, that is, as they are in relation to us as we experience them. This seems like a simple solution of a problem long supposed to be difficult, if not insoluble. But before we accept it, let us try to find out what it means. In spite of Professor Dewey's claim to be a naïve realist, it is very evident that he does not mean to assert that the physical thing is, independently of its being experienced and when not experienced, just what it is when and as experienced. The question of what the object is in its independent reality he rejects as a false and insoluble problem. It is evident that what he means to say is that things are what they are experienced as, not when they are not experienced or when they are otherwise experienced, but only, so far as we can say, *when and as they are experienced.* The physical thing has the shape and color it is experienced as having, when it is experienced as having them. This seems certain enough, but if this is all that is meant, one wonders why it should be identified with naïve realism, which is commonly understood to assume that things are experienced as they are independently of their being experienced. If Dewey means that things are nothing but what they are experienced as, when and as they are experienced, his position is simply a disguised psychological idealism, such as we have referred to above. If, as seems more probable in the light of later statements, and as Professor Murphy seems to mean, he means that there is an independently existing reality but that we cannot say anything about it as it exists independently of its being experienced, but only that when experienced under certain circumstances it has the qualities and relations it appears to have, the doctrine seems to be simply dualism and agnosticism, coupled with an unwarranted affirmation that the independent reality, of which we can know nothing, is what appears in our experience and has the qualities which we experience. When made more self-consistent this version of the view simply lapses into agnostic dualism, a position we have already sufficiently examined.

But let objective relativism be given its due. It may be that we cannot tell what the physical object looks like when no one is looking at it, but only what it looks like when it is looked at, or what it would look like if it were looked at under specified conditions. But this does not mean that we cannot gain *any* scientific knowledge of independently existing physical reality. We may not be able to say anything about colors or sounds except in relation to eyes and ears and perceiving minds; but the necessary relativity and conditionedness of sense-qualities does necessarily extend to mass and energy, quantitatively and causally considered. If, in spite of the fact that objective relativism seems to apply to some characteristics of the object, it does not necessarily apply to them all, then in spite of the fact that we cannot experience physical things except as clothed with sense-qualities, it is conceivable that through our sense-experience we may get immediate experience of some qualities and relations of physical things which do not depend for their existence upon their being experienced by us. In that case we may learn enough about independent things to be justified in saying not only that they exist, but that it is they which appear to us in sense-experience.

According to the view suggested, then, there would be a partial identity or coincidence of the directly experienced and the independently real. In perception of a physical thing, part of what is independently real would not be immediately perceived, and part of what is immediately perceived would not be independently real; but part of what is independently real would be absolutely the same existence as part of what is immediately perceived. Such a partial identity or coincidence of the immediately perceived and the independently real would be sufficient to make human knowledge of independent reality not only possible but actual. Let us see whether such a view is really tenable.

Some of the more important steps in the building up of a direct or monistic realism in critical form may now be set forth in a series of brief numbered statements.[10]

1. A theory of sense-perception, established for one sense, will presumably apply in its essential features to other senses. (This is at once a fundamental presupposition and a general working hypothesis, like the principle of the dependableness of nature.)

2. The human body is in real space-time, as real space-time as any we can know. (In speaking thus of "real space-time" there is no thought of denying the *facts* of relativity. Even if one were to assume an absolute space and time, they would of necessity be relative in perception and measurement. Absolute reality would have to be apprehended by us relatively, and so the necessary relativity of our apprehension does not necessarily prevent us from apprehending, in our own incomplete way, absolute reality.)

[10] Most of what appears in these numbered paragraphs is reproduced from my paper, "The Next Step in the Epistemological Dialectic," which appeared in the *Journal of Philosophy* for April 25, 1929.

3. Pain is when and where it is felt to be, and not when or where it is not felt to be—in the sore finger, for example, and not in the brain. It would be difficult to defend the proposition that pain exists when it is not felt, and why should it be thought a defensible proposition that it exists where it is not felt?

4. Combining (2) and (3) we get the conclusion that pain, being in some particular part of the body, is in the same real space-time as that in which the human body exists.

5. Combining (4) and (1), we arrive at the conclusion, which seems quite tenable in the light of the facts, that all sense-qualities of whatever sense exist when and as long as they are experienced, and are located just where they seem to be, namely, in the same real space-time continuum in which the body is, some of them being within the body, others on the surface of the body, and still others outside and at various distances away from the body.

6. In positive after-sensation, the patch of color which is the immediate datum, being discoverable in whatever direction in the real space outside the body it is looked for, is manifestly conditioned, as induction shows, upon processes in the psycho-physical organism, and not something which exists in real space-time independently of its being sensed.

7. Positive after-sensation is a mere fading continuation of the original sensation, produced in the same way, that is, as the temporarily persisting effect of the original stimulation.

8. Combining (6) and (7) we reach the conclusion that in the original sense-process, of which the after-sensation is simply the rapidly fading continuation, the patch of color sensed, although located outside of the body in real space-time, is nevertheless there as an effect of processes occurring in the psycho-physical organism.

9. Combining (8) and (3) with (1) we arrive at the conclusion that all sense-qualities emerge in connection with the psycho-physical processes involved in sensing,

and are given a locus in real space-time, either in the percipient's body, on its surface, or away from it. This confirms the conclusion arrived at in (5).

10. The particular colors and other sense-qualities produced in and through the processes occurring in a particular psycho-physical organism, or subject, though located in the same real space-time system as that in which the human body is, are not necessarily there in such a way as to be observable by anyone except that particular subject, and such facts as those of color-blindness indicate that each observer produces for himself and locates for himself in real space-time, either in his body, on it, or beyond it, the sense-qualities which he observes. In other words, while bodies are *independently* real in a space-time which is necessarily relative in perception and measurement, sense-qualities are *dependently* real in the *same* space-time.

11. The fact that color-blindness follows the Mendelian law of the inheritance of sex-linked characters calls attention to the fact that the capacity for producing certain sense-qualities on occasion of certain processes of stimulation has come to be an inherited capacity and that the first emergence of each new kind of sense-quality in the course of evolution must have been a fact of creative evolution.

12. The activities involved in (a) attention and adjustment of sense-organs sufficient to make us receptive to stimulation, (b) the production and location of specific sense-qualities, on occasion of specific stimulations, and (c) the overt psycho-physiological response to the stimulus under the guiding influence of the content of sense-experience, are more or less closely coördinated, and while the coördination between b and c is in large part an achievement of the individual, the coördination between a and b (selecting the stimulus and responding with the production of specific sense-qualities) seems to have been in the main an achievement of the race transmitted to the individual by natural inheritance. In visual sensation the direction of the location of sense-contents

seems to be determined by heredity, but ability to locate them at different distances, or at least expertness in locating them at the right distance, is acquired during the infancy of the individual. (The newly hatched chick makes the right response to the third dimension. This seems to indicate that in some animals the ability to locate sense-qualities correctly with respect to distance exists as an inherited instinct and not as a trial-and-error achievement of the individual.)

13. An important element in the explanation of the ordinarily correct (or practically correct) location of the sense-quality in space-time with reference to the events in the physical world from which the stimulation is proceeding may possibly be found in natural selection. Any animal which failed to locate sense-qualities fortunately, especially as to direction, but also as to distance, would be ill-fitted to succeed in the search for food or in flight from enemies, and so would be unlikely to survive in the struggle for existence. Accurate location of sense-qualities as to distance in the case of very distant objects, such as the sun, moon, and stars, has not been achieved, but this has not been a matter affecting survival in the struggle for existence. Appearances of such heavenly bodies were located accurately enough for primitive man's practical purposes when they were located up "in the sky" and beyond his reach.

14. In and through the sense-qualities which are psycho-physically produced and located, and with which I am related in that unique and immediate togetherness which I call my "awareness" or the object's "givenness," I discover the real thing which is and has been in the environment. In typical instances the sense-quality is located so accurately with reference to the thing from which the stimulation proceeded that the quality sensed comes to be the quality which the thing has (that is, for us) in our present experience. It is the finger that is sore, the flower that is red, the water that is warm. In no such instance is my brain or mind or consciousness

sore or red or warm. As a matter of fact in my immediate awareness of the pain in my finger I am likewise directly aware of my finger; when I immediately intuit or perceive the redness of the rose, I immediately intuit or perceive the rose which is red. Thus we are perceptually aware of independently existing things in real space-time. We perceive directly the independently existing physical thing, clothed with the colors which it has when perceived by us, but in the space-time in which it exists whether it is perceived by us or not. We get things in a perspective which varies with changes in the spatial relations between them and our organs of sense, but we get them as they exist in real, objective space. This is not knowledge in the form of deductive inference, of course, but knowledge as a practical achievement. It may be objected by the critic of this view that the space in which we locate sense-qualities is not absolute but relative to the observer; that colors are located at different distances, for instance, according as the observer is looking through glasses which correct for near-sightedness or is looking at the object without spectacles. But in either case the color is where, under the circumstances, the physical object is; it is no more in a plurality of spaces than the external thing is. In both cases we see the colored shape where we ought to, in relation to the other seen objects of the environment, in order to be truly informed as to where, in relation to them and to our own body, the external thing is. In short, we perceive relatively, but we *must* perceive relatively if we are to perceive truly.

The percept from this point of view, is the *perceptum*, the thing perceived. Perception lags a bit at the beginning and lingers on at the end; but in the case of objects near at hand, and especially for vision, the time-discrepancy between stimulus and percept is so slight as to be for ordinary purposes insignificant. At any rate ordinarily the percept throughout its whole duration, except perhaps for the last fraction of a second, is the existent perceived thing, in so far as it is perceived and with the appearance it takes on for the percipient when it is perceived.

15. In and through this immediate perception of independently existing reality the way is opened for the verification or refutation of at least some of our theories about that reality; adequate and adequately critical assurance of the presence of what is really present being in some instances possible, adequate and adequately critical assurance of the truth of judgments which are really true is consequently sometimes possible.

The theory outlined is free, I think, from self-contradiction and in harmony with the facts, and it has this further claim to our acceptance that, if it is true, it shows how we can really have the amount of knowledge of independently existing reality which we seem, as a matter of fact, to have. This is all that should be asked of a theory of knowledge. If our theory of knowledge be judged not to amount to *knowledge* that we have knowledge, but only to be *the most reasonable belief* about knowledge, and one which gives us the right to believe that in science and ordinary critical perception we have the knowledge we supposed we had, we have all that should be expected of an epistemological theory. Indirect confirmation of the theory that we can get true knowledge about independent reality is brought out in the next two points.

16. The shape and size of the patch of color or other content of sensation depends directly upon the shape and size of the part of the retina or other organ of sense stimulated, and this in turn depends for shape mainly on the shape, direction, and perspective of the stimulus, and for size upon its size and distance.

17. As a matter of fact, then, the size, shape, location, and duration of the patch of color or other content of sensation are valuable means of information with reference to the size, shape, location and duration of the stimulus.

18. The fact that we sometimes experience dreams

and hallucinations in which definite configurations appear to us without their having been conditioned by the usual external stimulus is not fatal to the view that ordinarily appearances are means of information about reality. In hallucination, at least in its most vivid form, the visual content exists in real space, though not with the same configuration of mass and energy as is ordinarily there when such a visual appearance is presented. But dreams and hallucinations occur only after the use of certain forms of thought and imaginations have become habitual, as a result, originally, of sense-experience and memory; and under certain peculiar conditions these forms of thought and imagination stir into activity processes of sensing such as would normally be aroused only by the appropriate external stimulation. Thus even the forms which appear in dreams and hallucinations are possible only because forms similar to these appearances, or at least to parts of them, have been in the real space-time environment and have stimulated and been experienced by us in the past.

19. As a critical realism holding without self-contradiction naïve realism's essential claim of immediate apprehension of independently existing reality, and as a natural realism critical enough to make room for all such facts as those of color-blindness, illusion, and hallucination, the theory may be called critical natural realism. Moreover, in spite of the fact that part of what is immediately perceived is not independently real and part of what is independently real is not immediately perceived, enough of the immediately experienced is independently real, according to our theory, and enough of the independently real immediately experienced, for the view to be classed as a form of epistemological realism and monism. We may therefore call it critical realistic monism, or more briefly *critical monism*. Seeking to remain, in order to understand the possibility of knowledge, as realistic and monistic as it may be while becoming as critical as it ought to be, it finds that it can hold on to the essentials of a direct realism as regards the existent thing and its

primary qualities by admitting an objective relativism in relation to its secondary or sense-qualities.

20. Such difficulties as there may be for contemporary thought in the theory are not, I think, epistemological, but metaphysical. In the older idealism we have become habituated to the idea of the creativity of mind in a non-realistic universe, and in the newer realism as well as in the older materialism we are familiar with the idea of the non-creativity of mind in a realistic universe; but this theory of the production of sense-qualities by and for psycho-physical subjects, or organisms, and their location in real physical space-time involves the creativity of life and mind in a realistic universe. Thus the metaphysical element in our critical natural realism or critical monism is one which points toward the same general world-view as is needed to do justice to the creative elements in such processes as those of emergent evolution in general and man's purposive free activity in particular. In fact, the location of sense-qualities where the stimulating object is, is simply a detail of their creative emergence. It is mysterious, but so is the creative emergence of consciousness in general, and indeed all real becoming. Why reality should be as it is is the ultimate mystery which must be accepted by philosopher and plain man alike "with natural piety."

Another way of showing the relation of critical monism to other views may be briefly indicated as follows. The "phenomenology (*Phänomenologie*) of Husserl and his followers may be regarded as the result of an attempt to get away from the controversies of current epistemology and ontology and to lay the foundations for any future metaphysics by taking up "an intuitive attitude toward the pure *what* of the world" (Scheler). In distinction from the *Gegenstandstheorie* of Meinong, which occupied itself indifferently with any possible object of thought, as such, and so not only with realities but with such unrealities as centaurs and such impossibilities as round squares and the square root of minus one, *Phänomenologie* undertakes to be a "first philosophy" of reality, setting forth the essential nature of the rationally possible. Naturally the content of perception falls within the range of these "logical investigations" but the data of perception are treated here not as existent things but simply as logical essences. All considerations of existence are "bracketed," set aside; phenomenology is philosophy "without (existential) presuppositions."

If philosophy were to remain on this unpretentious level of phenomenology a large measure of agreement among philosophers might ultimately be expected. But this is just because in these uncontroversial investigations most of the vitally interesting questions of philosophy are abstracted from, "bracketed." Phenomenology may be valuable as a philosophical propaedeutic, a scheme for getting a good running start for the tackling of the really important problems; but if it ends as it begins, never getting beyond these preparations for the encounter, the game of philosophy will soon lose its interest. In short, if philosophy is to remain one of the commanding human interests, it must break away from mere phenomenology and seek truth in the form of ontology. And in undertaking to do this it plunges at once into the highway of epistemology.

In setting up phenomenology existential assumptions were set aside. In order to get away from mere phenomenology let us deliberately make such existential assumptions as life and practice seem to justify. For while mere phenomenology might satisfy us if we were but spectators gazing at the passing show of things, as agents participating in the practical pursuits of life we must take account of existence.

1. As a first step then from phenomenology to ontology let us assume—or, more accurately, let *me* assume— the existence of my own self or mind. This done, the sense-data or sensa, which phenomenology treated simply as so many *whats*, or essences, now appear as my ideas, dependent contents of my own consciousness. This is the view known as solipsism, a theory which it seems

impossible logically to refute, however awkward and unsatisfactory it may be from a practical point of view.

2. But solipsism is not necessarily to be believed, even if on its own grounds it cannot be refuted. It resulted from adding to phenomenology a single existential assumption, that of my own existence. It remains solipsism only so long as no further existential assumptions are made. If then it seems too egotistical a doctrine, let me —or let *us*, as we may now say—see what happens when we deliberately make the further assumption of a plurality of existent minds in intercommunication with each other. From this point of view the so-called common object is either a conceptual construction in each of the minds aware of it, a mere permanent possibility of sensation, or perchance an idea in some permanently existing mind or minds. If it be asked how the intercommunication takes place, the answer may be given that it might conceivably have been by telepathy or in some other occult fashion, but that in practical life we assume that it is by means of a series of processes in an independently existing reality or world.

3. Let us add then to our previous assumptions that of an independently existing reality in order to explain the existence and sequence of our perceptual experiences. Here several varieties of view seem possible. (a) The external reality assumed as the objective cause of our sensations may be thought of as forever unexperienced and therefore an unknowable "thing-in-itself." Or (b) it may be thought of as a multiform physical world of events causally related among themselves and in some instances to sensations in our minds. And yet if this assumed multiform and independently existing physical world be forever unexperienced, how can it ever be known? There seem to be three possible interpretations of the view. (1) According to dualistic realism and phenomenalism sense-data are to be regarded psychologically, as ideas, contents of individual minds, and the physical as something totally different, an independent and forever unexperienced existence (Lovejoy, Sellars,

et al). (2) According to critical realism of the type advocated by Santayana, C. A. Strong and Durant Drake, sense-data are to be treated phenomenologically, as mere essences which have, as such, neither mental nor physical existence, while the physical is regarded existentially as an independent reality, but one which is never experienced and so can never be known, but only believed in by an act of "animal faith." (3) Finally, according to objective relativism (*e.g.* A. E. Murphy) sense-data are treated existentially as physical, but at the same time relatively. In other words in sense-data the independently existing physical reality is said to be directly experienced, but it is likewise maintained that there is no reason to suppose that the physical reality in its independent existence has any of the qualities, primary or secondary, which it has when directly experienced and perceived. But, we may ask, does not this mean that we do not know what the nature of the independent reality is, and furthermore that it is not the independently existing reality which we experience and perceive, but something different which we only *say* is the independently existing physical thing?

Unless, then, we make a further assumption to the effect that we have an immediate experience of independently existing physical reality in such a way that some at least of the qualities it has in its independent reality are experienced by us, revealed within the field of our direct awareness, we are forced to retrace our steps. Objective relativism [3 (b) (3)] cannot establish itself as against "critical realism" [3 (b) (2)]. For all that the objective relativist can say, sense-data may be mere essences of the physical and not the physical existent itself. This same critical realism in turn has failed to establish itself as against dualistic phenomenalism [3 (b) (1)]. The "critical realist" cannot disprove the view that sense-data are psychical products and thus mental existences, rather than mere neutral logical essences. Furthermore, (b) itself, the view that the independently existing reality is a multiform physical world, made up of a plurality of interacting elements, cannot establish itself as theoretically necessary as against the Kantian dualism and agnosticism, if it is still assumed that the independent physical reality is never directly experienced by the human subject. Nor is this all. The dualistic phenomenalism and realism cannot be shown to be theoretically necessary as against the idealistic phenomenalism, (2, above) which treats the "thing-in-itself" as an unnecessary fiction; for if the thing-in-itself has never been experienced why should it be assumed to be real? Finally, as has often been pointed out, if we have no experience of independently existing physical bodies of other persons, what convincing reason can be given for the assumption that the other minds, which seemed to be communicating with us through those bodies, are themselves independently existing realities? In other words, if we have no direct experience of independently existing physical reality, there seems no convincing reason, theoretically speaking, why we should not return to solipsism (1, above).

But while, without the assumption of immediate awareness of independently existing physical reality, it seems theoretically permissible to hold either (1) solipsism, (2) pluralistic idealistic phenomenalism, or (3) dualistic realistic phenomenalism, so that we are unable on purely theoretical grounds to vindicate (3) as against (2) or (2) as against (1), or indeed to make definitive choice of any one of the three positions, it has to be recognized nevertheless that the three successive assumptions—of my own existence, the existence of other intercommunicating minds, and the existence of an independent physical reality or world of interacting parts—have all worked very well and may reasonably be regarded as true. Why then may it not be a wise procedure to go on and make one more deliberate assumption, namely, that we have in our perceptual experience an immediate or direct awareness of the independently existing physical world? This is the assumption which we seem to need in order to protect the last two of our previous assumptions—

namely, that there is an independently existing physical world (as against mere idealistic phenomenalism) and that there is a plurality of intercommunicating minds (as against mere solipsism).

But is this assumption (4) that we have immediate perceptual experience of an independently existing physical world theoretically permissible? We have already seen that in its original unsophisticated form as (a) naïve realism, it is not tenable, nor even in its more philosophical form, as (b) the so-called "new realism." But it has been shown, we think, that in its more moderate form as (c) critical monistic realism, or critical monism, it is a theoretically permissible position. And, as we can now see, it has the tremendous value of enabling us to maintain that a realism of the physical world is the right view as against mere subjective phenomenalism, that a plurality of intercommunicating selves is the truth, as against solipsism, and that genuine knowledge of the physical world and of other minds is both a possibility and in some considerable measure an actuality.

But is all that can be said that critical monism, physical realism, and the doctrine of a plurality of intercommunicating minds are all mere assumptions, albeit assumptions which work practically as they might be expected to work if they were true? No, this is not all that can be said. It remains to point out that each of these theoretically permissible and practically workable assumptions is simply an explicit repetition of what originally comes to us not as a mere projected hypothesis but rather as a practical achievement of prephilosophical and prescientific cognition, an empirical intuition which is about as old and as universal as human consciousness itself. Our critical monistic realism then, besides accounting satisfactorily for the *fait accompli* which our prescientific and scientific knowledge of the world is, has this in addition to be said for it, that it has met and stood in a satisfactory way all three of our human tests of the truth of our ideas, namely logic, practice, and immediate intuition. As logically consistent, internally and externally, it is rationally *possible;* in practice it is found to be *necessary;* and in its principal positive features it is what has always been presented in man's immediate intuition as *actual.*

Critical monism may be applied to our knowledge of the self and of other selves, as well as to our knowledge of the physical world. From this point of view both our own consciousness and the mind or personal self which is its subject are real independently of our introspective awareness of them, but at the same time directly experienced and known (intuited) in the introspective complex of sensing, perceiving, and other mental processes. Similarly we become aware of other personal selves in the complex of our social experience, and particularly in the complex of their observable behavior. This, of course, presupposes that we are directly aware of their bodily organisms as existing independently in the same space-time continuum as that in which our own body exists.

Moreover, as in the case of the perceived physical object, so here in the cognition of selves there is a partial, but only a partial, identity of the independently real and the directly apprehended. This applies even to our knowledge of our own mind. There is a realm of mental life which is beyond the threshold of present consciousness, and on the other hand there are often contents of self-consciousness which are purely subjective, not objectively valid with reference to the real self. Still, to a very considerable extent what the mind or self is is immediately apprehended in self-conscious feeling and thought. Here again the partial coincidence or identity of the real and the experienced is the basis of verified knowledge.

When we turn to consider the possibility of a successful application of critical monistic realism in religion, what is suggested by the general form of the theory is (a) that not every quality or value which belongs to the object of religious interest in religious experience and appreciation is to be regarded as necessarily belonging to the divine reality in its independent existence, (b) that what is directly experienced of the divine is not necessarily to be taken as all there is of the divine in reality, and (c) that if there is to be empirical knowledge of an independently existing divine reality, there must be a partial coincidence or identity of what is immediately experienced and appreciated of the divine and a really divine independent reality. This partial coincidence or identity of the experienced and the real in the realm of the divine is obviously what must be found if any of our ideas of the divine are to be verified.

The question is suggested as to what criterion we have for the divine, whether as experienced or as real. Here the results of experimental religion in its more advanced and critical form are of importance. The "numinous" consciousness of mysterious reality is not necessarily an accurate criterion of divinity; the numinous sense gives us but the secondary qualities, as it were, of deity,[11] and in some instances what appears to be deity, because it elicits this numinous response, may (as when the unfamiliar is interpreted as supernatural) turn out to be largely religious illusion if not mere religious hallucination. On the other hand value-producing processes in the world may conceivably be the work of deity, but apart from religious experience and appreciation man does not readily recognize them as such; religiously speaking, they lie, at least at first, outside of the realm of religious knowledge. Rather is it where the numinous reality and the production of values overlap or coincide that we find our criterion of divine reality. And this overlapping or coincidence we discover, as a matter of fact, in *spiritual* religious experience. When we adjust ourselves in a certain way to the mysterious and numinous reality or higher power for the sake of promoting

[11] "The 'numinous quality' of which Professor Otto makes so much, being there in proportion as religious feeling finds it there, may be called the 'secondary quality' of God" (*The Reasonableness of Christianity*, 1925, p. 228, note). "If the spiritual world has been transmuted by a religious colour beyond anything implied in its bare external qualities, it may be allowable to assert with equal conviction that this is not misrepresentation but the achievement of a divine element in man's nature" (A. S. Eddington, *The Nature of the Physical World*, 1928, p. 335).

the production of spiritual values, we find that a difference for the better is made in relation to those values. An outstanding illustration is ethico-religious conversion, in which the turning to God in repentance and faith is part of the cause of the experience, even if it may be also itself part of the effect. Another illustration is genuine answer to prayer in which there is an essential coincidence of the answer and the spiritual effect.

This increase in the production of spiritual values through adjustment to numinous reality is both spiritual and numinous at once. Moreover, it is only the spiritual that dependably takes the form of the numinous in experimental religion; there seems to be no dependable experience of direct or immediate success or salvation in experimental religion save spiritual success, spiritual salvation. Physical and social success may follow, but only as after-effects of the primary experience, which is individual and spiritual. One might venture to put the matter thus: in the numinous we have the *form* of the divine, and in the spiritual its *content*,[12] and having discovered the divineness of spiritual values in a numinous ethico-religious experience, we subsequently tend to identify the divine rather more with that which agrees with its spiritual *content*—"the moral law within," for example—than with that which merely shares its numinous *form*—the "mysterious universe," for instance.

This matter is of such crucial importance that we may well give it special attention. Let us inquire a little further, then, into the religious interpretation of spiritual values and processes as divine.

Ideals, or values, such as rationality, and beauty and goodness of personal life, individual and social, which we may reasonably regard as valid ends always, everywhere, and for all persons, may be characterized as eternal and absolute ideals, or values, not in any altogether static sense of these terms, but in the sense indicated

[12] I find that Professor Otto himself sanctions this identification of the numinous with the form of the holy, and the rational (moral, etc.) with its true content (*Indiens Gnadenreligion und das Christentum*, 1930, p. 61; Eng. tr. by F. H. Foster, p. 82).

above, that they point out directions of development which are and, we may reasonably believe, always will be entitled to our absolute and wholehearted allegiance and devotion. Such absolute and eternal ideals or values, are, when considered purely qualitatively, in a certain sense divine. By this use of the term "divine" we do not mean to assume or imply either the existence of an ideal being or any theory as to the origin of the ideals in question, but merely to indicate their coincidence with the qualities of character which spiritual religion tends to ascribe to its object of worship and trust. But not only are the ideals specified qualitatively divine in the sense that they are worthy—as ideals—of our supreme or absolute reverence and devotion; it is also true that only as including them somehow could there be justly claimed for any being our absolute allegiance, worship and trust. But this much we can say with reference to reality: in so far as these qualitatively divine ideals or values are real in the actual world of human experience, their actualized presence there is a presence of something divine, a qualitatively divine presence.

There are in the world many processes in which divine ideals are being realized, divine values produced, as well as values and forms of being which are instrumental to divine values. Such processes are divine processes, and that reality, whatever it may be, which is related to this emergence of divine values in a divine process as its adequately potential cause is a divine reality. Without attempting to say as yet whether this reality is ultimately one or many, and while not maintaining that it is an all-inclusive reality, we may take it, in the light of its effects, as having at least some sort of collective and coöperative unity, so that we may speak of divine-value-producing reality as a divine factor. This divine factor we may call God, provided it be understood that in this immediate connection we mean to imply no further connotation of the term than such as is implied in this and the immediately preceding paragraph.

Obviously enough, the divine, in the sense in which we

have used the term, is conditioned by human behavior. Divine values and values which are instrumental to the same are produced more effectively on condition of certain right adjustments of persons to the world and to each other. In other words, there is in the universe a divine-value-producing factor (which we may call God) which works more effectively toward the production of divine values on condition of appreciation of spiritual values, scientific adjustment to the world, and intelligent and friendly coöperation on the part of human persons. But the divine-value-producing factor in the universe (God) works *most* effectively for the production of divine values, other things being equal, on condition of a certain right specifically religious adjustment. And by the right specifically religious adjustment we mean an adjustment to numinous reality or power for the promoting of values, such that it works to this end, and works dependably. And as a matter of fact, as we have seen, it is as directed toward spiritual values, primarily in the individual and ultimately in the social community, that specific religious adjustment dependably works. This indicates that the dependable numinous reality is favorable to spiritual values, and that in spiritual values we have a true indication of the character, not necessarily of everything which may arouse the numinous feeling, but of that particular numinous reality or power, called God, which can be depended upon through specific religious adjustment for the promotion of universally valid and desirable qualities of spiritual life.

This brings us back to the point from which we digressed a few paragraphs back. In the characteristic spiritual experience of dependably successful experimental religion we have not only revelation of the divine (the divine reality is revealed in all spiritual process) but revelation of the divine *as divine*, that is, as divine not only qualitatively but ontologically. We have discovered the criterion for which we were looking. The spiritual, especially the kind of spiritual which we can dependably have promoted in and through us if we persist in the right religious adjustment—this is the hallmark of the divine. Not the subjectively numinous is necessarily in every instance the truly divine in the full sense of the word, but rather the spiritual, the value-producing process in the universe. Historical religion has often gone astray and suffered religious illusion in being guided too exclusively by subjective numinous feeling. It is not to be denied that in some vague sense the term divine is not uncommonly used in connection with that ultimately mysterious cosmic reality (power and presence) toward which man feels constrained to take an at least potentially and perhaps incipiently religious attitude of conscious dependence, awe and wonder, accompanied, it may be, by humiliation and other states of consciousness which prepare the value-appreciating mind for attitudes and experiences which are distinctly and definitely religious. But it seems better, on the whole, to speak of this cosmic consciousness as potentially religious rather than as actually so.

Instances, then, of the production of spiritual value in the universe, primarily in connection with dependably effective experimental adjustments to numinous reality, but ultimately more generally, are perceived, appreciated, and rightly interpreted, in critical experimental religion, as instances of a divine process. As revelation of the divine they form the empirical data for a scientific development of theology. Generalizations as to the revelations (productions and discoveries) of the divine which are experienced and experienceable on condition of certain specific religious adjustments form the laws of theology as an empirical science. The right (because dependably successful) religious adjustment includes, as we have seen, (a) aspiration toward spiritual and especially moral ends; (b) concentration of attention upon God or religious reality, commonly identified with the awe-inspiring numinous reality, but necessarily regarded as a dependable source of help toward the realization of the spiritual ideal, and interpreted, especially in mature religion, as identical with the divine-value-producing factor in the universe and in history; (c) self-surrender to God; (d) an appropriating faith in the present help of the divine factor; (e) active response to the appeal of the moral ideal under the inspiration of this faith, and (f) persistence in all this long enough and wholeheartedly enough to bring the desired result or its equivalent.[13] The reality which dependably responds to this adjustment is the reality in which experimental religion is centrally interested, and that reality is what it calls God. The laws, then, of what the dependable religious object (reality, or factor in reality) can be depended on for, are theological laws at the same time that they are scientifically verified empirical generalizations.

In making the transition from scientific theological laws to scientific theological theory, the central process is that of inferring what a factor is from what it does. At least this much can be known about the dependable objective factor in religion, that it is the reality and the kind of reality which can be depended upon in such and such ways for such and such specifically divine effects. That on the basis of religious experience specific content can be put into this form of statement is a fact and it is enough to make empirical theology at heart essentially scientific. We have a certain amount of scientifically discovered religious knowledge.[14] If we know

[13] It may be well to point out that in general the most effective cue to an appropriate attitude or adjustment is not a detailed analytical description of the attitude itself, but rather such an idea or presentation of the object as will tend to produce the desired adjustment as the natural and appropriate response. There is good human psychology in the familiar rhyme:

> The centipede was happy quite,
> Until the frog for fun
> Said, "Pray, which leg comes after which?"
> This wrought him up to such a pitch
> He fell distracted in a ditch,
> Considering how to run.

It is quite likely that the elements specified above as belonging to the right religious adjustment will find place in the life of the individual much less certainly by being aimed at directly and self-consciously than when, whole-heartedly and with a minimum of introspection, one responds to some vivid and appealing presentation of an essentially valid God-idea, or to some revelation (discovery) in history or contemporary life of an objective divine process or reality.

[14] Cf. *Theology as an Empirical Science*, 1919, *passim.*

a real world and real human selves—and it is reasonable to believe that we do—we know a real divine factor at work in those real selves and that real world.

But in addition to our verified scientific knowledge, there is room for judgments embodying reasonable belief about reality. Within reasonable belief many degrees of reasonableness may be distinguished, varying from (a) what is almost demonstrably certain knowledge and (b) belief which is rationally necessary in the sense of being logically involved in what may be regarded on adequately critical grounds not only as theoretically permissible, but as practically necessary, to (c) what is merely rationally permissible, as not contradicting any known fact or anything which may be reasonably regarded as practically necessary.

In religion particularly, in addition to what may be regarded as fully verified religious knowledge, there is room for further belief in the form of practically justified and theoretically permissible judgments of faith. More especially, on the basis of an adequate appreciation of spiritual values (intellectual, æsthetic, ethical, social and religious) it is possible to construct in a logical way, i.e. by deductive inference, certain positively reasonable beliefs about reality, some of which have definite significance for belief about God. Some of these religiously significant beliefs about reality may be regarded as rationally necessary religious beliefs, the reason being that they are theoretically permissible in the light of available knowledge of fact and at the same time logically deducible from the validity of certain spiritual or ideal value-judgments (moral, social, religious, etc.) which we must regard as at once adequately critical and essential to life at its best. All such positively reasonable religious beliefs may be given a place in theological theory, but when this is done it would be well to keep these not fully verified elements distinct from the central core of scientifically verified religious knowledge.

Our thought about reality is often enriched by what is at first simply more or less questionable imaginative surmise. Beyond our verified knowledge and our definitely recognized ignorance, beyond our clearly distinguished beliefs and disbeliefs, there lies a penumbra of thought not definitely classifiable even as belief or disbelief but only as thinking (suggestions, surmises, hypotheses), much of which may be on its way to becoming belief or disbelief, or even, in some instances, knowledge. So, too, in religion, in addition to what is strictly known and what can be inferred logically about a divine reality as involved in an adequate appreciation of spiritual values, it is possible to formulate certain judgments in which to express our further surmises as to the nature of divine reality. Some of such judgments of surmise may eventually qualify for adoption as reasonably permissible beliefs, the reasonableness being found either in their theoretical probability or in their theoretical permissibility combined with some kind and degree of practical value.

Running across these divisions of our ways of thinking (knowledge, more or less reasonable belief, and surmise) there must be recognized the familiar distinction (not to be insisted upon too absolutely) between that which should be taken literally and that which can be accepted only in a figurative, symbolical, or poetical sense, whether originally intended literally or not. However, when what was originally intended as a simple straightforward statement of factual truth is later employed in a non-literal or merely symbolical sense, it is commonly desirable in the interests of intellectual honesty and understanding, that a clear distinction be made between the literal truth of the matter and the traditional symbolism in terms of which it may still find expression. In religion particularly there are elements in judgments of surmise about the divine reality which cannot be taken as they stand as literally true of the divine reality; they are true only as symbols, figures of speech, or poetry can be true. But even here it is sometimes possible to separate the thought into an element which can be regarded as literally true and others which cannot legitimately be so regarded.

It is here that a critically constructive theology or religious metaphysic finds a considerable portion of its difficult and dangerous task.

Religious thought, then, or, to speak more technically, theological theory, might be represented by a diagram of three concentric circles. In the innermost circle might be written the words "science" and "actuality"; in the middle ring, "rational faith" and "necessity"; in the outermost ring, "surmise" and "possibility." This diagram would represent what we still have to do. Under the caption of ontology we must seek to indicate in a general way, and as briefly as is consistent with clearness, what we scientifically know, what we must reasonably believe, and what we may be permitted to surmise about the object of our religious interest, God.

3. ONTOLOGICAL

We now turn from epistemology to ontology, but in doing so it must be confessed that the distinction between the philosophy of knowledge and the philosophy of reality is more easily maintained in theory than in practice. As we had to anticipate in some measure our theory of religious reality in dealing with the problem of religious knowledge, so in seeking to bring together whatever we may have to say about the religious object we shall have to refer from time to time to our epistemological distinctions between what we know scientifically and what we must or may reasonably believe or surmise. Moreover, in dealing with what we scientifically know a further distinction must be kept in mind, the distinction, namely, between our knowledge about *something* which *may* possibly be God and our knowledge (or rational faith or surmise) that this reality which we know *is* God. Our ontological part then may be expected to include a scientific part (the metaphysics of actuality), a pragmatic part (the metaphysics of necessity), and a speculative part (the metaphysics of possibility).

What we are undertaking is comparable to the attempt of the blind men, according to an old story, to gain knowledge of an elephant. One, touching the animal's side, said an elephant was like a wall; another, having felt its leg, thought it was more like a tree; a third gained from its trunk the impression that it was like a serpent; the fourth, from its tusk that it was like a spear; and the last, from its tail that it was like a rope. The impressions gained were very different and seemingly discrepant, but all were essentially true, about the same reality, and mutually supplementary. So it will be with us in the task before us. At best we shall be describing and seeking to think together into a unitary theory a number of different *aspects of Deity*. The task calls for such religious knowledge as can be derived from experience, such rationally necessary religious faith as there may be, and a considerable amount of imaginative surmise.

Let us first consider the religious significance of the object of our ultimate absolute dependence. We cannot escape from the fact that there is such a reality. With all our freedom and independence, we must come, sooner or later, to a recognition of a power above us with which we ultimately have to do, and upon which we are in the end absolutely dependent. Schleiermacher did well to suggest, as a substitute for "proofs" of the existence of God, the calling of attention to the universal human feeling of absolute dependence. In the complex of our experience as beings with an independence which ultimately encounters an absolute limit we are empirically aware of the object of our absolute dependence. And if this be God, we are sure of God as an existent reality.

But does not our feeling of absolute dependence arise in view of our relation to the universe? Is God then just the mysterious universe? Schleiermacher felt this difficulty, and confessed to an oscillation between the view which identified God with the universe and that which distinguished the two. If we gain our assurance of the existence of God from the inescapable consciousness of our absolute dependence, we find ourselves in a serious dilemma. God must be either identified with the universe, or distinguished from it. If God be identified with the universe, we avoid agnosticism but fall into pantheism, according to which there is no reality which is divine in any specific sense, no specifically religious adjustment called for, nor any specifically religious experience to be expected. If on the other hand God be distinguished from the universe as a power back of it upon which it is ultimately dependent, the question arises whether this is not to escape pantheism at the cost of making God unknowable.

But perhaps there is a third alternative. May it not be that that with reference to which we are ultimately absolutely dependent, while it is to be distinguished from the physical universe, and while it may be thought of as that upon which the universe itself is ultimately dependent, is at the same time expressed to some extent *in* the universe. May not God transcend the universe and yet be immanent in it? In other words may there not be a partial identity or coincidence, as it were, of God and the universe, so that while there may be that in God which is not completely to be found in the universe, and at the same time that in the universe which cannot be identified simply with God, there is also a divine element or process or factor in the universe, or, in other words, a phase of the universal process in which we can discover God. This suggests the value-producing process and factor in the universe as more specifically divine than mere cosmic power apart from value—a thought to which we shall have occasion to return at a later point in our discussion.

If the question be raised as to whether it is conceivable that a reality upon which the universe is dependent can be discovered *in* the universe, it may be suggested, by way of surmise, that if God be thought of as an intelligent power creatively producing and developing the universe as a body in and through which to express his divine life and purpose, it is quite conceivable that God should be discoverable as a divine factor at work in the world and yet be that upon which the world itself is ultimately dependent. But this is no more than permissible surmise, at least for the present; what we know is the reality of some object of our ultimate absolute dependence.

In some ways it might seem desirable to proceed at once to a consideration of the value-producing process in the universe, and then to go on to raise the question whether the remainder of the universe or the universe as a whole has any important meaning for religion; but we shall take the opposite course and begin with *the creative principle* (or process or factor) in the universe. This creative principle is not easily distinguishable from what we may call *the formative principle,* which we must also examine; in fact both principles seem to be involved through most of the cosmic process, so that they may be said to overlap or even to merge; and this seems a point in favor of the surmise that ultimately they are one and the same reality.

Physical scientists have startled the world by taking up once again another of those questions on the border line between science and religion which were discarded by science long ago and, it was supposed, permanently, as not being soluble by empirical methods. I refer to the problem of world-creation. There is a difference of opinion at the present moment between some of the most eminent physicists as to whether the available energy of the universe is disappearing, being radiated away as light without possibility of return, or whether there is a reverse process according to which the energy radiated away is being made available once more. On this question there has been developing a dispute between the British physicists, Eddington and Jeans, and the Americans, Millikan and Lewis. In astrophysics, as in theology and in the philosophy of history, Europe has chosen the pessimistic outlook (witness Barth and Spengler), while American astrophysics has become, as American theology remains, optimistic or at least melioristic, and the same thing would doubtless be true of American philosophy of history, if there were any such thing. The whole question is highly speculative, but Dr. Millikan is of the opinion that as at the center of the stars, under tremendous heat and pressure, electrons and protons are disappearing as such, being transformed into radiant energy, so in the depths of interstellar space, where opposite conditions prevail (extreme cold and rarefaction), radiant energy is probably being changed into electrons and protons, while these in turn are being built up into atoms of hydrogen, helium, and other heavier elements. As pointing to such a process of the creation of matter out of radiant energy, Dr. Millikan cites not only the well-known fact that the atoms of the various elements are almost exact multiples of the hydrogen atom and seem to have been built up out of units of hydrogen, but more particularly the fact that the energy of some of the recently discovered cosmic rays is the same in amount as would be liberated by the building up of helium out of hydrogen. From this point of view we have a new form of the old question as to which came first, the hen or the egg. Here the problem is as to which came first, electrons or light. Under present conditions of cosmological speculation a curious interest attaches to those classical prescientific surmises, that the first creative fiat, before the worlds were made, was "Let there be light!" and that in time to come the sun should be darkened and the elements melt with fervent heat. We should not be understood, of course, as attaching anything but a curious interest to these chance surmises of a religious past, nor even as attaching any crucial importance to the speculation of the American physicists. If in the end Millikan's theory should prove to have been mistaken, positive religious interpretation would no doubt tend to follow Eddington and Jeans in emphasizing the reality of spirit and minimizing the importance of the physical, while renewed attention would no doubt be given to the question of immortality.

In a very suggestive article entitled "A Realistic View of Theism," published in the *Crozer Quarterly* for January, 1930—an article which might well be read as an introduction to his contribution to the present volume— Professor W. K. Wright proclaims himself "quite ready to believe in the unending immortality of God and of ourselves if the astrophysicists will permit us to do so." He recognizes that possibly the physicists may some time find that there is a process compensatory to the second law of thermodynamics—some way in which energy is renewed and regenerated, so that it will then be reasonable to believe that God, as the immanent conscious and intelligent Life of the universe will endure forever. As cells are worn away and replaced in our own organisms while our conscious selves continue, so too, Professor Wright suggests, solar systems, as cells in the body of God, may be ever wearing away and ever being renewed without arresting the conscious life of God. This seems, in the present state of our knowledge, a reasonably permissible surmise; but in all this the assumption seems to be that the immortality of God as Spirit necessarily depends upon the immortality of the physical universe as God's body. But the prevalent belief in human immortality does not posit the immortality of man's gross perceptible body as essential, and there seems no sufficient reason, even on the assumption that at present the physical cosmos is the body of an immanent divine Life and Mind, to deny that this embodiment may be necessary only for the present stage in the existence and education of the human race. May it not be that the eternal, transcendent God became immanent in the physical world only for the creation and the first stage in the education of immortal human spirits, and that they, as well as he, will be able to persist without the present physical embodiment? In other words, if Millikan's theory of the creation of matter out of radiant energy should finally be shown to be untenable, religion would probably be free to maintain that the physical universe is but the nursery and kindergarten of immortal personalities, the primary grade in which only the first lessons are imparted by the immortal "Father of Spirits" who is also our never-to-be-superseded Teacher.

As a matter of fact the cosmological theories of the physicists to-day are not two, but three, namely, the materialistic or purely physical, the mathematical or purely idealistic, and what we might perhaps call indifferently the organic, teleological, functional, creative, or activistic.[15] Until recently most physicists held not only to the materialistic view, but to a completely mechanistic version of that theory. Now, however, in the light of quantum-physics, Heisenberg's "principle of indeterminacy," and other recent developments in physical theory, it is pointed out that there are events which no imaginable mechanical process will explain. On the other hand it is a fact that mathematical formulæ have been devised by means of which certain of these physically inconceivable processes may be correctly anticipated. Faced with this situation some physicists, among them Eddington and Jeans, have leaped to the conclusion that the universe is not really physical at all, but the thought of a Mathematical Thinker. The religious significance of such a view is obvious, but it would probably be a mistake to rest very heavily upon the authority of these eminent physicists when they leave their own special field and indulge in speculations in metaphysics and the philosophy of religion. If we may take a suggestion from our own human nature, in which there is an element of thought, an element of vital development and activity directed in part by thought, and an element of more or less completely mechanized habit, let us inquire whether a philosophy of organism somewhat like Professor Whitehead's may not be nearer the truth than either the materialistic or the idealistic extreme.

According to Whitehead's philosophy of organism the ultimate is creativity, a becoming rather than a static being. But in actuality this becoming is not a chaotic flux but a complex process ordered in accordance with certain "eternal objects," namely, mathematical and other rational forms, or "Platonic ideas." But how can eternal objects, which do not as such exist, but merely subsist and so have no power, determine the order of actual events? To solve this problem there is assumed

[15] Cf. F. S. C. Northrop, *Science and First Principles*, 1931.

as existing a first actual entity, eternally self-created and envisaging somehow within its conceptual experience the whole realm of eternal objects. This entity, denominated "the principle of concretion," or "God," is not regarded as the creator or efficient cause of the flux of events, but rather as the formal cause of the rational or mathematical order which it exemplifies and as the final cause of the evolutionary emergence in it of new forms of existence. In this way, it is held, an explanation is found for the ingression of the eternal forms into the flux of creativity and the consequent emergence of the ordered and intelligible world of events. "The concept of 'God' is the way in which we understand this incredible fact— that what cannot be, yet is." [16]

The concept is suggestive and may prove useful in our ontological construction; but as developed further by its author it presents serious difficulties both for thought and for religion. In his Gifford Lectures Professor Whitehead goes on to develop a "dipolar" view of the divine nature, according to which one side of the nature of God is "free, complete, primordial, eternal, actually deficient [i.e. deficient in so far as actuality is concerned] and unconscious," while the other side is "determined, incomplete, consequent, 'everlasting,' fully actual, and conscious." [17] As explaining the order of the world and the evolution of novelty God in his primordial nature is still spoken of as the principle of concretion; but by the consequent nature of God is meant God as evolving in conscious relation to the evolving world.

There are some features of this view which invite comment. Professor Whitehead has a horror of the "bifurcation of nature." In so far as he means by this phrase *epistemological* dualism, his antipathy is justified, if empirical knowledge of reality is to be regarded as at all possible. But from the point of view of religion his own philosophy is open to a similar criticism. As a philosopher of religion he bifurcates God. So great is

[16] A. N. Whitehead, *Process and Reality*, 1928, p. 531.
[17] *Ibid.*, p. 524.

the contrast not to say contradiction, between his "primordial nature of God" and his "consequent nature of God" that they fall apart into two apparently irreconcilable notions of God. Thus experimental religion in the form in which it has proved most efficacious for good tends to be undermined. The perfect, primordial God is represented as not conscious or even fully actual; and just how such a God, creating nothing outside of its own being, can be a formative principle in the world of creative evolution and real events is by no means made clear. On the other hand the fully actual and conscious God (or nature of God) is imperfect, a finite, evolving God, and thus quite possibly not qualified to be an object of absolute worship or trust. The two natures of God are taken too abstractly, but this is not all. The abstractness of the conceptions is virtually acknowledged by Professor Whitehead himself; but the trouble is that the characterizations given of the two natures are so mutually exclusive that the two abstractions cannot be thought into concrete unity again. Thus in the system before us religion falls to the ground between two stools. Two half-gods do not make one whole God any more than two half-men make a whole man.

Contemporary religious thought is greatly indebted to Dr. Whitehead for his fresh and suggestive interpretations, but one suspects that if his authority is trusted too implicitly in matters of religion it will be discovered that in contributing his idea—or ideas—of God to contemporary thought he has deposited a cuckoo-egg or two in the theological nest. It is not the first time such a trick has been played upon theology by a philosopher—witness Hegel's Absolute, for example. The idea which a critical, self-understanding religion is increasingly interested in is that of a single, self-consistent, actual, conscious, absolutely worshipful and trustworthy God, immanent and creatively at work in the world of our experience and yet always transcending it and us. Professor Whitehead is suspicious of the influence of religion upon philosophy, even upon the philosophy of religion and "the concept of God's function in the universe"; [18] but there seems room for the surmise that if God in his primordial, transcendent aspect were defined not as unconscious, deficient in actuality and non-creative in relation to the world, but as conscious, fully actual and creative, and God in his consequent and immanent aspect as not necessarily from the point of religion imperfect and incomplete, it would be possible not only to combine the two views of God in a unitary conception eminently satisfying to religion, but at the same time to square the resultant idea, certainly no less than the theological speculations and explanatory assumptions of the eminent Harvard philosopher, with the demands of a scientific view of the world. Meanwhile it seems both scientifically and philosophically reasonable to acknowledge a rational formative principle which is not necessarily "unconscious" or deficient in actuality, but an actual reality and active factor in the universe, determining the flux of events in accordance with the eternal mathematical forms of reason. This suggests the surmise that the universe is like a human organism in that it is a physical system permeated by a creative activity or life which is not mere thought-activity but activity (productive process) amenable to guidance by intelligent mind in accordance with mathematical forms. The view suggested is thus a synthesis of certain mutually compatible elements of all three theories of nature, the physical, the mathematical, and the functional.

And so from this modified point of view according to which Whitehead's primordial and consequent aspects of Deity—or something like them—are brought into unity, it is more than ever feasible to hold on to the teleological interpretation of nature upon which Whitehead himself so emphatically insists, [19] and that in spite of the fact that, like Bergson, he regards reality as fundamentally becoming, and man as an agent whose freedom is not to be explained away after the manner of the "soft deter-

[18] *Ibid.*, pp. 315-16.
[19] *The Function of Reason*, 1929, pp. 22, etc.

minists.'' But neither divine teleology nor human freedom is a matter of scientific knowledge; rather do they come under the categories of rationally necessary faith and theoretically permissible surmise. Human freedom is affirmed as a morally necessary faith which is at the same time theoretically permissible. Divine teleology, offered by Professor L. J. Henderson on a deterministic basis as something demonstrated, is rather a religiously necessary faith and a theoretically permissible surmise.[20] It may be shown, especially when we come to consider such facts as the value-producing process in the world, that such events are *as if* their production involved conscious purpose as a principle of intelligent benevolent guidance of some phases at least of cosmic becoming. From this point of view such not quite teleological concepts as Bergson's idea of creative evolution and General Smuts's ''holism'' are seen to be not only unsatisfactory religiously but also considerably less than might be affirmed as theoretically permissible in the light of scientific fact.

Professors S. Alexander and Lloyd Morgan are on fully scientific ground, however, when they describe the progressive emergence, in the course of evolution, of consciousness, intelligence, and personality; and one may even go further and claim essentially scientific knowledge of God as the principle of emergent evolution, if we mean by that term simply whatever creative principle is necessary to explain this progressive emergence of new and higher forms of existence which differ in kind from all that was explicitly contained in the earlier stages of the process. But when Lloyd Morgan calls this principle God in the sense of an intelligent being acting purposively, he rightly adds that he does this ''under acknowledgment,'' that is, as a surmise which is theoretically permissible at the very least. But when Alexander speaks of this principle of emergent evolution not

[20] *The Fitness of the Environment*, 1913, *passim*. For criticisms of Henderson's argument see R. B. Perry, *General Theory of Value*, 1926, pp. 65ff., and C. D. Broad, *Hibbert Journal*, XXIV, pp. 44f.

only as a *nisus* toward the forms which have appeared, but as a *"nisus* toward deity,'' he becomes not only unscientific but fantastical. The notion does not seem to be even a reasonable surmise. What might have been asserted with scientific justification was the existence of a *nisus* toward a divine humanity, *i.e.* toward a humanity with divine qualities in the character of the individual and of society ("the Kingdom of God"). The justification of this statement will appear in connection with our later discussion of the value-producing factor.

Before turning to that phase of our subject one more approach to the formative principle may be noted. This is to be found in the "nomotheism" of Theodor Ziehen,[21] according to whom God is neither more nor less than natural law. So stated, the position is no doubt very vulnerable, but it suggests the more defensible and highly important converse proposition that natural law is divine reality, in the sense that in the principle of concretion and the consequent order of nature—which last, if anything, we know scientifically—we discover divine reality. But as in the case of Whitehead's primordial and consequent God, so here our scientific knowledge needs to be supplemented by surmise and rational faith in such a way as to exhibit this abstract aspect of deity as being simply the method or expression of the activity of a real agent who is at the same time guided by the forms of rational thought. What we mean is much the same thing as Professor Pupin seems to have in mind when he speaks of "creative coördination"[22] as an activity characteristic of the human soul and presumably also of a cosmic creator.

But if, with Ziehen, we are going to take natural law as revelation of God, we ought to take the laws of the normative sciences in the same way. They are just as much laws of reality as the laws of the descriptive sciences. In fact, in so far as the ends of the normative and applied sciences are not absolutely imperative, the

[21] *Die Grundlagen der Religionsphilosophie,* Leipzig, 1928.
[22] M. Pupin, *The New Reformation,* 1927, p. 243.

laws of these sciences are simply groups of the laws of reality, selected for practical convenience in view of human interests and needs. As such they are revelations of the rational principle of concretion. But in so far as the ends of a normative science are imperative, as in logic and ethics, the laws are laws of reality in a double sense. Like any other laws they are laws of what reality requires us to do to realize the ends prescribed, and so are part of the divine constitution of reality. At the same time they are organic parts of what we have seen to be a qualitatively divine ideal, so that as such they are divine laws in the sense of divine requirements.

We must now turn to a consideration of the value-producing factor in the world, to which we have already more than once alluded. As intimated above, this factor may be evaluated as divine in quality in so far as the values produced are qualitatively divine. Divine in function also, by the same token, we may judge the divine-value-producing factor to be.

The value-producing factor and behavior in the universe, driving toward right adjustments on man's part even if he does not coöperate or opposes at first, tending to force him to the method of trial and error, or self-correction and success—this is a divine reality, whether it be one or many, personal, impersonal or superpersonal. The drive is going on in the universe anyway, whether we coöperate or not; if we coöperate, well and good; but if we oppose it, we cannot ultimately win; we are taught what is good and what reality requires of us by the long, roundabout way of trial and error and bitter experience. It is as when cattle are being driven through a gate; if they become obstinate and refuse to coöperate, they bring trouble upon themselves, and must learn their lesson and obey in the end. Like Margaret Fuller man does well to "accept the universe," particularly in its teaching aspect. There is a drive on in the universe, teaching man the value and even necessity of knowledge of the truth, of good character and conduct, of friendly social relations (international peace, for example), and the like. This is the drive from without toward divine values, and thus qualitatively a divine drive, the drive of a qualitatively divine factor.

But there is an internal as well as an external drive toward truth and good and right. This is the inner drive of conscience, which is also, qualitatively considered, a divine drive, a drive of a qualitatively divine factor. This is true even though the dictates of conscience are not infallible, for he who continues to be conscientious and keeps on learning from experience will infallibly be guided in the right direction in the long run. This inner divine factor is variously characterized as the higher self, the spiritual not-self within, the beyond that is within, a "theoid formation"[32] within the mind. When this inner divine reality is surmised to be in some way continuous with the divine reality known in other ways (or believed in on other grounds), it is appropriately called the Divine Spirit, or Holy Spirit. What we feel under absolute obligation to obey when we consider our duty, "the moral law within"; what reality must be in order to make the realizing of the moral ideal an imperative obligation—this is God in one aspect of his being.

Taking together the divine factor driving from without directly and indirectly toward truth, goodness, and other divine ideals, and the divine factor driving through conscience toward the same ends, we may say that God is scientifically knowable as a reality or factor (whether single or dual or multiple we do not yet say), immanent in the processes of producing universally and permanently valid values. Here we have what we may call in a very real and significant sense the "divine initiative" in human experience. Both in the inner impulse or drive toward right living from within and in the teaching through consequences, or the drive toward the same end from without, there is a divine initiative in the affairs of the human spirit comparable to the initiative of the external stimulus in the life of sensation.

[32] R. G. Milburn's expression.

But God is definable not only as a factor that makes toward human good whether man coöperates at first or not; it is also true that God is a factor that works more successfully and rapidly for human good on condition of man's scientific adjustment to the world and his conscientious, friendly and intelligent adjustment to his fellows. If man coöperates by regarding conscience and being careful to learn through experience, a comparatively short cut is taken by the divine factor in bringing him to an experience of true good.

In connection with this whole matter of the value-producing process and factor in the universe empirical realism in religion is greatly indebted to Professor Wieman, who, defining God as "that something, however unknown, which would and which does bring human life to the largest fulfillment when proper adjustment is made to it," points out that we "know with certainty" that God, as thus defined, is "truly existent in the total environment with which we interact," and that "its goodness transcends the goodness of everything else in the universe."[24] This has been hailed as meaning *the passing of atheism*. The question may well be raised, however, whether this is what it is, or whether it is not rather a way whereby it is made easy either to pass out of atheism or to pass into it. When one is given such an idea of God that he can know that God is real and can cultivate experimental adjustments to that divine reality, he seems to be given the opportunity of passing out of atheism. But when proof of the existence of what is called God is undertaken by defining God in such a way that even the person who hitherto has freely denied the existence of God can now affirm it without changing in the slightest degree either his opinions or his life, the way seems open to become or remain what has always been termed an "atheist," without any longer having to endure so opprobrious an epithet. In this connection these words of Professor Haydon, quoted from an article published in *Unity* (November 26, 1928) are significant:

[24] *The Wrestle of Religion with Truth*, 1927, pp. 59, 60.

To be called an atheist . . . has now become meaningless. If to live in dependence upon the cosmic and social environment for the achievement of our values is to have a belief in God, then there are no atheists, for we can live in no other way.

If the issue here were simply that of an ambiguous definition of God given by one of the most stimulating of recent writers on religion I should not think it necessary to dwell upon the point in this connection. But the problem raised is one that affects the worth of our whole achievement in Part III up to this point, in so far as it claims to be *knowledge* of God, as distinct from further conceptions introduced as surmise or rational faith. If we stop where we now are, especially in connection with our discussion of the value-producing factor, we lay ourselves open to the charge of proving the existence of God "by definition" (the phrase is Professor Wieman's). In a sense that is what we have been doing; we have been identifying God with something the existence of which almost no one has ever thought of denying, and unless all this leads up to something new in the way of religious adjustment, religious experience, and religious knowledge, it all becomes a fruitless process by which we discover nothing about reality, except that something familiar may be called by a name which we and others had always used with a different meaning—the proverbial giving of a stone to those who are asking for bread!

And yet what may be fruitless or even dangerous as leading to the abandonment of any further quest for religious experience and knowledge, may also be but the needed reassurance to encourage the taking of such further steps as will bring further acquaintance with divine reality and thus a closer definition of God without any diminution of the newly found certainty of God's existence. We may not only discover more fully through experience what this divine value-producing process or behavior or factor in the universe can be depended upon to do on condition of scientific and right social adjustment. We may canvass the possibilities of experience through discovering and maintaining the right specifically religious adjustment, that is, the most effective one discoverable among such as are reasonably permissible.

Accepting Professor Wieman's definition of God as that in the universe which yields the highest values when right adjustment is made to it, it is of the greatest importance that we interpret this right adjustment as including, besides scientific adjustment to the world of things and right social adjustment to other human beings, the right specifically religious adjustment. And even here it is important to note that the phrase "the right specifically religious adjustment" will mean, at least initially, different things according to the ideas entertained as to the nature of God.

To the non-theistic "humanist" it will mean nothing but adjustment to physical things and human persons, individually and socially, and possibly to ideas and ideals recognized simply as such. But to one who would agree with Dr. John MacMurray when he says (rather bluntly, but with much force from the point of view of Christian religious experience) that to argue that God is impersonal is "to defend an atheistical position and to deny that religion is objectively true,"[25] the right religious adjustment must seem to be an additional and very specific thing.

But the test of the right religious adjustment will be found, ultimately, not in the ideas which it presupposes in any particular case, but, assuming its theoretical permissibility, in the value and dependableness of the results which it brings. My own definition of God, similar as it is to Professor Wieman's, puts particular emphasis upon the specifically religious element, and then goes on to specify just what the principal features of the right specifically religious adjustment seem to me to be, judged in the light of historical, and especially of evangelical Christianity. God is "a Power not identifiable with ourselves, that makes for righteousness in and through us when we persist in the right religious adjustment," "a dependable Factor making for moral salvation and spir-

[25] *Adventure*, edited by B. H. Streeter, 1928, p. 184.

itual achievement, especially on condition of the right religious adjustment, whose existence is proved in experimental religion at its best.'' [26] The right religious adjustment is defined as aspiration after effective good will; [27] concentration upon an Ideal Being and Higher Power not identical with our actual self as we know it, and regarded as dependable and favorable to what is truly good; self-surrender to this Divine Being; an appropriating faith which lays hold of the divine help; a responsiveness which begins to act on this faith in line with what seems to be the true good, and persistence in all this long enough and wholeheartedly enough to bring the desired effect (effective good will and all that that makes possible). [28]

From the point of view of this definition of God, it is by no means true that everyone already knows that God exists. God is now defined as the factor which responds dependably to persistence in the right specifically religious adjustment (as defined), by promoting goodness of will and effectiveness in its activity, with such other phases of specific religious experience at its best (emotional, intellectual, physiological, social and *distinctively* religious) as are incidental to the fundamental experience. God is this and this is God, and the only way of knowing that God in this very important sense of the term exists is to know it in the light of the specific religious experience of spiritual and especially moral deliverance, uplift and achievement. The experience is one which is frequently to be observed in the lives of others, as well as being presumably for everyone a possible experience of his own.

This is not to give merely the name God to something the existence of which nobody, not even the atheist, would seriously question; it is to call attention to a verifiable

---

[26] *The Reasonableness of Christianity*, 1925, pp. 128, 131.

[27] Aspiration after more effective good will presupposes good will. Love to man facilitates approach to God. Forgiveness of man, as the Lord's Prayer teaches, preconditions forgiveness from God.

[28] "Prayer for strength of soul is that passion of the soul which catches the gift it seeks" (George Meredith, *Works*, XXVIII, pp. 237-38).

fact of which many are ignorant. Rather than being satisfied with proving the existence of God by so changing the meaning of the term God as to make it refer to something the existence of which nobody doubts, our procedure involves *proving the existence of God in essentially that specifically religious sense in which the term has been used throughout history* (as a reality which responds to man's religious attitude when it is the right one) *and proving this by a new and regenerating experience.* This, of course, is the normal way of proving existence—by experience. We learn that God exists and what he is, not by a mere shift of definition, but through a new discovery of reality.

We can now say that all of the "aspects of Deity" which we have set forth as *known* (rather than merely believed or surmised) are aspects of a total divine reality which has at least a collective and coöperative unity, however ignorant we may be as to the further nature of that divine totality (which is, of course, not necessarily to be identified with the totality of reality).

But have we not, so far as we have gone, a merely behavioristic theology?[20] We have essentially scientific knowledge of a process immanent in the universe and in man which is divine in value, a divine behavior of which we have discovered to some extent the conditions. But is this behavior, which may be termed qualitatively divine, or the factor which is the subject of this divine behavior, at all comparable with the self-conscious mind and will which we know by introspection to be the subject of our human behavior? If not, is it really God whose existence we have proved when we have pointed out this qualitatively divine behavior? May it not be said that what is proved, even in religious experience at its best, is simply that there exists a dependable factor, perhaps a very complex factor, or many factors, whose function is that which vital experiential religion ascribes to God, namely

[20] Professor Wieman significantly defines God as "the behavior . . . which preserves and increases to the maximum the total good of all human living where right adjustment is made" (*The Wrestle of Religion with Truth,* p. 62).

the function of regenerating the life and building up an
integrated spiritual personality, as well as promoting the
true well-being of man in general? And what more is this
than to say that there is in the universe a divine process
or behavior in which spiritual values are made real? It
is a further question whether this demonstrably real factor, which actually has the God-function in human experience, has also the spiritual or essentially personal nature
which historic religion has generally and Christianity
has always ascribed to God. In other words, in addition
to the behavioristic theology according to which we can
know God as a divine process or behavior in the universe,
can we find room in our religious realism for an animistic, spiritualistic or personalistic theology, according to
which the factor discernible in the value-producing process and in religious experience at its best may be reasonably believed to be a unitary, essentially spiritual, and
thus partly transcendent being? Is this an important
question? Is it one which can be answered, and if so,
what is the answer?

The question will seem a most important one to all
those of the Christian tradition and of other religious
traditions for whom worship has taken the form of communion with and adoration of a perfectly good and wise
invisible Companion. For all such Dr. MacMurray speaks
when he says that to argue that God is impersonal is
virtually to defend atheism. Moreover, even for maintaining the practical phase of religion which we have
called the right religious adjustment, there can be little
doubt that the idea of God as a being of ideal spiritual
character is of very great and perhaps even indispensable value. How, for instance, can we morally surrender
ourselves to an impersonal power? Can we have the
fullest faith in an impersonal power as dependably aid-
ing us in the production of spiritual values? And above
all, can we trust a mere unconscious, unintelligent something, however helpful it may have been up to date, to
conserve adequately throughout the future the spiritual
values which we and others like us may achieve? Even

if we may not be able to prove absolutely the essential personality of the divine factor, may we not be able to establish it as a reasonable religious belief, a conviction which, while not scientific knowledge, is at once our best philosophical wisdom and an assured religious faith? May we not find it possible to avoid the two opposite extremes within religious realism, the theological behaviorism which tends to deny the transcendence and spirituality of God, and the one-sided personalism which tends to conceive the independently real and personal God as being so completely transcendent as to be never in any sense comparable to the realities science deals with, never to any extent verifiable as a reality in the world about us or in the inner life of man?

There is nothing in the adoption of an essentially scientific attitude in religion to prevent one from adding to his scientific religious *knowledge* a reasonable religious *faith*. Professor John Baillie, following the Kantian tradition, has taken his stand on the side of rational religious faith as against empirical religious knowledge.[30] Professor Wieman, influenced by the neo-positivism of Dewey, seems to me equally one-sided in his minimizing of faith and his apparent determination to restrict religious affirmation to the realm in which full scientific verification is either actual or presumably possible. To Wieman, Baillie's faith seems a mere subjective escape from reality. To Baillie, Wieman's restriction of religious belief to the realm of the scientifically describable must seem to ignore all that is most characteristic and

[30] When Professor Baillie charges (*The Interpretation of Religion,* 1928, p. 223) that I destroy the element of faith in religion, and find no difficulty in making the sacrifice, certainly his "interpretation" of *my* religion misses the mark entirely! Why should it be supposed, when it is claimed that theological theory may include a core of verified religious knowledge, that what is meant is that it must exclude everything else, whether it be working hypothesis or faith, postulate or speculation? I know of no empirical science which does not include in its theoretical part a good deal that is not yet and perhaps never will be fully verified knowledge. Theology, broadly understood as a philosophy of religious reality, has room for reasonable faith and theoretically permissible surmise, as well as for what it ought to be fundamentally, namely verified religious knowledge. I trust that the present discussion will obviate any similar misconception as to my position. See also my book, *The Pilgrimage of Faith in the World of Modern Thought,* 1931.

vital in spiritual religion. Baillie's view, however, reminiscent as it is of the Kantian and Ritschlian development, gives large place also to elements of recent British idealism which involve an emphasis upon immanence and make his thought not so good an illustration of the antithesis to American neo-positivism as is the new "dialectical theology" or "theology of crisis" of Barth, Gogarten and Brunner. To the American school, religion is, on the intellectual side, essentially knowledge of an observable divine Behavior; to the European school, faith in an unseen divine Being. To the one, God is an immanent Process in the world and in man, and so not easily thought of as personal. To the other, God, although personal, remains forever transcendent and, except for an alleged supernatural revelation in "the Word," unknowable. But why should we be asked to take "either—or," instead of "both—and"? Is it too much to surmise that we can both scientifically know the immanent God, Producer of highest values, and rationally believe in the transcendent, essentially personal God, Conserver of highest values, and that these two, the transcendent and the immanent, the Producer and the Conserver, the known and the believed in, are ultimately not two different beings, but somehow organically and dynamically one?

In seeking to supplement our verified knowledge of a divine reality by exploring the possibilities, not of speculative surmise simply, but of a positively reasonable religious faith, let us begin with two negative propositions. In the first place, we may not, as reasonable beings, believe that everything is as it ought to be, nor that everything will turn out well, and just as well, in the end, whether we and other human beings do what we can to realize good ends or not. Neither is it reasonable, secondly, to believe that life is not and cannot be worth living, or that there ever will be a time when it will make no difference how anyone has lived. At least it is not reasonable to believe this, if any more wholesomely stimulating belief can be shown to be at least as reasonable, theoretically considered. Even in believing we ought to do as well as we honestly can.

We now proceed with affirmative propositions. We may reasonably believe that man, in view of the absolute moral obligation and responsibility of which he is morally certain, is, within whatever limits, a creative free agent, and consequently able to be a factor in securing the victory of good and right over evil and wrong. Moreover, it is not unreasonable to believe that if and in so far as man does his part, according to his ability, toward the elimination of evil and triumph of right, the reality upon which we are ultimately dependent may be trusted for whatever else most needs to be done for the ultimate well-being of human beings. This is confessedly a venture of religious faith, but one which appeals to the normal healthy mind and which is necessary for the fullest encouragement of the good life. It is open to us reasonably to build our lives upon it, unless and until it is disproved by the facts of experience. We have a right to believe as we must in order to live as we ought, if we can—logically and psychologically. This morally optimistic faith will logically involve the adequate conservation of the highest human values, even beyond the bounds of this life, and thus at the same time the conservation of the existence, beyond physical death, of all persons of actual (or even of potential and reasonably probable) good will. This reality or factor depended upon for this adequate conservation of spiritual values and of persons as the bearers of such values, a reality great enough and good enough to be reasonably trusted for whatever both concerns our true well-being and ought to be done (except for what man himself, as a free agent, ought to do), is God. In other words, God as a transcendent power, adequately conserving universally and permanently valid values, may be reasonably believed to exist.

It is reasonable to maintain that a power working as if intelligently toward moral and socially desirable ends is, in its own being, characterized by intelligence and

moral goodness, rather than by their opposites. As immanent producer of universally and permanently valid
values, a divine reality is known to behave as if intelligent and good. As transcendent conserver of universally and permanently valid values, a divine reality may
be reasonably believed to exist and to behave as if intelligent and good.[1] That this total divine reality, partly
known, partly believed in, behaves as if intelligent and
good because it *is* intelligent and good, and therefore
essentially personal spirit, however much more than that
it may also be, is a surmise which is not contradicted by
any known fact.

If religion at its practical best is valid, there must be
a reality which is the true Ideal realized, so as to be an
adequate object of absolute worship and trust. If the
universal and ineradicable human consciousness of moral
obligation and responsibility is valid, there must be a
reality which is not ideal and an ideal which is not yet
fully realized; otherwise there would be no moral obligation, nothing for man to do. These conclusions are recon-
cilable on the supposition of a God *whose will is perfectly good but whose good will is not yet fully realized
in man and in the world*. This furnishes a further consideration, at least from any non-pessimistic point of
view, in favor of the essential personality of God.

It is not unreasonable to surmise that the various
aspects of divine reality which we have set forth as either
knowledge, reasonable faith or permissible surmise are
unified in one and the same God. One God is enough
if that one is great enough. God under such various
aspects as the immanent producer of true values (known)
and the transcendent conserver of true values (believed
in), coöperating toward a worthy and harmonious end,
may be believed to be one God, though anything like a
fully satisfying comprehension of God in his unitary
being must be for us impossible. Moreover, intuitive
apprehension of a divine reality at work in the world in

[1] The problem of evil is treated, from this point of view, in Chapter
VII of *The Reasonableness of Christianity*, 1925.

and through the historic Jesus commonly leads to a surmise, accompanied by a very high degree of subjective certitude, that God is fundamentally like that intelligent good will in which, as a value-producing factor, he is so convincingly revealed.

It is not unreasonable to surmise that God as intelligent and moral personality or spirit may be related to the universe of physical energy and finite lives somewhat as the intelligent will of the human individual is related to its body and organic life. From this point of view our bodies and organic lives would be God's more fundamentally than they are ours, though we are permitted to use them for our purposes, within limits. From this point of view also man may be thought of as sharing not only the physical energy and life, but the intelligence and good will of the divine Spirit, the more fully as he learns to know the truth and do the right, and particularly as he enters into and maintains the right religious adjustment.

This analogy of the physical organism and its immanent intelligent life I should like to enforce by means of a parable which I have used in my classes and which, I find, is similar to an illustration used by Professor Boodin in his suggestive article entitled "God" in the *Hibbert Journal* for July, 1929. Let us, for the sake of our parable, take panpsychism seriously and suppose that electrons really are conscious. And let us stretch the theory to include the supposition that normally these conscious electrons are intelligent and good observers, and that some of them have received a modern scientific and philosophical education. We can imagine a metaphysically-minded but realistic and somewhat sceptical electron speculating as to the nature of man. The physical man would be to him a complex galaxy in which molecules and atoms would be comparable to our solar systems and worlds. They would be separated by such vast distances, from the electron's point of view, that it would seem fantastic to suppose that the whole human galaxy was a living organism controlled by a central intelligent mind. Man's inner conscious life would not be an externally observable fact. All that could be directly observed by the scientific electron would be certain fundamental processes, apparently quite mechanical, and, within the human cosmos broadly considered, a process of growth and a more or less dependable behavior. These might be interpreted by vitalistic electrons as indicating some super-mechanical principle, an entelechy directing the growth and a psychoid controlling the behavior; but even such theories would be regarded by many as ultra-metaphysical and going beyond the observable facts. Processes working toward recognizable ends would be pointed out, and it would be admitted that such processes were quasi-teleological, that is, *as if* they were the expression of conscious purpose; but it would be thought unscientific to imagine that they really were consciously purposive. Even in connection with the habitual modes of behavior it would be possible to point out, as an ingredient, certain eternal mathematical forms; and, in order to refer to this ingression of the eternal objects of reason into the flux of events, some mathematical and philosophically minded electron with a flair for introducing new terms into the vocabulary of philosophy might invent the name, "Principle of Concretion"; but while it might be deemed permissible to apply to this rather abstract Principle of Concretion some such symbolical term as Mansoul, it would be with the explicit understanding that in reality the principle of concretion, Mansoul in its primordial aspect, while ideally perfect, was not only not conscious but even deficient in actuality. And so the philosophical electrons might go on discussing endlessly the metaphysical nature of the human organism, and hesitating to attribute conscious mind to man for fear of being charged with projecting into the human galaxy their own sublimated libido. But whatever certain psychologist electrons might think of such "phantasy-thinking," it would be true all the while that man *is* intelligent mind and will expressing itself through his bodily behavior.

We human beings in relation to the universe are like these imaginary electrons in relation to man. We can discover a principle of concretion, the ingression of eternal objects into the flux of events, and processes working toward ends *as if* they were consciously purposive; and yet all we can observe directly is cosmic behavior; we are never able to observe from without the inner life of any supposed cosmic or divine mind. But if there were such a mind, the situation for us would be just what it now is. Perhaps there is, after all, a central mind and will in the universe.[22]

[22] In the words of Hans Driesch, "To see God in life we must study linked constellations as small as atoms and as large as Orion's belt." Cf. Raymond Dodge, in an Institute-of-Human-Relations publication, *Conditions and Consequences of Human Variability,* Yale University Press, 1931, especially pp. 159-61.

XII

RELIGIOUS REALISM AND THE TWENTIETH CENTURY

By
HELMUT RICHARD NIEBUHR
Associate Professor of Christian Ethics
Yale University

RELIGIOUS REALISM AND THE TWENTIETH CENTURY

AMERICAN religious realism claims a place in that constructive movement in twentieth century thought which, though sailing under various flags, has a common objectivistic interest and a general critical character. It is part of what appears from the perspective of the present to be a new orientation of the human mind—an orientation which is guided by similar interests and which is arriving at partly analogous results in the cognate realms of literature and art, of science and philosophy, of political and economic theory and practice. Hence the meaning of religious realism may be illuminated by the consideration of its relation to these kindred movements in our own civilization, to relevant tendencies of religious thought in other national cultures and to the fundamental attitudes which characterized the culture and religion of that past from which the new movements tend to distinguish themselves.

1

The nineteenth century, as an historical period rather than as a segment of chronological time, extended—it is generally agreed to-day—from the French Revolution to the close of the World War. The social experiences which, in association with its heritage of thought and custom, determined its character were the political emancipation of the individual, the industrial revolution in western Europe and America, the consequent rapid expansion of population and the rise of the middle class to power, the unparalleled increase of scientific knowledge and its application to the human control of nature, the growth of nationalism and its imperial extension.

413

The result of these experiences and of heredity was an attitude toward life which may best be designated as anthropocentric and—if the term be allowable, anthropocratic;[1] that is to say, the attitude was characterized not only by its evaluation of man as the central fact in reality but also by its ambition to subject all things to human control and by its assumption that such control is possible. A third feature of this philosophy of life was the optimism intimately associated with both of the other characteristics.

Anthropocentrism was expressed in the literature of the early nineteenth century as a romantic preoccupation with the human individual and his emotions or as a neoclassic emphasis on well-rounded self-realization as the goal of life. Lyric poetry and the novel, increasingly psychological in content—in contrast to the cosmic epic and the drama of some other periods—reflected the interest in man and his interior life. In political and economic thought man became the measure of all things; liberty and happiness were substituted for ideals of righteousness, of social harmony or of conformity to some superindividual, if not superhuman, standard, as the guiding principles of political practice while self-interest became the all-sufficient motive and controlling agency in man's pursuit of economic value. The popular result of the successful application of the theory of evolution to biology was not so much that of deposing man from his high estate as a special creation of God, but rather that of exalting him as the final product of a long travail and sometimes of leaving him in isolated splendor as the rational lord of a creation which though it began in no mind ended with the birth of human reason. In philosophy the period opened with Kant's reversal of the Copernican revolution and with the restoration of man as logical mind to the central place in the cosmos; it ended with critical naturalism and pragmatism, which

---

[1] This analysis of nineteenth century culture is indebted in many important points to Paul Tillich's *Religiöse Lage der Gegenwart*, Berlin, 1926, and to his *Religiöse Verwirklichung*, Berlin, 1930.

made the world a construct if not a more or less necessary fiction of the mind that was the final outcome of biological evolution and which performed its proper function in enabling man to live in and to control his universe. The idealism and positivism which flourished in the interval were alike anthropocentric and the latter was surely anthropocratic in its ambition to dominate the conditions of existence by means of scientific knowledge. Naturalism and Schopenhauer's pessimistic philosophy of the will brought the first evidence of revolt against this dominating tendency of man in his knowledge and control of the external world, yet the one was allied with an almost millennial expectation of human victory over the cosmos while both fell victims to the reassertion of anthropocentrism in neo-Kantian and pragmatic thought.

In religion the temper of the age appeared on the one hand in its concern for the culture of the inner life, in its pietism and evangelicalism, on the other hand in its moralization of faith. In both instances the emphasis lay upon religion as culture rather than as knowledge or revelation. Theology sought to approach its object by analyzing the religious subject, whether individual or communal, and so discovered the essence of religion in a feeling of dependence, or in a sense of duty, or in a value-judgment. Ultimately the tendency led to the effort to substitute psychology of religion for theology and to bring religion under control as an aid to the extension of man's autocracy over himself, his physical world and his society. In so far as the extreme statements of any period, its heresies, are symptomatic of its underlying philosophy, its orthodoxy, the efforts of Kant to define religion within the limits of reason, of Natorp to define it within the limits of humanity and of Durkheim to present it within the limits of social life are characteristic of the nineteenth century. Thus religion and theology were subject-centered; they were valued not as revelations or systematizations of reality nor as efforts to transcend the limits of reason and of humanity but as aids in the struggle for existence, in the self-assertion of the human spirit, in the control of life. The final fruit of this development is modern humanism with its elimination from religion of all but human objects and purposes.

Alongside of this anthropocentric and anthropocratic attitude the optimism of a period of expansion and increased control of nature flourished in most of the nineteenth century. The problem of evil assumed no tragic guise; evil itself appeared in no compact and resisting form. And this was especially true for that class which assumed leadership, the middle class; it found its wants increasingly satisfied, its power constantly augmented. The collective idea of progress, philosophical considerations to the effect that "there's nothing good or ill but thinking makes it so," and semireligious faith in the power of man's inconquerable soul to overcome whatever obstacles lay athwart his path to perfection, were alike expressive of the optimism of a generation and a class which were flushed with the sense of victory.

2

The anthropocratic and anthropocentric spirit of the nineteenth century is by no means exhausted. But a varied revolt against its dominance has arisen and despite the variety this revolt has a common realistic character. This realism is rooted in experiences no less significant than those which gave rise to anthropocentrism and idealism. If the latter represented the attitude of a youthful and ebullient individualism, then realism may be said to be the world-view of democracy which has come of age and which faces its problems with critical eyes. If idealism was the philosophy of a scientific age which gloried in the power of the human mind, then realism appears to be the attitude of a matured science which understands its limitations and the stark givenness of the facts which it seeks to understand. If idealism and the anthropocratic spirit were characteristic of a period of economic and political expansion and victory, then realism expresses the point of view of a time which has learned that failure is no less symptomatic of reality than triumph, decline no less significant of process than is progress.

Probably the first assertion of realism is to be found in literature. Breaking with the romantic glorification of human nature, a new cynicism which evaluated that nature as a frequently petty and sometimes filthy thing claimed the name of realism because it understood that the ignoble belonged to reality no less than did the noble, and that human nature was as often the product or the prey as the creator of its environment. Realism in art revealed again reality's stubborn independence of the eye of the beholder and moved on to suggest in symbolism a power or quality revealed in the æsthetic object which was not identifiable with some category in the mind of the beholding subject. Æsthetic realism became an æsthetic irrationalism, which presented its objects in their obstreperous, unidealized and actively independent forms. Realism, furthermore, has been encouraged by modern developments in science, which by "separating far more completely than hitherto the share of the observer and the share of external nature in the things we see happen," and by constantly adjusting its categories and its methods to its various objects has tended to remove the attention from the mind that understands to the reality that is understood. Modern science allows an idealistic as well as a realistic interpretation, to be sure, but its net result has been inimical to anthropocentrism; it has repeated, more effectively, the Copernican revolution with its dethronement of man and has increased the capacity for wonder in the face of a cosmos which is far less easily reduced to the terms of everyday experience and reason than anthropocratic naturalism imagined. Realism in philosophy is a part of this total objectivistic movement. Its varieties are many; it is a far cry from phenomenalism to American new realism; dualism and monism are at strife with each other within the confines of the total movement while critical realism—again in divergent forms—seeks to mediate between them. Yet certain common fundamental interests and orientations distinguish the realistic tendency as a whole from nineteenth century philosophy: the independence of the object, the subordination of mind to this independent reality, the fresh approach to values, the critical apprehension of the problem of evil and the rejection of a monistic assumption in metaphysics. And these common interests mark the movements in contemporary philosophy as part of the general revolt against the anthropocentric spirit of the past century.

In the realm of religion and theology realism in this broad sense is achieving increasing expression. Here also a large variety of movements—often at conflict among themselves—may be distinguished, but their common character and interest remain unobscured. Realism began in this sphere as the assertion and defense of religion as an independent type of experience, after the efforts of the nineteenth century to reduce it to a derivative from morality or science or the struggle for existence had failed. But the movement became definitely realistic in character and found its common essence when it turned from experience to the content of experience, from emphasis upon the religious subject to attention to the religious object, from religion to God. In actual religious practice these interests are expressed in the current attention to mysticism, in the cultivation of religious experience not for its own sake or its attendant emotions but for the sake of establishing relations with extra-human sources of power and insight, and in the instinctive or naïve reactions from relativism in faith and morals to traditional absolutism as set forth in religious and ethical dogma. In theology the realistic interpretation of religion varies according to the interests and the varying situations of the theologians. In the one instance the independence of the religious object from the religious idea is set forth; in another instance it is the availability of the religious object in experience which is the primary interest; in a third case the independence of God from all things mundane, from the whole order of human experience and control, is set into the foreground of interest. But all of these movements of religious realism are united by a common interest in maintaining the independent reality of the religious object. Hence they represent a movement distinctly different from nineteenth century liberal theology which found its center of gravity in the idea of the ethical value of religion. Though realism shares this ethical interest and accepts many of the critical results of liberalism, it has shifted the center of interest from the subject to the object, from man to God, from that which is purely immanent in religious experience to that which is also transcendent.

The varieties of religious realism and its distribution throughout Western Christianity are indicative of the spontaneous character of the revolt against anthropocentrism which is expressed in them. Variety at the same time promises interaction, mutual criticism and the consequent development of a more adequate theory than an isolated school of thought can present. Both of these points of view lead the theologian to a consideration of kindred movements in other countries; and for the Anglo-Saxon tradition in theology comparison with or criticism by no other type of thought appears more fruitful than the German. For modern German theology has produced tendencies that illustrate on the one hand the common realistic spirit of twentieth century religion, while on the other hand they criticize by their divergences the American movement.

3

From a purely epistemological point of view it may, indeed, be questioned whether there is such a thing as German religious realism. The movements which lay claim to this name seem to be associated with critical idealism and with phenomenology rather than with epistemological realism. Yet in the broad sense of the term realism both the theology of crisis and German religious

realism proper are entitled to the name. In common
with the general movement and in common reaction
against nineteenth century humanism their interest lies
in the claim to the objectivity of God and in the transfer
of the center of religion from the subject to the object.

The essential realism of the theology of crisis [2] is
expressed in its effort to distinguish the reality of God
from all ideas about him, from all experience of him,
from all natural theology, and to define revelation in
wholly non-psychological terms. Its central interest, to
be sure, is not epistemological but religious and ethical.
The distinction between God and the world which it urges
is not so much the distinction between object and subject,
between thing and idea, as the difference between good
and evil, sacred and profane, absolute and relative. But
in carrying through these distinctions it expresses in an
extreme form the modern reaction against anthropocentric and anthropocratic views of reality and religion.
God is God and man is man and only a complete separation between them in thought as well as practice seems
to this theology to offer an adequate basis for a true
evaluation of faith. In contrast to the doctrine of immanence which often resulted in the confusion of the divine
and the human and sometimes in the substitution of man
for God, of civilization for the "kingdom of heaven," the
theology of crisis sets forth a doctrine of transcendence
in which objectivism in religion is presented in extreme
terms.

The method which this theology uses to define its position is fundamentally inimical to its realistic interest.
If the nineteenth century, beginning with the subject,
could discover no way that leads from subject to object,
from man to God, then this twentieth century theology
beginning with the object fails to find a way to the subject, from God to man. If an anthropocentric mode of
thought tried to define religion within the limits of

[2] See especially Brunner, *Religionsphilosophie evangelischer Theologie,*
München, 1927; *Erlebnis, Erkenntniss und Glaube,* Tübingen, 1923; *Der
Mittler,* 1927; Barth, *Die Lehre vom Worte Gottes,* München, 1927.

humanity then this purely theocentric approach tends to present a faith within the limits of deity. After reducing all experience and reason in the religious realm to purely subjective processes the Barthian movement succeeds only in arriving at a Kantian agnosticism in which God remains forever unknown. To rescue itself from this position it must fall back, as it is doing to an increasing extent, upon authoritarian dogmatism. The wholly transcendent God can enter into human life only by means of a revelation which stands in contrast to all religious experience, to all history as well, and which can, in the last analysis, be accepted only as pure dogma. In effect, therefore, the theology of crisis is not so much a realism as a complete dualism which tends to become a dogmatism. Yet its realistic interest and its critical method remain as its significant meanings and the source of its religious strength. It represents in the exaggeration of its statements the extreme symptom of the objectivistic revolt in religion.

A philosophically more satisfactory form of religious objectivism is represented in German theology by Paul Tillich and his associates who have adopted the term "faith-realism" to designate their position.[3] Although the movement is more realistic in its epistemology than is the theology of crisis it justifies its claim to its name less by its theory of knowledge than by its general interest in objectivistic, non-romantic attitudes. In Tillich's case the term realism designates, first of all, an almost æsthetic interest in the independence of objects from control and subjection to general utilitarian categories, rather than from experience and idea. The apprehension of things as independent powers, as individualities, as existences which possess a sort of "mana"-like quality capable of calling forth wonder and appreciation in the beholder—the type of apprehension which is found in the realistic artist—is the recommended approach to real-

---

[3] See Tillich, *Religiöse Lage der Gegenwart; Religiöse Verwirklichung;* "Religionsphilosophie," in Dessoir, *Lehrbuch der Philosophie; Kairos; Protestantismus als Kritik und Gestaltung.*

ity. In the second place this realism is closely related in its origins and interests to historical realism which is similarly directed toward the knowledge of the unique event, the individual being. Both as æsthetic and as historical realism the movement directs its criticism less against the anthropocentric character of idealism than against the anthropocratic interests of "technical realism," which identifies objects with their utilizable, general relations and so seeks to dominate them. It believes that it represents the insights of the modern age as presented not only in art and history but also in a science which has learned that it cannot reduce reality to a few simple categories but must take account of organism, structure, "Gestalt," event of individual form as well as general category.

In its epistemology "faith-realism" represents an attempt to adjust critical idealism to these interests in the unique and the objective. It develops the critical method by absorbing, or seeking to absorb, intuitional and dynamic elements. It continues to attend primarily to the functions of the mind, and to seek truth by defining their norms rather than by turning to an objective world with which the mind deals. Yet the method does go beyond neo-Kantian and phenomenological analysis in seeking to apprehend the content as well as the forms of mental functions and in trying to do justice to the individual and creative as well as to the formal elements to be found in them. The substitution of a dynamic for a static view of mind, of a partly mystic, partly pragmatic view of truth for a purely formal one, appear to make this philosophy strain hard at the limits imposed upon it by the Kantian tradition and to incline its theory of knowledge more and more toward a realism comparable with that of the Anglo-Saxon countries.

Religion, in Tillich's definition, is direction toward the Unconditioned and as such it is implicit in every phase of culture and the mental life, explicit, however, only in faith. It is characteristic of all reality that it carries within it a self-transcending element, an intention or ref-

erence toward some ultimate source of being and meaning. Without this basis all individual events lose reality
and significance. The Unconditioned is the goal and presupposition of all thought and all reality; yet, in the
nature of the case, it transcends all reality and cannot
be regarded as an object alongside of others. Hence a
true realism, which apprehends things in their independence and individuality must see in them also this self-
transcending element, this reference to their unconditioned basis. True realism, therefore, involves an element of faith or must, at all events, be associated with
a faith that sees the individual not only as independent
of the beholder but as a function of the Unconditioned.
In the religious act reference toward the Unconditioned
is explicit, though it cannot be maintained that the Unconditioned itself ever becomes part of the religious experience. It remains transcendent; what enters into experience is the sacred symbol in which the claim of the Unconditioned becomes explicit and real, or in which the voice
of the Absolute is heard through the mediation of the
relative. At this point evidently, as in the case of the
theory of knowledge, the realistic interest has strongly
modified the idealistic approach. The result is a theological method as clearly distinguished from the psychological and historical method of the nineteenth century
as from the dogmatic method of the Reformation and
the theology of crisis. The task of theology is neither
the systematization of authoritative material nor the
description of the religious consciousness but the definition of that stratum of reality which religion intends.

Far removed as this "faith-realism" or "transcendental realism" may be in its philosophical technique from
American religious realism, the community of interest is
nevertheless apparent, as is the common turning away
from psychological and subjective views of religion
toward objective, theological definitions of its content.
Methodology varies, but a common attitude is expressed
in the various efforts to discover that methodology which
will lead theology and the philosophy of religion to pre-

cise definition of the religious object. In Germany as in America the dominant movements in theology indicate that "we advance inevitably from a religion of humanity to a religion of God."

When German and American religious realism are set side by side it is not only the likenesses which attract attention; the dissimilarities are even more striking and may be the more fruitful points of contact, so far as the development of an adequate and thoroughly tenable objectivism is concerned. Hence it is instructive to anticipate the criticism of American religious realism which is implicit in the German movement and is likely to become explicit as the two tendencies become more conscious of each other.

A preliminary criticism which the Old World philosophy directs against that of the New World—that the empiricism of the latter involves it in subjectivism and psychologism—may be dismissed in the case of religious realism as being due primarily to the differences in the connotation of the term empiricism when used within the sphere of the Kantian tradition on the one hand and within the sphere of Anglo-Saxon philosophic influence on the other hand. The objectivist interest and method of American theology is further underestimated by German thought when it regards empirical methodology as influenced primarily by the ambition to adjust theology to the methods of natural science.

An important point of difference between the two realisms arises, however, in their attitudes toward religious experience. From the point of view of German realism the American movement seems to be insufficiently critical of the empirical. This criticism may be directed primarily against all that sort of religious realism which seeks to derive a religious content from the experience of nature rather than from religious experience and does so by ignoring unduly the actuality of evil and chaos in the experience of the external world and by sacrificing important religious values which are to be found in faith but not in the natural theology based on such empiricism.

The lack of critical quality in American religious thought appears from this German point of view to be manifest also in the sphere in which theological realism is primarily interested, in the interpretation of religious experience proper. The theology of crisis in its consistent and extreme dualism condemns such experience as the realm of the relative and subjective. Faith-realism objects that the method of empirical realism is inadequate because empiricism always presupposes a knowledge of the essence which is to be abstracted from experience or, in other words, because the religious object cannot be gained from experience unless there is prior knowledge of the religious object. Furthermore, the inadequacy of the critical element in American religious thought appears, from this point of view, in its too ready objectification of symbolic elements in religious experience. What enters into experience for Tillich is never the Unconditioned itself but at best a "Gestalt" of grace, some structure in which the transcendent becomes effective but in which it is not contained. The content of experience in religion refers beyond itself to the absolute source of being and meaning. A religious realism which does not recognize the dualism resident in religious experience and therefore neglects the factor of faith by means of which the reference to the transcendent is made and so confuses the object in experience with that which experience intends appears to be insufficiently critical and in danger of falling back into subjectivism.

A further criticism which may be made of American theological realism from the point of view of modern German philosophy of religion is that our realism is still too much under the influence of a progressive and technological era which is interested in knowledge for the sake of power and which, in religion, is prone to define God in terms of his utilizable relations to the neglect of his uniquely divine or holy character. Hence it tends to define religion in terms of adjustment to divine reality for the sake of gaining power rather than in terms of revelation which subject the recipient to the criticism of that which is revealed. The revolt against anthropocentrism and anthropocratic tendencies seems insufficient; man remains the center of religion and God is his aid rather than his judge and redeemer. Hence also realistic theology in America seems to the German to pass over too rapidly into an applied science in which rules of procedure are formulated and a religious technique is elaborated by means of which men may use God in the service of interests which remain human, however much they may be criticized and refined.

Furthermore, German realism implies that American realism, being too optimistic about the availability of God *in* religious experience, tends toward an individualism which fails to recognize the importance of historical revelation, as the Barthians would say, or of the "Gestalt" of grace, as the faith-realists would be likely to urge. More specifically, German theology is highly critical of the apparent lack of concern in our theology about Christian doctrine in general and Protestant doctrine in particular. Germany's greater interest in the historical is partly due, it is evident, to historical reasons. The German theologian appears to live several generations nearer to the Reformation than does the American, since he is surrounded by a culture on which this movement has left its physical and spiritual impress in a fashion not possible in a new world civilization which received its Protestant heritage at second hand. But a deeper reason for the difference lies in the fact that German religious thought, with its dualism and transcendentalism, its pessimism and suspicion of all things phenomenal, finds ancient Christian doctrine and the thought of the Reformation more akin to its own spirit than does American theology. Transcendentalism and dualism, the rejection of anthropocentrism, disillusionment with the idea of progress and with humanism, lead it to a new appreciation of the meaning of faith, of justification and of mediation and so bring it into relationship to Platonic and Neo-Platonic philosophy and to ancient Christian dogma. From this point of view American thought appears too

optimistic and too individualistic, too much allied with
anthropocentric and positivist faith in the ability of the
individual or collective mind to know immediate¹ all
that is worth knowing and to accomplish whateve.
necessary for the redemption of man from evil.

The individualism of American thought in religion rest.
ultimately, the German believes, upon the lack of critical
analysis in dealing with experience. The American theologian or philosopher appears to abstract individual
experience unduly from its historic context and to be
inadequately aware of the cultural matrix out of which
his experience is born. Abstracting the experiencer from
his cultural conditions he ascribes to the content of experience a universal availability and validity which it
does not possess since it is in fact relative to a particular
historical nexus. The result is either the universalization
of Christian theology, which is regarded as available for
all rational human beings because they are rational and
human, or—what may amount to the same thing in the
long run—the reduction of the content of theology to that
which is abstracted from all particular historical connection, to the consensus of all religions or to a natural
theology gained by a process of inferences from man's
universal experience of nature, thought and morality.
Being inadequately critical and relativistic in its analysis
of religious experience American realism appears to discover the absolute within the relative more readily than
seems permissible; hence it fails to recognize the urgency
and difficulty of discovering the absolute and to appreciate the peculiarity of Christianity as revelation or of
faith as a divine *tour de force* by which the relative is
transcended. As the Barthian theology would put it,
our American religious realism fails to note the distinction between religion, as the universal human activity
directed toward God, and Christianity, which is not a
religion, but God's revelation of himself—the vertical
entrance of the absolute into time.

Ultimately, then, the differences between German and
American religious realism root in a divergent employ-

ment of criticism in the analysis of religious and moral experience. This divergence leads to a host of consequences which involve German theology in dualism, agnosticism, pessimism and dogmatism and American theology in optimism, monism, and rationalism. It is easy for the American to point out that German theology has pressed its critical principle to the point where it must choose between agnosticism and dogmatism and has, in fact, made a dogma out of the critical principle itself. On the other hand there is justice in the German criticism of the optimism and anthropocratic tendency in American religious thought. The acceptance of a more radical critical method than American religious realism has employed hitherto in most instances would not need to involve it in an agnostic dualism. The independence of God from experience does not imply his remoteness from experience; the relativity of historical experience does not imply the absence of an absolute content or point of reference; the presence of evil in more subtle and pervasive forms than is usually granted by American realism does not imply the absence of the good. If American religious realism is called upon to become more critically aware of the subjective and the relative, it is also challenged to be critical of the critical dogma, to be as critical of every attempt to reduce the absolute to the relative as of every effort to exalt the relative into an absolute.

A truly critical realism appears to offer, therefore, not only an opportunity for developing a philosophy adequate to the insights and interests of the modern world in its reaction against the excessively humanistic tendencies of the nineteenth century, but also a field in which the theological and philosophical movements of divergent cultures, such as the American and the German, may cooperate to set forth an interpretation of religion and religious reality which may have more than relative significance, which may represent not only the experience and the spirit of the twentieth century but contain within it as much of that which is common to all the centuries as it is possible for a philosophy or a theology to contain.

XIII

GOD AND EMERGENT EVOLUTION

By
WILLIAM KELLEY WRIGHT
Professor of Philosophy
Dartmouth College

GOD AND EMERGENT EVOLUTION

1. GOD, according to religious realism as acknowledged by the present writer, exists independently of human thought about Him. He is a Person, accessible to men in prayer and other forms of religious worship. He performs no miracles in violation of the laws discovered by natural science; yet He affords human worshipers courage, self-control, better coördinated judgments, æsthetic joy, and the peace that passeth understanding. In a spiritual sense, He is a very present help in time of trouble.

(a) How defend such a creed? The most obvious answer is, by an appeal to religious experience. Men believe in God partly because of the testimony of others,—the witness of saints, prophets, apostles and martyrs. Most of all, men believe in God because of their own personal religious experiences, and those of other persons whom they know, love and revere. A man may believe in God because he recollects an adolescent religious awakening which gave his life an added significance; or because when engaged in religious worship he has at times felt a calm assurance of the presence of another Person; or because he has received moral and spiritual benefits from prayer—courage for a difficult day's task, or a changed disposition eliminating some defect of temper, or comfort in bitter sorrow and restored confidence that there still is something for which to live. It is on account of personal religious experiences like these that men affirm the objective existence of the God of religious realism. Probably very few people believe in the existence of a personal God who can be worshiped, who have not had some experience of this kind.

On the other hand, a critical inquirer, confronted by the psychological and sociological explanations of religious experience, will desire additional evidence for the existence of God drawn from sources extraneous to religious experience.

Let us see why this is the case. Psychologically, religious experience is attributed to the action of the subconscious and of autosuggestion. William James thought that the nervous system has reserve layers of subconscious energy that, when tapped, release forces which appear to the individual to come from outside of his own organism, and which certainly do come from outside the scope of his consciousness. James himself was inclined to the view that in such experiences energy is imparted to the individual by a God external to the worshiper, that is, by what we should call a realistic God. But James' conception of the subconscious was not such as to necessitate the interpolation of the hypothesis of God into a causal description of religious experience. Energy stored in the cells of the brain and nervous system, and suddenly released during the religious experience, would be a sufficient scientific explanation of the reason why the individual believes that he has received strength from a source extraneous to himself. It may be said that James' psychology and physiology are crude; for instance what does he mean by "subconscious energy" and how can it "enter consciousness"? No doubt our modern behaviorists would interpret the phenomena of religious experience in other language—perhaps in terms of verbalizations?—but they would be sure to be naturalistic, and to leave no place for a realistic God in a purely scientific description of religious experience. Psychological explanations by Freudians and psychoanalysts are also purely naturalistic. We cannot look to any school of psychologists for support in the belief that in religious experiences men have veridical percepts of a realistic God, who exists independently.

Sociologically, the school of Durkheim has taught us that much which seems to us to come from outside is due to the unconscious sense of social pressure. We feel impelled to emotions, beliefs, and conduct by a force outside of ourselves that we know is not purely physical. We do not realize that this force is simply that of human society, so we suppose it to be supernatural, divine; whereas all that the sociologist needs to recognize is that it is superindividual.

The believer in the reality of the God of his religious experiences can reply to psychological critics who object that the Alter of religious experience is not God, but simply energy stored in nutritive cells, and to sociological critics who say that it is simply society and its collective representations, with the observation that neither the psychological nor the sociological explanation necessarily excludes belief that God really exists. The psychological and the sociological explanations may both be true, and the present writer believes that they are so. But he believes that he can accept these explanations as adequate for scientific purposes, and yet supplement them by the philosophical over-belief that through the subconscious and through social evolution and through the development of collective representations, God reveals Himself to mankind. Granted, for instance, that Amos gained his religious and moral insight through the release of subconscious energy and through the social outlook and traditions of his time: it can be added as a philosophical surmise that it was through these media that God made Himself known to Israel.

It will at once be objected that my philosophical surmise, as a religious realist, is indeed possible but not proven; and that it is both good philosophy and good science to employ the fewest hypotheses that will cover the observed facts; that to affirm the existence of God when the facts can be explained without it is to entertain a needless and superfluous hypothesis. It will be further objected that probably there is no god, ghost, bogey, demon, fairy, spirit, elf or brownie in all religious or folk lore that someone cannot be found to testify that he has heard, seen and handled, with his ears, eyes and hands, respectively. It will therefore be asked, "Can you mean to affirm that every supernatural being experienced and worshiped by every cult, actually exists? How can all religions be true, since each of them in many respects contradicts the others?"

A religious realist cannot reply to such objections in the manner of an absolute idealist or philosophical Brahmin, who might say that each of these supposedly supernatural beings possesses some degree of truth and reality, and occupies a place in the hierarchy of appearances, and is a phase in the life of the Absolute. For the realist does not believe in degrees of truth and reality; to do so would seem to him to juggle between truth and error, between existence and non-existence. Since the religious realist cannot attribute actuality to all of the gods, does it follow that he must accept the conclusion that none of them exist?

It seems to me possible for a religious realist to reply that he believes that there actually is a personal God in the universe, and that He has revealed Himself to all of mankind through their subconsciousnesses and their social milieux as well as in other ways. He could say that men have understood this objectively real God very imperfectly, and so have confused Him with their subjective fancies, hence the great variety of objects of worship in the various religions. Yet, as men have become more reflective and discriminating, they have gradually substituted the belief in one God for that of many gods; and the one God, in the most advanced religions, has been believed to conserve the highest moral ideals, and to be spiritual, loving, personal, a Father. Thus men have been gradually gaining clearer insight into the nature of the true God who actually does exist. Our knowledge of God is still imperfect, and conceptions of Him in the future will alter with added experience. But our present belief in a realistic God, who is a personal, loving Father, accessible to men in their religious experiences, and who, without violation of physical laws, comes to their aid in their efforts to attain the highest values, is the closest approximation we have yet attained to the character of the real God.

That the idea of God has developed, and will continue to do so, need not disturb the realistic believer in God. The same could be said of any of the elementary conceptions of science. No scientific or philosophical realist, for instance, supposes that electrons or atoms or molecules actually exist in precisely the manner in which they are described in contemporary literature. But these conceptions are the closest approximations to the absolute reality independent of our intelligences that human scientific inquiry has yet been able to reach. Matter and energy (or space-time, or whatever may be the ultimate physical reality) exist independently of our thought. But with the progress of science, our conceptions of ultimate physical reality are coming closer to the truth. In a somewhat analogous manner, advancing religious experience and reflection are growing more accurate in their characterization of God.

At least this much could, I think, be derived from a critical study of religious experience for belief in a real God. There are no facts and no adequate explanations, psychological or sociological, that necessarily *exclude* such a belief. On the other hand, the testimony of religious experience shows that those who have had such experiences believe them to have come from an external source—and in the highest religions this source is believed to be God. Some weight certainly must be attached to such testimony. Professor A. N. Whitehead has taught us to be suspicious of hypotheses that are over simple. The psychological and sociological hypotheses are simple; they may prove to be inadequate. In any case they do not render the existence of God impossible. The theistic hypothesis may also be true, and may furnish a supplement to scientific accounts of religious experience. If evidence favorable to belief in God could be found in some domain entirely independent of religious experience, the arguments based on the latter would be furnished with external support and would become more persuasive.

(b) Where shall we expect to find evidence for the

existence of God, outside of religious experience itself?
Two time-honored philosophical types of argument—the
ontological and cosmological or causal—in the opinion
of most philosophers were thoroughly shattered by Hume
and Kant. Hume seems to have accepted the teleological
argument, according to some interpreters of the *Dialogues on Religion,* while Kant accorded to it a limited
and hesitant recognition in the *Critique of Judgment.*
But when the cruder but better known eighteenth-cen-
tury versions of the teleological argument in the sense of
design, as set forth by Paley and the *Bridgewater
Treatises,* were thoroughly demolished by the evolutionists of the nineteenth century, many inferred (I think
wrongly) that all types of teleological argument had been
refuted.

The nineteenth-century evolutionists certainly succeeded in establishing that the hypothesis of God is not
needed for scientific explanations. Laplace, at the beginning of that century, was able to offer an account of the
evolution of the earth in terms of the nebular hypothesis
which made no use of the conception of God. In the
thirties Lyell succeeded in explaining geological changes
in the earth's surface by natural causes. In the middle
of the century Darwin showed that the hypothesis of
common descent from one or a few original species, and
later migrations, will better explain the present geograph-
ical distribution of flora and fauna than the hypothesis
that the various species owed their separate origin to
divine creation. He maintained that the remarkable
adaptation of plants and animals can better be accounted
for by chance variations preserved by natural selection
than by divine creation. Since the time of Darwin, therefore, the hypothesis of God has no standing in biology.
Later astronomers have advanced accounts of cosmic evolution different from Laplace's nebular hypothesis, later
geologists have disagreed with Lyell in details, and some
of the later biologists have advanced other interpretations of organic evolution in place of natural selection.
To-day, however, no physical or natural scientist thinks

of divine intervention as a legitimate causal explanation
of any phenomena studied by his science.

Conceptions of evolution have been equally destructive
of Kant's own arguments for the existence of God, as
advanced in his *Critique of Practical Reason*. The consciousness of moral obligation, which to Kant seemed
such a mystery as to warrant the postulation of God and
immortality, can now be explained psychologically and
sociologically. Psychologically, duty implies conflicting
impulses and anticipation of the results of acting on different alternatives, and a feeling of pressure to prefer
remoter but ultimately more satisfactory goods rather
than more immediate gratifications. William James in his
Principles of Psychology, and William McDougall in his
Social Psychology have worked out detailed explanations
of this process of volition, in response to moral obligation, along what at first seems the line of most resistance.
Sociologically, Spencer, Clifford, Durkheim and others
have shown that duty, or moral obligation, is a feeling
induced in the individual by the authority and prestige
of his social groups. The contents of his judgments of
right and wrong are in the main expressions of the moral
traditions and collective representations of his groups.

Psychologists and sociologists differ somewhat in their
detailed explanations of duty and moral obligation, but
no psychologist or sociologist to-day would think of either
as the miraculous voice of God, or as in any way supernatural in character.

(c) Interpreted by psychologists and sociologists, religion itself becomes a natural phenomenon, due to the
subconscious and to social influences on the individual.
In neither the psychology nor the sociology of religion
does the hypothesis of God occupy a legitimate place.

When we think over the matter, we can hardly regret
that God no longer is an hypothesis in any physical, natural, or social science. To explain a phenomenon by divine
action is not to explain it at all, for any practical purpose.
How unsatisfactory to say that God or angels move the
earth about the sun, that God by floods and other catas-

trophes has miraculously washed out river valleys and implanted fossils! It seems equally unscientific in spirit to say that God created the first forms of plant and animal life; it is better to study the colloids and organic chemistry, and to try to trace the evolution of protoplasm from inorganic matter. Nor is it scientifically satisfying to say that God created each separate species and put it into its particular habitat; Darwin has better explained matters. The emergence of consciousness and of reasoning powers in man are puzzling; but what scientist to-day would explain either by saying that God at a certain stage in the embryonic development of every human being miraculously implanted a soul! Who, taking up a book of history, would like to find the author saying that God inspired Thomas Jefferson to write the Declaration of Independence, or Woodrow Wilson to propose the Covenant of the League of Nations, and its adoption by the American Senate! The reader desires legitimate historical explanations of events, by which he means, explanations in terms of natural, or if one pleases, secondary, causes. If a reader is not satisfied with Gibbon's list of the causes for the spread of Christianity in the Roman empire, it is not because they are naturalistic, but because they seem superficial, and he probably turns to Harnack in hope of finding a more convincing but not less natural or causal explanation. In the psychology of religion we now expect to find conversion, prayer, inspiration, and mysticism described, and so far as possible, explained as natural phenomena; we do not expect to find them attributed to miraculous action. Religious educators and others who wish to spread and inculcate religion look to psychologists for analysis of the character and conditions of religious experience. These are of most help to the practical religious worker. This is because, by revealing the natural causes in operation, they make it possible to predict, and in some measure to produce and to control the manifestations of religious experience. But to describe and explain events thus is to do so without introducing the hypothesis of God.

It does not follow from the fact that God is neither a necessary nor a legitimate hypothesis in any science that He does not exist. It merely means that in the interpretation of phenomena from the standpoint and for the purposes of science the hypothesis of God has no function. The possibility that God does exist is neither denied nor affirmed; except that if He does exist it is assumed that He does not set aside the laws of nature thus far discovered and formulated—such as gravitation, the conservation of energy and the like in physics, nor the laws of economic production, supply and demand, and marginal utilities in political economy, nor those of any other science. God, if He exists, does not move on the plane of natural causation. He must be discovered in another dimension.

We now seem to be in a predicament. The facts of religious experience at most raise a certain presumption in favor of the existence of God. They do not suffice to establish it. The old philosophical arguments have become destroyed with the advance of explanations in terms of evolution. All the sciences to-day are silent on the subject. Where, then, shall we look for evidence?

Idealists of an older generation at this point might have turned to epistemology. They might have endeavored to show, like Berkeley, that we must assume God to explain the continued existence of the objects of experience which we attribute to the outer world. Or else they might have argued, like Royce, that two persons could not recognize a common object even sufficiently to quarrel about it unless they and the object were all included within a common Mind. The arguments of the idealists were legion, but in some form or other realists believe that all of them were fallacious. They begged the question by assuming as a matter of initial predication the points needful to be proved; as they progressed, they became more and more entangled in the egocentric predicament; they narrowly escaped solipsism; if they thought their premises out to the logical end, as Bradley did, their reasoning terminated in skepticism. The Personal Idealists of our own time, to be sure, retain a conception of God that is religiously attractive, but, true children of Berkeley as they are, they deny the existence of matter and in consequence fall into the naïve fallacies of the good Bishop. Absolute Idealists were more subtle, some of them, like their master Hegel, being so ambiguous and involved in their expositions that it is almost impossible to decide whether they believed in God in any genuine sense at all. Bradley and Bosanquet affirmed an ineffable Absolute who is not God, and who cannot be worshiped; what humans call God and worship is an anthropomorphization of the Absolute and is not ultimate reality but only a high form of appearance. The failure of idealists to find satisfactory arguments for God in epistemology reconciles the religious realist to the fact that his general standpoint makes a recourse to epistemology impossible in his own case.

Where, then, shall we turn? Since we cannot find evidence bearing on the problem of the existence of God in the data of the separate sciences by the employment of scientific methods, let us see if anything can be done by a more synthetic approach. Let us compare the data of the different sciences dealing with Evolution, and see if in their combination we may not discover a thread of argument favorable to the hypothesis of God.

2. To simplify the discussion of Evolution, let us review, in what Professor Lloyd Morgan would call a "plain tale," the scientific facts regarding the evolution of our particular planet, the Earth, and of its inhabitants.

(a) Originating, let us suppose, in undifferentiated nebulous material, the Earth proceeded through a course of integration, differentiation and increased definiteness in some such way as is sketched by Spencer. Land and water, mountains and plains, rivers and lakes became differentiated. The earth's surface gained in heterogeneity as well as in integral unity and definiteness. All this occurred in accordance with purely mechanical laws capable of formulation in terms of physics, chemistry, and geology.

In the course of inorganic evolution, prior to the emergence of life, in a manner set forth in treatises of physics and chemistry, the various chemical elements and compounds evolved. They can be safely assumed to have possessed the various "primary qualities"—mass, extension, motion, rest, number, figure, and any other qualities and properties which a scientific account of inorganic matter finds it necessary to attribute to them. It is unwarranted to impute to them, for extra-scientific reasons, such as considerations of epistemology, any of the secondary qualities, like color, temperature, odor, and sound, in the psychological sense of these terms.

Presently, in some natural manner as yet unknown, but which will doubtless some time be discovered, low forms of life emerged. Living organisms come into existence and endure so long as they maintain an equilibrium of anabolism and katabolism—so long as they assimilate the proper materials from their environment as rapidly as they wear it out, so that waste and repair are equalized. Such are facts, known or highly probable, which science has sufficiently established.

(b) It is also to be noted that living organisms, although their existence involves the maintenance of physical and chemical elements in definite combinations, contain new qualities (internal characteristics) and properties (relations to one another and to their environment) that are not found except in living organisms. It is further to be noted that they rearrange the constituents of their physical environments to their own advantage in accordance, to be sure, with the laws of the inorganic sciences, but in ways that are nevertheless unique. All living organisms have the functions of digestion, circulation, excretion, growth and reproduction. In addition, animals have powers of locomotion, and have distance receptors which enable them to adjust themselves to stimuli originating in objects remote from themselves. All this means that, supplementary to the processes of inorganic matter, whose organization in a specific manner their life involves, living organisms have their own distinctive processes, which latter furnish the laws of the biological sciences.

There is a sense in which all the constitution and behavior of organisms is ultimately describable in terms of physics and chemistry; and to effect this description is of the utmost practical value for the cultivation and maintenance of organisms. A visit to any agricultural experiment station or any medical laboratory or clinic would make this evident enough. On the other hand, there is a sense in which biology never can be reduced without remainder to physics and chemistry. For inorganic elements and compounds, unless united in the peculiar combinations that constitute living organisms, do not have the qualities and properties of life. Such terms as metabolism, struggle for existence, natural selection, determinants, etc., have no significance other than highly metaphorical, if applied to non-living matter. Furthermore, animals are conscious. Whatever conscious behavior may be, and whatever organization of nerve cells, atoms and molecules it may involve, it has its own distinctive qualities and properties. Animals, being conscious, respond to sensory stimuli with movements appropriate to the interests of nutrition, reproduction, and security, to mention only three obvious and universal ends of animal behavior.

It is a problem for animal psychologists to determine, at what points in the phylogenetic series animals first acquired sense organs which enable them to respond to external stimuli of a different character with sensations of temperature, color, sound, odor, and other secondary qualities. The secondary qualities as such have no existence in inorganic matter except when it is perceived by organisms. It is not necessary to assume that on occasion of their perception by conscious organisms with specialized sense organs material objects spontaneously acquire new properties corresponding to the secondary qualities. As Durant Drake has pertinently pointed out, there is no scientific evidence that when material objects effect stimulation of organisms through sensory receptors any returning mechanical movement proceeds toward these objects, such as might alter or add to their properties.[1] The reactions of organisms are modified in response to external objects when secondary qualities are perceived. The secondary qualities are attributed to the objects. Color is perceived in objects, not in the brain nor in the eye, sound is perceived in a bell or in an automobile horn, not in the ear or the temporal lobes of the cortex. But what exists in the objects and in the space between the objects and the organism are forms of matter and energy which are perceived by the organism as secondary qualities of a different character than the properties that actually exist in the physical relations between the organism and the objects responsible for stimulation.

The situation seems different in the case of pain and other sensations referred to parts of the organism itself. The pain is actually in the tooth or the finger, because that is where the sensory receptors are situated. It seems, therefore, reasonable to suppose that organic tissue, in relation to sensory receptors, acquires a new property which it did not previously possess. With the cessation or interception of conscious pain, or other organic sensations, the tissues no longer possess these new properties, but continue to have the primary qualities, which on stimulation of the sensory receptors are responsible for the emergent properties of pain and other organic sensations. Temperature felt in the hand is actually there, but temperature attributed to the ice which the hand touches does not exist in the ice in the form in which it is perceived.

Men at least, and other animals to a greater or less extent, in their response to sensory stimulations react in a manner that indicates the utilization of past experience. A percept implies an addition of some kind to the sense data furnished at the immediate moment. Men, and to a much less extent, certain of the higher animals, have conscious memory images involving retention, recog-

[1] Durant Drake, *Mind and Its Place in Nature*, pp. 17-20.

nition and recall of past experiences; they form free images that are not precise duplications of any particular past experience; they reason, solving problems and adapting themselves to moral situations.

Men are persons, each with a distinct character of his own. Men live in social groups, and each is modified in his desires, habits, interests, and ideals by his contemporaries and by the social traditions of his groups. The social sciences that deal with human conduct—psychology, sociology, economics, politics and the rest—cannot be reduced to the biological sciences since they treat of qualities and properties peculiar to man—except that a few of the higher animals share these characteristics to a less degree.

Persons stand on a unique level of emergent evolution, a level that can only endure so long as the lower levels which it involves continue to maintain the unique combination that makes personality possible—including as we now know various chemical elements supplied by ductless glands. To understand more completely the laws of this unique combination will be one of the great achievements of science in the coming generation. Such knowledge will prolong and heighten the duration, welfare, and efficiency of human persons. It will be of inestimable benefit, enabling physicians, educators, psychiatrists, criminologists, social workers, and even clergymen to assist persons to realize the higher values for themselves and for society.

Yet when all this is admitted, it none the less remains true that each of the social sciences deals with qualities and properties that are peculiar to persons, and exist on no lower level. So these sciences can never be reduced to biology.

Persons are conscious of values. By intellectual judgments they seek to know reality and so appreciate truth. By moral judgments they seek to know and sometimes to do what will most promote their own welfare and that of other persons, and so appreciate goodness. By æsthetic judgments they seek to know, produce and to enjoy objects of physical nature and of human art that will afford them satisfactions of unity and self-expression, and so they appreciate beauty. Do values exist apart from persons? No. External reality exists on the lower levels independently of persons, but truth value only emerges when persons pass judgments that agree with it. Goodness and badness can exist only as personal welfare is promoted or impeded; beauty and ugliness only when æsthetic desires are furthered or retarded. Values are properties peculiar to the relations of persons to one another and to their physical environment, and they exist only in the experience of persons. Persons, however, with their powers of imagination, conception and aspiration, can strive to actualize in their experience values that as yet exist only in their ideas. This is why faith and achievement are possible.

In our greatly simplified account of emergent evolution we have observed three distinct levels—matter, life, and personality. Each of the latter two involves the levels beneath it. The members of each level manifest increasing integration, heterogeneity, and definiteness. Members of each of the upper two levels modify to some extent—and in the case of man to a very considerable extent—the events that occur on the lower levels. Mechanists are guilty of the fallacy of materialism when they suppose that the higher levels can be reduced without remainder to lower levels. At the same time it must not be forgotten that increased knowledge of the sciences dealing with the lower levels makes possible more efficient maintenance and improvement of the members of higher levels. On the other hand, it is a fallacy of idealism to argue, since the higher levels have evolved from the lower ones, that some, or all, of the qualities and properties of the higher levels must be attributed to lower levels. Illustrations are pananimism and panpsychism, which assume that inorganic matter must in some sense be alive and even have mind, because living and conscious persons have emerged from it.

Thus far I have advanced what seems to me a "plain

tale" of emergent evolution, to borrow the term which Lloyd Morgan has made famous in *Life, Mind and Spirit*. Only the most obvious facts of each level have been accepted, and I have rejected all proposals for reductionism, whether materialistic, which would reduce higher levels to lower ones, or idealistic, which would raise the lower levels to the higher ones.

The levels, so far as one adheres strictly to a scientific account, must be "accepted with natural piety," in the phrase which Alexander has borrowed from Wordsworth and employed in *Space, Time and Deity,* in many respects the most important philosophical treatise that has yet appeared in the present century. The characteristics of a higher level cannot be deduced from those of a lower level. So science cannot tell us *why* higher levels emerge; it can only note the precise circumstances under which they do. This is why it is said that a scientist who had complete knowledge of the laws of any level would be unable therefrom to predict what novel qualities and properties would appear in a new level that had not yet emerged. Once, however, the new level had made its appearance and its qualities and properties been observed, together with the exact combination of elements on the lower level requisite for its emergence, a scientist would be able to predict that, whenever the combination should again occur, a new level with the same characteristics would emerge. So Emergent Evolutionism is not necessarily committed to indeterminism; it is compatible with complete determinism also; which position or which compromise between the two he may prefer, will be decided by any individual emergent evolutionist on other grounds than the mere fact that he believes in emergent evolution. In any version of Emergent Evolutionism, so far as I know, it is conceded that once a new level has emerged, the laws of its combination, like those of the Medes and Persians, remain fixed ever after.

Sublevels manifest themselves upon the levels of emergent evolution. Atoms are a higher sublevel than electrons, molecules than atoms, and so on. It has been suggested that the appearance of each new biological species is the rise of a new sublevel. In human history, perhaps the rise of each new race, nation, culture, and religion involves emergence, in that new characteristics appear that are not deducible from anything that has gone before. So, too, in the life of the individual; one arrives at times at new outlooks, in which the elements of one's past experience take on novel significance. Indeed, any instance of creative synthesis might be regarded as one of the emergence of a sublevel. But sublevels differ, as it seems to me, fundamentally from levels. Each level involves those that have preceded it and the levels form a progressive hierarchy. This is not true of all sublevels. Chemical compounds, biological species, human races and cultures can be better represented diagramatically by the branchings of a tree than by the steps of a pyramid. On the broad base of any level multitudinous sublevels may simultaneously emerge at different points. But only one higher level can emerge from a lower one; at least this has so far been true of terrestrial evolution.

In a "plain tale" of emergent evolution restricted to accepted facts of science, there seems no occasion for imputing life or mind in any Spinozistic sense to matter as its correlate, attribute or anything of the kind. The contrast between inorganic matter and organisms is sharp, and furnishes the reason for believing in emergent evolution. There is certainly no scientific reason for imputing mind to inorganic matter. Both life and mind either are, or depend upon, functions of matter organized in certain ways. Apart from such peculiar organization it is hard to see how they can exist in any object of less extent than the whole Earth itself—and more probably than the Universe as a whole. There is nothing in the inorganic phenomena, observed by themselves, to warrant the supposition that they are in any sense conscious, subconscious, or alive.

(c) It will be observed that for the third level of emergent evolution I have designated Persons, instead of Mind, as is usually done. This is for several reasons. It is difficult to infer from objective observation at what point in the phylogenetic series either mind or consciousness first appears. If we assume that no plants have mind and that all animals do, then mind must be presumed to have emerged very early in the evolution of life, and if mind be regarded as a higher level than life that the further evolution of vegetable life proceeded on a lower level subsequent to the emergence of the higher level of mind. It is still a controversial question precisely what part mind or consciousness performs in the life of an organism: is it an epiphenomenon; is it a soul or some other kind of stuff or substance that interacts with the body; is it a quality of the highly developed organism or of its central nervous system; or is it a relation between the parts of the organism? If mind were a distinct level there ought not to be so much doubt about its qualities and properties. On the other hand, the demarcation between persons and lower organisms is much clearer and more readily defined.

Peculiar to persons are the capacities to make tools, to reason, to speak, and to form religions. Perhaps all four are derivatives from the power to form free images and ideas, if we follow the older psychology; or the other three are results of verbalization if we prefer behaviorism. None of these capacities is possessed by non-human animals except to a very slight extent (and to this slight extent we may concede to certain lower animals anticipatory or quasi personality). Persons are members of societies, and many of their characteristic features are consequences of their social relationships. Without societies there could be no persons.

It may be asked why Society should not be reckoned as the third level of emergent evolution. So to designate the third level would make its relation to the second level more analogous to the relation of the second level to the first. For, as organisms are unique combinations of material particles, so societies are unique combinations of human organisms. The higher level of Society could be said, in Lloyd Morgan's language, to "involve" persons, while persons "depend" on society. This would be a capital illustration of Lloyd Morgan's doctrine that the higher level to some extent modifies those beneath it. The emergence of society transforms human organisms into persons; without society men would not be persons but mere animals. It must be confessed that the temptation to choose Society for the third level is attractive.

But this temptation must be resisted. A society has no distinct and unique corporate capacity. Only in a figurative sense does it possess organic structure and functions. It does not bear the same relation to individual persons that organisms bear to the cells of which they are composed, or to their more ultimate physical and chemical constituents. A society exists only as it is recognized by the persons who compose it. The same person belongs to many different societies. No one society is inclusive of all persons and other societies within a given area, unless it be the State, and to regard the state as the third level would hardly do. Its absolute sovereignty, including its alleged omnipotence and omnicompetence, have been gravely disputed in recent years. The State, as Maciver has shown, is the creature of the Community. And the community is certainly too vague a social unit to be designated as a level.

The facts—established or highly probable—of the past history of emergent evolution on the Earth have been summarized thus far in the paper without proceeding out of the domain of the sciences, or at least of inferences apparently implied in them. These facts of emergent evolution should be accepted in a realistic sense. It is no necessary implication of the truth of these facts that they have been, or now are, perceived or thought by any human mind. The first two levels passed through a long history before any human mind was in existence. Man is a late arrival on this planet. So far as science is concerned, the assumption that all the levels are present to a divine mind is not excluded, but is in no way called for. So far as the existence of God is concerned, science is, and ought to be, agnostic. The plain tale of emergent evolution can be outlined without including God. There is no necessity for that hypothesis so long as we stick to science.

3. While the "plain tale" of emergent evolution based on science does not include a rôle performed by God, there is nothing in it that necessarily excludes the possibility of the existence of God. The question now is, whether we as philosophers, seeking more ultimate explanations than the sciences attempt, may not properly formulate an interpretation of emergent evolution in theistic terms, provided the evidence seems to point that way. Our philosophical synthesis must of course in no way contradict the facts, assumptions and methods of any of the sciences, physical, biological or social. It may however, be more broadly speculative than a scientist could be in his professional capacity. It may prove to be the case that the methods of science and the data which it establishes force it to a positivistic position, while a more boldly speculative interpretation of the same evidence may be shown to indicate a considerable weight of probability in favor of the existence of the personal God of religious realism.

Before attempting such a philosophical interpretation or synthesis of the "plain tale" of emergent evolution, let us first repeat what it is and what it is not legitimate for us as philosophers to attempt in such an undertaking, in order that there may be no misunderstanding.

(a) Philosophers in a speculative synthesis or interpretation of scientific data must not introduce any conjectures that the established or even the fairly probable conclusions in any science either exclude or tend to exclude. A philosopher if he is a realist will not feel himself competent to criticize the assumptions of the sciences, or to attempt the rôle of an arbiter or supreme judge, or try to establish by decree the proper domain of any science. He cannot presume to tell a scientist that the latter's investigations deal with the "merely phenomenal" or "merely existential," or with "appearances," while he, the philosopher, discloses the "noumenal," the "ultimately real," the "absolute" or the "intelligible."

(b) On the contrary, the realistic philosopher accepts scientific facts, established or probable, and the fairly certain implications of these facts, as immeasurably more certain than any speculations that any philosopher, even a realist, can devise.

(c) Nor can the philosopher properly advance an *argumentum ad ignorantiam,* and contend for the truth of any religiously attractive belief merely on the ground that scientists at present cannot definitely prove that the belief is not true, although the drift of scientific thought may be unfavorable to it. The philosopher who seeks a substantial foundation for the house of religion cannot be contented with a sandy bar of nescience which the future floods of scientific discovery are liable to sweep away at any time. A reconciliation between science and religion that assigns to religion the ever-shrinking circle of the unknown which must perpetually recede as science advances, will not meet the requirements of a philosophy of religion.

(d) To describe the constructive task of the philosopher who is a religious realist in more positive terms. He should survey the facts and more probable theories of the various sciences synoptically, and not hesitate to advance as speculatively probable whatever generalizations seem to him on the whole to be indicated by the evidence. His efforts must to a large extent be mere inferences, perhaps not more than surmises, and they can rarely if ever gain the certitude of facts established by observation. But if they in no way contradict the established and probable facts of science and accord with the direction in which scientific advance seems to be moving; and if, in addition, the weight of empirical observations and abstract reasoning appears to be inclined in their favor, at least some measure of probability can be claimed for them.

It is in this spirit that we must as philosophical realists interpret the "plain tale" of emergent evolution, and ask ourselves whether this tale probably implies, or probably does not imply, the presence of the personal God of theism.

4. We are therefore now ready to attempt a philosophical synthesis or interpretation of the "plain tale" of emergent evolution.

(a) First, let us consider whether any future higher level of emergent evolution on the Earth seems in prospect, such as that to which Alexander gives the name of Deity, which would be as markedly different from persons as persons are from organisms, or organisms from non-living matter. No positive answer can of course be given to such a question, but for my part, I see no prospect of such a level emerging. Society is not, and will not develop into such a level for reasons already pointed out. No combination of persons into larger units that might be called "deities" or "angels" seems likely, or quite conceivable. Nor does it seem probable that a new species of supermen will ever emerge from the descendants of man, as high above man as man is above the apes, as conceived by Nietzsche in *Thus Spake Zarathustra*. Natural selection in the human race long ago virtually ceased. The progress in historic times has been in the improvement of mechanical tools, social institutions, cultures, and in moral, æsthetic and religious traditions. There has been no radical alteration of human nature itself, whether in its bodily constitution or in its mental capacities. Something may be done, when the science of eugenics becomes further developed, to prevent degeneration and to conserve the better stocks. Social, cultural and religious progress may result in the emergence of new sublevels of various kinds. A more satisfactory economic order, an international federation of states, a unification of some of the world's religions, are possibilities. But none of these would mean sufficient modification of persons as we know them to constitute a new level that would bear a relation to persons analo-

gous to that of persons to organisms. So the prospect of
the emergence of deities or angels or supermen on the
Earth seems to be excluded.

(b) We must ask ourselves whether as philosophers
we should posit life or mind at a lower level than that
on which they appear to emerge in the plain tale of
emergent evolution furnished by science. We have already seen that there is no scientific warrant for insert-
ing life and mind at the level of inorganic matter. We
should be very conservative in making philosophical in-
terpolations for which there is no scientific warrant. We
shall, indeed, later on find occasion for doing so. But the
burden of proof rests wholly upon us as philosophers,
whenever we add supplements to the plain tale of science. The chief philosophical argument in favor of imputing life and mind to inorganic matter is to secure
continuity in evolution, to avoid the jumps in evolution
which appear to occur at the points where the qualities
and properties of new levels and sublevels emerge. The
fact that, once these qualities and properties have been
observed at a new point of emergence, it can be predicted
that they in the future will ever be observed to appear
under like conditions suggests determinism. This determinism is, it is urged, more readily accounted for by
supposing that life and mind and other emergents were
already implicitly present at lower levels, although not
explicitly observable. But what does "implicit" really
mean when used in this sense? No one so far as I know
has offered any plausible explanation.

On the other hand, the hypothesis that inorganic matter is in some inferior way alive or that it possesses some
very low order of "subconscious" or "unconscious"
mentality, has never led to the slightest suggestion how
or why life and mind at the points at which they are
observed have come to emerge from their hypothetically
implicit states. The organic chemists are apparently
making some progress on the road to an explanation of
the origin of life, although they doubtless have a long
road to travel. But such hypotheses as pananimism or

hylozoism seem utterly unfruitful in offering suggestions for attacking the problem.

The outstanding fact for common sense and naïve realism is that one of the sharpest bifurcations in our universe is that between inorganic and living matter, between things that are dead and those that are alive. Paulsen [2] once ridiculed materialists for the attempt to classify mind as a form of matter by saying that one might as well call iron a form of wood. He meant, I suppose, that if one were to call iron a form of wood, there would be two kinds of wood to distinguish, the iron kind of wood and the ordinary kind. They could not remain less different, and the relationship between them could not in the least be clarified by giving them a common name. Paulsen, who was an advocate of panpsychism, did not realize that to call matter a lower form of life or of mind is just as unsatisfactory. It is merely to give a common name to two heterogeneous classes of objects, and can do nothing to establish a common relationship, much less show how one could have emerged from the other.

The reason therefore for rejecting theories of panvitalism and panpsychism is that on philosophical no more than on scientific grounds do they appear to be fruitful hypotheses. They throw no light upon the real problems. The philosopher is justified in adding a supplement to the plain tale of emergent evolution furnished by science only when by so doing he can advance a speculative explanation or interpretation from which inferences can be drawn that throw some light on experienced facts. [3]

(c) A consideration of the levels of emergent evolution suggests to many interpreters some kind of nisus or tendency in the whole of things pressing toward the actualization of higher levels, and in progress on each level

---

[2] F. Paulsen, *Introduction to Philosophy*, trans. by Frank Thilly, p. 82.

[3] An interpretation that meets this requirement has been advanced by Professor W. P. Montague, who shows that the qualitative discontinuities of emergent evolution have been generated through quantitatively continuous changes (*Essays in Honor of John Dewey*, pp. 257-73).

toward higher sublevels. To adapt Lloyd Morgan's apt figure of a pyramid to the version of emergent evolution set forth in this paper, while as yet the Earth consisted only of matter, there was a latent tendency in the matter, a process of organization or integration, accompanied by increased differentiation or heterogeneity and increased definiteness, toward the emergence of organisms. To be sure, to acknowledge such a tendency or nisus is a philosophical surmise, an inference, an imputation, a distinctly speculative addition to the "plain tale" of scientifically established facts. Still it does not seem an unwarranted surmise, and it is made in different ways by Alexander,[4] who combines this notion of *nisus* with his conception of God who includes all the universe thus far in existence, by Lloyd Morgan,[5] who identifies the

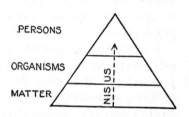

nisus more simply with God, and by Sellars,[6] who, most naturalistic and unspeculative of the three, makes no more of it than the observed fact of "organization."

(d) The vital question for the philosophy of religion at this point is just how much we can safely surmise regarding this nisus. Here, if anywhere, we shall find God in emergent evolution. To recognize any nisus at all is to go beyond scientifically established facts and theories though in no way to contradict them either in letter or in spirit. It is hard to see how science can ever have anything at all decisive to say on the subject. It certainly has nothing to say at present, so far as I can see.

(e) It has long seemed to me that in the general course of terrestrial evolution we do observe a teleological tendency. We ought at least to be able to call the nisus a teleological tendency. As Professor L. J. Henderson[7] called to general attention some years ago, there existed

[4] *Space, Time and Deity.*
[5] *Emergent Evolution.*
[6] Most simply in his elementary *Principles and Problems of Philosophy.*
[7] *Fitness of the Environment, etc.*

on the Earth's surface and in its atmosphere ages before
the appearance of life the precise combination of chemical elements and compounds—hydrogen, oxygen, carbon,
nitrogen, water and carbonic acid—that would be most
favorable for the subsequent emergence of life. No conceivable form of metabolism could have developed so
advantageously from any other combination. Yet there
was only one chance in millions of millions that this precise combination should have taken place rather than
any other. It seems to follow that in the evolution of
the Earth, from the beginning of the history of the
planet, there was a pattern, a teleological order, not to
be accounted for as mere chance or on purely mechanical
principles.

No convincing answer to this argument has ever been
advanced, so far as I am aware. It has indeed been
pointed out that this planet is only one of millions of
millions of celestial bodies in the universe, and the possibility has been suggested that this may be the only one
on which life has actually emerged. Such a suggestion
merely calls attention to one speculative possibility, to
the truth of which astronomy can supply no positive
answer at present, although, I suppose, there are a few
indications that life exists on two of the planets nearest
us—Mars and Venus. Again it has been suggested that
solar systems may be very rare in the universe; that
most stars may not possess satellites of this character.
Even if our Earth should be the only heavenly body in
the universe on which emergent evolution has advanced
to the level of persons, this would not exclude the inference that on our Earth, at any rate, there is a nisus or
teleological tendency in operation.

If it be suggested that perhaps life everywhere emerges
from inorganic matter, whatever be the combination of
elements and compounds, although life of a totally different nature from any that we know, a realm of wide speculation is entered. Professor Henderson insists that the
organic chemist can conceive of no metabolism that would
be nearly so favorably circumstanced. But even if he

should be wrong, the answer still could be made that such a suggestion assumes a universal teleology—that matter everywhere, in all its possible combinations contains within itself an implicit tendency to effect the emergence of life. The nisus would not be confined to the Earth, but be omnipresent, and in one sense, omnipotent.

If it be claimed that whatever happened in the later evolution of the planet, whether life emerged or only further combinations of matter, mountains and rocks and sand dunes, anyone regarding its history might choose to infer a latent nisus striving to consummate precisely the outcome that actually occurred, it can be replied that an inference of this kind could hardly be made unless life emerged. An evolution that did not ultimately produce organisms which struggle for existence and manifest a preference for some ends rather than others could in no sense be reckoned teleological. There would be no design or pattern in such an evolution, unless it were attributed to the mind of an external manufacturer, such as the God of Deism. And even such an inference would have no ground, unless the outcome could in some sense be supposed to accord with the purposes of such a Deity.

Or, if it be said that there is no teleology in matter itself, but life somehow emerges and shapes matter to its ends, we have implied a dualism somewhat in the manner of Bergson, and life is, or contains, or is directed by a nisus or an *élan vital*. By denying teleology to matter, this interpretation does not fail to concede it to life.[8]

Once life has emerged, the immanent teleology in organisms seems indisputable. Organisms struggle for existence. Even the amœba exercises choices in its movements. Plants turn their roots in favorable directions into the soil, and they shoot upwards, if necessary sideways, into the air. All organisms show an adaptability to environmental conditions that never contradicts mechanical principles, but is never describable entirely

[8] W. K. Wright, *A Student's Philosophy of Religion*, pp. 314ff.

in mechanical terms. To say this is not necessarily to be a vitalist. It is unnecessary to assume a *vita,* an *élan,* an entelechy, or any other non-material substance operative in organisms. One need only call attention to the facts, and insist that in the organism is manifest a novel form of relatedness, not present in the inorganic world. Explain it if you will, in terms of tropisms, reflexes, or whatever mechanistic principles you choose, the lowliest vegetable and animal organisms secure nutrition, reproduce themselves, repair injured parts if injuries are not too great, and modify their immediate environments in such ways as they can in accordance with their interests. And higher animals do a great deal more.*

The history of man reveals a marvelous progress in mechanical control of his environment, through the invention of tools, agriculture and industry, in order to secure increased length and breadth of life. His advances in social organization, in culture, in morality, and in religion are too striking and well known to require extensive exposition.

(f) Looking at the course of emergent evolution on the Earth, it seems that no one who is not willfully blind to obvious facts can fail to see in it a teleological pattern. Perhaps the chief reason why this is ever disputed is because some religious apologists wish to claim that a more perfect pattern exists than the facts indicate.

It must be conceded that the teleological pattern is by no means perfect. The Earth is not an ideal environment for the successive rise of the different levels of emergent evolution. Think how much of its surface—mountain, desert, regions covered by ice and snow or subjected to perpetual heat—is ill-suited to the emergence of life! Think of the bitter struggle for existence among organisms in their battles with the physical environment, with other species, and with rivals of their own species! Consider how many species have perished altogether, or have become lost in blind alleys whence neither retreat (because of the law of orthogenesis) nor further advance

* On all this, cf. J. A. Thomson, *System of Animate Nature.*

were possible. Many, like the amœba, have failed to advance at all; some have actually degenerated. Reflect how many branches of the human race have made no real contribution to human progress, and how few individuals even in the best nations have really been creative or in any high way admirable. Most of the great men and civilizations have arisen within those portions of the Earth's surface where climatic conditions have been unusually favorable, and these portions comprise only a small fraction of it.[10] As one of the seven sages of Greece long ago observed, ''Most men are bad.'' The Earth cannot therefore be claimed to be an ideal or entirely successful place for the development of persons to realize the higher values; nor has the general course of emergent evolution on its surface been the actualization of a transcendent pattern of complete rationality and beauty.

It is by no means strange, therefore, that many, dismayed by the imperfect teleology of real life have turned away from the world before them and taken refuge in compensatory religions and idealisms of their own imaginations, and so found in blissful contemplation of visions and ecstasies or in rational speculation upon Platonic ideas or eternally subsistent values a means of escape from reality with all its evils and horrors. Nor is it strange that some disillusioned religionists and philosophical idealists, like Buddha and Schopenhauer, have concluded that all human life is inevitably doomed to frustration, and so have become pessimists. For a pessimist is only an idealist *in excelsis*—or would it be better to say, *in extremis?*—who tries to break entirely with life and the world as they are and seeks final and complete submergence in an imaginary Absolute in which he hopes to be at rest.

(g) Nor is it necessary to go so far as to insist that emergent evolution on the Earth reveals the unfolding

---

[10] This assertion seems warranted on the basis of the data gathered by Professor Ellsworth Huntington in *Civilization and Climate* (cf. map on page 142) and *The Character of Races* (especially Chapter XV).

of a pattern that was perfect in its original ideal conception, but which it was impossible to carry out completely because of physical obstacles. The teleological pattern itself may have been frequently modified not only to meet emergencies, but also because new improvements were thought of by God. The teleology of emergent evolution on the Earth is not suggestive of what Aristotle meant by evolution, nor of that which Newman claimed for the development of Catholic doctrine, an entirely logical unfolding of an implicit plan. It is more Bergsonian in spirit.[11] It is suggestive of the teleological productions of human persons. No one carries out a project precisely as he had previously conceived it; he has to overcome unforeseen obstacles, or he conceives of improvements in the original plan. Terrestrial evolution is analogous to the development from the original plans of St. Peter's at Rome or of our national Capitol at Washington, or to that which takes place in successive generations of city planning in Paris or Chicago.

But while a review of the course of Emergent Evolution does not disclose a teleological pattern that is perfect, either in original conception or in execution, none the less the existence of a pattern is unmistakeable. Higher levels have emerged from lower ones, and persons have advanced from savagery to civilization. Man has ascended from eolithic monsters to the civilized humanity of the twentieth century.

(h) Theodicies have been able to justify some of the seemingly dysteleological features in the course of terrestrial evolution. The struggle for existence was necessary in order that the fit might survive. And as a rule, though with exceptions, the biologically fittest have also in the long run proved the morally and æsthetically fittest. Nor has the struggle for existence been so invariably

[11] Bergson himself in *Creative Evolution* uses such terms as teleology, finalism, etc., to indicate reversed mechanism, which is a kind of evolution similar to Aristotle's and Newman's. Bergson's own conception of evolution—an *élan vital* with constantly growing and expanding though sometimes thwarted purposes, is more like the type of teleological evolution favored in this paper.

brutal and bloody as is sometimes supposed. There has been coöperation between members of the same species and between specific plant and animal species, as Kropotkin and Patten have shown.[12] Severe climates and other adverse conditions have been beneficial in developing resourcefulness and character; man has progressed most in regions where he has had great but not excessive obstacles to overcome. Character and moral values imply freedom of choice, and the latter implies that some will choose wrongly, hence sin and error are inevitable in an advancing world.

(i) Now we have to face the crucial question for the religious realist who seeks evidence for God in the course of emergent evolution. Can evidence of a nisus, of a teleological pattern, warrant us in inferring the existence of God?

Demonstration here is of course impossible. However, there are some considerations that need to be taken into account. If we are agreed upon acceptance of a nisus and of a teleological trend, we must at this point choose between two alternatives. Either the nisus and the trend are impersonal manifestations of an Earth that is at bottom mechanical and material on the first level, and yet when the first level alone existed effected the emergence of the next higher level; or else there was a directing Intelligence that guided the course of evolution and brought the higher levels into existence. The higher levels either owe their duration and development wholly to the continued action of inorganic matter or else in part to the support and guidance of such an Intelligence.

Choice between the two alternatives must be made by each reader for himself. Proof is impossible. He must decide which of the two seems to him the more reasonable, the more thinkable, the more probable.

This is not, I think, properly the place for a moral appeal, to urge the reader to consider "was für ein Mensch man ist," nor for an exhortation to exercise a

[12] P. Kropotkin, *Mutual Aid a Factor in Evolution*. William Patten, *Grand Strategy of Evolution*.

"will to believe" and to accept what would be the more pleasing or comforting or inspiring alternative, or what would most assure the conservation and triumph of values. If the choice could be made upon such considerations, there indeed could certainly be little hesitation. An Earth governed by a personal God would best answer all of these requirements.

The reader must exercise intellectual honesty, and come to his decision by rational and empirical logic regardless of emotional or volitional preferences or prejudices. He must follow the argument wherever it leads him, and reach his conclusions honestly. To do otherwise would be to obscure the light of reason which is our only ultimate guide between truth and error; or, in theological parlance, we might call it the sin against the Holy Ghost. And however one decides upon the evidence, he must be just, tolerant and respectful of those whose judgment leads them to decide differently. And it must be remembered that those who decide adversely toward the claims of religion are at least as likely to be prejudiced as those who decide favorably. Fanaticism and bigotry are not monopolies of the orthodox.

For my own part, it is much more difficult to conceive of an Earth composed of inorganic matter manifesting a *nisus* toward integration and organization, and effecting the emergence of higher levels, including that of conscious, willing persons with appreciation of moral, æsthetic and religious values, than it is to assume such an evolution to be the work of a Mind, or Intelligence or Will of some kind,—in short, a psychical Agent.

Now, if any kind of a psychical Agent at all is assumed, to this Agent should be attributed the characteristics of a Person. (At least, so it seems to me—I cannot speak for others; it is so much a matter of personal judgment, and the objective evidence is not conclusive, else philosophers would not so widely differ.) A psychical Force that struggles blindly in manifestations of inertia and gravity, that strives only a little less blindly in plants and the lowest forms of animal life, and only comes to self consciousness on this particular planet in man, is more difficult to conceive in the light of the facts open to us than is a personal God.

A teleological pattern, including in its origin a happy combination of chemical elements and compounds that would make life possible, the emergence of abundant plant life to sustain an evolution of animals, a progressive evolution of animals that has reached its apex in man, who can think, love, form ideals and in some measure realize them—all this is more readily conceivable on the assumption that a Person plans all these developments and brings them about through his own efforts, than by any alternative hypothesis.

Taken all in all, and notwithstanding the difficulties that stand in the way, this seems logically the simplest and philosophically the most plausible interpretation of the "plain tale" of emergent evolution on the Earth.

5. Early in this paper we found that the testimony of religious experience affirms the presence of a personal God, conceived in terms of religious realism. We found that this evidence, though not strong enough to be decisive, is not without weight. We have now, however, considered an entirely independent argument for the God of religious realism, based on a philosophical interpretation of the "plain tale" of emergent evolution. The two independent arguments, taken together, are stronger than either would be in isolation. While proof in such matters is impossible, it seems to me, at any rate, that we can claim a balance of probability in favor of the existence of the personal God of religious realism. It will be recalled that emotional appeals, *argumenta ad ignorantiam,* and exhortations to exercise "the will to believe" were conscientiously avoided. The conclusions drawn are nowhere, it is believed, in conflict either with the letter or the spirit of scientific inquiry. Although they are admittedly speculative, they are acknowledgments that are not devoid of rationality, nor of empirical probability.

Let us try to state this conclusion a little differently. On the hypothesis of a personal God in the direction of terrestrial evolution and occupied with the effort to consummate the achievement of higher values on the Earth, should we not expect Him to have brought into existence on this planet conscious persons who could in some measure appreciate higher values and endeavor to realize them? Would not the best way to effect the presence of these higher values be to do so with the coöperation of such persons?

And would not such a personal God reveal Himself to the lesser persons on the planet as rapidly and as effectively as it would be possible for them to become conscious of Him? And is not all this precisely what has occurred in the history of human religious experience? Savage man could only become conscious of God as *mana* or *numen,* as totem or spirit, and he would only look to such an Agency for assistance in the attainment of those simpler values which he knew—food, victory in war, safety for himself and his family, posterity, counsel through medicine men, lots, tokens, oracles, and the like. As man became more reflective, higher values would emerge within his ken. He would ultimately come to seek purity of heart, peace, love, divine communion and all the finer goods of a spiritual life which the best and most profoundly religious men have sought in their intercourse with God.

The means by which God would communicate with men, and by which men would seek intercourse with Him, would be the processes which the psychology and sociology of religion are making known to us. God would be experienced as a larger Self, with whom men come into relationship in worship, and the medium through which this would occur in persons whose conscious processes are functions of a brain and nervous system would be through the release of energy stored in nutritive cells, and through the action of the subconscious. Men would interpret God in the light of their own personal and social experiences. When men lived under kinship organization, God would be thought of as a patriarchal chief. When men lived under authoritarian social organization, God would be a king. In our modern democratic social and political organization the crudeness of patriarchal and authoritarian conceptions would gradually be overcome, and to God would no longer be attributed love of blood revenge and delight in despotic powers and attributes. On the contrary, in intensified and purified degree, would be ascribed to him those tender and personal qualities of which men in no age were wholly ignorant—because men have always lived in families—the traits of a personal and loving Father.

6. We have seen that values exist only for persons, and in the "plain tale" of emergent evolution based on science, that values only emerged with persons. In our philosophical interpretation, however, we are justified in interpolating values earlier in evolution if we can find good reasons for doing so.

If we decide to believe that one Person has been continuously in direction of emergent evolution, purposes and values have existed in His mind as long as there has been a teleological pattern in emergent evolution (and that may have been forever if cosmic evolution has gone on forever). Values as objects of aspiration and endeavor on the part of human persons prior to their realization in human experience have no material but only ideal existence. To what extent may we suppose that God experienced values in terrestrial evolution prior to the emergence of human persons? He must have felt the æsthetic satisfactions in the order and regularity of physical matter which are now enjoyed by mathematicians and physicists. He perceived æsthetic features as yet unknown to men, for there is doubtless more order, regularity and beauty in the inorganic world in relation to a perceiving mind than our scientists have yet discovered. And He experienced truth value, for He knew things as they were. But moral values could only to a limited extent have been experienced by Him if He was then a solitary Individual. If, on the other hand, we suppose that God was not a solitary Individual prior to the emergence of man, but that He participated in the society of angels or other persons inhabiting other portions of the universe than the Earth, His experience included all the moral values implied in all the social relationships then in existence. In any case, with the emergence on the Earth itself of persons who could share in the appreciation of values, divine and angelic enjoyment of terrestrial values must have been enhanced, and supplemented by the emergence of new values. With the further advancement of human persons, the divine appreciation of values must be still further promoted. This can be assumed to be true, without implying that the Earth is a planet with an extraordinary development. Persons on other planets eons ago may have advanced further than humanity will ever attain. Even so, no matter how humble may be the values and other attainments of men on earth, they must enrich the lives of whatever other inhabitants of the universe are cognizant of them, and sympathize with them. Human parents find increased enhancement of values when their children discover them for the first time. So it must be with God the Father.

Without arguing in a circle, I think it can be said that if a teleological pattern exists and reveals a tendency toward the emergence of human persons who appreciate values, we can argue that a divine Person must have thought out the pattern, and, at least in idea, to some extent have anticipated the values that thus far have become actualized in the individual and social lives of humanity on this planet, and those that shall hereafter become actualized. If values can only exist as they are experienced by persons, and if emergent evolution prior to the advent of man manifests a tendency toward the realization or actualization of values, there must have been a supreme Person who (perhaps gradually) conceived the values. For values cannot exist or subsist without persons any more than valleys without hills or circles without diameters and circumferences.[13]

Does God, in idea, eternally anticipate all the values that shall be realized by Himself or by other persons on this planet or anywhere else in the universe? Is there an absolute and eternal frame of values which subsists in His mind?[14] Is the teleological pattern which emergent evolution on the Earth imperfectly realizes, itself an approximation, the best possible under the circumstances, to an absolutely perfect frame of values? There are some questions about the nature of God which even a philosopher may not have the audacity to attempt to answer. But it may seem that any Person, even He, learns and profits by experience; and that He, in the course of evolution, may not only modify His plans for making ideal values actual, but may reconstitute the ideal values themselves. A Person that can never grow intellectually, and can only progress in achieving better instruments for the actualization of values in the lives of lesser persons, would seem less happily circumstanced than a Person whose life constantly expands with enlarging insights. Perhaps there may be no perfection, even in idea, for the divine Person, that will not be transcended in His future thought, arising out of His expanding experiences.

7. We must next consider a few of the more obvious difficulties in the conception of a personal God, as thus derived, primarily from terrestrial evolution, and secondarily from religious experience.

(a) There is the problem of Dissolution. Evolution seems everywhere on the Earth to be attended by dissolution. The processes of evolution, to be sure, at present have the upper hand; but, as Spencer predicted, this

---

[13] The dependence of values upon persons and the necessary inference that cosmic values imply the existence of God has been convincingly shown by W. R. Sorley (*Moral Values and the Idea of God*) and by J. A. Leighton (*Man and the Cosmos*).

[14] C. Lloyd Morgan uses the term "frame of values" with reference to human experience (*Life, Mind and Spirit*, pp. 265, 270, 273; but he does not definitely impute such a frame of values to God in the following chapter).

state will be followed by an era of equilibrium, which will be succeeded by a period of dissolution. To be sure, this time of disaster will not arrive so soon as was formerly supposed, before it was known that not all of the energy released by the sun is due to contraction. Except in the advent of some unlikely catastrophe, like collision with another heavenly body, man will survive and progress upon the Earth at least one hundred and fifty million years longer, and more likely a million million years, in the opinion of Sir James Jeans.[15] But, sooner or later, the natural resources of the Earth will be exhausted, despite all the increased ingenuity of human invention and utilization of resources which we do not know how to exploit. The Earth itself will grow cold. Man will degenerate and finally perish. The level of persons will thus be dissolved. Later, the level of organisms will also disappear. The higher sublevels of matter will be dissolved into lower constituents, and the Earth will return to the nebulous material from which it came. What then?

Frankly speaking, this prospect is not nearly so damaging to the practical interests of religion as at first appears. If God now exists, if men now can commune with Him and in coöperation with Him can in future millenniums attain achievements of which no one can now dream, it makes no practical difference in the conduct called for on the part of the religious believer to-day if the process cannot endure forever.

It is possible that when the Earth shall finally dissolve with the rest of our solar system, from the resulting nebula a new sun and planets will ultimately evolve. The process of alternate evolution and dissolution may go on forever. If God be in some sense the soul of the solar system, there may be some way in which His personality can survive the shock of the dissolution of one solar system and continue to direct the ensuing evolution of the succeeding system. And in directing the teleological pattern in this future system God may profit by the achievements of the present system. Human persons learn by

[15] *The Universe around Us,* pp. 329f.

their past experiences. Why not He? Moreover, our personal immortality may somehow be conserved in His, and we may survive with Him.

But why suppose God to be limited by the fortunes of the Earth, or of our solar system? Why not suppose that He guides, and is immanent in the evolution of our whole galaxy of stars, and of whatever other galaxies there may be in the universe? And may not the evolution and dissolution of solar and galactic systems go on forever? May not the relation of planets and stars to the life of God be analogous to the wearing away and restoration of cells in our own bodies? Cells continually pass away and are repaired, and yet our conscious life continues unimpaired. We have long known that the distances between electrons within the atoms that constitute the cells of our bodies are, in proportion to their masses, astronomical. So the remoteness of stars from one another is no objection to such an analogy.

(b) But what of the second law of thermodynamics, variously known as Carnot's law, entropy, and the degradation of energy? Energy is continually running down within our solar system; in time will it not be true that none of it will be available for future evolution? In reply it may be suggested that this law is not known to hold universally throughout the heavens. In other celestial regions some compensatory process may be discovered.

It is possible, therefore, that evolution and dissolution succeed each other endlessly throughout all space. While evolution prevails in one sun and its satellites, dissolution may triumph in another, and *vice versa*. In all parts of space there may be occasional planets in which higher levels emerge from matter or energy, in some cases perhaps higher levels than have emerged, or are likely to emerge, in the history of the Earth. If these possibilities be true, they are favorable to the orthodox belief that God is eternal in time and omnipresent in space.[16]

[16] Sir James Jeans, however, thinks that the present indications are unfavorable to the possibility of cyclical evolution of this kind. *Op. cit.,* pp. 308-12.

(c) Nor need we be unduly disturbed at the fact that we find no perfect teleological pattern in even terrestrial evolution. The imperfections of terrestrial evolution may imply that God is limited in power. This is perhaps the best of possible worlds that He could produce under the limitations of terrestrial matter, and the necessity of affording freedom of will to human persons, if they were to develop the moral qualities that were an essential part of the scheme of values which He desired to consummate on this particular planet.

But why do religious men balk at the thought that God may be limited in power? When we think of the cruel monstrosities that such theologians as Augustine and Calvin have substituted for God in consequence of the inexorable logic that seemed to them implied in His infinite power, and when we think of the unsatisfying emptiness of the Absolutes of Oriental pantheisms and of Western Absolute Idealism, shall we be reluctant to believe that God is not an Absolute, but a Person, even though this implies that, like all other persons, He is limited by the presence of other persons, as well as by inorganic matter?[17]

Persons can arise only in societies, in the give and take of social intercourse. Perhaps God, in order to be a Person, must limit Himself by producing other persons in the world. And as these lesser persons realize their personalities in social intercourse and mutual service, so God realizes His personality in communion with them. Religious worship may be a service to God as well as to ourselves. We may be fellow workers with God in the effort to achieve a more perfect society, in which ever higher values may be conceived and actualized.

The conception of an ever-evolving world, in which even God is a Person, and learns by social intercourse, seems to some to lack all stability. They desire to believe in an eternal and unchanging God who stands aloof from

[17] The arguments in this and some succeeding paragraphs may be said to contain an emotional appeal. Their only purpose is to reconcile the sentiments of those who wince at the conclusions previously drawn from a dispassionate consideration of the evidence.

all time and space, evolution and dissolution, in Brahma-like self-sufficiency. A God of this kind, however, would not be a Person. Persons only exist in societies. Unless God is a Person, how can persons worship Him, commune with Him, love Him as a Father, and serve Him as their Master?

(d) On the other hand, if God be a Person, shall we not have faith in Him, even if we believe Him to be limited in power? Even so we may look forward to a future of indefinite and possibly of unending progress. The Being who has effected the teleological pattern that terrestrial evolution has thus far disclosed, who has guided inorganic matter in its evolution upward to man, and of savage man to civilized man, who has given us Jesus—shall we not believe Him great enough and good enough for us to love, and trust and obey? For us he is "practically" infinite and absolute. We have far more reason to have faith and confidence in Him than children have in the best of fathers and mothers.

8. Let us now answer some questions that may suggest themselves in the light of the conclusions at which we have arrived with regard to the nature and attributes of God.

(a) Is God, as with Professor Whitehead, to be regarded as a principle of concretion?[18] I am not quite sure of what he means but I shall try to make clear my own position, which agrees with his at least in affirming that God exists in a realistic sense, that He is limited, and that He brings order into things. For me certainly God is not merely a principle of some kind. He is a Person. All cosmic processes that reveal purpose, appreciation of values and the endeavor to make them actual, are manifestations of the activity of God. On the other hand, the merely orderly and regular processes of physical nature operating along mechanical principles in accordance with such natural laws as inertia, gravitation and the conservation of energy do not of themselves suggest the presence of God. Inorganic matter, apart from

[18] A. N. Whitehead, *Religion in the Making.*

its actual or possible relations to persons, is morally and æsthetically neutral, neither good nor bad, neither beautiful nor ugly.

(b) How is God related to evil? Matter is inert, it lacks plasticity and does not readily evolve into the higher forms that God desires. This explains the presence of physical evil. There is no active force or principle of evil in nature, no personal devil, that, in a manner analogous to the activity of an organism or a person, resists God. We are speaking figuratively when we say that matter resists God, somewhat as an Aristotelian speaks figuratively when he says that matter resists form. The analogy of the relation of an artist to the material which he uses, is appropriate here. No artist can produce any creation—a statue, a painting, or a building, without using materials. And every kind of material in some way resists and limits the scope of his efforts. The sculptor cannot use a variety of shades and colors. The painter has to produce his effects on plane surfaces. The architect is limited in his designs by the characteristics of his building materials, their strength, durability, plasticity, and the like. So God is limited by the nature of His materials, and cannot effect a complete realization of a teleological pattern in emergent evolution. Yet no artist, not even God, can produce a creation without materials. I am unable to conceive of creation out of nothing. Moral evil is due to the freedom of the wills of lesser persons, a freedom indispensable to their character as persons, but a freedom which they do not always use as they should. Hence the presence of sin in the world.

(c) Is God infinite? Whether God extends infinitely in space and has unending duration in time, are questions which the philosopher cannot answer until more information is available from astrophysics. If space and time themselves are infinite, if evolution and dissolution are universal and unending processes, if teleological patterns appear in the emergent evolution of many planets, then God may be presumed to be infinite in these respects. Otherwise not.

Infinite in power God certainly is not. As a Person, He is limited as all persons are, by physical matter and energy, and by the wills of other persons. But since good gradually prevails in evolution, and higher values in the long run more often are realized, God's power is evidently increasing.

(d) In what sense is God omniscient—infinite in knowledge? If He is infinite in spatial extension and temporal duration, it may be inferred that His mind comprehends all present and past events. In addition to the actual, He knows much of the possible—subsistents as well as existents, unrealized values as well as facts. That He knows *all* possibilities may be doubted; it may be that His knowledge of what is possible and what is practicable increases with His experience, that He, like other persons, learns by doing. As has been already intimated, His knowledge and appreciation of values increases with the number of other persons in the universe, and the closeness of their communion with Him.

(e) Is God transcendent or is He immanent? God is transcendent to man in the sense that He exists elsewhere in the universe in His own right apart from all human thought about or activity with reference to Him. Man does not create God in his own image; what man creates in his own image are human thoughts about God. As man advances in knowledge, and especially in religious experience, his ideas of God bear increasing resemblance to the true God, who realistically exists independent of human thought.

God is immanent in whatever processes of nature are achieving the realization of purposes and values apart from the efforts of other persons, or to a greater extent than could be achieved by their efforts alone. God is immanent in the lesser persons of the universe in the sense that He knows their thoughts and purposes. "O Lord, Thou hast searched me and known me!" However, all lesser persons have freedom and moral responsibility; they may or they may not be aware of His presence, and of what He desires them to do; if conscious of both, they may or may not act in accordance with His wishes. When, however, in prayer an individual enters into communion with God, He is in an additional sense immanent in his mind; in religious worship we find God within ourselves. God is therefore immanent in the minds of persons in communion with Him, in an additional sense to that in which He is present in minds indifferent to Him. God indeed knows the thoughts of the red-handed slayer and of the doubter, but in a further sense He is present wherever the hymn of faith is sincerely sung.

The hope of immortality for men lies just here, in the possibility that our minds may somehow be included within His mind, and yet remain independent personalities. In no other manner could immortality be possible, in view of the fact that a human conscious life, except in so far as it may inhere in God independently of other circumstances, involves the functioning of the brain and nervous system of a living organism.

This conception of God is theistic, not pantheistic, in that it affirms the personality of God, and the independent existence of matter and the other persons of the universe, to the extent that the former passively and the latter actively may resist His wishes. On the other hand, the immanent view of God is accepted to the extent that God is believed to be present wherever in the universe teleological patterns are manifested in emergent evolution, and whenever lesser persons have religious experiences.

(f) In contrast to man, God may be said to possess qualities and attributes that are infinite and absolute in the sense that the French sometimes colloquially use these adjectives and their corresponding adverbs. God is ''practically'' infinite in relation to man. Man can look toward Him in entire confidence and trust. Man should love and obey Him implicitly. Man should be confident that, if he commits his will to Him, He will never fail him. For practical purposes man's attitude toward God should be one of as complete loyalty, devotion and confidence as in the times when no qualifications were attached to the absoluteness and infinitude of the attributes imputed to Him.

We might revise what some of us in our youth were taught about God into some such formulation as this: *God is a Spirit, practically infinite, eternal and unchangeable in His being, wisdom, power, holiness, justice, goodness and truth, and* (let us add what our fathers overlooked) *in His love.*

XIV

GOD AND THE COSMOS

By
JOHN ELOF BOODIN
Professor of Philosophy
The University of California at Los Angeles

GOD AND THE COSMOS [1]

ARE religious values and ideals but the iridescence of a blind world of matter? So says materialism. Are they the mere shadow of man projected on the abyss of the future? So says humanism. Religious realism says that the object we worship in religion is a reality independent of ourselves—a reality with which we can enter into rapport. This religious reality is not something remote from us. It is a reality which we feel as we feel the sunshine, which we share as we share beauty. This does not mean that all share it. Some people are color blind and some people are insensible to beauty, yet those who experience color and beauty do not doubt the reality of them. The divine is not merely a creation of human experience, a projected social ideal, but an eternally existent, enveloping reality.

Religious experience, like all experience of reality, presents an immediate aspect of awareness and a mediate aspect of interpretation. The immediate experience of reality in religion is a unique fact, as the experience of music is a unique fact. No doubt this immediate experience is complex for analysis, but it is nevertheless a fact of its own kind. Religious experience is not just fear, for we have many kinds of fear without having religious feeling. It is not just shudder, for we may shudder at a rattlesnake without feeling religious. It is not just thrill, because there are thrills which are not religious. It is not resolvable into social feelings whether of sex or family or tribe, because we can have these feelings without any religious consciousness. Nor is it a combination merely of these various feelings, because we

[1] See in this connection the article, "God," July, 1929, and the article, "The Universe as a Living Whole," July, 1930, in the *Hibbert Journal.* A fuller statement will appear in a forthcoming book, *God and Creation.*

may have a complex of such feelings without having any religious consciousness. These and many other feelings may enter into the religious consciousness and no doubt enter in at various times, but the religious consciousness itself is a unique attitude and feeling which points to a reality of its own, as the consciousness of light points to a reality of its own.

But religion is not mere feeling. Imagination and thought enter into the religious attitude as well as feeling. Just as in our experience of nature the immediate feeling furnishes the stimulus for interpretation, so in the case of religious experience. To say that we have immediate experience of religious reality does not mean that we comprehend it, any more than to say that we have an immediate experience of light and beauty means that we comprehend these. Being imaginative, we strive to furnish a setting for our immediate experience. We try to understand what we feel. By understanding I mean that we enter creatively into the reality which we live, in order to interpret its meaning. If it can be said of sense experience that we half create what we perceive, so it can be said of religious experience. Religious interpretation does not involve merely one part of human nature, whether sense or feeling or thought or will; it involves the whole of human nature. It is a creative reaction of our whole personality to the unseen. The whole gamut of our minded organism takes part in our religious experience. All the mechanisms which have to do with feeling and emotion, all the mechanisms of memory, all our capacities for imagination and logical construction are focused in religious appreciation and furnish a basis for the interpretation of religious reality.

In some sense, the religious conception of the universe is animistic, since nature for the religious consciousness is not mere dead lumps of matter but alive with spirit. But religion is not mere primitive animism; and primitive animism was not necessarily religious. Not all the objects, interpreted as animated, were given religious reverence; most of them were treated as matters of fact.

Nor is mysticism to be confused with the religious consciousness. Mysticism is no doubt a genuine type of experience, but it need not be religious. If mysticism were the same as religion we could produce religion by means of drugs. The mystical state as such is the same, however produced. Animism and mysticism must be invested with a religious quality; they must have a religious object, in order to be religious experience.

There are two methods of interpreting religious reality, as there are two methods of interpreting reality generally. There is the *a priori* method and the empirical method. The former starts with certain assumptions as regards the object of religion and then develops the consequences of these assumptions. An outstanding example of this method is Scholasticism which started by assuming that God is omnipotent and omniscient, the source of all existence, everything depending upon God. It also made certain moral assumptions, such as absolute justice and absolute goodness, which it tried to square with the former assumptions. But Scholasticism did not grow out of the religious experience of human beings and therefore was not capable of interpreting the religious experience of human beings. It moved within the circle of its own assumptions. The empirical method, on the other hand, starts with the historical experience of the race and strives to understand its implications. For the empirical method religious interpretation is experimental. It asks the question: What sort of conception of reality will satisfy human religious needs? From the empirical point of view there can be no finality in religious concepts, any more than there can be finality in practical and scientific interpretation. It is therefore no criticism of religion that its concepts have been relative and that they have varied with the development of man. We might as well criticise science because its concepts have been in perpetual development. It has been said that science is the history of error, and the same has been said of religion. But this overlooks the fact that, with the advance of human experience, the concepts of both science and religion have shown themselves more adequate to meet the needs of man. In neither case can we hope that our human version of reality will be more than an approximation to the reality which it strives to grasp.

The religious consciousness points to a power greater than ourselves which can coöperate and is willing to coöperate with us in the realization of our ideals—a power which possesses actually what we strive to realize in our individual and social experience. This power must be ubiquitous in space and time. In primitive religion this ubiquity was conceived as many local presences with which the individual or group could come into rapport and satisfy its needs. In the advance of religion this Presence has been conceived as one universal Presence, the same everywhere and at every time and ready to enter into relation with man as he is prepared. Furthermore this Presence must possess many attributes in order to answer the needs of human nature. Early religion conceived these attributes as vested in separate personalities to which man addressed himself in accordance with his special needs. In the advance of religion these various attributes were conceived as vested in one personality who responds variously according to the conditions of man. Historical religions have not conceived these attributes as stereotyped but as creative relations in which the divine reality reveals itself variously according to the development and capacity of the worshiper. Thus light responds variously and affects things variously according to their condition. Light may be constructive and healing in the processes of nature when these are in rapport with light. But it may also be destructive to things not in rapport with light. In the creative relation between man and the divine, the divine may be stern or gentle, just or merciful according to the conditions of man. God may be policeman or schoolmaster or father or the lord of the group or the great ideal of humanity according as man is prepared to react to God.

In the religious experience of man, God has been conceived as being present on all varieties of occasions and at all times and places without including all things in himself. Pantheism and Deism are both speculative theories. Neither expresses the religious consciousness of man. Pantheism includes everything within God in the sense that everything is a part of God. This destroys the selective relation which the religious consciousness implies. For the religious consciousness the divine is not the whole of things but the better part of reality with which we can get into rapport and thus realize our best. Pantheism destroys the quality of the object of religious worship and thus must necessarily fail as a religion. Deism, on the other hand, makes the presence of God external to the finite individuals and thus fails to establish the intimate relation which must exist between the individual worshiper and the divine. The divine Presence must permeate the individuals. It must be present in its own essence in all individual things, though it is not the essence of the individual. The light of divinity always illuminates our soul and everything, but it only becomes *our* light when we are prepared. To conceive a divine reality which is present to and in things everywhere we may be helped by thinking of the analogy of space. Space must be conceived as a universal medium in which all things exist, yet space is not things but something immaterial. But in order that space may be more than analogy we must conceive of this universal medium as spirit—pervasive, sensitive, creative genius which operates everywhere in its own essence. When we thus conceive of the divine Presence we need not be troubled by the vastly increased magnitude of the universe which modern science has revealed to us. The divine Presence is the same on the small scale of human personality and in the vast reaches of the cosmos.

The modern concept of evolution presents no problem to a religion which conceives the divine Presence as we have indicated. We may for descriptive purposes view the process as emergence, where new structures and new levels of structures pass in succession within the particular history such as our geological history. Emergence emphasizes that the later stages of evolution cannot be adequately described in terms of earlier stages. A molecule cannot be adequately described in terms of its constituent atoms. Life cannot be described adequately in terms of inorganic matter, though this precedes it in our geological history. Society cannot be described adequately in terms of biological organisms. The spiritual creativeness in art and science cannot be described adequately in terms of the mere routine of habit, however complex. New categories are required at every stage of development to give an adequate description of that stage. We need find no fault with the concept of emergence so long as it is taken as a description merely and not as an explanation of the series of stages in evolution. To understand the creative advance of nature we must have more than just the succession of stages. We require a principle or field which can furnish the rationale of the creative advance. It is impossible to see how nature can be measured everywhere into the same fundamental units without some conception of a control which is not that of the units themselves. Nor can we understand the architecture of nature which repeats itself everywhere in the atoms and molecules and the molar masses of matter when the conditions are similar. We can only understand such similarity of architecture over the vast spaces of the cosmos when we conceive the cosmos as the architecture of pervasive genius. This genius must be of the character of mathematical genius and of æsthetic genius because the universe lends itself to mathematics and it is in rapport with our æsthetic capacities. When we find nature manifesting itself as creative thought and creative appreciation, which can enter into the structure of nature and make this structure its own meaning and value, we are obliged to think of the genius in nature as somehow akin to creative thought and creative personality, however much it may exceed our capacity. As we must feel that our finite existence, even at the highest level of development which we know, is still imperfect and in the process of evolution, we may conceive of this cosmic genius as a nisus which guides the process onward and beyond to further levels, but it must be not merely something in the future but present actuality in order to be the guiding field of the advance.

The history of religious experience implies the coöperation of the finite individual and God. The pluralism of individuals must be taken as an ultimate fact, as well as the pervasive and unitary presence of God. Advance in evolution is conditioned upon the willingness and capacity of the individual at every stage of development. We have gotten rid of the idea of inert matter and are thinking instead in terms of energy. The lowliest types of individuals in the economy of nature are active and sensitive entities with a certain indeterminateness in their behavior. The individual, even at the level of electrons, is not a mere function of the field but reacts with a certain initiative of its own. The structure, within which the individual acts, has indeed its determinateness, but the individual is not obliged to fall automatically into this or that structure. It is impossible for us to characterize nature at its lowest levels, but we may with Leibnitz assume the principle of continuity in nature. This does not mean identity in nature. We cannot ascribe the mind of man to the lower stages of biological evolution, nor can we ascribe all the characteristics of the organism to the inorganic stages of nature, yet there is some continuity through the various stages in nature. There is something psychological about the lowest stages of life and there are some lifelike characteristics in even the simpler stages of nature. It is certain at any rate that nature at its lowest levels is active and sensitive, and it behaves as though in some sense it exercised initiative and preference, however far removed from the meaning of those terms in our own experience. What is clear is that plurality and initiative are fundamental in nature. At every stage of nature it is necessary to overcome the inertia or cosmic laziness of the *status quo*. Willingness seems to be an ultimate fact in nature from the highest stages to the lowest. Cosmic genius furnishes the field for advance and the grace for advance, but the advance is conditioned upon the willingness or venturesomeness of the individual at every stage. At every stage the vast number of individuals remain in the *status quo*. Only a small part of the individuals at any stage are willing to risk a new stage in nature. Some religions and philosophies have thought it necessary to assume an evil principle or principles in nature in order to explain the refractoriness of nature, especially human nature, to advance to a higher level. But I believe that the principle of cosmic laziness is a sufficient explanation for the tardiness and refractoriness of nature. On the one hand, for any advance to a higher level there must be what theology has called grace—the active presence of something higher at work in nature—but on the other hand grace cannot be effective to produce something higher and nobler unless there is the willingness of the individual. This seems to be the philosophy of evolution and of human history.

There is no doubt a great deal of predestination in the evolution of nature. The individual cannot be regarded in separation from history. It is part of a route of advance, and these routes of advance are in their general features predetermined in the later stages of development. These routes are diverse. Thus at an early stage in our solar and planetary evolution material routes were established of atomic series and molecular and molar structures. Then came life with its new plasticities and new possibilities; the different routes of plant development and the different routes of animal development were established. In the course of the ages human development became a possibility; and going back into the vast ages there have been different routes of human development, most of which are extinct. The creative possibilities of the individual are determined, therefore, in a large measure by the route of development in which he finds himself. A plant form cannot be an animal form or an animal form a plant form, and in the many routes of each type of organic life the particular individual is conditioned by the route of which it is a part. An oak seed cannot become an elm seed, a cat cannot become a dog. A human individual is part of the human route of development, and his creative possibilities are conditioned by the biological stage in which he finds himself and, to a large degree, by the stage of civilization in which he participates. Anaximander may have had as great a genius as Newton; but he could not be a Newton, because he did not have the history of scientific development which Newton had at his command. But while it is true that the type of structure which an individual may assume, whether a certain kind of crystal or a certain kind of flower or a certain kind of animal or a certain type of human being, is thus prescribed, yet at every stage there are the possibilities of individual initiative according to the capacity of the individual and the conditions in which he finds himself. At every stage there is the call to advance, the stimulus to new organization, to new creativeness; and at every stage advance is conditioned upon the willingness and capacity of individuals, whatever their route may be. In every case it holds that many are called but few are chosen.

The significance of the vast cosmic drama, as I view it, is the possibility of spiritualization—the development of higher types of individuality. This may not be the best possible world in the sense of a perfect world. If the individual is an ultimate factor in the creativeness of God, the world is better or worse for the willingness and earnestness of the individual to coöperate in the creative process. It is the sort of world where the individual may fail and sometimes and often does fail. But it is also the sort of world where the individual may be a bridge for further advance, a link toward a higher destiny. It is a world of venture, of risk and opportunity. The important thing is not that the world shall be more or less perfect, but that soul shall be created in the cosmic process and spirit salvaged. We cannot understand the plan of the whole, but if the genius of the whole operates within the world to create spiritual patterns, we may believe that this genius in his own way and for his own ends will conserve within his spiritual economy the individuals who have the willingness and the insight to realize within their limitations the divine destiny and thus furnish potentiality for further realization.

The fundamental note in the history of religion is a certain sense of wrongness and a desire to establish harmony. This sense of wrongness has sometimes taken the sterner form of the moral consciousness of the Hebrew prophets, sometimes the gentler form of the æsthetic consciousness of the Greeks. It may have been, and to a large extent has been, a sense of ceremonial wrongness, of failure to fulfill the demands of customary religious practice; or it may have been concerned with the inner attitude of the will to a conscious ideal of conduct. But in any case the religious consciousness has been a striving to establish harmonious relations with what has been conceived as the divine part of the universe. This sense of wrongness has been the spring of individual and social activity. It has also been the basis of man's construction of a cosmic scheme. Man has required the conception of a universe which has a bias for such conduct as leads to harmonious relations of individual with individual, of individual with group, of group with group, and of man with the universe. In the struggle of man with hindrances within and without, he has felt the inadequacy of his own individual efforts and the need of reinforcement from the unseen. The companionship which man requires in this striving cannot be the mere statuesque God who, while perfect in himself, remains aloof from human concerns. In man's highest religious consciousness at any rate he has conceived of God as not merely perfect in himself but as entering into the process of history and sharing the life of man. He has conceived of God as incarnate in human history—laboring, suffering, dying in the heroic effort to lift human life to a higher level. And he has had faith that this struggle is not in vain but that, though the human God may be crucified, he is also the resurrection of man's fundamental hopes and ideals.

Theology has had little to say of this temporal God who becomes incarnate in the life of the world. It has emphasized God as eternal and immutable. It has seemed somehow as though the timelessly eternal were more perfect than the ideal which must be realized in the process of struggle and death. But is not the temporal personality of Socrates worth more than a syllogism or a system of geometry? In some way we must find the eternal in the temporal. The eternal must somehow incarnate itself and reincarnate itself in history. It is indeed true that the human soul craves the conception of a God who is perfect and eternal. There can be no evolution of God, for in that case there can be no guidance, no impetus to higher evolution. God must therefore, it seems, be transcendent in the world and perfect in himself. But at the same time the human heart craves the conception of God as bearing our sorrows, as having compassion with our needs as one sharing our life with us and not as a mere contemplator of human history. We cannot hope to reconcile these two needs of the human mind. But where our human insight fails, we must still hold fast to what is of ultimate importance for our living. If this seems unsatisfactory to the rational consciousness, we may learn modesty from the procedure of science. The scientific mind does not hesitate to work with irreconcilable conceptions if they seem to be required by experience. Thus science is confronted with a dualism in the case of both radiant energy and material energy. Both have a dual aspect. Light for example must be taken for some purposes as wavelike (as in refraction and interference of light rays). For other purposes light must be treated as corpuscular. It acts as individual particles. Both aspects seem to be fundamental in nature; and science for different purposes recognizes both aspects. Why should we assume that we are wiser in dealing with the vaster mysteries of spiritual reality than science in dealing with sensible reality? If we must for

our human purposes conceive of God both as eternal and
perfect in himself, and also as incarnate in history—
striving, suffering, dying and rising again—we must reverently hold both these concepts as true.

Closely associated with this conception of the duality
of God, as both temporal and eternal, is the conception of
the duality of God in his own eternal essence. It is a
sublime conception that God expresses Himself in kind—
God of God, Light of Light—in perfect equality of
essence and perfect fulfillment in mutual love. If the
essence of God is love, it must be the essence of God to
be loved. For love without reciprocity is only half love.
The reciprocity of love in relation to the finite and imperfect cannot be a complete fulfillment. Complete fulfillment of a perfect love requires equality. It is so in
human relations; and the highest human relations are
our only key to that which is higher than human relations. The Christian intuition has been sound, but its
theology has been intellectualistic and barren. Since it
was fashioned in the days of the patriarchal family, it is
natural that it should conceive divinity as masculine. It
speaks of persons in divinity, but these are mere substan-
tiations of abstractions, the Father being conceived as
power, the Son being conceived as intellect. To these two
abstractions it added a third abstraction, that of love, as
the Holy Ghost, a procession from the other two abstractions, in order to hold them together. It is no wonder
that such abstract logic has left the human heart cold.
If we must use the analogy of the highest human consciousness to give content to our conception of God, then
we must take account of the emotions as well as the intellect; and historical religion has always conceived God
as having emotion. It has not evaporated love as a mere
abstraction. As human personality can only be realized
in social relations, so we must conceive divine personality as realized in social relations.

Aristotle tells us that man is a social animal and that
a being that is not social is either a brute or a God. For
Aristotle God is a completely self-centered being, con-

templating only his own perfection and completely satisfied in himself. The ultimate characteristic of God is self-sufficiency. But the divine reality of the historical religious consciousness has not been merely a statuesque thing of beauty to be admired, as is Aristotle's God; nor a mystically self-intoxicated being as is the One of Neoplatonism; nor a self-complete system of ideas as in Hegel's Absolute. Such a conception of God can never answer the needs of human beings. The need for reciprocal love is as fundamental as the logical and æsthetic needs. A supreme mathematical genius or a supreme artist cannot suffice as an object of religious worship. Christian theology has followed the Greek tradition and emphasized the self-sufficiency of God. But such self-sufficiency does not appeal to us as an ideal of human beings. It is egoism apotheosized. A normal human being loves and craves to be loved in turn. It is not in supreme self-satisfaction that man realizes his highest personality, but in the creative sharing of his thought and emotions with the noblest of his kind. Man cannot find full satisfaction in the companionship of a dog or even a child, much as he may value these. He requires a friend who can share his highest aims, his joy in the creative life. If we must approach the reality of the divine through our highest human realization, then we must believe that God, however much he loves the finite creation below him, must realize his perfection by sharing his life with a being of his own quality, who returns God for God, perfect love for perfect love. Only so is the divine drama complete.

XV

THE TRINITY

A Speculation

By

WM. PEPPERELL MONTAGUE

Professor of Philosophy
Barnard College, Columbia University

THE TRINITY

A Speculation

To reinterpret the categories of one age in the light
of another is probably a bad business, certainly it is a
business that has been much overdone during the past
hundred years in which "modernism" after "modernism," refusing to abandon the ancient concepts of religion, has yet striven to adapt them to new presuppositions which, in some cases, are in direct contradiction to
those from which the beloved concepts originated. The
doctrine of the Trinity is one of these ancient notions
and the sort of reinterpretation which I have in mind to
attempt might well appear more than ordinarily sterile;
first, because most of those calling themselves liberals
to-day find it sufficiently difficult to believe in even the
vaguest theistic ground for the universe, not to mention
one that is in an especial sense triune; and secondly,
because when once the strictly orthodox idea of the Trinity is departed from, we are beset by a mass of analogies,
as loose as they are trite, which the number three has
suggested and which have been tediously exploited by
philosophers from Plotinus and Porphyry to Hegel and
Freud. And the prospect of a further addition to these
analogies would seem peculiarly uninviting.

In the face of such objections I am nevertheless
impelled to suggest a new conception of trinitarian theism and for the following reasons:

The world of things as they are is not self-explanatory; it bears the earmarks, if not of a manufactured
product, at least of a thing that has been derived from
something other than itself. Now I am well aware that
this indictment of reality on the ground of its rationalistic insufficiency has been answered by angry demurrers,

in which we are told that causality is a category whose application is at best interphenomenal and intramundane, and that to extend it by a kind of transcendental extrapolation and make it apply to a supposed relation between the world and something else, is an outrageous abuse of logical procedure. All creationists have of course been in some measure guilty of this act of extrapolation, but Anselm, and later, Fichte and Hegel committed the crime, if crime it be, on a grand scale. Not content with explaining natural existence by supernatural existence, they propounded the conception of existence as itself derived from purely logical being or essence. We remember the bitterness with which Schopenhauer attacked this notion of *causa sui* particularly in its Fichtean form, and also the devastating criticism to which Kant subjected the Anselmian argument. As to the Empiricists, they have since the days of Hume objected to the category of causality even as applied to intramundane phenomena, and any suggestion that it be extrapolated and used to explain the origin of the world from a supernatural existent or still worse from a mere logical essence appears to them the height of absurdity. Whether the world seems to us self-explanatory or the opposite is an accident of our own mental constitution, they will tell us, and in neither case are we justified in going beyond the realm of experiential data. To attempt it will only make a bad matter worse.

Despite this momentous opposition I feel, as I have already confessed, an urgent need of going beyond the world to explain the world, and I refuse to recognize the validity of any *a priori* limitation or censorship of our use of explanatory categories. Whether we gain or lose by extrapolating a concept such as causality is a question that can only be answered pragmatically, by trying and seeing.

The world of things as they are comprises the realm of subsistence or essence and the realm of existence or spatio-temporal particulars. The domain of existing things seems to consist of protons and electrons, the unit

masses of positive and negative electricity. Recent
physics in its wave-mechanics suggests that the protonic
and electronic units may themselves be composed of units
still smaller and wavelike in character; and that in any
event the mass factor which they embody is reducible to
and interchangeable with the more fundamental factor
of *energy*. But whether the ultimate elements of the
material world are the hard little atoms of old, the
protons and electrons of the Bohr atoms of yesterday,
the Schroedinger waves of to-day or their as yet un-
guessed successors of to-morrow, the outstanding fact
about them is their diffusion over all space and their
amazing similarity. And we are moved to ask: *What
is the probability that such a situation of widespread
diffusion of homogeneous units could exist unless those
units had originated from a single source?* Such a probability would, it seems to me, be very small, and the
greater the number of primary elements (*i.e.* elements
underived from one another) the smaller it would be, and
consequently the greater would be the counter probability that they had been derived from a single cause. In
short the principle of *one ground for similars,* if not an
axiom has about it a strongly axiomatic flavor.

When we pass to the further question as to whether
any element of consciousness or personality can be
ascribed to an originating or First Cause of the primary
existential elements, I can see no ground for answering
in the affirmative. It seems rather that the thing or
principle responsible for the origin of nature as we find
it was a power of fecundity, self-repetition or increase
and that the only hope of ascribing to it *mind* or *life*
would depend on showing that those categories are interpretable as later phases, "emergent" yet inevitable
developments of the principle of development itself.
Following upon the increase of being by mere number
and extent there would be an increase of the second order,
consisting in the harmonization of the earlier elements
of being. This secondary growth would be intensive
rather than extensive, and would consist in the removal

of interferences or negations exerted by the units of being upon one another.

If then we take the principle of growth as Hegel took his principle of *Negativität,* and study its "dialectic," we find it involving at first a phase of mere multiplication and conservation of sheer being. And then, if further growth is to be realized, organized existence will succeed mere existence and an intensive increase of being through harmonization will supervene upon the earlier extensive phase. And this harmonization would at its maximum involve life, consciousness, and finally personality. Such would seem to constitute the "immanent dialectic" of the concept of increase or growth, a *That* whose *What* consists of *being ever more than itself.* Of all our concepts this notion seems to me best suited for a first principle or absolute *Prius.*

Now if we turn from existence to subsistence and survey that Realm of Essence which has been discovered by Plato, carefully explored by Husserl and gloriously proclaimed in all its dimensions by Santayana, we find, I think, traces of that same principle of fecundity, self-increase or growth to a maximum which we postulated at the core of the naturally existing world of matter. That the realm of essence contains all that is possible, is a truth that is three quarters a truism. This maximum totality of forms or natures is a level of being that is logical and timeless and so by its very nature immune to genesis in any ordinary or temporal sense. Now in that little section of the domain of subsistence consisting of the number series, the higher integers do not attain their timeless being at any later moments than the integers one and two; yet the being of those higher integers presupposes the being of the lower, as logically though not temporally prior to their own. Could we but see as only God can see the expanse of subsistence in its entirety, and with the same clarity with which we see the island of number that is contained within it, I believe that we should see also a single thread of dialectical genesis which would constitute its structure a logical hierarchy.

And that arch essence would then I believe be found to
be not the principle of *Negativität* which Hegel used so
bravely, but something more like that ideal of the Good
held to by Plato, Anselm and Leibnitz. This ideal I
should wish to formulate as a principle of growth or
increase to a maximum. And as before on the existential
level, so now on this level of essential being, the first
phase of dialectical development would be sheer wealth
of qualitative variation resulting in the totality of possi-
bles, while the second dialectical phase would be the
integration or harmonization of this All in its collective
aspect into a single organic unity of maximum compossi-
bility equivalent to a complete subsistential personality.

Let us now make a bold quasi-Leibnizian and quasi-
Herbartian postulate and assume that any possibility
tends to be compossible or actual, and fails only to the
extent that it is inhibited by others, so that the world
of existence is a sort of vector resultant of the tendencies
to exist of all the essences. From this it would follow
that the totality of essences in its collective unity and
integrated personality would (as Anselm believed) entail
its own incarnation in existence.

We should have then as the outcome of a cosmic *Prius*
consisting of the principle of unlimited increase or
growth: first, "God the Father," a preconscious and
prepersonal power expressing itself in the production
of mere existential and subsistential being in maximum
abundance. Taken in their distributive plurality, these
beings would constitute the World; second, there would
be that same existential and subsistential totality of
things, but now taken collectively in its integrated and
personal unity; this would be the Logos or "God the
Son." Now, if the *Prius* of "maximum increase" is to
be true to itself, there would be a third phase of its
"immanent dialectic" which would consist not of an
entity but of an unending *activity* by which the independent and self-willed constituents of the world had
their several natures increased or enhanced by being
brought more and more into harmony with one another

and with the personality of the totality. This Third Phase of the creative power would be "God the Holy Ghost" expressing itself in what we recognize as "evolution," but evolution interpreted as the working of God in that World which is within him—the spirit of the Whole fructifying and organizing its own independent and self-existing parts.

This last phase of Deity is inferable from reasons less abstract and dialectical than those invoked to prove the two phases preceding it. For our world exhibits not only (1) things evil and nonpurposeful and (2) things good and purposeful, but (3) a mighty *trend,* slow yet unmistakable from the nonpurposeful to the purposeful. And these three aspects of the world would seem to indicate that the world-ground is correlatively threefold: first, a transcendent originating cause, second a concretely actualized person, and, third, an immanent and progressively more pervasive partner in the company of its own effects.

If I may use a simile to make my meaning clearer, it is as if there were in the beginning a seed from which grew a stalk with an abundant welter of boughs, branches and twigs, each self-existent and endowed with something of the primary causality and sheer spontaneity of the originating seed. From the central stalk there then came as a second creation a blossom and a fruit which was the actualized perfection of what was in the seed potential only. Following upon these primary and secondary epochs of creation, there came a third in which the boughs and branches partly of themselves and partly aided by the central life of the stalk began in their own right to develop blossoms, each after its kind.

By way of conclusion, I wish briefly to point out in what respect my speculation as to the triune world-ground differs from what I understand to be the orthodox conception of the Trinity.

My First Phase differs from "God the Father" in being not personal but impersonal or prepersonal; for, as I tried to make plain, the first phase in the dialectical development of a principle of increase would be mere multiplication of entities, existential or quantitative and subsistential or qualitative. Personal or integrated being emerges from the impersonal as its Second Phase, the continuance of growth on a higher dimensional level. Thus God does not consciously create the world with its disorder and evil, he creates himself and *awakens* to his own existence to find a world within him as an earlier product of that primordial ontological gestation of which his own conscious personality or Logos was the climactic phase. "In the beginning" were Chaos and Old Night, but upon that Chaos, Cosmos supervened. God looked upon the world within him and saw not that "it was good" but that *it was to be made good;* and as personality had supervened upon mere life, so the evolution of the world in its distributive plurality supervenes upon the personalized perfection of its unified totality.

This conception of the world-ground resembles the Plotinian rather than the Christian Trinity, in making the First Phase non-personal. But it differs from the scheme of Plotinus in not regarding the First Phase or the One as ineffably *higher* but rather as *lower* than the Logos and the World-soul. Hence Nature and life are not to be thought of as a descent or falling away from God with the implication that the goal of life is escape from the world and reabsorption in the One or Brahma or Nirvana. On the contrary, the goal of life for us as for God is endless increase and enhancement and furtherance of a more and more individuated worldly existence.

As to the Second Person of the Trinity, there is little difference, metaphysically speaking, between the conception of Plotinus and that of the Church. Historically and concretely, there is of course the immense difference in the emphasis upon the earthly life of Jesus of Nazareth. All I can say on this subject is that just as an author might put himself into his book as one of its characters, so there would be nothing absurd or impossible in the belief that the Soul of the World had literally embodied itself in one of its own members; and the fact that the utterances ascribed to Jesus and his life as told in the Story (even when freed from the conventional and distastefully improbable claims of a lack of any earthly imperfections) contain elements of supreme and infinite beauty would make it possible to believe that he was an incarnation of God in some less figurative sense than another man could be, even if he were equally good. But while such a supposition seems to me conceivable, I think that it is more probable, and perhaps more in accord with the spirit of Christ and the meaning which he attached to his own mission to think of his divinity as consisting in what he made of his life by his own efforts as a mortal man, rather than to impute to him the physical and metaphysical advantages of a miraculously inherited nature.

Finally with regard to the Third Phase of the world-ground, I believe that Nature as revealed by science gives broad and clear evidences of an upbuilding or synthesising agency which expresses itself not only in the genesis and ascent of life upon our planet but in the far more widespread evolution of inorganic compounds from their simpler elements. How can we accept the intolerably arbitrary conception (recently advocated in high quarters) of a God who created the world some quadrillions of years ago, all wound up with a maximum of complex organization and a minimum of entropy, and then left it to run down and dissipate its substance in a sea of insignificant and impotent waves of radiant energy? Is it not more plausible to believe that the world's failure to have run down by this time is due not to the accident of its youth but to a factor as yet undiscovered by astronomy and mechanics, but continuously operative in all nature and indirectly manifested in the development of living individuals and in the evolution of their species? Such a factor would be the steady foe of entropy or decay. And this *anti-entropic* agency which builds the atoms and their inorganic compounds and the still stranger protoplasmic organisms might also as the immanent God or Holy Ghost build up and strengthen with grace the hearts of men.